Social Entrepreneurship and Innovation

Social Entrepreneurship and Innovation

Carole Carlson
Brandeis University

Los Angeles | London | New Delhi
Singapore | Washington DC | Melbourne

FOR INFORMATION:

SAGE Publications, Inc.
2455 Teller Road
Thousand Oaks, California 91320
E-mail: order@sagepub.com

SAGE Publications Ltd.
1 Oliver's Yard
55 City Road
London, EC1Y 1SP
United Kingdom

SAGE Publications India Pvt. Ltd.
B 1/I 1 Mohan Cooperative Industrial Area
Mathura Road, New Delhi 110 044
India

SAGE Publications Asia-Pacific Pte. Ltd.
18 Cross Street #10-10/11/12
China Square Central
Singapore 048423

Acquisitions Editor: Maggie Stanley
Editorial Assistant: Lauren Younker
Production Editor: Vijayakumar
Copy Editor: Christobel Colleen Hopman
Typesetter: TNQ Technologies
Proofreader: Benny Willy Stephen
Indexer: TNQ Technologies
Cover Designer: Gail Buschman
Marketing Manager: Jennifer Jones

Printed in the United States of America

Library of Congress Cataloging-in-Publication Data

Names: Carlson, Carole (Economist), author.

Title: Social entrepreneurship and innovation / Carole Carlson.

Identifiers: LCCN 2021052390 | ISBN 9781071811597 (paperback) | ISBN 9781071811627 (adobe pdf) | ISBN 9781071811603 (epub) | ISBN 9781071811634 (epub)

Subjects: LCSH: Social entrepreneurship. | Entrepreneurship–Technological innovations. | Business planning. | Leadership.

Classification: LCC HD60 .C337 2022 | DDC 361.7/65–dc23/eng/20211208

LC record available at https://lccn.loc.gov/2021052390

This book is printed on acid-free paper.

22 23 24 25 26 10 9 8 7 6 5 4 3 2 1

BRIEF CONTENTS

Preface xv

Acknowledgments xvii

About the Author xix

CHAPTER 1 • Social Entrepreneurship and Leadership 1

CHAPTER 2 • Innovation and Idea Generation 32

CHAPTER 3 • Shaping Social Venture Opportunities 59

CHAPTER 4 • Building Social Impact Teams and Ecosystems 86

CHAPTER 5 • Creating Alignment and Measuring Impact 113

CHAPTER 6 • Legal Structures and Financial Plans for Social Ventures 140

CHAPTER 7 • Scaling and Expansion 173

CHAPTER 8 • Entrepreneurial Operations and Marketing 202

CHAPTER 9 • Business Plans and Pitches for Social Ventures 235

CHAPTER 10 • Social Entrepreneurship in a Global Context 264

CASES

Case 1 • Genesis: Seeding a Social Enterprise 291

Case 2 • Sanergy: Using Social Entrepreneurship to Solve Emerging Market Problems 299

Case 3 • WorkAround: Starting a New Global Venture 312

Index 331

DETAILED CONTENTS

Preface xv

Acknowledgments xvii

About the Author xix

CHAPTER 1 • Social Entrepreneurship and Leadership 1

Learning Objectives 1

Defining Social Entrepreneurship 1

The Promise of Social Entrepreneurship 3

Entrepreneurial Leadership 5

Characteristics of Entrepreneurs 5

Entrepreneurial Motivation 7

Profile: Bill Drayton at Ashoka 8

How Social Entrepreneurs Achieve Impact 9

What Do Social Entrepreneurs Actually Do? 9

What the Critics Say 11

Three Types of Social Entrepreneurs 12

Innovators 12

Scalers 13

Ecosystem Builders 15

Transitions Between Roles 18

Finding Your North Star 19

A Few Key Questions 19

Self-Assessment Options 19

Chapter Summary 21

Key Terms 21

In-Class Exercises 22

Exercise 1.1: Defining Your Entrepreneurial Purpose 22

Exercise 1.2: Entrepreneurial Leadership Self-Assessment 24

Short Case: Linda Rottenberg—Supporting High-Impact Entrepreneurs at Endeavor 25

Discussion Questions 28

CHAPTER 2 • Innovation and Idea Generation 32

Learning Objectives 32
The Role of Entrepreneurial Insights 33
Chance Favors the Prepared Mind 33
Innovation and Social Ventures 33
Divergent and Convergent Thinking 34
Where Ideas Come From 36
Elements of Creativity 36
Enhancing Creativity 38
Honing Discovery Skills 39
Profile: Neal Bermas and STREETS International 40
Innovating for Social Impact 41
Problem-Focused Solutions 41
Opportunity-Focused Solutions 42
Factors Supporting and Constraining Innovation 44
Macro-Level Factors 44
Micro-Level Factors 44
Using Ideation to Unlock Creativity 45
Brainstorming 46
Braindumping 46
Brainwriting or Brainwalking 47
Other Ideation Approaches 47
Chapter Summary 49
Key Terms 49
In-Class Exercises 50
Exercise 2.1: Using the Double Diamond Model 50
Exercise 2.2: Innovating Solutions 52
Short Case: Rakib Avi and Innovation at BRAC 53
Discussion Questions 57

CHAPTER 3 • Shaping Social Venture Opportunities 59

Learning Objectives 59
From Idea to Opportunity 59
Initial Market Assessment 62
Validating Market Potential 64
The Importance of Learning From Failure 65
How Are Business Models Developed? 67
What Is a Business Model? 67
Creating a Business Model Canvas 68
Profile: John Harthorne at MassChallenge—From Concept to Launch 71
Hypothesis-Driven Entrepreneurship 73

Why Is a Minimum Viable Product (MVP) Important? 74
Avoiding Cognitive Bias 74
Design Thinking 75
Chapter Summary 77
Key Terms 77
In-Class Exercises 78
Exercise 3.1: Business Model Canvas 78
Exercise 3.2: Hypothesis Development and Testing 80
Short Case: Majd Mashharawi at SunBox 81
Discussion Questions 83

CHAPTER 4 • Building Social Impact Teams and Ecosystems 86

Learning Objectives 86
The Benefits of Founding in Teams 86
Navigating Formation Challenges 88
Wasserman's "Four R's" 88
Heterogeneous and Homogeneous Founding Teams 89
Attracting Talent to Social Ventures 90
Managing Social Venture Teams 92
Profile: Ohad Elhelo—From Soldier to Entrepreneurial Peace Builder 94
The Importance of Ecosystems for Social Entrepreneurs 95
Boards of Directors and Boards of Advisors 100
Contracted Professionals 102
Partners 102
Universities as Incubators 103
Chapter Summary 104
Key Terms 104
In-Class Exercises 106
Exercise 4.1: Design Your Culture 106
Exercise 4.2: Map Your Ecosystem 106
Short Case: Cheryl Dorsey at Echoing Green—Supporting Bold Ideas 107
Discussion Questions 110

CHAPTER 5 • Creating Alignment and Measuring Impact 113

Learning Objectives 113
Why Measure Outcomes and Impact? 113
The Planning and Learning Cycle 114
Using a Theory of Change or Logic Model 115
Why Use Models and Evaluation Tools? 115
Theory of Change 116
Logic Model 118

Impact Measurement 120
Why Do We Measure Impact? 120
Different Approaches to Measurement 120
Measuring From Multiple Perspectives 124
Which Measurement Approach Should Social Entrepreneurs Choose? 125
Profile: Matt Forti—Driving Impact at the One Acre Fund 126
Impact Measurement Pitfalls 127
Measuring the Wrong Things 127
Measuring Without Regard to Cost 128
Measuring Without Analyzing or Acting 128
Calculating Social Impact 128
Chapter Summary 132
Key Terms 132
In-Class Exercise 133
Exercise 5.1: Create a Logic Model 133
Short Case: Reinvention and Planning for Impact at HopeWell 134
Discussion Questions 138

CHAPTER 6 • Legal Structures and Financial Plans for Social Ventures **140**

Learning Objectives 140
Choosing a Legal Structure 140
A Tale of Three Ventures 140
Legal Forms of Organization in the United States 141
Legal Forms of Organization Globally 145
Which Form to Choose? 146
Financing Decisions 146
Sources of Financing for Mission-Driven Ventures 148
Funding Strategies 148
Sources of Initial Capital and Expansion Funding 149
Sources of Funding for Operations 153
Profile: Tracy Palandjian at Social Finance 155
Different Ventures, Different Strategies 156
Matching Mission and Financing Strategy 156
Funding Models for Nonprofit Organizations 158
Chapter Summary 160
Key Terms 160
In-Class Exercises 163
Exercise 6.1: Legal Structure 163
Exercise 6.2: Financial Model 163

Short Case: Prosperity Candle 167
Discussion Questions 171

CHAPTER 7 • Scaling and Expansion 173

Learning Objectives 173
What Do We Mean by Scale? 173
Scaling for Mission-Driven Organizations 174
Scaling and Organizational Evolution 176
Deciding to Scale 177
Initial Questions to Ask 177
Reasons to Scale 178
Disadvantages of Scaling 179
Scaling Models 181
Meeting Untapped Demand by Expanding Locally 181
Expanding via Owned Branches or Subsidiaries 182
Expansion via Franchising or Affiliate Structures 183
Licensing 185
Scaling via Mergers or Acquisitions 185
Scaling Impact via Knowledge Dissemination and Network Creation 186
Scaling via Intrapreneurship 186
Profile: Louise Langheier: Driving Impact Through Scale at Peer Health Exchange 187
Issues to Navigate 188
Assessing Readiness 188
The Importance of Fidelity 189
How a Social Venture's Financing Model Affects Growth 189
Thinking Long Term 190
Chapter Summary 192
Key Terms 192
In-Class Exercises 193
Exercise 7.1: Scaling Plan 193
Exercise 7.2: What's Your End Game? 195
Short Case: GreenLight Fund—Scaling for Social Impact 196
Discussion Questions 200

CHAPTER 8 • Entrepreneurial Operations and Marketing 202

Learning Objectives 202
Connecting Strategic Thinking and Entrepreneurial Execution 202
Entrepreneurial Operations 204
A Short History of Operations Management 205
New Approaches: Lean and Agile 206

Designing for Entrepreneurial Operations 208
Lean Design in Action: Ekal Vidyalaya 208
The Role of Experimentation 210
Leveraging External Resources 211
Management and Culture 212
Entrepreneurial Marketing for Social Ventures 212
Marketing Basics 212
What Is Different for Entrepreneurial Organizations? 213
What Is Different for Social Ventures? 214
Refining Your Marketing Strategy 215
Profile: Catherine T. Morris at BAMS Fest: Using Arts and Culture to Catalyze Social Change 218
Digital and Social Media Marketing for Social Ventures 219
Chapter Summary 224
Key Terms 224
In-Class Exercise 225
Exercise 8.1: Marketing and Operations Plan 225
Short Case: Brenna Schneider and 99Degrees—Operations Under Fire 229
Discussion Questions 232

CHAPTER 9 • Business Plans and Pitches for Social Ventures 235

Learning Objectives 235
Creating Business Plans 235
What Are the Benefits of Creating a Business Plan? 237
What Are The Drawbacks of Creating a Plan? 238
What's in a Business Plan? 238
Section Content 239
Social Venture Pitches 242
The Value of Effective Pitches 242
The Science of First Impressions 243
Tell a Great Story 244
Elevator Pitch Basics 244
Pitching With Slides 246
The Pitch Process 247
Tips for Presenting Virtually 250
Profile: Rutopia—Creating the Perfect Pitch 251
Protecting Intellectual Property 252
Types of Intellectual Property Protection 253
Working With University Technology Transfer Offices and Other University Resources 254

Chapter Summary 255

Key Terms 255

In-Class Exercises 257

Exercise 9.1: Pitch Practice 257

Exercise 9.2: Advanced Pitch Challenges 257

Short Case: Shruti Sehra and Amina Fahmy at New Profit—Selecting High-Impact Entrepreneurs 258

Discussion Questions 262

CHAPTER 10 • Social Entrepreneurship in a Global Context 264

Learning Objectives 264

The Economic Impact of Entrepreneurship 264

Global Entrepreneurial Impact 264

Entrepreneurship in Emerging and Developing Economies 265

The Importance of Institutional and Cultural Context 266

Entrepreneurial Motivation 267

The Promise of Global Social Entrepreneurship 268

Entrepreneurship and the UN Sustainable Development Goals 270

Factors Supporting the Growth of Global Social Entrepreneurship 272

Constraints to Global Social Entrepreneurship 272

Resources Supporting Mission-Driven Ventures 273

Characteristics of Global Social Entrepreneurs 273

Profile: Michael Sly at Wilding and Co.—Leveraging a Global Market to Meet Local Goals 276

Different Types of Mission-Driven Ventures 277

Local Ventures Serving Local Needs 277

Local Ventures With a Global Market 278

Regional Ventures 280

Global Ventures 281

Chapter Summary 282

Key Terms 283

In-Class Exercise 283

Exercise 10.1: Entrepreneurship and the Sustainable Development Goals 283

Short Case: Tanya Accone at UNICEF—Promoting Intrapreneurship and Global Innovation at Scale 285

Discussion Questions 288

CASE 1 • Genesis: Seeding a Social Enterprise 291

Personal Background 291

Genetics and Closed Communities 292

Accelerating the Idea 293

The Business Plan and the Return to Israel and Palestine 296
Moving Forward—and a New Challenge 297
Discussion Questions 298

CASE 2 • Sanergy: Using Social Entrepreneurship to Solve Emerging Market Problems **299**

New Year, New Challenges 299
A Sanitation Crisis in the Developing World 300
Sanergy's First Location in Nairobi, Kenya 301
Sanitation in the Nairobi Slums 301
Sanergy Operations 302
Measuring Impact 304
Competition 305
Scaling Sanergy 306
Expanding to New Markets 307
Auerbach's Resolutions 309
Discussion Questions 310

CASE 3 • WorkAround: Starting a New Global Venture **312**

The Genesis of WorkAround 312
The Global Refugee Crisis 313
The WorkAround Solution 314
Early Successes 315
Incubating the Venture 315
The Challenge at MassChallenge 318
The Big Event 319
What Happened Next? 320
Discussion Questions 322

Appendix 1: WorkAround Team Bios 322
Appendix 2: Worker Demographics 323
Appendix 3: WorkAround Business Model Canvas 324
Appendix 4: WorkAround Pitch Deck 325
Appendix 5: MassChallenge Selected Judge Feedback (Anonymized) 328

Index **331**

PREFACE

Over nearly two decades teaching and coaching aspiring social entrepreneurs and during my tenure directing the Social Impact MBA program at Brandeis University's Heller School (a top 10 ranked social policy school), I was often frustrated by the lack of relevant classroom material. I had what I describe as a Goldilocks problem: I found that the material available was either too hot (well focused on entrepreneurship but missing the social dimension) or too cold (insufficiently rigorous or lacking real-world applicability) and only rarely just right. Inspired by current students and recent alumni and their experiences founding social ventures, I set out to write a series of cases that would further students' understanding of social entrepreneurship. That work became the inspiration for writing a textbook that would provide theory, real-world examples and a valuable tool kit.

This book provides a practical, current overview of social entrepreneurship in three ways. First, it connects the dots to include basic theory in related academic fields as diverse as leadership, entrepreneurial finance, legal structures, impact measurement, operations, and marketing, all intended to bring rigor to the often poorly defined field of social entrepreneurship.

If there is one thing I have learned by teaching over 25 courses in entrepreneurship, it is this: the best way to give students a realistic view of what it takes to become a social entrepreneur and the breadth of opportunities is to expose them to role models who have chosen that path. The most popular part of my courses in *Social Entrepreneurship and Innovation*, *Global Social Entrepreneurship*, *Business Plans and Pitches*, and *Health Care Entrepreneurship* is hearing from a diverse array of guests that share their on-the-ground experience founding and growing social ventures. To bring their experiences to this book, I interviewed over 50 successful social entrepreneurs and ecosystem participants from around the world. Collectively, they offer examples of what to do (and what not to do) when launching and growing high-impact ventures. This book also profiles a more diverse and global set of entrepreneurs than I have seen in other cases or books with an emphasis on young entrepreneurs, many of whom started their ventures while students.

Finally, recognizing that university courses in social entrepreneurship should provide a foundational tool kit to students who are considering entrepreneurship as a career, this book emphasizes practical applications through in-class exercises that build towards a semester-long project. The intent is to help students create mission-driven ventures that are financially feasible, scalable, agile, and efficient. I hope that readers will quickly learn that just having a compelling idea is not enough. In addition, they need to rigorously develop and then continually test and refine their concept, assemble a supportive group of stakeholders, pitch their ideas effectively, and compete in a real-world context to give it life.

To help students learn from the experience of social entrepreneurs, each chapter contains both a profile of a social entrepreneur or team that includes their advice for aspiring social entrepreneurs. Each chapter also includes a topic-related short case for classroom discussion. To reinforce student learning and help them gain hands-on experience with the tools they will use if they choose to launch a social venture, each chapter also includes classroom activities that will help students apply the lessons from each topic area to their venture concepts.

I hope that this book has conveyed my excitement about social ventures and their potential for large-scale impact and, in particular, my enthusiasm for the work of young social entrepreneurs. Social entrepreneurship is a hard path to follow but one with enormous potential for both personal growth and satisfaction as well as benefit to society. It is my hope that by providing foundational learning, inspiring examples, frameworks, and application experiences, I can help social entrepreneurs along this path. In closing, I would like to thank the many contributors to this work and gratefully acknowledge the important work of instructors who join me in seeking to guide and inspire aspiring social entrepreneurs.

DIGITAL RESOURCES

Instructors, go to **www.sagepub.com** to access the instructor support materials that accompany this text.

ACKNOWLEDGMENTS

I would like to acknowledge the external reviewers whose valuable feedback and suggestions helped to shape this book. My thanks go out to Jason Brennan (Georgetown University), Samuel L. Brown (Old Dominion University), Caroline E.W. Glackin (Fayetteville State University), Richard Filley (Arizona State University), Tim F. Burke (Fontbonne University), Tammi C. Redd (Ramapo College of New Jersey), Adela Z. Ghadimi (Florida State University), Sarah Kimakwa (The University of Texas Rio Grande Valley), Steve Rundle (Biola University), Marcus D. Harris (University of Michigan Dearborn), Angeline Nariswari (California State University, Monterey Bay), Inessa Korovyakovskaya (Savannah State University), Justin Gandy (Dallas Baptist University), Janelle Kerlin (Georgia State University), Veronica Gutierrez (Arizona State University), Tom J. Sanders (University of Montevallo), and Justin Peart (St. Thomas University). I'm also grateful for the support provided by my editor Maggie Stanley and her colleagues Sarah Wilson and Lauren Younker.

I had the benefit of receiving input and advice from many of my colleagues at Brandeis University including Professors Joel Cutcher-Gershenfeld, Elif Sisli Ciamarra, Xin Wang, and Laura Beals, Senior Fellow Della Hughes and colleagues Rajnish Kaushik, Rebecca Menapace, Bethany Romano, Karen Shih, and Bozhanka Vitanova.

Over 50 social entrepreneurs and ecosystem participants, including many former students, generously shared their knowledge and experience with me, and you will read about them throughout this book.

Many thanks are due to current and former students who have helped me by contributing research, ideas, and examples as well as editorial advice. I'm particularly grateful to Norman Abbott, Rachel Blau, Christa Bogdanow, Matthew Kriegsman, Iwona Matczuk, Elizabeth Nguyen, and Monica Oxenreiter. I'm also grateful for the inspiration that all of my students provide and for their willingness to test and help refine many of the exercises and cases included here.

Finally, I would like to acknowledge the support of my husband David and our daughter Amelia, both of whom were my most critical and constructive readers.

ABOUT THE AUTHOR

Photo by Evgenia Eliseeva

Carole Carlson is the Director of the MBA program and Senior Lecturer at the Heller School for Social Policy and Management at Brandeis University, a US News and World Report top 10-ranked social policy school. There, she teaches courses in in *Social Entrepreneurship and Innovation*, and *Global Social Entrepreneurship* in the MBA program, a course on *Business Plans and Pitches* in the Our Generation Speaks incubator, and an executive education course on *Health Care Entrepreneurship*. Prior to teaching at Brandeis she was a Principal at the Parthenon Group (now Parthenon E&Y) where she advised senior leaders of Fortune 500 and high-growth middle market companies and leading nonprofits to help them create effective strategies and steer operational improvements. She has led the design and delivery of numerous innovative entrepreneur-oriented programs and has authored or coauthored dozens of case studies, mainly on entrepreneurship and social ventures. She has mentored over 50 entrepreneurial ventures, and continues to mentor young entrepreneurs. She holds advanced degrees from Harvard Business School, where she was a Baker Scholar, and the Massachusetts Institute of Technology.

CHAPTER ONE

SOCIAL ENTREPRENEURSHIP AND LEADERSHIP

On the first day of class on Social Entrepreneurship, when I ask students "who sees themselves as a social entrepreneur?" about half of the students raise their hands. When I then ask: "who sees themselves as a major contributor to a social venture?" a majority do. There are multiple roles for those who want to contribute to mission-driven ventures; the most important thing to do is to understand what kind of contribution fits you best.

Entrepreneurial leadership can take many forms but social entrepreneurs who succeed display common characteristics that include courage, adaptability, and opportunity obsession. Whether you are an inventor, a scaler or an ecosystem builder, or a supporter who enables others to succeed in these roles, you should be ready to utilize all your talents to innovate to create organizations that benefit society. We hope you enjoy the adventure.

Learning Objectives

- Define social entrepreneurship. Identify key attributes and distinguish it from other approaches to achieving social goals.
- Describe how social entrepreneurs create value.
- Identify important characteristics displayed by entrepreneurs and social entrepreneurs.
- Explain the core activities of social entrepreneurs and examine criticisms of social entrepreneurship.
- Compare different approaches employed by social entrepreneurs and identify the potential for transition between roles.
- Identify your core motivations and answer important questions social entrepreneurs should address about their motivations and abilities.

DEFINING SOCIAL ENTREPRENEURSHIP

When they attempt to define social entrepreneurship, most scholars start with the concept of entrepreneurship. Entrepreneurs have multiple characteristics but the ones that are cited most frequently are tenacity, creativity, a bias to action, and an unrelenting interest in creating something new or different that addresses an unmet market need.

In their 2007 article in *Stanford Social Innovation Review*, strategist Roger Martin and Skoll Foundation CEO Sally Osberg went further and identified an important quality of entrepreneurs. They observe a suboptimal situation (for example, lack of credit access for the poor) and create a venture that leads to a permanent shift to "a new stable equilibrium, one that provides a meaningfully higher level of satisfaction for the participants in the system."[1]

Longtime Harvard Business School Professor Howard Stevenson defined entrepreneurship a little bit differently, calling it "the pursuit of opportunity without regard to resources controlled."[2] By this, Stevenson meant that entrepreneurs look outside their immediate context to assemble resources in original and different ways to create new value.

What about the "social" in social entrepreneurship? In short, it means that the organizations social entrepreneurs found prioritize social benefits before profit. Social ventures *can* be profitable, but the primary goal of the social entrepreneur is to use those funds to further social good.

Professor Gregory Dees, one of the earliest and most influential thinkers in the field, expanded on Howard Stevenson's ideas by defining social entrepreneurs as individuals who play the role of change agents in the social sector, by:

- Adopting a mission to create and sustain social value (not just private value)
- Recognizing and relentlessly pursuing new opportunities to serve that mission
- Engaging in a process of continuous innovation, adaptation, and learning
- Acting boldly without being limited by resources currently in hand, and
- Exhibiting heightened accountability to the constituencies served and for the outcomes created.[3]

Let's add to this definition with three additional themes:

- Focused on society's most pressing social problems
- Committed to offering new ideas for wide-scale change
- Interested in applying practical, innovative, and sustainable approaches

In their 2008 article, Martin and Osberg distinguished between entrepreneurship and social entrepreneurship based on the way that value is distributed. "For the entrepreneurs, the value proposition anticipates and is organized to serve markets that can comfortably afford the new product or service and is thus designed to create financial profit."[4] In contrast, the social entrepreneur "neither anticipates nor organizes to create substantial financial profit for his or her investors—philanthropic and government organization for the most part—or for himself or herself. Instead, the social entrepreneur aims for value in the form of large scale, transformational benefit that accrues either to a significant segment of society or to society at large."[5]

This is also what Dees meant by mission-related impact rather than wealth creation being the central criterion for social entrepreneurs, writing that for them, "the social mission is explicit and central" and that "wealth is just a means to an end for social entrepreneurs."[6]

Martin and Osberg further define social entrepreneurship by distinguishing between it and two other activities. One is **social service** provision, which has social benefits but is focused on immediate benefits not broad change. A second is **social activism**, which is intended to create change by influencing others to act, but not necessarily to create value through entrepreneurship.

Social entrepreneurship is also distinct from **stakeholder capitalism** and **environmental, social, and governance (ESG)** investing, although both have received attention in the past decade as customers and investors have increasingly demanded that companies they interact with act with transparency and consider social impact.

- *Stakeholder capitalism* is a corporate orientation to serve the interests of multiple stakeholders, including shareholders, employees, suppliers, and the communities in which they operate. Rather than maximizing shareholder value, the intent is to enhance long-term value for a variety of stakeholders.
- *Environmental, social, and governance (ESG)* describes a set of criteria used by investors that evaluate the positive social impact of an organization's activities. These could include the organization's pay structure, environmental impact, protection of shareholder rights, or provision of other social benefits.

While stakeholder holder capitalism and ESG have raised awareness of the responsibility of private organizations to consider objectives beyond profitability, they are distinct from social ventures in that they do not make social impact their central goal.

A related concept is the **triple bottom line**, which is the idea that companies should also measure environmental and social benefits in addition to profit. Efforts to balance the three elements—profit, planet, and people—exist at triple bottom line companies as diverse as Ben & Jerrys (now owned by Unilever) and the LEGO Group.

THE PROMISE OF SOCIAL ENTREPRENEURSHIP

It started with a little amount of money. So little that you can laugh at it looking back. A total loan of $27 for 42 people—not even a dollar a person.[7]

–Muhammad Yunus

This was the simple beginning of Grameen Bank, an organization that has changed the world under the leadership of economist Muhammad Yunus, Grameen's former CEO and the 2006 winner of the Nobel Peace Prize.

Yunus created Grameen Bank after he observed that people living in rural villages in Bangladesh were unable to lift themselves out of poverty because they lacked access to banking and credit, despite having all the drive and potential of their higher income counterparts. After his $27 experiment, he tried to expand by offering himself to banks as a guarantor; they were not willing to lend to the poor, so he funded loans personally. Based on this experience, he turned lending upside down, challenging the conventional wisdom (loan to men, concentrate on urban areas, require collateral) and did exactly the opposite. This new way of thinking evolved into Grameen Bank, which today works in every village in Bangladesh and has 8.5 million borrowers, 97% of whom are women. And unlike most other lending institutions, borrowers own the bank.[8]

Yunus was not the first to see promise in the concept of microfinance. The creation of community-based and informal financial institutions had existed for hundreds of years prior to Grameen Bank's launch in 1983. In Ireland "loan funds emerged in the 1720s using peer monitoring to enforce the repayment in weekly installments of initially interest-free loans from donated resources."[9] In Germany, the first thrift society was established in 1778, and by the mid-1800s, spurred by a mid-century famine, credit cooperatives were formed in both urban and rural areas.[10] But we credit Yunus with adapting the model in Bangledesh, growing Grameen to create a much more ambitious organization.

In addition to providing loans, Grameen has worked to foster a culture of self-sufficiency. For example, Yunus described how after observing limited sanitation in Bangladesh villages, "We made a rule that if you want to join Grameen Bank you need to dig a hole (for a privy) and use it. After that, we started to give loans for decent sanitary facilities. This influenced the women in well-off families—who asked "why the beggar woman has a latrine and we don't."[11] Social pressure created a new standard in these communities, enabling rural villages to dramatically increase access to sanitation.

Yunus also expanded Grameen's scope beyond loans and other financial services. He created a low-cost health insurance program for borrowers and their families. He teamed up with French food conglomerate Danone to form Grameen Danone Foods, and created a yogurt with micronutrients, which helps serve children in Bangladesh—half of whom are malnourished. Grameen created a nursing college, to provide education and increase the supply of good-quality nurses. It started a water company to deliver clean water to rural areas and, understanding that going barefoot makes people vulnerable to parasitic diseases, Grameen created a shoe manufacturing company that produces shoes for under €1.

Yunus believes that creating social businesses—where impact, not profit, is the goal—can solve many of the world's most pressing problems. He said: "Whenever I see a problem, I design a business to solve the problem."[12] In his view, all of the UN Sustainable Development Goals, including reduction of poverty, achieving health goals and improving education, "are also excellent social business ideas."[13]

His vision also extends to education:

> Why should, in this day and age, anybody still be illiterate, tell me? There is no reason. The illiterate person has a phone in her hand. If you can come up with good software like games and things which are fun, people will be having fun and at the same time they will learn to read and write. You don't need a school, you don't need teachers any more, because technology provides all these facilities. We're looking (to create) social businesses to make this technology, and many technology companies are paying attention to it. Education for everybody is possible. The education for the children of the richest families in the world and education for the children of the poorest families in the world should come from the same source.[14]

Grameen Bank has launched multiple enterprises including Grameen Shakti (Grameen Energy), Grameen Telecom, Grameen Shikkha (Grameen Education), (Grameen Fisheries), Grameen Baybosa Bikash (Grameen Business Development), and the Grameen Foundation.

What can we learn from this serial social entrepreneur and his groundbreaking organization? Among many lessons, key ones include the values of thinking differently, challenging conventional wisdom, and working to extend boundaries to create even more social good.

Yunus famously said that he hopes that in the future, there will be a "museum of poverty; a building where the children of the future would go and marvel at the phenomenon of poverty. They would ask questions which couldn't be answered: 'There was great wealth and prosperity, and everyone was splurging, so why were others poor and dying?'"[15]

ENTREPRENEURIAL LEADERSHIP

Characteristics of Entrepreneurs

While there is no single, innate personality characteristic that defines entrepreneurs, there is agreement about some of the attributes that help make them successful.

Professor Jeffry Timmons and Stephen Spinelli in their book *New Venture Creation Entrepreneurship for the 21st Century* analyzed more than fifty studies and identified seven desirable attributes of effective entrepreneurs:

- *Commitment and determination*—characterized by persistence and tenacity
- *Courage*—characterized by moral strength and the ability to face conflicts
- *Leadership*—shows up as the ability to motivate and inspire others
- *Opportunity obsession*—seen as intensively focused by problem-solving and value creation
- *Ability to assume risk and operate with ambiguity*—expressed as tolerance for uncertainty and lack of structure
- *Adaptability*—characterized by the ability to adapt, pivot, and change
- *Motivation*—results and achievement orientation[16]

But they also cite William Lee, adding that "there is no evidence of an ideal entrepreneurial personality. Great entrepreneurs can be gregarious or low-key, analytical or intuitive, charismatic or boring, good with details or terrible, delegators or control freaks. What you *do* need is a capacity to execute in certain ways."[17]

Longtime business author Joseph Mausco at the Center for Entrepreneurial Management conducted a study identifying demographic, psychographic, and behavioral characteristics that predispose an individual towards entrepreneurship based on a survey of 3,000 entrepreneurs. The top five were as follows:

- Offspring of self-employed parents
- People previously fired from more than one job
- Immigrants or the children of immigrants
- People previously employed in businesses of fewer than 100 employees
- The oldest child in the family[18]

These observations make intuitive sense—the presence of entrepreneurial role models, attraction to smaller enterprises, and (likely) early socialization around responsibility align well with what we know about entrepreneurial behavior. Does this mean that someone needs to have a particular family background to become a successful entrepreneur? The answer is obviously not—early exposure can help to foster an orientation, but these capabilities can also be developed through exposure and experience. In my entrepreneurship class we have an ongoing debate—are entrepreneurs *made* or *born*—and students consistently surface examples to prove that either can happen.

Entrepreneurial Motivation

Tim Butler, Senior Fellow at Harvard Business School and Advisor to the Career Center, is a psychologist who has spent the past four decades understanding the career paths and motivations of business leaders. His research examined the psychological tests of 4,000 entrepreneurs in multiple countries and contrasted them with 1,800 general managers who did not identify themselves as entrepreneurial. Intriguing patterns emerged that help to both refine our knowledge of the entrepreneurial mindset and overcoming some long-held stereotypes. In a recent article in the *Harvard Business Review*, he shared his findings that entrepreneurs are not necessarily more creative than the sample of managers as a group, but instead are "curious seekers of adventure, learning and opportunity."[19] Butler found that "openness to new experiences" is the trait that distinguishes entrepreneurial leaders. He also found that entrepreneurs are not, as they are commonly portrayed, risk seekers. Instead, they are more comfortable with risk and are motivated by unpredictable and ambiguous environments.[20]

Professor Howard Stevenson joins Butler in debunking the idea that entrepreneurs are risk lovers, explaining during an interview that "back in 1983, people tended to define 'entrepreneurship' almost as a personality disorder, a kind of risk addiction. But that didn't fit the entrepreneurs I knew. I never met an entrepreneur who got up in the morning saying, 'Where's the most risk in today's economy, and how can I get some?'"[21] Instead, he characterizes entrepreneurs as those who effectively recognize, evaluate, and manage risk, not those who blindly embrace it.

Butler also assessed ambition as a characteristic, but found that for entrepreneurs, the motivation was less about authority and more about a need for ownership—having control over the product of their efforts. Finally, he highlighted how entrepreneurs are natural salespeople, utilizing confidence and persuasiveness to sell ideas to partners and supporters.[22]

What do our decades of observation tell us about social entrepreneurs? They suggest that social entrepreneurs, while a diverse bunch, tend to have the same qualities as mainstream entrepreneurs plus one more: an unwavering focus on creating a positive benefit for society. The sectors that interest these ambitious entrepreneurs may vary, the methods and strategies they employ may differ, and they may employ a range of corporate and organizational structures, but the common thread is an unrelenting vision for social change.

PROFILE: BILL DRAYTON AT ASHOKA

Bill Drayton is CEO of Ashoka: Innovators for the Public and is a pioneer in the field of social entrepreneurship. He is described in David Bornstein's seminal book *How to Change the World* as an "usually determined and creative individual."[23] It is hard to overstate the influence Drayton and Ashoka have had on the field of social entrepreneurship. In addition to coining the term "social entrepreneurship," Ashoka supported thousands of the early role models in the field and created a mutually supportive network that has sustained system change around the world. When Drayton started Ashoka, his vision was to identify and support the world's leading social entrepreneurs, learn from the patterns in their innovations, and mobilize a global community that embraces these new frameworks to build "everyone a changemaker world."

Drayton's interest in public service and social change emerged at an early age. As an undergraduate student at Harvard, among other initiatives, he launched an organization called Ashoka Table, a discussion group that invited prominent public leaders for off-the-record dinner conversations during which students could ask how things really worked. The name Ashoka was inspired by the Sanskrit word Ashoka that means the "active absence of sorrow" and by the Indian Emperor Ashoka, a revolutionary social change agent who ruled from 269 to 232 BC.

In 1970, Drayton began his career at McKinsey and Company in New York City. He then spent four years during the Carter administration as Assistant Administrator at the US Environmental Protection Agency, where he launched emissions trading and other reforms. In 1980, he founded Ashoka (while working at McKinsey), but discovered that the concept of social entrepreneurship was too new and unusual to gain foundational support. "For the first five years of Ashoka I could not get one public foundation in United States to support us with one cent. None. It was not because this is a bad idea or because I was inarticulate… Not one of them would risk any money on this idea."[24] This all changed when in 1984 Drayton received a $200,000 MacArthur Genius grant, enabling him to work full-time to establish Ashoka. He also secured financial support from the Rockefeller Brothers Foundation and this helped to convince other foundations that the Ashoka concept was worth investing in.

Ashoka's early work involved selecting fellows in Brazil and then Mexico, Bangladesh, and Nepal and supporting them as they pursued their visions. It used a distinctive selection process to identify high-potential social entrepreneurs, using five criteria: whether the entrepreneur possessed a truly new idea, whether the idea was compelling and impactful, whether the entrepreneur was creative in both vision and problem-solving, whether the entrepreneur was relentlessly driven and possessed ethical fiber. Selected social entrepreneurs received a stipend to support their living expenses while developing their initiative (typically for three years). During the 1990s Ashoka expanded to select fellows in Asia, Africa, Latin America, and Central and Eastern Europe and in 2000, anxious to move beyond its reputation as a development organization, it also began operating in the United States. By the late 1990s Ashoka had achieved its goal of establishing social entrepreneurship as a movement. It had selected more than 1,000 social entrepreneurs and supported them by providing training, counseling, and venture advice and it had created a fellowship of mutually supportive social entrepreneurs.

Ashoka was first in what would become a groundswell of organizations that grew to support social entrepreneurs both in the United States and globally, including Echoing Green (established in 1987), the Schwab Foundation for Social Entrepreneurship and New Profit (both established in 1998), the Skoll Foundation (1999), and many others. In 2005, Drayton was selected as one of America's Best Leaders by US News and World Report and Harvard's Center for Public Leadership.

Today, Ashoka operates in more than 90 countries and has elected more than 3,500 Ashoka Fellows worldwide. Drayton estimates that "three quarters of the Ashoka Fellows have changed the pattern in their field at the national and/or international level within five years."[25]

Starting in 2005, Drayton expanded Ashoka's vision even further. Not content to simply select and support visionary social entrepreneurs, it launched its "Everyone a Changemaker" initiative, observing that "everyone needs to become a changemaker in order to thrive; and everyone should be equipped with the qualities that most define social entrepreneurs. Ashoka has unlocked this strategy by drawing on the inspiration, depth of knowledge and expertise, accumulated experience and collective insights from the Fellows' work that enables a broader flowering of effective social change."[26] In 2008, Ashoka launched the AshokaU program, which catalyzes social innovation in higher education by assembling a global network of change teams composed of entrepreneurial students, faculty, and community leaders. Soon after, in 2012, it launched the Changemakers Schools program to create a global community of leading elementary, middle, and high schools that prioritize empathy, teamwork, leadership, and problem-solving.

Drayton's vision for Ashoka going forward is to create even larger scale social change. Currently, he is deeply concerned about the acceleration of global inequity. To help address this, he is pushing Ashoka to work with both young social entrepreneurs (he calls them "jujitsu partners") and leaders within established institutions that will leverage the "pattern recognition" that comes from its network of the world's best social entrepreneurs to create consensus for regional and national change. For example, in Brazil, Ashoka is working in the education sector with young changemakers, unions, schools, and select political units to create a more equitable education sector (B. Drayton, personal interview, November 3, 2020).

His advice to nascent social entrepreneurs is simple—"give yourself permission." He observes that great entrepreneurial ideas aren't all that complicated, they just require the use of problem-solving skills and intense focus. "By ignoring the naysayers and persistently pursuing your vision, you really can change the world" (B. Drayton, personal interview, November 3, 2020).

HOW SOCIAL ENTREPRENEURS ACHIEVE IMPACT

What Do Social Entrepreneurs Actually Do?

As we mentioned above, social entrepreneurs are a diverse group, but two essential qualities stand out: an orientation towards using **innovation** to change the status quo and an obsession with creating value through social change (Figure 1.1).

Figure 1.1 Innovation and Impact

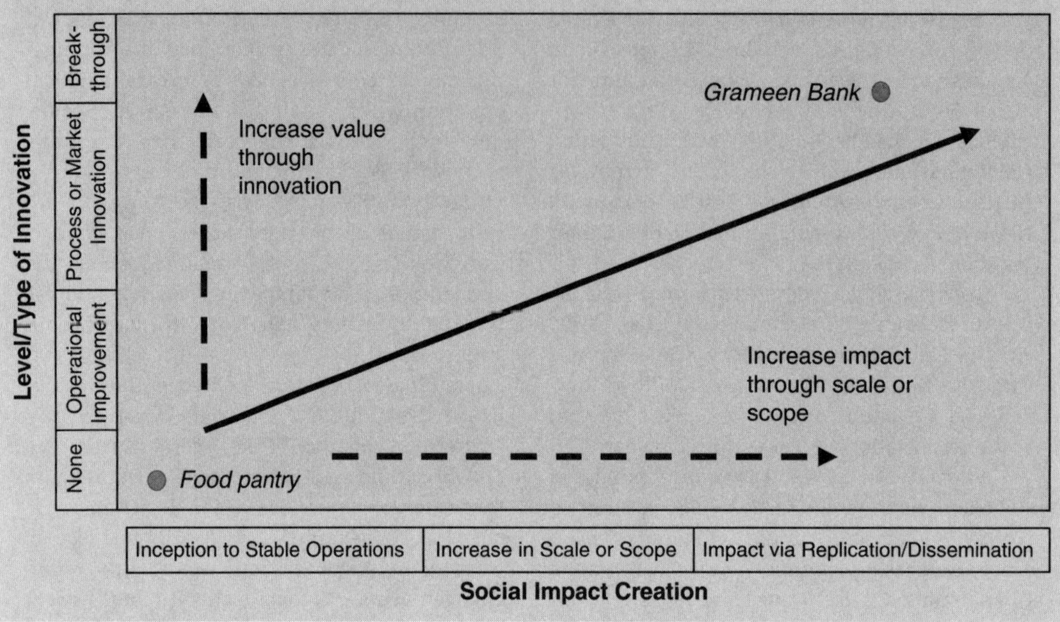

Mapping these elements graphically illustrates the difference between types of ventures. Consider, for example, a food pantry. While it provides an important benefit to the community, the basic model—collecting food and financial donations and distributing food to those in need, it is not especially innovative and is almost always local. While these organizations provide critical resources to individuals and families, they do not have a high impact outside their immediate communities and therefore are placed in the lower left of the image. That said, some food pantries have developed a larger, regional vision. And some entrepreneurs, like Doug Rausch, founder of Daily Table (discussed later in this chapter and in Chapter 3) have taken an entrepreneurial problem-solving approach to reducing food waste and food insecurity while also developing innovative and higher impact offerings.

Some entrepreneurial ventures fall towards the left side of the graph because their growth or innovation level is constrained by geographical limitations or the nature of the problem they seek to address. For example, Genesis, founded by Dr. Yasmeen Abu Fraiha, provides premarital genetic testing to Bedouin teenagers and young adults to reduce the very high prevalence of genetic birth defects in Bedouin communities. With 21 million Bedouins (and 3 million sick children) worldwide, there is a large addressable market but potential for additional expansion is limited. To be sure,

Dr. Abu Fraiha could expand to provide services to other similarly closed communities, but this is unlikely because of her focus on benefiting her community.

Let's contrast this with Muhammad Yunus at Grameen Bank. Yunus' initial insight—that the poor were good credit risks but did not have access to credit—enabled him to innovate by creating new credit products for an unserved market. He did this not just by providing funds but also by inventing a new approach. Grameen sits at the top right in our diagram because of how it innovated to create microlending because of the scale of its impact. It did this by increasing both its **scale** (increasing the number of borrowers served) and **scope** (by introducing other products to help the poor). In addition, it inspired the development of a new industry of microlending organizations around the world. Today, there are nearly 1,000 microlenders worldwide meeting the credit needs of 140 million borrowers, 80% of whom are women and 65% of whom are located in rural areas.[27]

Other ventures fall at different points on the spectrum, but effective entrepreneurs are always seeking to accelerate innovation and increase impact (whether via scale, scope, **replication**, or **dissemination**). An important question for nascent social entrepreneurs to ask themselves is why should they ever be satisfied with being at the bottom left rather than aspiring to the upper right? Constantly pushing on the dimensions of innovation and social impact—sometimes concurrently, sometimes sequentially—is what separates high-impact social entrepreneurs from their less effective peers.

What the Critics Say

While we celebrate the important work done by social entrepreneurs, there are a few caveats. One is that we tend to idolize solo entrepreneurs. As we discuss in Chapter 4, most ventures are team-founded and rely on a supportive ecosystem, so the successful solo player is the exception rather than the rule. A recent study published in the *Journal of Social Entrepreneurship* analyzed the results of 40 interviews with successful social entrepreneurs and concluded that while leading social entrepreneurs are indeed motivated by social responsibility they also show "an iconoclastic need to redefine the world based on their own values." The authors also observed that "ego is often a driver."[28] Aspiring entrepreneurial leaders should work hard to ensure that their solutions are well grounded in deeply understood social problems.

Another criticism of social entrepreneurs comes from journalist and policy analyst Anand Giridharadas in his influential book *Winners Take All: The Elite Charade of Changing the World* in which he raises concerns that social entrepreneurship can compromise momentum for broader social progress. He argues: "When elites put themselves in the vanguard of social change, it not only fails to make things better but also serves to keep things as they are."[29]

In addition, there is substantial disagreement about how to define social entrepreneurship. Not everyone agrees that the primacy of social goals is central to the definition. In a recent article in the *Journal of World Economics*, coauthors Ana Maria Peredo and Murdith McLean review research on the question and draw a continuum that ranges from ventures focused entirely and exclusively on social impact to organizations where social benefits are further down the list of organization objectives. For example, they include organizations that use "cause branding" in their marketing.[30] The authors conclude that "there is no exact way of fixing the border below which the importance of social goals fails to quality something as social entrepreneurship."[31] A broad approach to defining social entrepreneurship has benefits (it allows for a wider range of activities to be considered) and drawbacks (if the definition is too broad it may lose meaning.)

THREE TYPES OF SOCIAL ENTREPRENEURS

Recognizing that there are many ways to categorize social entrepreneurs, we have grouped them into three categories: innovators, scalers, and ecosystem builders.

Innovators

Innovators are individuals or teams that see a dysfunction in society that they want to solve by using a novel solution. These leaders are characterized by their interest in creating something new that solves a persistent social problem. But as we can see from the examples below, the nature of the problem and solution can differ substantially.

Innovating to Solve a Persistent Problem: Daily Table

Doug Rausch, founder of Daily Table, noticed an opportunity in the market to provide affordable, nutritious food for lower income households while reducing waste. As the former president of grocery retailer Trader Joe's, he knew full well how much food is wasted in the conventional retail system. He observed that in the United States "We have one in six Americans that are hungry, and we're one of the richest nations in the history of the world. Meanwhile, somewhere between 30% and 40% of the food we grow is just going to waste—it's not being consumed."[32] Rausch envisioned a supermarket that would sell fresh, wholesome food and healthily prepared foods at or near cost to residents in low-income neighborhoods.

Daily Table works with a large network of growers, supermarkets, manufacturers, and other suppliers who donate their excess, healthy food to Daily Table, or provide them with special buying opportunities. Some, but not all, of the food is near its sell-by date but is still safe and healthy. The goal is not only to offer affordable groceries in lower income communities but also to sell healthy ready-to-cook meals and hot grab-and-go items at prices that compete with "cheap" fast food. Since establishing its first store in

Boston's Dorchester neighborhood, Daily Table has expanded in the Boston area and has its sights on eventual expansion to Detroit, Los Angeles, New York, and San Francisco.

Daily Table is a nonprofit organization, but it runs like a business, sustaining itself without financial donations. Rauch observed that they could raise a massive amount of charitable contributions and sell food at a discount but in his view this was not a scalable model.

Realigning Systems to Create Social Value: Sanergy

Another way to innovate is by identifying a unique recombination of resources that creates social value. This is what Sanergy did (discussed in depth in the full-length case at the end of this book). By rethinking human waste collection in the Nairobi's slums and realigning the toilets and waste collection processes, the founding team brought together elements that previously had been separated and combined them to create a self-supporting and scalable model. Sanergy's network of low-cost sanitation centers, franchising model, and production of organic fertilizer created a new and valuable system. Later, the addition of waste-based products such as insect-based animal feed and briquettes further reinforced its financial viability and impact.

What is the common theme in these examples? In short, innovators spot opportunities to launch new ventures that create social value that others have overlooked. Innovators harness emerging technology, demographic, or political change. They might also import ideas from one context to another. For example, Yasmeen Abu Fraiha's technology for premarital genetic testing was not new—it had been used previously in the orthodox Jewish community by nonprofit Dor Yeshorim. Her insight was that if social barriers to implementation could be overcome, it could also be effective in Bedouins' communities.

Other innovators who have developed novel solutions to solve social problems include BRAC and STREETS International (Chapter 2), One Acre Fund (Chapter 5), Prosperity Candle (Chapter 6), 99Degrees (Chapter 8), and Wilding and Company (Chapter 10). UNICEF is featured as an intrapreneurial innovator. Innovators that have solved social problems by importing solutions from other contexts include SolarBox (Chapter 3) and Social Finance (Chapter 6).

Scalers

Scalers are entrepreneurs who take a socially beneficial innovation and grow it to expand impact. As we discuss in Chapter 7—Scaling and Expansion, typical ways to accomplish this are increasing the scale of the venture (by serving more people, often by expanding geographically), increasing the scope (by proving more services or expanded services to its customers), or both. Scalers are characterized by their tenacity and ability to attract the resources required for expansion. Many, but not all, founders that start as innovators become scalers. Many also find their niche in one role or the other, with those that remain innovators often expanding impact in another way by becoming serial social entrepreneurs.

Scaling Impact by Expanding Services: Management Leaders for Tomorrow

John Rice, CEO of Management Leaders for Tomorrow (MLT), is a classic scaler. A former executive with Disney and the National Basketball Association, he received a BA with honors in Latin American Studies from Yale, where he was a three-year starter on the basketball team. Rice used his sports background to devise how MLT should work. He noticed that in sports, people get coaching and a playbook for what is expected and a network of peers and mentors each step of the way, but that this doesn't exist as formally in the professional world.

While Rice was getting an MBA at Harvard Business School in the early 1990s, he was disheartened by the lack of minority students in the program. He observed that while Black Americans make up 13% of the US population, there are only five black CEOs of Fortune 500 companies.[33] This led him to develop a business plan for a new venture that would bolster minority talent at schools and in management positions.

Rice created Management Leaders for Tomorrow in 1994 and launched it in 2002 with a mission to prepare men and women of color for high-trajectory, postcollege jobs that deliver economic mobility for them and their families. MLT started by working with college students, and then created the Career Prep program that provided fellows with a "winning professional playbook," 18 months of one-on-one coaching and a network. Eventually MLT expanded to MBA access and preparation (standardized test guidance, seminars and one-on-one coaching for early career individuals interested in pursuing an MBA). The addition of MBA professional development and career advancement programs expanded their impact by offering services throughout an individual's career.

MLT's success and outcomes are undeniable. 95% of Fellows in MLT's college program received highly competitive job offers prior to graduation and 75% of the professionals in MLT's midcareer advancement program received promotions within one year of completing the program. Today, MLT serves over 8,000 students and professionals nationwide and is a leading source of minority talent at its 150 blue-chip partner companies like Google, Goldman Sachs, and Procter & Gamble. Meanwhile, Rice has been named as one of Forbes Top 30 social entrepreneurs in the world.

MLT's growth relied on increasing both scale and scope. Initially, MLT launched with a program narrowly aimed at college students but, as the organization gained resources, it expanded programming. Starting with just a few external partnerships, it developed relationships with 150 leading companies to extend its impact in the workplace. By leveraging its alumni, who frequently say they feel a responsibility to help those that are coming after them, it continues to broaden and grow its impact.

Creating a Large Footprint to Address Education Gaps: Ekal Vidyalaya

Ekal Vidyalaya is another example of how social entrepreneurs rethought a problem to create a practical solution that was able to rapidly expand. The nonprofit organization was originally formed in 1986 in response to the enormous gap in educational opportunities facing rural children in India. In India in the 1980s, there were few government-funded schools in small, rural villages. Many families also depended on their children to help with farming and household chores. Among children aged 6–10 in rural India, only 38% of boys and 25% of girls attended school.[34]

The founders of Ekal Vidyalaya responded by creating a concept called "One Teacher Schools" that was designed to address the realities facing rural village families. To establish a school, the team worked with a village to identify a local resident who could serve as the teacher and set up a school in their home or outdoors. Schedules were designed to enable children to attend while still meeting family responsibilities. An established curriculum and significant support for teachers (many of whom had only a high school education) enabled them to teach a common curriculum.

A series of national government policies guaranteeing rural education supported the expansion of rural schools, and by 2013, primary school attendance for rural children reached 82%. In areas with high-performing government-funded schools, Ekal adapted by providing a curriculum that supplemented these efforts, and in areas where gaps still existed, it continued its traditional curriculum. In 2013 they were the primary source of education in 20% of the villages where they operated and by 2014 Ekal had expanded to a network of 50,000 schools spread across India. Their lean model meant that each school's budget was only USD$1 per day, a small fraction of the typical cost of government schools. Ekal's schools are funded by a combination of donor contributions and funding from the villages and towns served.[35]

Today there are over 100,000 schools in the Ekal network educating 2.7 million children. What can we learn from this impressive scaling story? Among other things, that a low-cost model, a lean approach to operations and a customer-centric design can help social entrepreneurs translate a simple idea into enormous social impact.

Other scalers featured in this book include One Acre Fund (Chapter 5), Peer Health Exchange (Chapter 7), UNICEF (Chapter 10), and Sanergy (case). Aspiring scalers include SolarBox (Chapter 3) and WorkAround (case).

Ecosystem Builders

Ecosystem builders are individuals and organizations that create infrastructure that enable social entrepreneurs to be more successful. These supportive systems take many forms. One is identifying high potential entrepreneurs and connecting them with resources and a supportive community. The Skoll Foundation, New Profit, and

Ashoka are examples. A second is creating an infrastructure that promotes social entrepreneurship and enables an entrepreneurial community to thrive. Examples include the Bridgespan Group (nonprofit consulting), the Schwab Foundation, and the Ākina Foundation.

Supporting Disruptive Leaders: Echoing Green

When Cheryl Dorsey (who we profile in more detail in Chapter 4) took the helm of Echoing Green in 2001, she was ready to build on its legacy of helping leaders including Wendy Kopp (founder of Teach for America), Vanessa Kirsch (founder of Public Allies and later founder of New Profit), and Vikram Akula (founder of SKS Microfinance) launch their ventures. This was at a time when public awareness of and support for social entrepreneurs was in its infancy.

Echoing Green's fellowship program used an intensive selection process to choose from hundreds of applications each year. Finalists were invited to a selection weekend in New York so that they could present their "bold idea for social change," participate in interviews, and pitch their ideas in front of other finalists and a panel of judges.[36] As Dorsey observed: "We are really good at picking winners. People come to us with an interest in taking on the status quo, saying 'Things aren't working in the field I care about, so I'm going to do something different.' And, at Echoing Green, we say 'great idea—we're not sure it will work but we'll take a chance on you and see what you can do.'"[37]

As of 2020, selected fellows receive a two-year $80,000 stipend ($90,000 for partner applications), personalized coaching, well-being support, an expert advisor and thought partner. They also gain lifelong access to Echoing Green's alumni network, retreats, networking events, and pro bono legal and investing advice as well as other professional support. According to Echoing Green, 80% of the fellows they have supported still work in the social sector and 70% of the organizations they have funded are still in operation today. Meanwhile, their reach continues to grow, and they have helped to found over 800 organizations in 86 countries across the globe.[38]

Partnering to Create a Social Movement: Ākina Foundation

New Zealand's Ākina Foundation has a different approach to ecosystem building. The foundation partners with the New Zealand government to use public funding to further their shared economic development objectives. Named for the native Māori word that means "to challenge," Ākina was created with the goal of building a prosperous and inclusive New Zealand.

Led by CEO Louise Aiken, Ākina was founded in 2008 by the Todd and Tindall Foundations to support practical action on climate change and the environment. Its mission evolved to focus on five impact areas: transportation, housing, consumption and waste, land and ecosystems, and energy. Ākina's team also built an incubation model that supports a range of social enterprises and social entrepreneurs throughout the country. Over time, they saw that social enterprise could provide a powerful vehicle for driving transformation and change.

New Zealand is an island nation of 5 million people that regularly shows up as number 1 in the World Bank's Ease of Doing Business report. Despite its small size, it is well known for its tourism and education sectors, as well as its focus as a nation on environmental sustainability. Aitken joined Ākina in 2016, following a successful corporate career that included the management of the country's largest corporate social responsibility program. She also sits on the board of the Impact Enterprise Fund and on the National Advisory Board for Impact Investing Network Aotearoa New Zealand.

One of New Zealand's national priorities has been to build its economy with a focus on fostering a strong entrepreneurial sector. By partnering with the New Zealand government, Ākina has supported social innovation and entrepreneurship and together, they are helping to create the conditions for a thriving social enterprise sector in New Zealand. Ākina does this by promoting social enterprise contributions to the government's economic, social, and environmental goals and by working directly with entrepreneurs to test changes that would grow their ventures.

In 2014, New Zealand's government announced funding to expand Ākina's incubation and development services for high potential social enterprises across New Zealand. By 2018 they had been named as the strategic partner to the government in a three-year program to further develop the sector. Ākina's team worked with ventures to help build their capacity, define and report their impact, reduce legal barriers to growth, and increase their market opportunities as well as working with change-makers from Māori enterprises. As a close partner with the government, Ākina has gained the support they needed to grow both the infrastructure for and the national conversation on the social sector.

In 2017 Ākina, alongside partners, raised NZ$8 million for New Zealand's first impact investment fund. Ākina made the choice to prioritize financial returns alongside impact returns. "There is a lot of philanthropy in New Zealand, and a lot of financially motivated investment in New Zealand, but less understanding that the outcome of both of these actions can be achieved with the same dollar. We, therefore, decided to make a finance first impact fund to help the financially motivated people understand they can generate strong returns as well as impact. As these investors become more familiar with impact, we hope that over time they show interest in investing in impact first funds while still receiving a financial return."[39]

Other ecosystem builders featured in this book include Ashoka (Chapter 1), MassChallenge (Chapter 3), Our Generation Speaks (Chapter 4), and the Greenlight Fund (Chapter 7).

Transitions Between Roles

Many people with great ideas and an obsession with solving a social problem do not initially see themselves as visionary social entrepreneurs. When Muhammed Yunus loaned $27 to women to help them start ventures that would enable them and their families to escape poverty, he thought was solving in immediate problem, not creating a movement. But he was just getting started.

Social entrepreneurs often move between the innovator, scaler, and ecosystem builder roles. For example, Yunas started as an innovator, became a scaler, and ultimately became an ecosystem builder. Others find their passion in one category, like Ashoka founder Bill Drayton, who is profiled in this chapter. Drayton dedicated his career to building an ecosystem to support social entrepreneurship. Or consider Margaret Hall and John Simon, the cofounders of the Greenlight Fund. GreenLight operates as an ecosystem builder that helps nonprofit organizations scale. But in order to achieve this, the fund's founders needed to themselves be effective scalers, expanding GreenLight's presence to multiple cities to increase its impact.

As we discussed at the beginning of this chapter, there are multiple opportunities for those who want to make a difference in a mission-driven entrepreneurial organization. Founders are the people we think of first when we discuss entrepreneurial leaders and nearly all entrepreneurial ventures have an inspirational person at the helm that provides the external face of the organization. But many externally focused founders balance their efforts by collaborating with individuals who bring a critical internal management perspective. For example, while Our Generation Speaks (profiled in Chapter 4) was created by Ohad Elhelo, a founder with fundraising and external engagement capabilities, it is now run by Lobna Agbaria, an attorney and former fellow who both leads and ensures that the operations run smoothly to support future growth. After seven years at the helm of 99Degrees, Brenna Schneider (the subject of a short case in Chapter 8) was anxious to recruit an outstanding COO who would help to shepherd the next stage of growth. Cheryl Dorsey's work at Echoing Green would not have been as successful without the collaboration and organizational development work of Senior Vice President Lara Galinsky, and other internally focused contributors.

Finally, while many aspiring social entrepreneurs are motivated to start their own ventures, they should consider whether society is better served by contributing their efforts to an existing venture. Playing a supporting role can help them learn how to be most effective when they strike out on their own. For example, Linda Rottenberg learned key skills while first volunteering to help Wendy Kopp recruit college seniors for startup Teach for America, and then by working with Bill Drayton at Ashoka. These experiences helped her develop her vision for Endeavor. Indeed, many aspiring private sector entrepreneurs piece together entrepreneurial apprenticeships using bootcamps, incubators, accelerators, mentors, and other resources to help them gain experience, establish networks, and hone their capabilities.[40]

FINDING YOUR NORTH STAR

A Few Key Questions

In his classic article "The Questions Every Entrepreneur Must Answer," Tufts University Professor and entrepreneurship scholar Amar Bhide lays out a few crucial questions that anyone who considers themselves an entrepreneur needs to be ready to address.[41]

We've added an additional question at the beginning aimed at social entrepreneurs: *Am I truly committed to solving the social problem that I am targeting?* Founding a new social venture requires a high level of persistence and flexibility, and aspiring mission-driven leaders should be confident that they and their stakeholders are willing and able to make the kinds of sacrifices required to move their forward.

The second question, posed by Bhide, is *Where do I want to go?* Aspiring entrepreneurs should carefully consider whether launching the proposed venture aligns with their personal goals. Many ventures are "all in" particularly during the start-up phase. Ventures that work in developing markets are usually ill-served by founders that are based elsewhere.

Bhide's next question is: *How will I get there?* Prospective founders should realistically consider whether their strategy is sound and whether their venture is likely to achieve a scale that will make their efforts worthwhile.

Finally, entrepreneurs should ask: *Can I do it?* For social entrepreneurs, answering this question requires a clear-eyed assessment of whether you have the right capabilities, network, and access to capital, as well as other key resources that may be needed. Evaluating the success (or lack of success) of similarly positioned social entrepreneurs can help to answer this question. Candid advice on this question from mentors is also invaluable.

Self-Assessment Options

As they consider entrepreneurship as a path, aspiring social entrepreneurs may want to consider two approaches to self-assessment. Luckily a few good thinkers have created some structures that can help.

Jim Collins, in his classic management book *Good to Great*, described what he called the "hedgehog" concept for organizations—the intersection between three intersecting circles, and then subsequently applied the idea to individuals. The first describes what you are deeply passionate about. The second involves finding what you can do uniquely well (he calls it what you are genetically encoded for). The third circle examines what you are engaged in that is of social or economic value.[42]

A related approach comes from the thousand-year-old Japanese concept of Ikigai, which translates to "a reason for being" or that which creates satisfaction and a sense of meaning. An Ikigai diagram, illustrated below in Figure 1.2, has four intersecting circles. Similar to the hedgehog concept, three circles involve defining that which you love, that which you are good at, and that which you can be paid for. The fourth circle is that which the world needs. In an exercise at the end of this chapter we use the Ikigai approach to help you develop a perspective on understanding your passion.

Finally, in their excellent *Harvard Business Review* article, "From Purpose to Impact," authors Nick Craig and Scott Snook offer advice for determining your leadership purpose and translating it into action. They recommend mining your life story for themes. A few questions they urge readers to consider are what you enjoyed doing as a child, what challenging experiences have shaped you, and what you enjoy doing now. They advise crafting a clear statement of your leadership purpose and envisioning the impact you can have.[43]

Founding or contributing to an entrepreneurial social venture requires a high level of dedication, persistence, and flexibility, and aspiring mission-driven leaders should be confident about moving a venture forward. Or to take another piece of advice from Craig and Snook: "Clarify your purpose, and put it to work."[44]

CHAPTER SUMMARY

Aspiring entrepreneurs benefit from the work of earlier leaders in the field. As scientist Isaac Newton wrote in 1675, "If I have seen further, it is by standing on the shoulders of giants."

The same is true for social entrepreneurs. Today's social entrepreneurs are able to follow in the footsteps of visionaries like Muhammad Yunus, William Drayton, Linda Rottenberg, and countless others to establish ventures that can change the world.

While there is no single, innate personality characteristic that defines social entrepreneurs, a number of characteristics have been found in successful entrepreneurs such as courage, adaptability, opportunity obsession, and an unwavering focus on creating a positive benefit for society. These individuals can often be classified as one of three different types of social entrepreneur: inventors, scalers, and ecosystem builders. Inventors like Doug Rausch of Daily Table can be identified by their interest in creating something new that solves a persistent social problem. Scalers like John Rice, CEO of Management Leaders for Tomorrow, are entrepreneurs who take a socially beneficial innovation and grow it to expand impact. Ecosystem builders like Cheryl Dorsey of Echoing Green are individuals and organizations that create infrastructure to enable entrepreneurs and the initiatives they create to be more successful. For new ventures, it is possible to either move between categories or find your passion in just one.

There are also multiple ways to contribute to a mission-driven entrepreneurial organization. While founders are often the individuals we think of first because they are the venture's external-face, other roles are also crucial. Execution-focused managers contribute by concentrating on making the venture efficient and ecosystem developers accelerate social entrepreneurship but do not themselves aspire to be entrepreneurs.

Before getting started with your social venture, remember there are a few questions you should ask yourself. Consider first if you know your objectives and are truly committed to the issue at hand. Founding a new social venture requires a high level of dedication, persistence and flexibility, and aspiring mission-driven leaders should be confident that they and their stakeholders are willing and able to make the kinds of sacrifices required to move it forward.

And if you are—we hope you enjoy the journey!

KEY TERMS

Dissemination: the ability to spread a product or idea beyond the initial bounds of its conception.

Ecosystem builders: individuals and organizations that create infrastructure to enable entrepreneurs and the initiatives they create to be more successful.

Environmental, social and governance (ESG): uses criteria that extend beyond profit to evaluate potential investments. The measures examine an organization's relationships with other organizations, pay structure, environmental impact, social benefits provided, and protection of shareholder rights.

Innovation: the process of seeing dysfunction or inefficiency in society that can be solved by using a new or unique solution and doing so.

Replication: the duplication of a certain service, venture, or product.

Scalers: entrepreneurs who take a socially beneficial innovation and grow it to expand impact.

Scope: what is covered or not covered by a venture or service.

Social activism: intended to influence others to action, but not create value through entrepreneurship.

Social service: actions or ventures that have social benefits but is not designed to scale.

Stakeholder capitalism: describes a corporate orientation to serve the interests of multiple stakeholders, including shareholders, employees, suppliers, and the communities they operate in. Rather than maximizing shareholder value, the intent is to enhance long-term value for a variety of stakeholders.

Triple bottom line: the idea that companies should also measure environmental and social benefits rather than simply pursuing profits (the traditional bottom line for companies).

IN-CLASS EXERCISES

Exercise 1.1: Defining Your Entrepreneurial Purpose

(Estimated time: 20–30 minutes)

Purpose

Social entrepreneurs can focus their energy by inventorying their skills, interests, and intended impact to better define their purpose.

Preparation

Provide a blank copy of the template in Figure 1.2 for each student.

Process

1. Individually, each student takes 5 minutes to answer the four questions in the template.
2. Break into groups of 3–5 students.

3. Each participant presents the results of their analysis. Others in their group ask questions to help the presenter refine their ideas. Assign one person to summarize the results and report back to the class. (That person should verify whether or not results should be presented anonymously.)
4. Class debrief: After returning to class, the designated reporters for each group summarizes their discussion for the class:
   - Where were there points of similarity?
   - Where did differences exist?
   - What unique learnings/insights did you note about yourself and your purpose?
5. If time allows, a few volunteers can present their self-assessments to the class.

Alternate Approach: Pre-class Assignment

Use as a pre-class activity. Students complete the template and post their results on a shared site prior to class.

Figure 1.2 Map Your Purpose Using the Ikigai Framework

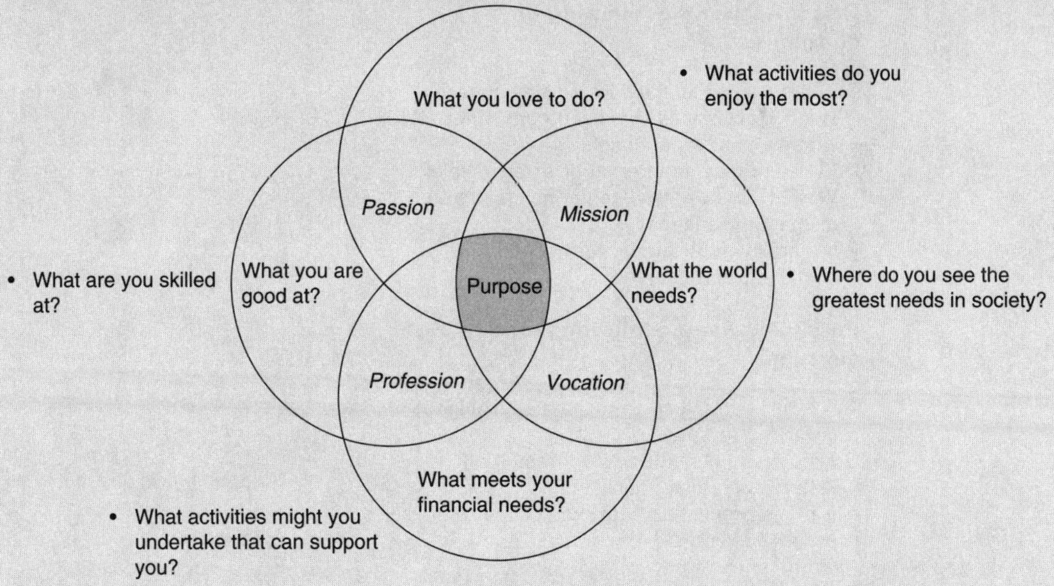

Source: Adapted from Ikigai by Bodor, D., & van Deurzen, E. (2015). *Wikimedia commons*. Retrieved from https://commons.wikimedia.org/wiki/File:Ikigai-EN-optimized-PNG.png. CC-BY-SA 4.0.

Exercise 1.2: Entrepreneurial Leadership Self-Assessment

(Estimated time: 20–30 minutes)

Purpose

Forward-thinking social entrepreneurs should rigorously assess their motives and realistically assess their assets and capabilities to increase their probability of success.

Preparation

Have blank copies of Table 1.1 below.

Process

1. Individually, take 5 minutes to answer the questions in the template.
2. Break into groups of 3–5 students.

Table 1.1 Entrepreneurial Leadership Self-Assessment

Question	Response
Part 1: Answer the following three questions: Do I see myself as a leader or a manager? Why? How has as this been consistent with my past experience? Do I like to play an internal or external role? Why? How has this been consistent with my past experience? What are my motivations for becoming a social entrepreneur?	
Part 2: Answer the following four questions: Am I truly committed to the social problem I am trying to solve? Does starting a venture to address it align with my personal goals? Am I being realistic about the scale of the proposed venture? Will it make enough of a difference to be worth of my efforts? Do I have (or can I secure) the right resources including my capabilities, access to capital, access to networks, and other key resources?	

3. Each participant presents the results of their self-assessment. Others in their group should ask questions to probe each presenter's logic. (Assign one person to summarize the results and report back to the class. That person should verify whether or not results should be presented anonymously or with attribution.)
4. Class debrief: After returning to class, the designated reporters for each group (or volunteers, as time allows) takes ~3 minutes to present summary results to the class, touching on the group members' answers, questions that were raised, and overall themes.
5. Post-class: Individually, continue to consider the questions and evaluate what this implies for the future.

SHORT CASE: LINDA ROTTENBERG—SUPPORTING HIGH-IMPACT ENTREPRENEURS AT ENDEAVOR

Linda Rottenberg has been described as an "Innovator for the 21st Century" by *Time* magazine, as one of "America's Best Leaders" by US News, and as "The Entrepreneur Whisperer" by ABC and National Public Radio. A high-energy, hands-on social entrepreneur, she is the cofounder of New York City–based Endeavor, a global organization that enables economic growth by supporting high potential entrepreneurs.

The concept for Endeavor grew out of a meeting between Linda Rottenberg and serial entrepreneur Peter Kellner in early 1997. At the time, Rottenberg was working in Latin America where she was leading a Southern Cone expansion strategy for Ashoka. In 2017, she met Kellner, a private sector entrepreneur and emerging markets investor, during a Harvard Business School recruiting trip. They immediately recognized their shared interest in supporting entrepreneurs in emerging markets and through their conversations concluded that in multiple countries many entrepreneurs have enormous potential but lack the support systems to launch and grow their ventures. After sketching out the initial concept and overcoming initial skepticism from family and friends, Rottenberg and Kellner set out to create Endeavor. As she explained the concept to prospective stakeholders, Rottenberg became known as *la Chica Loca* (the crazy girl), for insisting that high-impact entrepreneurs exist in emerging and developing markets.

Endeavor is a nonprofit organization that creates economic growth by finding and supporting high-impact for-profit entrepreneurs. Rottenberg launched its first local offices in 1997 in Chile and Argentina and by 2001 Endeavor was operating in five countries in Latin America—having added Brazil, Mexico, and Uruguay. The organization provides support by identifying and nurturing high-impact entrepreneurs through a highly competitive selection process. One of Endeavor's early picks was Wences Caseres. Caseres was the son of an Argentinian sheep rancher. During college, he experimented with founding various ventures and decided to create a financial services portal called Patagon. When he first met Rottenberg, he had been turned down by 33 investors as he looked for expansion capital. Endeavor bet on Caseres' vision for Patagon, selecting him out of hundreds of applicants. After participating in Endeavor's mentoring program, he learned how to create a business plan and raise capital. Less than five years later, Patagon was acquired by Banco Santader for $750 million. Caseres became a role model for aspiring entrepreneurs in Argentina and stepped up to serve on the Endeavor board.

Of the 50,000+ entrepreneurs screened since 1997, fewer than 3% have been selected as official Endeavor Entrepreneurs.[45] But Endeavor's promotion of entrepreneurship does not stop with selection: Rottenberg believes that it is also important to create a cultural narrative on the necessity of understanding entrepreneurship in the countries the team works in. To do this, Endeavor trains journalists in emerging markets on how to cover stories related to innovation and startups. Endeavor has also assisted in the creation of over 170 case studies centered on their entrepreneurs that are taught in business programs around the world.[46]

Throughout its existence, Endeavor's focus has primarily been on high-impact entrepreneurs. According to Rottenberg, "We noticed that there was a huge gap for entrepreneurs in what we call the missing middle."[47] Traditional sources of funding such as loans and venture capital were only available to connected or wealthy founders, while microfinance was typically reserved for poorer individuals. "No one was focusing on creating a middle class…We began to consider whether you could transform and build strong economies by providing high growth companies and high impact entrepreneurs the support they needed to compete in a global economy."[48] In her *New York Times* bestselling book *Crazy is a Compliment: The Power of Zigging When Everyone Else Zags*, Rottenberg describes high-impact entrepreneurs as "individuals with the biggest ideas, the likeliest potential to build businesses that matter and the greatest ability to inspire others."[49]

Each Endeavor country has its own office, which is organized as a separate nonprofit entity with its own local leadership and board. Each office is financed by donations from local business leaders and benefactors. The global office provides connections between them, supports expansion, and develops cross-country initiatives. The Endeavor network concentrates on creating five different types of capital: financial capital, human capital, intellectual capital (nearly 1,500 patents or patent applications have been filed by Endeavor Entrepreneurs since 1997), social capital (including mentoring and advising), and cultural capital (including media mentions, business awards, events, and university partnerships).

Today, Endeavor has established a presence in nearly 40 markets across Latin America, Asia, Africa, the Middle East, and underserved areas of Europe and the United States. As of 2020, Endeavor companies were generating $24B in annual revenues and had created 4.1 million jobs.[50]

Endeavor has augmented its work supporting entrepreneurs by creating investment funds, using its extensive knowledge of what makes new ventures successful. In 2010, Endeavor began to raise donations for its first proof of the concept, Endeavor Catalyst Philanthropy, using tax-deductible charitable donations. For Endeavor, the returns became an important source of operating funds; while its country offices were largely self-supporting, it was challenging to raise funds for their headquarters and for global operations. The investment fund was a huge success, returning seven times its initial capitalization (L. Rottenberg, personal interview, November 25, 2020).

In 2013, Endeavor launched Endeavor Catalyst I with a different model. Upon exit, the fund would distribute 20% of the upside to private investors, and the balance would support Endeavor. In 2020, Endeavor announced the final closing of its third fund, Endeavor Catalyst III. Seeking to treat the investors more like partners, the fund used a 50/50 return structure. Since launching Endeavor Catalyst in 2012, the fund has invested in more than 150 Endeavor Entrepreneur-led companies across 30 different markets.[51] "Within the Endeavor Global Board there was an increasing recognition that Endeavor was evolving toward a new 'hybrid' business model with a nonprofit mission and an increasingly for-profit sustainable funding model."[52]

According to Rottenberg, "Reaching $250M in assets under management is an amazing milestone…When we created Endeavor Catalyst eight years ago, we had a big dream: to build the world's most founder-friendly investment fund that could be truly of, by and for entrepreneurs. Today, we are well on our way to making that dream a reality!"[53] Investing follow-on capital vs. early-stage venture capital also meant that Endeavor was not crowding out other investors in the market.

Rottenberg's personal motto is "go big or go home," so it is not surprising that she has been working on an even bigger vision. She had noticed that the highest impact Endeavor Entrepreneurs often outgrew support networks in their home countries and needed global role models and a network of true peers in order to meet their full potential. In April 2018, with support from JP Morgan and Silicon Valley Bank, Endeavor launched a new initiative to provide tailored support to the entrepreneurs that are leading the fastest-growing companies in its global ecosystem. Rottenberg called these founders Endeavor Outliers. Endeavor Entrepreneurs with over $100 million in annual revenues and growth rates of 25% or more were qualified to be part of this group. They received leadership development support from Endeavor Global and peer-to-peer coaching to enable them to multiply their impact—not only within their local ecosystems but also across Endeavor's global ecosystem.

Rottenberg also had her eye on a group of "Emerging Outliers," founders of companies that have $20M+ in revenue and revenue growth rates of over 75% per year. If they continue their trajectories, they will soon be in the outlier category. For both groups, she sees a "virtuous circle" where, in addition to supporting the entrepreneurs, Endeavor also learns even more about what it takes to create high-impact ventures, which further informs its selection and support processes (L. Rottenberg, personal interview, November 25, 2020).

Rottenberg is enthusiastic about the future of global entrepreneurship. She believes that the majority of problems are best solved by private sector solutions and observes that the problems entrepreneurs are creating solutions for—using technology-enabled innovation in areas as diverse as finance, medicine, and education—are making the world a much better place. She also sees entrepreneurs in emerging global markets—like Argentina and Lebanon—as having a built-in advantage. Since they created their initial ventures in markets that experienced a high level of volatility, they are in a favorable position to create solutions in developed markets which are now experiencing unprecedented rapid changes. "The COVID pandemic showed us how fragile many businesses are, and it is developing market entrepreneurs with their bias towards agility that will have the greatest potential to be successful in the future" (L. Rottenberg, personal interview, November 25, 2020).

Discussion Questions

1. What do you think has made Endeavor so successful?
2. What is your perspective on Rottenberg as a leader? How did she innovate?
3. Do you support the concept of supporting high-impact entrepreneurs? Why do you think Endeavor has concentrated in this area?
4. Why do you think Rottenberg launched Endeavor's investment funds? How does it contribute to their mission?
5. What can Endeavor learn from the Outliers? In Rottenberg's shoes how would you capitalize on this network?

NOTES

1. Martin, R. L., & Osberg, S. (2007). Social entrepreneurship: The case for definition. *Stanford Social Innovation Review*, *5*(28).
2. Eisenmann, T. R. (2013). Entrepreneurship: A working definition. *Harvard Business Review Blog Post*. Retrieved from https://hbr.org/2013/01/what-is-entrepreneurship.
3. Dees, J. G. (2001). The meaning of "social entrepreneurship". Retrieved from https://centers.fuqua.duke.edu/case/wpcontent/uploads/sites/7/2015/03/Article_Dees_MeaningofSocialEntrepreneurship_2001.pdf.

4. Martin, R. L., & Osberg, S. (2007). Social entrepreneurship: The case for definition. *Stanford Social Innovation Review*, *5*(28).
5. Ibid.
6. Dees, J. G. (2001). The meaning of "social entrepreneurship". . Retrieved from https://centers.fuqua.duke.edu/case/wpcontent/uploads/sites/7/2015/03/Article_Dees_MeaningofSocialEntrepreneurship_2001.pdf.
7. TEDx Vienna. (2012, January 18). *A history of microfinance*. [Video]. YouTube. Retrieved from https://www.youtube.com/watch?v=6UCuWxWiMaQ.
8. Yunus, M. (2016, May 13). *Grameen Bank* [Carlson strategy class visit]. Waltham, MA: Brandeis University.
9. Seibel, H. D. (2003). History matters in microfinance. *Small Enterprise Development – An International Journal of Microfinance and Business Development*, *14*(2), 10–12.
10. Ibid.
11. Yunus, M. (2016, May 13). *Grameen Bank* [Carlson strategy class visit]. Waltham, MA: Brandeis University.
12. TEDx Vienna. (2012, January 18). *A history of microfinance*. [Video]. YouTube. Retrieved from https://www.youtube.com/watch?v=6UCuWxWiMaQ.
13. Gehrke, M. (2013, April 29). Muhammad Yunus: 'Put poverty in the museum'. *DW*. Retrieved from https://www.dw.com/en/muhammad-yunus-put-poverty-in-the-museum/a-16778589.
14. Ibid.
15. Broomhall, K. (2006). The Nobel winner who wanted to make poverty a museum piece. *The Guardian*. Retrieved from https://www.theguardian.com/news/blog/2006/oct/13/thenobelwinne.
16. Ibid.
17. Lee, W. (2009). What successful entrepreneurs *really* do, cited in Timmons, J., & Spinelli, S. *New venture creation: Entrepreneurship for the 21st Century* (8th ed.). New York, NY: McGraw-Hill.
18. Manusco, J. (1993, May 1). Who's most likely to go it alone?, cited in Bianchi, A. *Inc.* Magazine.
19. Butler, T. (2017). Hiring an entrepreneurial leader: What to look for. *Harvard Business Review*, *95*(2), 85–93.
20. Ibid.
21. Schurenberg, E. (2012, January 9). 'What's an entrepreneur?' Here's the best answer ever. *Inc. Magazine*.
22. Ibid.
23. Bornstein, D. (2004). *How to change the world: Social entrepreneurs and the power of new ideas*. Oxford: Oxford University Press.
24. Ibid.
25. Meehan, W. F. (2019, November 22). Bill Drayton and social entrepreneurship: How a social movement is changing the world…*and* launching another: Everyone a changemaker. *Forbes Magazine*.
26. Ashoka United States. (2020). *Ashoka's history*. Retrieved from https://www.ashoka.org/en-us/story/ashokas-history.
27. Convergences. (2019). *Microfinance Barometer 2019* [Brochure]. Retrieved from https://www.convergences.org/wp-content/uploads/2019/09/Microfinance-Barometer-2019_web-1.pdf.

28. Christopoulos, D., & Vogl, S. (2014). The motivation of social entrepreneurs: The roles, agendas and relations of Altruistic economic actors. *The Journal of Social Entrepreneurship, 6*(1), 1–30.
29. Giridharadas, A. (2019). *Winners take all: The elite charade of changing the world* (p. 8). New York, NY: Alfred A. Knopf.
30. Predo, A. M., & McLean, M. (2006). Social entrepreneurship: A critical review of the concept. *Journal of World Business, 41*(1), 56–65.
31. Ibid.
32. Jacobs, S. (2018, May 17). Trader Joe's former president launched an even cheaper grocery store and has a huge vision for changing how Americans buy food. *Business Insider.*
33. Von Hoffman, C. (2017, October 30). *Giving minorities a playbook for career success*. Harvard Business School. Retrieved from https://www.alumni.hbs.edu/stories/Pages/story-bulletin.aspx?num=6425.
34. Drake, D., Bhattacharya, N., Godbole, P., & Amrita Saigal, A. (2016). *Ekal Viyalaya: Education for rural India*. HBS Case No. 617021. Harvard Business School Publishing.
35. Ibid.
36. Battilana, J., DeLong, T., & Weber, J. (2009). *Echoing green*. HBS Case No. 410-013. Harvard Business School Publishing.
37. Dorsey, C. (2009, April 23). *Echoing green* [class visit]. Boston, MA: Harvard Business School.
38. Echoing Green. (2020). *Discovering tomorrow's leaders today*. Retrieved from https://echoinggreen.org/fellowship/.
39. Dana Philanthropy Blog. (2020). *No ordinary business with Ākina foundation*. Retrieved from https://www.danaphilanthropy.com/blog/2018/7/29/005-no-ordinary-business-with-kina-foundation.
40. Applegate, L. M., & Carlson, C. (2014). Entrepreneurship reading: Recognizing and shaping opportunities. In L. M. Applegate (Ed.), *Core curriculum readings series*. Boston, MA: Harvard Business School Publishing.
41. Bhide, A. (1996). The questions every entrepreneur must answer. *Harvard Business Review, 74*(6), 120.
42. Collins, J. (2001). *Good to great*. Random House Business Books. See also: Collins, J. (2018). *Question #5: Have you found your hedgehog – your personal hedgehog?* [Video]. YouTube. Retrieved from https://www.youtube.com/watch?v=ERcF9HKmjh0.
43. Craig, N., & Snook, S. (2014). From purpose to impact: Figure out your passion and put it to work. *Harvard Business Review, 92*(5), 105–111.
44. Ibid.
45. Sahlman, W. (2010). *Endeavor creating a global movement for high impact entrepreneurship*. HBS Case No. 810049. Harvard Business School Publishing.
46. Ibid.
47. Rottenberg, L. (2010), cited in Sahlman, W. *Endeavor creating a global movement for high impact entrepreneurship*. HBS Case No. 810049. Harvard Business School Publishing.
48. Ibid.
49. Ibid.
50. Endeavor. (2021). *Impact: Endeavor makes its impact by providing and fostering financial, human, social, intellectual and cultural capital*. Retrieved from https://endeavor.org/impact/.

51. Endeavor Blog. (2020). *Endeavor catalyst announces full deployment of its $80M+ fund II and plans for fund III*. Retrieved from https://endeavor.org/blog/catalyst/endeavor-catalyst-raises-134m-fund-iii/.
52. Applegate, L. M. (2019). *Endeavor in 2019: Leading through inflections*. HBS Case No. 820031. Harvard Business School Publishing.
53. Endeavor Blog. (2010). *The best business school you've never heard of*. Retrieved from https://endeavor.org/blog/network/best-business-school-youve-never-heard/.

CHAPTER TWO

INNOVATION AND IDEA GENERATION

Learning Objectives

- Explore what propels innovation and the different types of thinking that support it.
- Describe the different factors that support creative thinking.
- Identify where entrepreneurial ideas that can create social impact come from.
- Differentiate between micro- and macro-level factors that affect innovation.
- Compare different strategies for unlocking creativity through ideation processes.

Innovation is at the heart of social entrepreneurship. And innovation begins with ideas—ideally lots of them. But where do ideas come from? As discussed later in this chapter, ideas might come from thinking deeply about a problem. This is particularly true for social entrepreneurs who are obsessed with a particular problem in society. Or ideas may come from seeing an opportunity that is created by a gap in the marketplace, observing that customers or recipients are poorly served by existing offerings. Ideas can also come from changes in context—for example, technology or information flow that enable new solutions to address old problems.

What do we mean by social innovation? *Stanford Social Innovation Review* authors define it as:

> *A novel solution to a social problem that is more effective, efficient, sustainable, or just than existing solutions and for which the value created accrues primarily to society as a whole rather than private individuals.*[1]

How should nascent social entrepreneurs position themselves to generate valuable innovations? First and most important is to be ready to recognize and then act on ideas that have value, and discard those that do not. Proximity—being close to the problems that need to be solved—is usually the best way for a prospective entrepreneur to be well poised to generate actionable insight.

THE ROLE OF ENTREPRENEURIAL INSIGHTS

Chance Favors the Prepared Mind

Consider Louis Pasteur, the nineteenth-century chemist that first proposed germ theory—the theory that germs caused disease. This theory became critical to advances in medicine and in particular, the development of vaccines. As Pasteur famously said, "Chance favors the prepared mind." What Pasteur meant by this is that chance discoveries—often found through experimentation—are critical to innovation, but it is critical that the inventor be well prepared to understand what the observations mean and how to use them to create value.

Pasteur is best known for inventing pasteurization, a process of heating liquids to destroy pathogens in milk and other beverages. Prior to pasteurization, consuming milk (and other beverages) was risky because of the presence of bacteria. Most people think that Pasteur was solely responsible for creating a new process aimed at solving this problem. History, however, is a little more complicated. Pasteur, a prolific scientist, invented his life-saving pasteurization technology when trying to develop a method for extending the shelf life of beer, and it was German Chemist Franz Soxhelt who suggested the process be applied to raw milk.

Credit aside, their readiness to embrace and disseminate a new technology has saved millions of lives. Chance (the application of germ theory and invention of a heating method) favored the prepared minds of Pasteur and Soxhelt. But the story is incomplete without mentioning the contribution of New York philanthropist Nathan Straus, who had dedicated himself to distributing food and coal to New York's tenement dwellers during the 1892–1893 depression. Seeing an opportunity, he funded and operated milk stations that helped to popularize the life-saving benefits of pasteurized milk. Through public health regulation, pasteurized milk eventually became the standard.

Innovation and Social Ventures

Put simply, an entrepreneurial insight is a flash of understanding that sparks the development of a new venture. It can come from a unique understanding of a problem or connecting patterns, trends, or ideas in a unique way.

The example of pasteurization demonstrates how entrepreneurial ideas are developed. Often it is a new way of looking at a problem (in Pasteur's case, the insight that germs cause disease and can be foodborne) or the invention of a new technology that presents an opportunity. The migration of an idea from one context (beer) to another (milk) creates value. The development of new technologies (liquid heating machinery) can propel a social benefit from idea to adoption. And, as we will discuss in Chapter 4, the dissemination of new entrepreneurial ideas is usually a team process in which other players (in this case, Strauss creating a distribution system and others creating new laws on food quality) enable an innovation to realize its full potential.

Neal Bermas, who founded STREETS International and who is profiled later in this chapter, built STREETS on the insight that street children in Vietnam had limited employment opportunities but could easily be trained to access well-paying opportunities in the hospitality sector. Brenna Schneider, whose organization 99Degrees Custom is described in Chapter 8, had the insight that garment production was being "reshored" in the United States due to demand for customization, and that this trend could be leveraged to create jobs and career paths. Doug Rausch, former president of grocery chain Trader Joe's, had the insight that food was routinely wasted in the United States while families went hungry and that wholesome food near its expiration date could be resold at low prices. This led to the creation of Daily Table, a nonprofit grocery retailer.

Innovation for social ventures tackles critical societal problems by mobilizing and transforming existing resources and human capital to create new business models. These solutions create benefits for society as they address seemingly intractable issues. Some of these solutions are small or local, while others are global.

Examples of areas ripe for social innovation are vast. Take, for example, renewable energy solutions that mitigate climate change or innovations that reduce poverty, hunger, and homelessness. Innovation can also address challenges such as improving social justice for marginalized communities, reducing inequality and oppression, or finding solutions to major diseases and epidemics and improving access to medicine and quality health care.

Divergent and Convergent Thinking

Entrepreneurs rely on two types of thinking to develop initial ideas and then evolve them to business concepts: divergent and convergent thinking.

- *Divergent thinking* involves generating creative new ideas. If addressing a problem, it means developing multiple possible solutions. When we talk about brainstorming, we are using divergent thinking. Divergent thinking is important for entrepreneurs because it enables them to use their creative skills to generate multiple options.
- *Convergent thinking* is the process of narrowing ideas. It is an essential skill for determining concrete solutions to problems, and involves weighing the benefits of potential options, determining feasibility, and making decisions about which options to move forward with.

As illustrated in Figure 2.1, a combination of divergent and convergent thinking skills can be applied sequentially to the problem arenas (where an entrepreneur defines

Figure 2.1 Divergent and Convergent Thinking

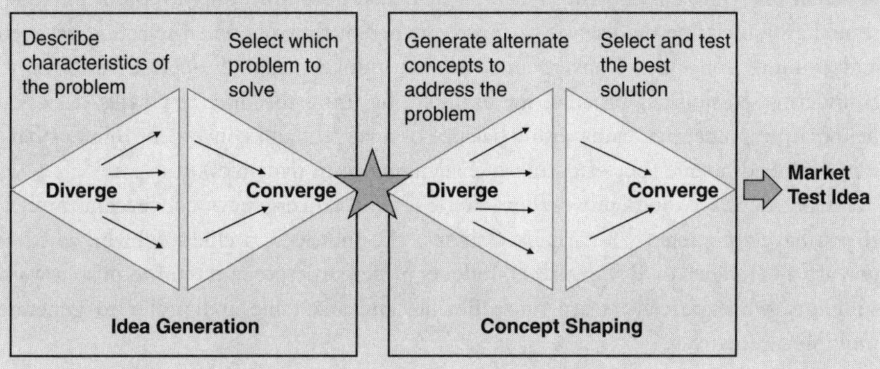

Source: Adapted from British Design Council. (2021). *The double diamond: A universally accepted depiction of the design process*. https://www.designcouncil.org.uk/news-opinion/.

the nature of the problem they plan to address) and the solutions arena (where an entrepreneur brainstorms multiple solutions and determines which ones to pursue.) This model is an adaptation of the Double Diamond Model popularized by the British Design Council and developed based on 1996 work by Hungarian American linguist and UC Berkeley Professor Bela Benathy.

During the idea generation phase, brainstorming enables the entrepreneur to fully understand the problem and typically follows a divergent process, starting with a problem symptom and then expanding as innovators describe different dimensions of the problem. For example, an entrepreneur might start with an observation about, for example, the prevalence of child malnutrition in a given location and then expand to consider problem elements that might be contributing to it such as poverty, limited access to fresh foods, children's eating habits, and other factors. Once the dimensions of the problem are well understood, the entrepreneur can then use convergent thinking to identify the specific part of the problem they intend to address.

During the concept shaping phase, an entrepreneurial concept is developed and refined. For example, the entrepreneur might have settled on limited access to fresh food as the addressable problem and can then employ divergent thinking to brainstorm potential solutions. In our nutrition example, they might consider opening grocery stores in areas that lack access to food retailers, providing food delivery services, initiating programs to improve affordability of fresh foods, improving transportation access, or investing in in-school meal programs. After brainstorming potential solutions, they can apply convergent thinking, narrowing choices by considering likely market acceptance and financial and technical feasibility.

While people can participate in both divergent and convergent thinking, they usually have a preference. Aspiring social entrepreneurs should try to recognize their tendency and compensate. Those who are skilled at brainstorming (divergent thinking) should also discipline themselves to apply convergent thinking when selecting between and refining concepts. Convergent-dominant thinkers should open themselves to considering possibilities broadly, for example, by using the discovery skills discussed below. Entrepreneurial teams with a balance of divergent and convergent thinkers have a powerful advantage (but often more challenging team dynamics).

Consider for a moment whether you tend to be a divergent or convergent thinker. If you have completed your Myers–Briggs Type Indicator, a clue might be whether you are a J (Judger) or P (Perceiver). Judgers prefer structure and tend to push toward solutions, while perceivers are more flexible and adaptable and prefer to generate multiple alternatives.

WHERE IDEAS COME FROM

Individuals generate ideas in different ways. In 2014, *Inc.* magazine surveyed the CEOs of its *Inc.* 500 list of the fastest-growing private companies in the United States. The results were surprising. When asked where they got their best ideas for new products and services, the largest proportion (28%) mentioned their customers. Over 26% said "myself," followed by 16% via employees, another 16% from dedicated teams, and 7% from business partners.[2] Clearly, leaders of fast-growth companies use multiple methods for idea generation.

An earlier survey of 100 founders of Inc. fast-growing companies also yielded interesting results. Over two-thirds reported that they replicated or modified an idea that they had encountered through previous employment and applied the thinking to a new opportunity. One-fifth "discovered" ideas serendipitously and only 4% discovered it through systematic research.[3]

Elements of Creativity

Harvard Business School Professor Teresa Amabile's research on creativity provides a useful structure for thinking about creativity and entrepreneurial discovery. She identifies three basic components of creativity: creative thinking skills, expertise, and motivation, and suggests that all are important levers for ensuring new venture success.[4] We've added a fourth dimension—passion—to expand our thinking about creativity among social entrepreneurs (see Figure 2.2).

- *Creative thinking skills* are skills related to imaginative problem-solving—ways of thinking differently that enable entrepreneurs to develop unique solutions.

Figure 2.2 Four Components of Creativity for Social Entrepreneurs

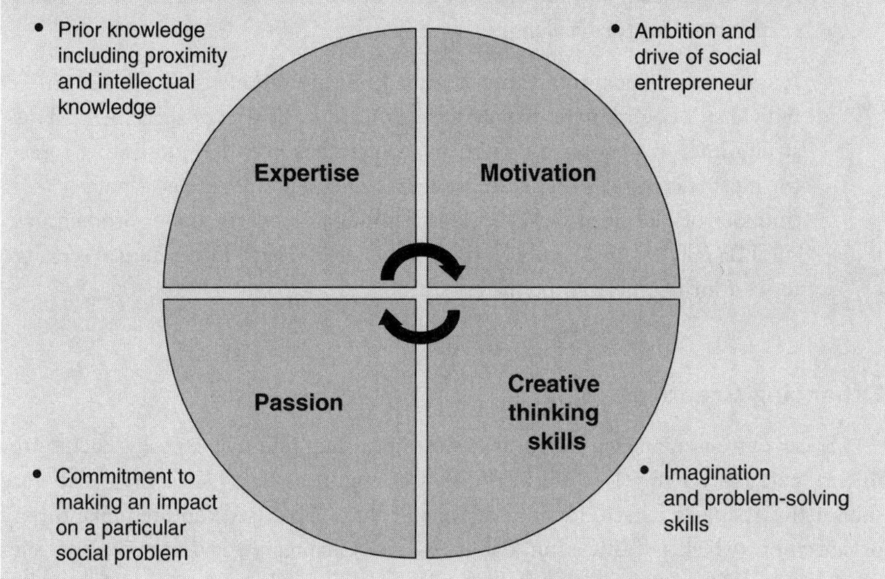

Source: Adapted from Amabile, T. M. (1998). How to kill creativity. *Harvard Business Review* 76, no. 5.

An important part of creative thinking is skills pattern recognition—the ability to observe an idea in one context and imagine its potential in another. Consider the example of One Acre Fund, a nonprofit provider of agricultural services that we profile in Chapter 5. The inputs that support higher levels of farm production—high quality seeds, fertilizer, water, and crop rotation. But the ability to provide these as low-cost bundled services to smallholder farmers in sub-Saharan Africa enabled the founders to create an impactful new organization and rapidly expand it.

- *Expertise* involves understanding the context well (often through proximity) or having specific technical, procedural, or intellectual knowledge.[5] It is no surprise that most successful entrepreneurial ventures replicated or modified an idea encountered through previous employment.[6] For example, Ted Barber and Amber Chad, the social entrepreneurs behind Prosperity Candle, a venture that help refugees and women in conflict regions export and sell handcrafted candles, relied on their collective expertise importing crafts and selling through catalogues to test the viability of their products and then launch their new venture.

- *Motivation* describes the force that enables entrepreneurs to persistently pursue ideas. Amabile also distinguishes between extrinsic motivation (which is often financial) and intrinsic motivation which is an inherent interest in certain activities or challenges.[7]
- *Passion* is a personal motivation founded in a set of beliefs that drives an individual's commitment to solving a problem in an area of social need. This strong interest in solving a singular problem has been the motivating force for most successful social entrepreneurs, whether Muhammad Yunus (founder of Grameen Bank) seeking to mitigate poverty among women in rural Bangladesh or Wendy Kopp (cofounder of Teach For America) seeking to transform American public education.

Enhancing Creativity

Social entrepreneurs who want to stay creative often find that exposing themselves to new cultures via travel or work in different countries helps keep their discovery skills active. Vanessa Kirsch, founder of New Profit, a US-based venture philanthropy organization (which is featured in a short case in Chapter 9), had founded two successful nonprofit organizations—Public Allies and the Women's Information Network—when she took a year off to travel the world and interview individuals and social entrepreneurs in 22 countries. Her insights about the need for growth capital was the impetus for founding New Profit. Travel helps entrepreneurs be more open-minded, culturally adaptive, and attuned to what consumers and stakeholders in other places consider important. This benefit has also been observed in the private sector where researchers have found that the more countries a person has lived in, the more likely they are to leverage their experience to innovate.[8]

Another approach to generating ideas is to keep an idea diary, where an individual can record ideas, observations, intriguing technology, and other things. This book of "inspiration" enables aspiring entrepreneurs to revisit ideas from time to time to create new ideas or identify connections between observations.

Teamwork is another powerful way to generate ideas. Teams can be critical for bringing together the perspectives and insights needed to create breakthrough ideas. Consider the cofounders of Sanergy—a Nairobi-based company that operates a network of over 2,000 franchised pay toilets and uses the products generated to create fertilizer, energy, and animal feed. The team met in a course at the Massachusetts Institute of Technology called the Poverty Action Lab and over the course of a semester generated a creative and sustainable approach to improving sanitation in urban slums. Team discussions or problem-solving can spur creative thinking. Some examples of team approaches to unlock creativity are suggested in the exercises later in this chapter.

Honing Discovery Skills

Discovery skills are the skills entrepreneurs draw upon to find and explore new ideas.

In their article "The Innovators DNA," Innovation experts Jeffrey Dyer, Hall Gregersen, and Clayton Christensen identify five key discovery skills that enable prospective entrepreneurs and innovators to cultivate idea generation capability: *associating, questioning, observing, experimenting, and networking*.[9]

Associating: Associating is the ability to connect seemingly unrelated questions, ideas, or problems, often drawing on insights from different fields or disciplines. As Dyer and his colleagues note, "Association is like a muscle that can grow stronger by using the other discovery skills. As innovators engage in those behaviors, they build their ability to generate ideas that can be recombined in new ways."[10]

Questioning: Questioning is a particularly important skill for social entrepreneurs. It involves continuously challenging the status quo, asking "why?" or "why not?" or "how might we?" Asking questions and considering alternatives can help the entrepreneur develop novel solutions to seemingly intractable social problems. Consider Fazle Hasan Abed, founder of BRAC, who questioned how to support people living below the poverty line. Or Yasmeen Abu Fraiha, who founded Genesis, a provider of premarital genetic tests, after she wondered why Bedouin teenagers entering arranged marriages were not able to screen partners for shared genetic defects.

Observing: Observing customer behavior or other common phenomena can produce important insights. These insights can reveal important opportunities to create new products or services or modify existing ones to create or increase social benefits. Forward-thinking social ventures have also used this principle to harness the ability of shared insights. Patients Like Me was an information sharing platform created to help patients suffering from muscle wasting Amyotrophic Lateral Sclerosis (ALS), also known as Lou Gehrig's disease, to share strategies for improving their quality of life. Patients Like Me quickly expanded to include dozens, then hundreds, of diseases and enabled patients to engage with each other.

Experimenting: Experimenting involves tinkering with ideas, and sometimes pilot testing them to learn more about their impact and how they can be refined. For example, the founders of Owlet, producers of a wireless baby monitor, started in 2013 by creating a sock-like device designed to monitor infant heart rate and oxygen levels while sleeping, reducing parent anxiety and the potential for Sudden Infant Death Syndrome (SIDS). Their unconventional approach to experimentation involved observing customers in baby stores to see how they purchased baby monitors.

Networking: Networking is the final discovery skill. The most productive social entrepreneurs are voracious networkers. They are always on the move, sharing ideas and building relationships. They recognize that networking with a diverse group of other individuals enables them to develop perspective, access resources, and form important partnerships. We will discuss ways to network and build teams and ecosystems in more detail in Chapter 4.

PROFILE: NEAL BERMAS AND STREETS INTERNATIONAL

Neal Bermas' experience as a high impact social entrepreneur demonstrates several important lessons: First, it is never too early or too late to become a social entrepreneur. Second, social entrepreneurs bring diverse experience, but by applying their expertise, passion, and motivation to creatively identifying opportunities, they can have an astonishing impact on the lives of others.

Bermas was born in the 1950s in New York City. After earning a PhD in social policy and management at Brandeis' Heller School, he had a fulfilling career in management consulting primarily in the hospitality sector, working with such clients as the Walt Disney Company, Le Meridien, and Sheraton. He also taught hospitality and management courses at NYU and New York Institute of Culinary Education. His dual passion for hospitality and education provided the inspiration for STREETS International, an entrepreneurial social enterprise that provides culinary and hospitality training for street kids, orphans, and other disadvantaged youth across Southeast Asia. Indeed, his experience is a perfect demonstration of Pasteur's observation: "Chance favors the prepared mind," as his professional experience and education orientation enabled him to spot an opportunity for social impact and then create an organization to act on it.

During a visit to Vietnam in 1999, Bermas was deeply affected by seeing children begging for basic foods rather than money. To him, this was a poverty beyond what we see regularly in the United States. His entrepreneurial insight was that in developing economies, one of the first industries that takes hold and grows is hospitality. The hospitality industry also offers well-paying careers that can be filled by motivated but less educated workers. He saw this combination of factors as an ideal opportunity to create economic opportunities for impoverished youth.

In 2007, Bermas founded STREETS International, a US-based nonprofit that provided education and apprenticing opportunities for disadvantaged youth in Vietnam. STREETS International focused on disadvantaged, orphaned, out-of-school, trafficked, and other impoverished youth between the ages of 17 and 22 years old. Program participants came from all over the country and STREETS provided a no-cost 18-month residential program teaching hospitality and culinary skills. The program training included supervised housing, medical care, clothing, transportation, English language education, and life-skills training. The objective was for all graduates to start their careers at international hotels and resorts in Vietnam, and 100% of STREETS International trainees had been hired by target employers within 30 days of program completion. The impact also extended to participant's families. "Many of the youth in our program did not finish high school because their families lacked resources. We routinely see that their younger brothers and sisters can stay in school because their older siblings can help pay for their school meals, books and uniforms" (N. Bermas, personal interview, February 19, 2020). The program had a commitment to gender equity in enrollment and program training, and prioritized students from ethnic minorities who are at a higher risk of being trafficked.

To found STREETS, Bermas analyzed country economic and tourism trends with in-country tourism professionals and collaborated with recognized hospitality academics, chefs, and experts from his own network to design the curriculum and program structure. STREETS International Café was the initial economic engine that drove the enterprise while it provided the apprentice site for trainees to practice and develop their skills. Oodles of Noodles was created as a second revenue-generating enterprise, providing an additional apprentice site for culinary trainees to hone their English-speaking skills and confidence. At Oodles, tourists are taught to make local rice noodles, while trainees practice their English and their culinary skills. Together, these two enterprises allow STREETS to be largely financially self-supporting.

In describing his motivation, Bermas says, "As a New Yorker I am tenacious. I have always had a lot of energy and am passionate about what I do" (N. Bermas, personal interview, February 19, 2020). He also credits his upbringing, during which he learned important early lessons centered about "always caring about those that have less" (N. Bermas, personal interview, February 19, 2020). He acknowledged that he needed to learn some new skills to launch the venture. "I had never run a school before. But I drew on my experience as a part time academic to figure it out" (N. Bermas, personal interview, February 19, 2020). As we discuss in this chapter, Bermas combined the four elements of creativity—expertise, passion, motivation, and creative thinking skills—to develop the STREETS concept and then used experimentation to grow the venture.

Bermas advises aspiring social entrepreneurs: "Don't wait until you have it all figured out. If you have a good idea and vision, go for it" (N. Bermas, personal interview, February 19, 2020). He also believes that "a social enterprise is best built by someone with a business background. Someone with this knowledge can integrate financial strategies and operations in a way that benefits a community while making profits" (N. Bermas, personal interview, February 19, 2020). And for those who, like him, have extensive professional experience, he adds "Give up your money-making career for at least a few years and devote yourself to something important...it's not so difficult at a certain point to walk away."

INNOVATING FOR SOCIAL IMPACT

Building on our discussion of *divergent and convergent thinking* earlier in this chapter, there are two ways to view how solutions emerge from social venture ideations. There are two sources of solutions: those that arise from problems and those that respond to opportunities.

Problem-Focused Solutions

Problem-focused solutions are generated by social entrepreneurs who want to make a difference in a specific area. This may evolve from a personal connection with a country, community, or context. Problems can also often arise from global social challenges or local challenges. Examples of *global* challenges include the following:

- *Climate Change:* identifying renewable energy and solutions to mitigate climate change

- *Human Rights:* ensuring equal rights for all people
- *Poverty:* reducing inequality, the wealth disparity, homelessness, and hunger
- *Social Justice:* addressing institutional oppression, such as racism and sexism
- *Health Care:* improving maternal and infant healthcare, solving major epidemics and preventing or mitigating diseases
- *Education Access:* enabling access to quality education to all children, regardless of social economic backgrounds
- *Environment:* protecting the natural environment and biodiversity.

Local challenges are those that affect a specific geographic community, or a population subgroup, for example, rural children or subsistence farmers. Examples of local challenges addressed by social entrepreneurs include the high prevalence of genetic disease among Bedouin families in Israel, or the lack of employment opportunities for women in Haiti.

An example of a successful organization created to address a problem-focused solution is Equal Exchange, a pioneer in fair trade certified worker-owned cooperatives, who sought to improve the livelihoods of farmers by introducing fair trade coffee products to the United States. Equal Exchange founders Rink Dickinson, Jonathan Rosenthal, and Michael Rozyne observed the plight of low-income coffee farmers (an estimated 80% of whom live below the poverty line) and wanted to directly influence the supply chain so that each step was more sustainable and equitable to all of their stakeholders including their farmers and consumers. Equal Exchange is now one of the largest worker-owned coffee operations in the United States.

Opportunity-Focused Solutions

Social entrepreneurs who create opportunity-focused solutions see an opportunity to start a venture that is created by a change. This might be an increase in consumer demand, shifting demographics, a legal or policy change, or a technology advancement that makes it possible to create additional value for consumer or offer current solutions in a more efficient way.

Consider the case of WorkAround. Founder Wafaa Arbash believed that advancements in technology would enable her to create an online platform that could link companies with remote workers to perform microtasks. As "gig economy" companies such as Uber, Airbnb, and TaskRabbit were becoming more common, WorkAround learned from them and founded a company that creates value for corporate clients while addressing the global refugee crisis by providing skilled and educated workers with employment opportunities and an ability to establish a work history with a US company. Initial customers included America's Test Kitchen (which hired WorkAround to identify pirated content) and Zoominfo (which needed human judgment about the relationships between companies appearing in online postings.)

The "opportunity" behind opportunity-focused solutions can come from multiple shifts:

- *Technology:* new ways of performing work or making connections. WorkAround is a good example of this.
- *Demographic shifts:* changes that alter the demand for a social venture's initiatives. For example, an aging population can drive demand for services for older individuals
- *Economic changes:* changes in the feasibility of offering certain solutions. For example, the cost of a key resource might drop, making a previously infeasible solution practical. On the negative side, a financial crisis could increase the need for a social good.
- *New operating approaches:* more efficient ways of operating can displace existing providers
- *Financial changes*: changes in the availability of financial resources (for example, via microloans or crowdsourcing)
- *Political and policy changes:* changes in government funding or shifts removing or creating regulatory barriers

In his book *The Little Black Book of Innovation*, leading innovation thinker and author Scott Anthony suggested three questions that can help aspiring entrepreneurs identify early signals that the context is changing (and creating opportunities):

1. What do underlying trends suggest about potential future states?
2. Where do small but growing trends tell us?
3. What do analogies and metaphors reveal?[11]

Sometimes new ventures have both a problem and opportunity focus. For example, Patrick Lawler founded Youth Villages in Memphis, Tennessee, in 1980 when he was asked, as a 24-year-old youth counsellor, to take over a small, operationally challenged residential treatment center for disadvantaged youth. His passion was to help emotionally and behaviorally challenged children reintegrate into society. His *problem-focused solution* was to develop a service that met the needs of participants. However, early in his leadership he discovered an evidence-based model that used intensive around-the-clock services for youth and their families that enabled children to stay in their homes while overcoming their challenges. This approach had significantly better results at a much lower cost. The *opportunity* was using a novel approach that displaced higher-cost residential treatment options while improving outcomes. Today, Youth Villages serves 30,000 youth in 21 states and has 3,000 employees.

FACTORS SUPPORTING AND CONSTRAINING INNOVATION

Macro-Level Factors

The 2015 development of the UN Sustainable Development Goals created a "universal call to action to end poverty, protect the planet and improve the lives and prospects of everyone everywhere"[12] and the significant traction we have seen toward meeting them has demonstrated the power of innovation (including through entrepreneurship) to make progress addressing society's most intractable problems.

On a macro level, innovation is cultivated when entrepreneurial activity is encouraged, motivating entrepreneurs as they begin to develop their businesses. The economy and government play a role. For example, countries such as Ecuador and Peru have recognized the importance of innovation and created governmental incentives such as tax exemptions to support social entrepreneurs.[13] Similarly, the "Chilean government provides equity-free investments to select startups that meet rigorous requirements for scalability and social impact," which has helped set Chile apart as a city for entrepreneurs with innovative ideas.[14]

There are also macro-level factors that challenge innovation. Societal expectations can impede innovation for social ventures. The social problems that entrepreneurs tackle are often major challenges that have no clear solution, and which may appear to be "too big to solve." Another challenge that impacts social innovation is the expectation that collaboration among a complex web of stakeholders will be too difficult. Solutions related to heavily regulated industries like health care present particular challenges. For example, consider the complexity encountered by One World Health, the first nonprofit pharmaceutical company in pursuing the mission of providing drugs in developing countries. The initiative required continuous conversations with governments, private companies, donors, health-care professionals, scientists, and countless others in its initial stages and throughout its implementation and evolution.[15]

Micro-Level Factors

On a micro level, factors that support innovation include an expansion of the number of nonprofit or for-profit organizations that support entrepreneurs by providing financial and development resources, as well as the existence of a robust infrastructure. Supporting organizations include incubators, accelerator organizations, as well as other types of pitch and funding competitions that support entrepreneurs by connecting them to investors or providing them with mentoring, training, and resources. Such resources may include helping entrepreneurs scale up their social enterprise. We will discuss these supports more in our Chapter 4 discussion of ecosystems.

There are also micro factors that directly impact founders including the inherent financial risk involved with innovation. Social entrepreneurs may have limited access to financial resources to start or expand their businesses and find that traditional sources of social capital, such as foundations, are reluctant to take risks on early-stage ventures. While social innovators may have creative solutions with viable business models, they are often not able to access investors who can help them get their business off the ground. An exacerbating factor is the gap between the potential for earnings and wealth creation of for-profit counterparts and what nonprofit entrepreneurs typically earn. Since financial gain is not a motivation it is unsurprising that only the most passionate and tenacious individuals become nonprofit social entrepreneurs.

USING IDEATION TO UNLOCK CREATIVITY

Where do creative ideas for innovations come from? Sometimes, ideas come naturally from entrepreneurs seeing a problem or opportunity but take hold because of collaboration with a group or team. To help generate ideas, there are a number of tried-and-true ideation techniques—all which can be a part of a fun ideation session. Ideas can emerge from a single person (for example, Wendy Kopp's concept for Teach for America) or from a group (for example, the team collaboration that led to the formation of Sanergy).

Creativity often doesn't happen naturally. Individuals are usually most effective thinking creatively in teams since multiple perspectives lead to new insights. American educational theorist David Kolb developed two theories about learning styles that help explain why team-based creative processes are so powerful and why bringing together individuals with different styles can solve problems more easily by leveraging different approaches. Kolb observed that individuals have very different learning styles.

- *Diverging styles*—are able to look at things from different perspectives
- *Assimilating styles*—use a logical, thinking approach
- *Converging styles*—are oriented towards practical problem-solving solutions
- *Accommodating styles*—rely on intuition and leveraging information provided by others.

It is easy to see why a combination of these styles can be used to generate and then sort through ideas.

Kolb also described an experiential learning cycle that enables individuals to process information and reach conclusions. The cycle starts with concrete experience (reinforcing the importance of experience and proximity discussed earlier in this chapter), followed by reflective observation, followed by abstract conceptualization (learning from the experience), and leading to active experimentation (planning and trying out what you have learned).[16] This perfectly encompasses what entrepreneurs try to achieve when they generate, cull, and experiment with ideas.

Experts in creativity and design thinking have leveraged this cycle to create a group of processes that help to unleash innovative thinking and idea generation collectively called "ideation." Three common types of ideation activities include brainstorming, braindumping, and brainwriting (or a variant called brainwalking.)

Brainstorming

To brainstorm, teams typically start with a group of challenges, goals, or "how might we" statements and address one problem at a time. This can be done through conversation, drawing, acting, or writing out ideas, with the goal of blending together ideas to create stronger ones. A useful technique, borrowed from improvisational comedy, is to use "yes, and" statements to encourage participants to build on each other's ideas.

> Brainstorm example: A team member facilitates a conversation around climate change. She challenges her teammates to all think about ways communities can reduce using plastics. Each team member considers how they would achieve this goal then shares ideas in a group discussion. While one participant thinks that that plastic bottles should be redesigned, another focuses on changing people's habits by creating an app. The team then lists and weighs the solutions.

Braindumping

This approach uses a challenge, goal, or "how might we" statements, but focuses on writing ideas on sticky notes individually before working in a team environment to move forward with chosen ideas.

> Braindump example: A team member knows that certain people on her team have great ideas but are sometimes too nervous to speak in large crowds. She asks all of her teammates to write ideas for expanding their business into

international markets on sticky notes and places them on a board. She has another team member come up and sort the sticky notes for duplicates before opening the floor to review the options. Then the group votes on which ones seem viable.

Brainwriting or Brainwalking

This approach uses a "round robin" style writing process to write the challenge, goal, or "how might we" statements and to expand on team member's ideas each round, with an optional aspect of physically moving around.

Example: The facilitator is planning a session for after lunch and wants to encourage participants to move around the room. She starts by having all of her teammates write ideas for ways to improve a process on sticky notes and places them on a board. Everyone is given sticky notes to expand on each other's ideas.

Other Ideation Approaches

During any ideation process, participants should be sure to remain open-minded to all ideas (and capture all of them), including ideas that may seem infeasible or even crazy. Favoring quantity over quality helps create many ideas, and this helps ensure that a few feasible ideas emerge from the ideation.

Other approaches to ideating are described below in Table 2.1. We encourage aspiring entrepreneurs to experiment with several of these.

Table 2.1 Seven Other Ways to Ideate

Ideation Approach	Process
Storyboarding	Develop visuals to help creativity laying out pictures and information on a large surface to help participants see end-to-end connections and stimulate thought. This is particularly helpful for visual learnings
Mission Impossible	Participants generate ideas using challenging questions. For example, "How could we reduce poverty in New York City by 10% in 18 months?"

(Continued)

Table 2.1 Seven Other Ways to Ideate *(Continued)*

Ideation Approach	Process
Reverse or Opposite Thinking	Instead of discussing how to solve a problem, participants discuss how it might not work. (This builds on a normal tendency to be more comprehensive finding problems than solutions.) Then, participants discuss how to solve the problems
Role plays	Participants adopt a character and develop ideas from the character's point of view. This is a good way to break common thinking patterns
Dot Voting	After participants have generated ideas, they use small colored dots to vote to determine the most effective ideas
Mindmapping	Participants map thoughts from a key phrase, focusing on word connections as the map expands
Mashups	Create a list of existing technologies and innovations and then merge them to create innovative combinations

CHAPTER SUMMARY

In this chapter, we've covered fundamental ideas about how social entrepreneurs generate ideas. These ideas form the basis for both entrepreneurial insights—the deep understanding of how a social problem might be solved with an entrepreneurial solution—and other ideas that help to make a concept practical.

Both divergent thinking (generating new ideas) and convergent thinking (the process of narrowing options) are important to social entrepreneurs. Failure can also be critical to learning and entrepreneurs who rapidly learn from failure are typically the most successful.

For aspiring social entrepreneurs, the combination of four elements—*creative thinking skills, expertise, motivation, and passion*—works together to fuel creativity. To maximize creativity, entrepreneurs can work to hone their discovery skills to cultivate their ability to generate ideas.

Steve Jobs, Founder of Apple, famously observed that "creativity is just connecting things. When you ask creative people how they did something, they feel a little guilty because they didn't really do it. They just saw something. It seemed obvious to them after a while; that's because they were able to connect experiences they've had and synthesize new things."[17] One way to connect and synthesize is to use ideation, a process that provides different approaches to using ideation to generate creative ideas.

KEY TERMS

Associating: the ability to connect seemingly unrelated questions, ideas, or problems, often drawing on insights from different fields or disciplines.

Braindump: this approach uses a challenge, goal, or "how might we" statements, with a focus on writing ideas on sticky notes individually before working in a team environment to move forward with chosen ideas.

Brainstorm: starting with challenge, goal, or "how might we" statements. Teams move towards addressing one problem at a time with the goal of blending together ideas to create stronger ones.

Convergent thinking: a process of narrowing ideas. It is an essential skill for determining concrete solutions to problems and weighing the benefits of potential options, determining feasibility, and making decisions.

Creative thinking skills: skills related to imaginative problem-solving—ways of thinking differently that enable entrepreneurs to develop unique solutions.

Divergent thinking: generation of creative new ideas and developing multiple possible solutions.

Experimenting: tinkering with ideas and sometimes pilot testing them to learn more about their impact and how they can be refined.

Expertise: understanding the context well or having specific technical, procedural, and intellectual knowledge.

Motivation: impetus that enables entrepreneurs to persistently pursue ideas.

Networking: process of interacting with others to exchange information and develop professional or social contacts.

Observing: process of observing customer behavior or other common phenomena to produce important insights.

Opportunity-focused solution: opportunity to start a venture that arises from a gap, likely through the inefficiency of current players.

Passion: personal motivation founded in a set of beliefs that drives an individual's commitment to solving a problem in an area of social need.

Problem-driven solution: solution generated by social entrepreneurs who want to make a difference in a specific area.

Questioning: a particularly important skill for social entrepreneurs that involves continuously challenging the status quo, asking "why?" or "why not?"

IN-CLASS EXERCISES

Exercise 2.1: Using the Double Diamond Model

(Estimated time: 45–60 minutes)

Purpose

Practice idea generation and concept shaping, and practice divergent and convergent thinking skills in teams.

Preparation

Break into teams of 4–6 students. Assemble in a space (ideally breakout rooms but could be classroom corners). Whiteboards or flip charts and markers can be used to improve the conversation.

Process

1. Each team selects a major problem "arena"—a large-scale social issue that requires attention. A good place to start is with the Sustainable Development Goals (discussed in Chapter 10 and copied below) or teams may choose their own.
2. Each team takes 10 minutes to brainstorm the characteristics of the problem arena, and write them down. (Participants will naturally want to move towards problem selection and solutions—we advise holding back.)
3. Each team takes 5 minutes deciding which of the problems they have generated they would like to solve. Teams identify their logic for selecting the specific problem (for example, importance to society.)
4. Each team takes 10 minutes to generate as many potential solutions to the problem they have identified as possible.
5. Each team takes 10 minutes to evaluate their potential solutions (criteria might include level of impact and feasibility) and identify their three most highly ranked solutions.
6. Each team identifies a spokesperson to debrief the process by presenting their team's work. Each spokesperson starts by listing their team's three top solutions, and then works backwards to describe how the team culled from a larger number or solutions, how they generated solutions, how they decided to focus on a specific problem, and the initial problem ideas they identified. It is often easiest to illustrate this on a blackboard, whiteboard, or posted paper.
7. The class provides feedback on the team's process and whether the solutions provided meaningfully address the original problem.

List of UN Sustainable Development Goals[18]:

- No Poverty
- Zero Hunger
- Good Health and Well-being
- Quality Education
- Gender Equality
- Clean Water and Sanitation
- Affordable and Clean Energy

- Decent Work and Economic Growth
- Industry, Innovation and Infrastructure
- Reduced Inequality
- Sustainable Cities and Communities
- Responsible Consumption and Production
- Climate Action
- Life Below Water
- Life on Land
- Peace and Justice Strong Institutions
- Partnerships to achieve the Goal

Exercise 2.2: Innovating Solutions

(Estimated time: 45–60 minutes)

Purpose

To gain exposure to and practice with ideation methods.

Preparation

Break into teams of 4–6 students. Each team assembles in a space (ideally breakout rooms but could be classroom corners). Whiteboards or flip charts and markers can be used to improve the conversation.

Process

1. Half the teams select a problem from the list of problem-focused solutions in Table 2.2; the other half selects sources of opportunity from the list of opportunity-focused solutions.
2. Teams spend 15 minutes exploring solutions using each of the techniques (brainstorm, braindump, brainwrite) described in this chapter to generate ideas. If teams have cycled through their problem quickly, they can select another problem to address or to move from problems to opportunities (or opportunities to problems) and repeat the process.
3. Return to class to debrief the process. Discuss what was hard and easy about the process

Table 2.2 Problem- and Opportunity-Focused Solutions	
Problem-focused solutions: Social entrepreneurs want to make a difference in a specific area. This may evolve from a personal connection with a country, community, or context. Sources of problems: • Climate Change • Human Rights • Poverty • Social Justice • Health Care • Education Access • Environment	*Opportunity-focused solutions:* Social entrepreneurs ideating through an opportunity-focused solution see an opportunity to start a business that arises from a gap, likely through the inefficiency of current players. Sources of opportunities: • Technology changes • Demographic shifts • Economic changes • New operating approaches • Financial changes • Political and policy changes

SHORT CASE: RAKIB AVI AND INNOVATION AT BRAC

Rakib Avi entered the BRAC Headquarters building in Bangladesh and took the elevator to the Social Innovation Lab (SIL) on the 20th floor. Because of his dual role as a program coordinator in the SIL and strategist in the Executive Director's Office, he was in a unique position to understand the role of innovation at BRAC. In his 7 years of working at BRAC, he had seen and promoted many innovations, and was anxious to ensure that BRAC's expertise innovating in service of meeting the needs of the poor continued and accelerated.

BRAC (the Bangladesh Rural Advancement Committee) has grown tremendously since its inception in 1972. Avi was confident that innovation was critically important to BRAC's ability to both continue to grow and serve its many stakeholders, including funders/partners, staff, and program participants. Preparing to present a list of suggestions for the BRAC senior leadership to consider in the next 5-year strategy plan, he gathered his innovation team of 12 people in the conference room, looked at the motto to "Generate ideas, design prototypes, and test our solutions" and started to create some solutions.

The Origin of BRAC

Founded in 1972 by former Shell Oil executive Sir Fazle Hasan Abed in Bangladesh, BRAC is now the world's largest nonprofit organization. BRAC employs over 100,000 people, mostly women, in 11 countries in Africa and Asia. Their work had reached more than 110 million of the poorest people around the world. BRAC's 2018 annual operating budget was over $US1.2 billion.

BRAC's mission is to "empower people and communities in situations of poverty, illiteracy, disease, and social injustice,"[19] which they seek to accomplish by scaling antipoverty innovations to help millions of people. BRAC's emphasis on innovation, integrity, inclusiveness, and effectiveness was evident across their multifaceted program portfolio that was geared to address social challenges, including eliminating poverty, increasing access to health care, enabling food security, and women's empowerment and economic empowerment through social enterprises and microfinance. Their impact had been tremendous: Since 1972, BRAC has supported 2 million women and their families—8 million people in total—break free from extreme poverty. BRAC has made $4 billion in microloans to over 7 million borrowers in 2018. BRAC's schools have reached over 12 million students from primary and preprimary schools in Asia and sub-Saharan Africa, with nearly 3.17 million students and members currently enrolled in its 36,000 schools and centers across Bangladesh.[20]

In 2017, responding to the Rohingya refugee crisis, BRAC transformed from an international development organization into a humanitarian aid organization to serve refugee settlements in Bangladesh. BRAC provided over 1 million services to Rohingya refugees, focusing on health, nutrition, and treating communicable diseases. As the refugee settlement became more permanent, BRAC continued to create a holistic community for the refugees through their work by making the area safer for children to learn and creating gardens to enable healthy eating habits.

Social Enterprises for Sustainability

From the beginning, founder Sir Fazle wanted BRAC to be financially self-supporting and not rely exclusively on charitable donations to operate. Instead, BRAC uses surplus from its microfinance operations and social enterprises to fund close to 80% of its expenses. BRAC's operation included 13 different social enterprises such as Aarong, BRAC Dairy, BRAC Seed and Agro, BRAC Nursery, and BRAC Fisheries which had earnings that supported BRAC initiatives, while also providing direct benefits such as providing small farmers and producers with markets for their products and an ability to earn a sustainable income.

According to Abed, "Often people are very skeptical of nonprofits running social enterprises, and with good reason: It requires two vastly different cultures to coexist side by side. Our social enterprises are successful because we run them like businesses while at the same time staying focused on our nonprofit mission." Abed's vision for BRAC to be both an NGO and a social enterprise has fueled its growth and increased its impact across rural areas of Bangladesh.

Rakib Avi Background

Avi started his career at BRAC in 2012 after completing a BA in Business Administration at University of Dhaka. His first role was as a member of its communication department where he managed large-scale communications project related to public health, women's empowerment, youth, and technology. He was part of the team that developed BRAC's first global communications strategy. Avi championed key initiatives at BRAC including the first hackathon organized by a development organization in Bangladesh and an initiative to recognize grassroots-level innovators.

After working closely with the SIL since 2012 and assuming a leadership role in 2017, he supporter the Lab's contribution as the knowledge and experimentation hub at BRAC. His portfolio of projects included mobile financial services for women, digital tools for development, youth development, incubating social enterprises, and institutionalizing human-centered design principles. He also focused on scaling successful social innovation and identifying high growth potential opportunities for BRAC's emerging social enterprises.

BRAC's Social Innovation Lab

Since 2011, BRAC's SIL had operated as a knowledge and experimentation hub, creating a cross-disciplinary platform to generate and share scalable innovative ideas for BRAC. The goal had been to test new ideas, design prototypes, and learn and share what works and what does not in solving the most complex social problems. The lab has seeded innovation through three channels:

Lab generated ideas: SIL scanned the innovation space and identified innovative ideas in the private, public, and nonprofit sectors to determine partnership and best practices in these spaces.

BRAC generated ideas: With its global mandate of empowering all employees at BRAC, SIL has to promote innovation in staff at all of its countries and affiliates. This occurred through hosting internal forums to capture and share ideas, via learning events such as the Frugal Innovation Forum, and funding *intrapreneurs* and their ideas.

Externally generated ideas: SIL also engages external partners, helping them to use BRAC's footprint to test and experiment with innovative ideas. By working with the SIL, entrepreneurs have scaled their product or service, often pitching to BRAC Investments for support. Some entrepreneurs have also participated in a SIL-sponsored 6-month incubator program that helped them access resources to create new social impact ventures.

SIL's Problem-Solving Approach

BRAC's SIL used an approach called human-centered design to solve problems and develop innovations. In BRAC's view innovation was not just about products. It also involved creating new approaches to systems, experience, and services. BRAC's process was divided into three steps: simplify, innovate, learn. "Simplify" descried the process of seeking to understand the problem from the user perspective. "Innovate" meant making sense of what was learned and identify opportunities for prototyping and testing. "Learn" involved prototyping and piloting to evaluate ideas and pivoting to refine them based on test feedback. BRAC's innovation manual described the human-centered design process in detail, starting with ground rules of respect (putting the users first), responsible processes, and open-mindedness. BRAC's innovation process required solution designers to deeply engage with those they intended to help, using patient listening and in-depth inquiry to develop insights on the nature of the issues they faced. A central tenet was using prototyping to test, refine, and iterate potential solutions. Finally, the SIL encouraged pilot projects to test the long-term impact of each solution prior to scaling.[21] SIL shared this approach in the field and provided training to help human-centered design become an organization-wide capability.

Example: Mobile Money as a Way Out of Poverty

An example of innovation in action at BRAC is their work in mobile money. Starting in 2013, BRAC articulated the benefits of mobile money seeing a strong opportunity to help the ultra-poor, who lack critical access to financial services. The idea, according to Avi, was to determine how that mobile money could help give the unbanked access to essential financial services. According to the World Economic Forum, "an overwhelming body of evidence shows that providing people with the ability to save and borrow efficiently and securely improves well-being and encourages enterprise, ultimately reducing global poverty and increasing economic growth."[22]

In early 2014, the SIL launched its first challenge to generate ideas about how access to mobile money could help its clients. They received over 100 ideas within a month and selected seven to pilot. (The next year, there were 400 ideas out of which seven additional pilots were selected.) After experimentation, three concepts were selected for scaling: establishing a monthly savings program as an added offering to microfinance clients, creating "digital wallets" for schoolteachers, and introducing a suite of mobile finance services in remote wetland regions of rural Bangladesh.

Unsurprisingly, BRAC encountered multiple design and implementation challenges including the need to orient and train users, break cultural taboos, and overcome distrust. As they continue with implementation (and experimentation), BRAC expects the momentum will continue, enabling its clients to use mobile money as a powerful tool to help them escape poverty.

Innovation Challenges

Avi was faced with a dilemma: He wondered how BRAC should continue to build on their impressive legacy of innovation given their scale. He knew that in the past when BRAC was smaller, the organization had more appetite for testing and piloting individual pilot ideas, sometimes working with over 20 ideas at the same time but that as BRAC had grown, this had become more and more challenging.

While he was proud of the SIL's reputation as the "custodian of innovation," Avi feared that if SIL was not more fully integrated into BRAC, it would miss opportunities. As he joined his team on the 20th floor, he wondered: with the diversity of BRAC programs in multiple countries, how should the SIL focus continue to innovate? How should he integrate its work into BRAC's on-the-groundwork? And how should he best manage and motivate his team to create, collect, and respond to opportunities that would optimize BRAC's impact going forward?

Discussion Questions

1. Why is innovation important to BRAC's work?
2. What has BRAC done successfully so far to foster innovation?
3. Can an organization as large as BRAC really be innovative?
4. Where do you see the most promise for generating ideas—within the SIL, within BRAC as a whole, or externally?
5. What should Avi do to maintain an innovation culture going forward?

NOTES

1. Phills, J. A., Deiglmeier, K., & Miller, D. T. (2008). Rediscovering social innovation. *Stanford Social Innovation Review*, *6*(4).
2. Krasney, J. (2014). Where entrepreneurs get their brightest ideas. *Inc. Magazine*. Retrieved from https://www.inc.com/jill-krasny/where-entrepreneurs-get-their-brightest-ideas.html.
3. 1989 Interviews with the founders of 100 companies on the *Inc.* "500" list of the fastest growing private companies in the United States, cited in Bhide, A. (1994, March 1). How entrepreneurs craft strategies that work. *Harvard Business Review*, *72*, 150–161.
4. Amabile, T. M. (1998). How to kill creativity. *Harvard Business Review*, *76*(5), 76–87.
5. Ibid.
6. Bhide, A. (1994, March 1). How entrepreneurs craft strategies that work. *Harvard Business Review*, *72*, 150–161.
7. Amabile, T. M. (1998). How to kill creativity. *Harvard Business Review*, *76*(5), 76–87.

8. Ibid.
9. Dyer, J. H., Gregersen, H., & Christensen, C. M. (2009). The innovator's DNA. *Harvard Business Review, 87*, no. 12.
10. Ibid.
11. Anthony, S. D. (2012). *The little black book of innovation: How it works, how to do it*. Boston, MA: Harvard Business Review Press.
12. United Nations (n.d.). *The sustainable development goals*. Retrieved November 25, 2020, from https://www.un.org/sustainabledevelopment/.
13. Arsht, A. (n.d.). *Spotlight: Social entrepreneurship in the Americas*. Atlantic Council. Retrieved February 9, 2020, from https://publications.atlanticcouncil.org/socialentrepreneurship.
14. Ibid.
15. Martin, R. L., & Osberg, S. (2007). Social entrepreneurship: The case for definition. *Stanford Social Innovation Review, 5*(28), 29–39.
16. Kolb, D. A. (1984). *Experiential learning: Experience as the source of learning and development*. Englewood Cliffs, NJ: Prentice-Hall.
17. Wolf, G. (1996, February 1). Steve Jobs: The next insanely great thing. *Wired Magazine*.
18. United Nations (n.d.). *The 17 goals*. Department of Economic and Social Affairs. Retrieved November 25, 2020, from https://sdgs.un.org/goals.
19. BRAC (n.d.). *Our vision our mission our values*. Retrieved November 25, 2020, from http://www.brac.net/vision-mission-values.
20. BRAC (2021, March 26). *Bangladesh at 50: A global model for poverty reduction*. Retrieved from https://bracusa.org/bangladesh-50-global-model-poverty-reduction/.
21. BRAC Social Innovation Lab (n.d.). BRACORON: The BRAC way of designing with users. *Internal Training Manual*.
22. Driver, M. (2017, April 20). Why financial inclusion is key to ending global poverty. *World Economic Forum*. Retrieved from https://www.weforum.org/agenda.

CHAPTER THREE

SHAPING SOCIAL VENTURE OPPORTUNITIES

Generating ideas may well be the easiest part of creating a new mission-driven venture. In contrast, evaluating and shaping ideas is hard. The path from an idea to a venture concept supported by a viable business model is complicated and challenging. It involves carefully articulating each interrelated part of the business while efficiently testing key assumptions, adapting the plan, and then often abandoning it and moving on to the next idea. As discussed later in this chapter, there are some powerful tools to help with this process. But aspiring social entrepreneurs need to steel themselves to be objective and agile because when they vet and improve their plans, they will inevitably find out that they need to adjust their vision.

While this process sounds challenging—and it is—the benefits are enormous. When they are just starting out, the two most precious resources an aspiring social entrepreneur has are almost always time and money. Careful planning and use of experiments to design their venture preserves both, dramatically increasing the odds of a successful launch.

Learning Objectives

- Describe how to assess the viability of new venture ideas and validate market potential.
- Explain how failure is a key part of the entrepreneurial discovery process.
- Refine business model elements using a business model canvas.
- Test and modify ideas using hypotheses and minimum viable product development.
- Identify circumstance where design thinking can be used to create new products and ventures.

FROM IDEA TO OPPORTUNITY

The value of a raw idea is almost always at or near zero. The process of shaping a venture, attracting stakeholders, and ultimately execution is where an idea gains value. Social entrepreneurs seeking to address a particular opportunity should start with many ideas, as we mention in Chapter 2, and then begin a careful process of winnowing to identify the concept that is most likely to work.

A historical example of a great idea generator (and great idea culler) is Thomas Edison, who once famously said, about his invention of the light bulb: "I have not failed 10,000 times—I've successfully found 10,000 ways that will not work."[1]

What made Thomas Edison one of the most successful innovators in American history was that he pursued many, many ideas. While the light bulb is his best-known invention, we also credit Edison with inventing other innovative new products that included the wax cylinder phonograph, the celluloid strip motion picture camera and projector, the printing telegraph, synthetic rubber, cement mixers, and talking dolls. Not only did he tinker with ideas (which often failed), he also created an early **makerspace** to process ideas. Located in West Orange, NJ, Edison's facility included a chemistry lab, a film studio (that pivoted on a turntable to capture natural light), an enormous machine shop with overhead scaffolding, and multiple workshops. Leonard DeGraaf, an archivist at the Edison National Park, says, "One of the things that makes Edison stand out as an innovator was that he was very good at reducing risk…if one idea or one product (didn't) do well he has others…that can make up for it."[2]

Today, aspiring social entrepreneurs can follow Edison's example by recognizing that the first step in the shaping process is to sort through ideas—and quickly discard those that have a low probability of success. Ideas might fail to gain traction for many reasons including technical infeasibility, limited customer demand, regulatory barriers and competition (including recognizing that other organizations may already be addressing a social need) among other issues. What is left is a shorter list of concepts to pursue, or perhaps a single concept. Successful entrepreneurs constantly evaluate customer feedback and adapt the business model to adjust to market conditions to survive—even (and perhaps especially) in the social sector (Figure 3.1).

At the early stages of venture shaping, successful social entrepreneurs rely on a combination of *agility* and *tenacity*.

Agility refers to the willingness to adapt an idea—sometimes significantly—when the entrepreneur learns that parts of the emerging concept will not work. While doing this, aspiring social entrepreneurs also must keep a clear eye on the mission they seek to achieve, ensuring that adaptations don't compromise their overall goals.

Tenacity is an ability to work through initial barriers, relentlessly pursuing an opportunity. It takes discipline, focus, and a good measure of optimism to successfully develop a new product or service. That said, entrepreneurs recognize the value of their time and have the discipline to shed time-wasting activities.

While these two qualities may initially seem to be in conflict, they can actually be complementary. An entrepreneur can engage in rigorous debate with colleagues, advisors, and team members about how to adapt a new product or service while being tenacious in developing an improving the ideas. A good entrepreneur also knows when to move on.

Consider the experience of the team behind Owlet, an early-stage venture that we introduced in Chapter 2. The team's initial plan was to develop a wireless version of

Figure 3.1 How Early Ideas Turn Into Venture Concepts

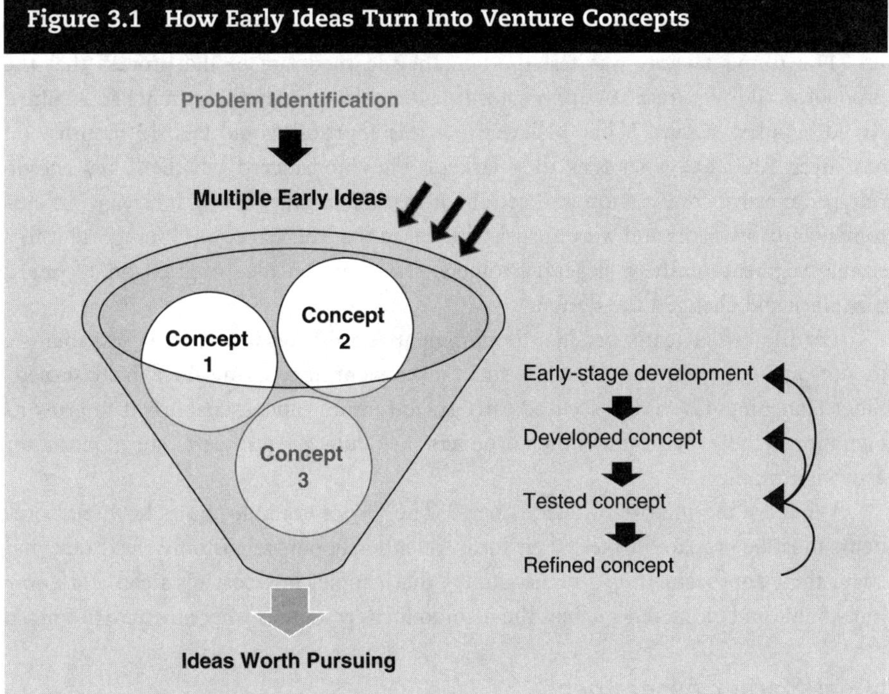

Source: Adapted from Applegate, L. M., & Carlson, C. (2014). Entrepreneurship reading: Recognizing and shaping opportunities. *Core Curriculum Readings Series*. Boston, MA: Harvard Business Publishing.

pulse oximetry monitors found in hospitals and doctors' offices, believing that it would improve the patient experience. To validate this, they interviewed over 50 nurses and found that nearly all of them favored the product. But when they spoke with hospital administrators, there was little purchase interest. As the founders explained it, they learned a very important lesson—your user is not always your customer.[3]

The team showed *agility* by pivoting based on the personal experience of a team member and decided to instead create an in-home anklet style product that measured infant blood oxygen levels and was linked to the parent's smartphone. With a concept that could reduce the rate of sudden infant death syndrome and an addressable market of 4 million US births per year, they believed that the market was large enough to move forward. To validate interest, they surveyed over 100 mothers and 96% said they would use the product.[4]

The team's initial plan was to distribute the product through hospitals using a rental model, but inexpensive early market research encouraged them to pivot to a retail purchase model. After they built a beta version website, they were surprised when it was discovered by potential customers. This led to a flood of inquiries from eager buyers and potential partners. This affirmed their belief that a purchase model was feasible.

The team's *tenacity* was tested when they learned late in the process that the product would require FDA approval if it had an alarm, something they had assumed would be a key feature. They believed that this approval would take 12 months and cost over $200,000, resources they lacked. They considered whether they should release an alarm-free version and set about market testing this by interviewing customers in baby stores and were surprised to learn that the alarm was unimportant to a sizable segment of their target customers. They also made progress on technical feasibility and changed the design.[5]

For the Owlet team, product development and market testing took less than six months and cost less than $1,000, a small investment in ensuring their likely success. Since launching, Owlet has secured early-stage venture capital, enabling it to grow its operations, and expand into other products including a fetal heart rate monitor for expecting mothers.

What are the important lessons here? The Owlet example shows how entrepreneurs must be prepared to test their ideas, relentlessly pursue customer feedback, and adapt their approach. It also demonstrates that simple, low-cost tests can add enormous value and ultimately enables the team to focus resources where they matter most.

Initial Market Assessment

One of the first questions a social entrepreneur should ask is, "is there actually a market for my product or service?" Many founders have learned the hard way that they cannot assume user acceptance and interest even if the product is beneficial and distributed for free or greatly subsidized. Mirroring commercial marketplaces, consumer decisions are complicated, and founders must objectively consider whether the buyer is willing to take the time to learn about, acquire, accept, and use a product or service. The entrepreneur might start by asking:

- Does the customer actually want the product?
- Is it accessible to them?
- Can customers be more readily satisfied by competitors or by substitutes?
- Do customers believe in the product and the organization behind it?

Many well-funded ventures have failed because the founding team failed to ask these simple questions.

The process of rigorously assessing and testing the market starts with a well-constructed *value proposition*. Value propositions are brief descriptions of a product or service and the value it provides. It explains why a product or service is superior to other choices and why a customer should choose it. Writing a value proposition helps an aspiring entrepreneur focus on the value they are creating in the eyes of a customer or beneficiary.

With a well-defined value proposition in hand, the entrepreneur can turn their attention to three fundamental questions:

- Is there a genuine need for this product or service?
- Is the value proposition sufficiently compelling to ensure key stakeholders (customers, recipients, funders) will purchase the product or provide financial support?
- Are implementation obstacles fully understood and can they be managed?

Consider the example of Daily Table. The venture was started in 2015 by Dave Rauch, former President of Trader Joe's, a North American grocery chain. According to Rauch, "I got worn out from ceaseless travel and I recognized it wasn't as much fun for me to manage a business as it was to grow it."[6] He immersed himself in a year-long fellowship at Harvard University seeking to develop a social venture. Realizing that over 40% of food in America was discarded while at the same time that one in six families experienced hunger, he decided to draw on his expertise to start a not-for-profit grocery store offering healthy and convenient foods to low-income residents of Boston. Daily Table operates in the Roxbury, Dorchester, and Central Square neighborhoods of Boston and Cambridge, and keeps its prices low by selling soon-to-expire packaged foods, and "ugly" produce items that would not make it to the shelves of conventional grocery stores.

Despite having an experienced founder and a compelling value proposition, Daily Table immediately became mired in controversy. Critics were concerned that the organization was exploiting its customers by selling spoiled food to buyers with limited choices. Meanwhile, potential customers were concerned about the safety of expired or near-expired groceries.

Daily Table's team showed *tenacity*, overcoming these criticisms and driving demand by providing high-quality fresh foods and prepared meals at consistently low prices. Word of mouth and an attractive retail environment helped them to overcome initial concerns. They showed *adaptability* by adding value by offering low-cost take-away food items, recognizing that their target buyers often worked multiple jobs and did not have time to prepare healthy meals. Today, Daily Table is on track to become financially self-supporting, with plans for both local and national expansion.

While Daily Table was able to build confidence among its target customers, many well-meaning ventures have not been as fortunate, failing to launch or closing their doors after discovering that their market size projections were overly optimistic, key stakeholders were unwilling to make investments, or consumers did not want the product. But as we saw with the Owlet team, with a little creativity these pitfalls can be avoided via inexpensive and fast efforts to validate market potential and other critical assumptions.

Validating Market Potential

To verify interest in a new offering, social entrepreneurs should follow Owlet's example by challenging themselves to size and segment the target market. Sometimes this can be accomplished using third-party data, but hands-on research is often required as well. Market data have another important use: when seeking external funding, it is usually essential for gaining the support of donors or investors. When validating market potential, founders will need to have answers to several key questions:

How Large Is the Market for This Product or Service?

Entrepreneurs should estimate the number of potential consumers in the marketplace and then realistically assess how much of the market they can capture. Basic demographic information can be meaningful and can be supplemented by customer surveys and focus groups and small experiments can validate (or refute) market potential.

How Is the Market Changing Over Time? Is It Growing? Shrinking?

Entrepreneurs should consider how the addressable market for their product or service is changing over time. Migration, demographics, changes in technology, shifting economies, and other factors can dramatically affect market potential. Markets are rarely static: some are growing, others are shrinking, and still others are shifting in terms of tastes, demand levels, and other factors. Understanding changes in the marketplace will help the social entrepreneur determine how to position themselves, both at formation and going forward.

Are There Segments? Do They Have Different Needs or Attributes?

Consumers can be diverse and have both easy to identify characteristics such as age and gender and more difficult to identify ones such as health status or interest in technology. Wise social entrepreneurs carefully segment their target markets and tailor their value proposition or offer different value propositions to different customer groups. This affects not only the product or service but also how customers are reached and served.

Who Competes With Your Venture? How Successful Are They? What Are Their Plans?

Social entrepreneurs should carefully assess the competitive landscape, evaluating both direct and indirect competitors. Founders of nonprofit organizations in particular sometimes ignore the fact that they are competing for both consumer and funder attention and that they may be competing against both for-profit and nonprofit players. Another overlooked source of competition is nonconsumption—a consumer's choice to not consume at all. For example, a hidden competitor for college access programs is the choice by students or parents not to participate in a program or not to pursue college. When assessing whether nonconsumption is an important constraint, social entrepreneurs should look beyond the benefits of their solution (which they are convinced of) and remember the challenges of changing human behavior and habit, even for a product or service that offers compelling value.

Who Will Use the Product or Service? Who Will Pay for It? At What Price?

As Owlet and Daily Table show us, determining the right approach to pricing is important. Sometimes in order to meet a venture's mission, a product is offered at a subsidized rate or at no cost. For example, SunBox (profiled in a short case at the end of this chapter) provides their home solar systems at roughly half the cost of production, making up the difference via crowdfunding and grants. In other cases, ventures pursue a revenue model where some consumers pay full price while others pay a discounted price or receive the offering for free. We'll address the question of pricing in more detail in Chapter 8, but the "bottom line" is that an aspiring entrepreneur's successes depend in large part on getting the economics right.

THE IMPORTANCE OF LEARNING FROM FAILURE

Most new ventures fail. According to the Kaufmann Foundation, which has studied entrepreneurship for over three decades, about half of small businesses survive their first five years.[7] According to CBI Insights, the leading cause of failure for small businesses was "no market need" (42%), followed by "ran out of cash" (29%), and "not the right team" (23%).[8]

But Kaufmann author Emily Fetsch also reports that approximately 84% of nonprofits survive the first five years. She proposes that more stable revenue sources and higher levels of sectoral support leads to higher survival rates.[9] Another reason may be that nonprofits often delay launching until they have secured philanthropic funding, while private sector entrepreneurs often take the leap with personal resources and are solely dependent on investors and market revenues for success.

Either way, failure is important for mission-driven organizations because embedded in failure is the opportunity to learn. Current mantras in new venture formation—"fail fast" or "fail smart" underscore this assertion. As we discuss later in this chapter, the key is to break down assumptions, and experiment and learn from early failure to refine a venture's business model prior to launch when the consequences are smaller and costs are lower. This is equally true for both commercial and social entrepreneurs.

Harvard Business School Professor Amy Edmonson is a leader in helping organizations think about and learn from failure. She distinguishes between three types of failure: preventable failures in predictable operations (which are bad but easy to diagnose and fix), unavoidable failures in complex situations (which should compel an organization to analyze their operations and learn from mistakes), and intelligent failures at the frontier (when experimentation is necessary because answers are not knowable in advance). This last category, which she describes as "good failures," are those where innovative organizations learn rapidly from experiments and outcomes, enabling them to learn quickly thereby tailoring their solutions to meet the needs of their stakeholders and using their resources wisely.[10]

BRAC (Bangladesh Rural Advancement Committee), an innovation leader in antipoverty solutions that we described in a short case in Chapter 2, has fully embraced the process of learning from failure. In both 2018 and 2019, BRAC's Social Innovation Lab published a "Failure" Report" on their website. As they mentioned in their 2019 report: "Analysing our failures helps prevent us from repeating the same mistakes again, and also enables us to strategise how to do things better the next time around. It saves finite resources and increases overall effectiveness. It can mitigate harm and maximise positive impact for those we serve. If we remain uncomfortable with the idea of failing, then we cannot truly be comfortable with testing new ideas, learning, and iterating."[11] This report included four case studies of initiatives that failed and for each they profiled the project's intent, analyzed what went wrong, and evaluated what could have been done differently.

One of the projects they profiled was Bhumi Bondhu. Responding to the frequency of land disputes in Bangladesh, the Bhumi Bondhu team set out to devise a way to increase transparency surrounding land disputes. The initiative intended to provide a wide range of services that included tax calculations, counselling, and legal aid related to land ownership. The failure report concluded that while most team members were seasoned development professionals, they had limited business expertise. Skipping a detailed market assessment meant that their business model and marketing plan lacked critical customer input. The result was a poor product–market fit. Reflecting on what could have been done differently, the case study discussed the importance of thorough market analysis and rigorous customer segmentation. They concluded that adding personnel with strong business acumen to the team early in the process would have helped to avoid some of the pitfalls the team encountered. They also observed that closer consultation with government land service providers would have enabled the team to launch a product that was complementary to existing offerings. Tips for future teams included ideas on conducting in-depth market research and launching pilot projects and iterative trials.[12]

BRAC's 2019 failure report ends with an invitation to others within BRAC to collaborate on analyzing case studies. This open invitation to investigate points of failure is emblematic of BRAC's commitment to being a learning organization. It is also an important reminder to social entrepreneurs to embrace and learn from failure as a way to be a good steward of resources, enable learning, and increasing the probability of successful ventures moving forward.

There are important differences between failure at mission-driven and commercial ventures that create additional responsibilities for social entrepreneurs. One is that social entrepreneurs, if they attract external funding, are using scarce philanthropic resources that could fund other social ventures. Accordingly, they have an obligation to use capital wisely. The second is that social entrepreneurs are often providing goods or services to vulnerable populations who will be worse off if the venture fails. For example, 99Degrees Custom, which we discuss in a short case in Chapter 8, provides jobs and skill building for hard-to-employ garment workers. If the venture closed, the negative impact on employees would be considerable. Realizing this, founder Brenna Schneider paid special attention to the durability of her business model.

Below we discuss some techniques—business model canvas development, hypothesis-driven entrepreneurship, and design thinking—that are intended to help aspiring entrepreneurs think carefully about their business model (fail smart) and accelerate the failure cycle via experimentation (fail fast) to avoid postlaunch failure.

HOW ARE BUSINESS MODELS DEVELOPED?

What is a Business Model?

A *business model* is a design for a business venture. It describes the products and services the venture is offering, the value the product or service creates and for whom, and how the venture will operate and support itself. These elements are individually important, mutually reinforcing, and must be defined for both social impact ventures and any new business venture.[13]

The foundation of a good business model is a unique strategy—one that differentiates it from the competition (even in a social venture). The model requires choices about *where* to participate (the industry to compete in and specific market to serve) and *how* to participate (product offerings, pricing, and operational choices.)[14]

In their article, *What are Business Models and How are They Built?*, Clayton Christensen and Mark Johnson describe a business model, Shown in Figure 3.2, as four interdependent elements that collectively create value.[15] These include the following:

- *Value proposition:* an offering that helps customers do something they care about more easily

Figure 3.2 The Business Model

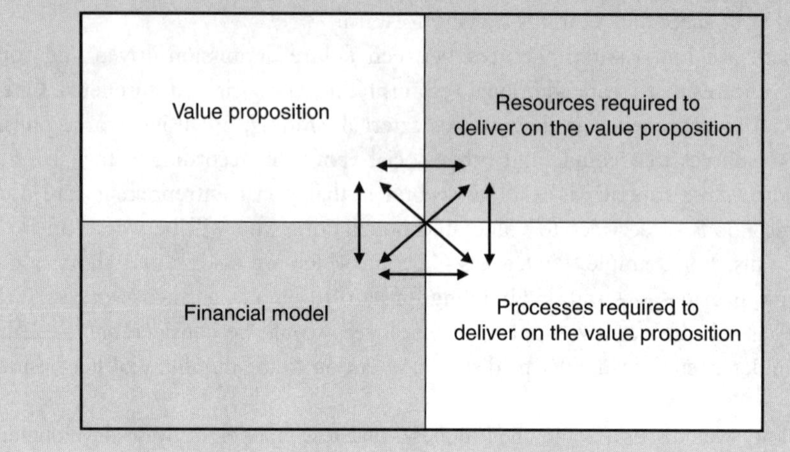

Source: Adapted from Christensen, C., & Johnson, M. (2008). *What are business models and how are they built?* Harvard Business School Module Note.

- *Resources:* the elements that the venture must put in place to deliver the value proposition, for example, technology, equipment, people, and products
- *Processes:* the way a company uses its resources
- *Profit formula:* the revenues and costs of the venture, and how they interact to create a profitable outcome

Each of the four different components is interconnected. Aspiring entrepreneurs planning a new venture should consider how to fill the boxes and assess whether all the elements have been well thought through and whether they are mutually reinforcing.

Creating a Business Model Canvas

A very popular way to refine a basic business model, and test the assumptions behind it, is to lay it out on a "canvas." The concept of a business model canvas was proposed in 2010 by Alexander Osterwalder, Yves Piner, Tim Clark, and Alan Smith, in their book *Business Model Generation.* In this influential book, the authors identified nine segments that represent the building blocks for a venture's business model on a single page. The canvas ensures that all aspects of the business venture receive adequate consideration early in the business development process. This helps to avoid an important pitfall: entrepreneurs often have strong skills in one area (for example,

Figure 3.3 Social Business Model Canvas and Key Questions

Mission: ______________________________

Activities and Resources

- What are our main activities?
- How do we operate to support them?
- What resources are required to deliver on our value proposition?

Partners

- Who are our key partners?
- What is our relationship with them?

Competitors/ Complements

- Who competes in this market?
- Who participates?
- Complements?

Value Proposition

- What is the value that the enterprise creates for key stakeholders?
- For customers / recipients?
- For funders?
- For other stakeholders?

Customer Segments and Relationships

- What are customer segments?
- What is our sales and marketing approach?
- How do we maintain customer relationships?

Intended Impact

- What problems are we addressing?
- Who do we intend to benefit?

Impact Measurement

- How will we measure impact?
- Direct and indirect?

Revenue Stream

- What are our sources of revenue? Donations? Earned income?
- What are revenues on per unit basis?

Cost Structure

- What are our costs?
- What fixed and variable components exist?
- What drives costs on per unit basis?

Organization What is the basic organization form? Nonprofit? For profit? Hybrid?

Source: Adapted from Osterwalder, A., & Yves Pigneur, Y. (2010). *Business model generation.* John Wiley & Sons.

customer acquisition or operations), and this can lead them to naturally favor problem-solving in that domain while overlooking other equally critical areas.

The social business model canvas is an adaptation that makes the canvas relevant to social entrepreneurs. It includes the mission of the organization, prompts the entrepreneur to articulate the value proposition in social impact terms, and adds sections relevant to social ventures. It also specifies the legal form of the organization since this is an important initial decision that affects how a venture interacts with stakeholders and secures funding (Figure 3.3).

Let's look at these components in detail:

Mission

When completing this canvas, the first task for the social entrepreneur is to articulate the mission of the organization, both to be clear when the venture is described to others and to check to make sure the other elements, as they are developed, are supportive of the mission. As we will discuss in Chapter 5, methods of planning for impact such as developing a theory of change or logic model enable the entrepreneur to dive more deeply into the intended impact of a new venture and how it is achieved. But for the canvas a simple statement of mission is sufficient.

Value Proposition

This element of the business model canvas is at the center for a reason. Most new ventures that fail do so because of poor product–market fit. In other words, what is proposed does not create enough value for stakeholders including customers, funders, suppliers, or partners. Social entrepreneurs should avoid this pitfall by considering the value proposition from the point of view of each key stakeholder.

Activities and Environment

The three boxes on the left-hand side of the canvas (activities and resources, partners and competitors/complementors) define the organization's main activities and the environment in which it conducts them. Activities include a description of what the organization does to create value and what resources are required, while the partners and competitors segment describes external elements that support the production of these activities (by, for example, supplying key resources.) For example, a food bank relies on food donations. Competitors are product or service providers with competing value propositions. Complementors are nonpartner organizations that makes it easier for a venture to deliver its value proposition. For example, public transportation services are a complementor to youth employment programs because they enable job seekers to access employment opportunities.

Customers, Value Delivery, and Impact

The three boxes on the right define who the customers are and identify major customer segments. As mentioned earlier, understanding the unique needs of various segments is important since it enables a venture to deliver a tailored value proposition. In this section, founders describe how customers will be secured (via a summarized sales and marketing plan) and which channels they will be served by (by, for example, online or in person). Finally, this section includes sections for defining the desired social impact and for describing how impact will be measured.

Financial and Organizational Approach

The bottom three boxes describe the proposed financial structure of the organization. In the revenue stream box, sources of revenue are identified. When doing so, it is important in this section to ask hard questions, for example, if the model relies on selling a product, is it realistic to assume consumers or others will be willing to pay at the expected level? If not, how will gaps be filled? If the venture relies on donor funds, can the venture realistically secure them?

The team should also ask hard questions about the cost structure, for example, what will it *really* cost to operate the venture? What initial investments in property, equipment, or technology will be required? What will the cost of producing the good or service be at different production levels? How much will need to be invested in overhead, including customer acquisition, fulfillment, and management? What compensation is required for the founders and employees?

As discussed in detail in Chapter 6, Legal Structure and Financial Plans for Social Ventures, the decision about whether to be a nonprofit, for-profit, or hybrid (and if so, what type) is important as it informs where revenue will come from and what the cost structure will be.

It is not unusual for an entrepreneurial team to develop the top half of the canvas and then realize that the venture they have envisioned is not financially feasible when they reach the lower boxes. This should trigger an iterative process where the team reworks elements of the value proposition, activities, and customer targets to develop a financially viable plan. It might also trigger the team to reimagine the financial structure.

PROFILE: JOHN HARTHORNE AT MASSCHALLENGE—FROM CONCEPT TO LAUNCH

John Harthorne cofounded MassChallenge in 2009 with fellow Bain consultant Akhil Nigam. In fewer than ten years, MassChallenge had become a global network of zero-equity start-up accelerators. Described as the "most startup friendly accelerator on the planet," by 2020, MassChallenge had assisted over 2,300 entrepreneurs who collectively had raised over $4 billion of investment, had generated over $2.7 billion in revenue, and had created over 140,000 jobs. Harthorne had been recognized as one of Boston's 50 most influential business leaders, the World Economic Forum recognized him as one of their Young Global Leaders, and Ernst & Young had voted him as 2013 New England Social Entrepreneur of the Year.

As an MBA student at the Massachusetts Institute of Technology (MIT)'s Sloan School, Harthorne "fell in love with startups" (J. Harthorne, personal interview, February 10, 2000). At MIT, he competed in the school's $50K startup competition, ultimately winning with his plan to commercialize a robotic cancer diagnostic product. At Sloan, he also ran the Global Startup Workshop which organized a conference to teach the world how to emulate the catalytic impact of MIT's start-up competition, giving him important foundational knowledge that he later used at MassChallenge. After graduating with significant student debt, he became a consultant for Bain & Company where, as a member of their private equity group, he regularly evaluated potential investments and acquisitions by private equity firms. His intent was to learn additional skills and pay down his loans, enabling him to leave to launch his own start-up.

The entrepreneurial insight that led to Harthorne's creation of MassChallenge came in late 2008. Witnessing the human impact of the financial crisis, he reflected on the positive benefits that entrepreneurship could make in the economy by creating "growth, wealth, optimism, hope, and jobs" (J. Harthorne, personal interview, February 10, 2000). His flash of insight came early one morning. Half asleep, he realized several things in rapid succession: "First, someone should be trying to fix the economic malaise and pain created by the financial crisis. Second, entrepreneurship had the potential to do just that. Third, due to the financial crisis and recession, the resources needed by entrepreneurs to be successful—office space, labor, legal support, mentorship, and other key resources—were all available in excess supply; and, finally, that he was 'someone' and was actually very well positioned to take a leadership role" (J. Harthorne, personal interview, February 10, 2000).

Despite being confident that he had identified an obvious answer, the creation of Mass Challenge required hard work, agility, adaptation, and persistence. The cofounders' first vision was for a global, for-profit investment fund and ecosystem aimed at identifying and scaling high potential start-ups. Initially they targeted funding from the US federal government, expecting support from federal economic stimulus funds that had become available. Harthorne and Nigam prepared a pitch deck and as they received feedback, evolved the concept. The next iteration maintained the for-profit ecosystem approach but after realizing the importance of high-touch services for entrepreneurs, the venture was reconceived as a local (Metropolitan Boston) concept. This was also in accord with lessons they had learned while seeking financial support: they would be much more likely to get state funding because the federal government was too siloed (and byzantine) to support a generalist vs. industry-specific model. As they learned more, they continued to adapt. By the time it launched, MassChallenge had evolved into a nonprofit accelerator with a composite funding model (philanthropic and government-supported) which would initially focus locally but would maintain national and ultimately global ambitions.

How did Harthorne and Nigam evolve Mass Challenge so quickly? As Harthorne recounts, they initially pitched the idea at MIT and Harvard and then reached out and refined their concept through dozens—ultimately hundreds—of meetings. He recounts: "We got smarter at every meeting, and as we were able to adapt and answer more questions, we realized we were ready to pitch to increasingly high-profile individuals" (J. Harthorne, personal interview, February 10, 2000). By the time they were able to secure a meeting with legendary high-tech entrepreneur, venture capitalist, and philanthropist "Desh" Deshpande they believed they had a compelling story. But Deshpande put them through a "series of tests," assessing their commitment, sales and marketing ability, ability to leverage other commitments, and ability to spend resources wisely. Once they had satisfied his concerns, Deshpande became a critically important mentor and founding board member. He also co-invested to enable the venture to launch and helped provide and secure additional funding at numerous critical points as they grew. After negotiating no-cost space in Boston's Seaport District, selecting their first class of entrepreneurs in 2010, and assembling a talented and committed team, they were poised to make a massive impact.

Harthorne offers the following advice to aspiring social entrepreneurs: "Focus primarily on understanding the problem you want to address, and the impact you want to create, and less on tactics and mechanics. Have a bias towards action and know in advance that no plan is perfect initially. Even with a great idea, expect to adapt and figure it out as you go. But get started on your initial hypothesis as soon as reasonably possible so you can start learning and improving right away" (J. Harthorne, personal interview, February 10, 2000).

HYPOTHESIS-DRIVEN ENTREPRENEURSHIP

Steven Blank, a professor at Stanford University and cofounder or early employee at multiple start-ups, observed three important things in his seminal article, "Why the Lean Startup Changes Everything." First, business plans rarely survive first contact with customers. Second, five-year plans and forecasts are a waste of time. And finally, start-ups are not smaller versions of large companies and do not unfold via master plans. Instead, successful start-up ventures moved quickly from failure to failure while they adapt their ideas and learn from customers.[16] Mission-driven ventures are not exempt from these lessons. Indeed, they may need to pay more attention to these principles given resource scarcity.

How should an aspiring social entrepreneur ensure that their process is lean? The answer is to use a methodology called hypothesis-driven entrepreneurship that guides founders to test key assumptions, enabling them to avoid the pitfall of discovering that they have invested significant resources to create a product without a viable market, revenue, or cost structure. The methodology hinges on developing small, inexpensive tests of key elements of the business model. The approach suggests an entrepreneur with a vision for a new product or service develop a *minimum viable product* (MVP), which is a scaled down product or service that presents the smallest set of features needed to either prove or disprove key assumptions.

The MVP enables entrepreneurs to measure value to customers via experimentation, enabling them to learn from product tests and act upon the data. The results allow them to *persevere* if the information suggests they should go ahead with their plans, *pivot* if they should keep some elements of the plan while readjusting others, or *perish* if the outcome supports abandoning the venture. We encourage entrepreneurs to use a series of prioritized tests that validate all of the key assumptions behind the business model.

The steps of the lean start-up method are as follows:

1. Develop a vision
2. Translate the vision into hypotheses
3. Specify tests of a minimum viable product
4. Prioritize tests to sequence them based on high-priority rise elimination
5. Learn from minimal viable product tests
6. Act on the data: persevere, pivot, or perish; and if hypotheses are validated
7. Scale and optimize the venture[17]

Why is a Minimum Viable Product (MVP) Important?

Testing a MVP enables the entrepreneur to verify or refute hypotheses with minimal resources, thereby avoiding the expense of failing after making significant investments. Tests enable the entrepreneur to learn about the market and cooperate with potential users to craft the final offering. The approach also saves time, often the entrepreneur's most valuable resource. Different types of MVPs include prototypes, demonstrations, landing pages, crowdfunding, and mini-launches. In each, the venture offers a product that appears to be developed but lacks some features or functionality or has a minimal back end. The reason this method is more successful than other more resource-intensive launch approaches is that it allows for course corrections and adjustments throughout the product development process.

Returning to the Owlet baby monitor example, the founders were successful because of their ability to pivot when they determined that their product and market were not aligned. The Owlet team was rigorous about laying out their hypotheses, prioritizing them, and then testing them in a disciplined way. This saved them time and money as they evolved the final product.

After creating an initial MVP, they were able to iterate and adjust as needed. They decided to pivot when they realized that hospital administrators were not interested in their original monitor product and then pivoted again when they ran into additional roadblocks (for example, their original anklet design proved infeasible, and when they learned regulatory approval was required if their product had an alarm). The Owlet founders also elected to persevere when they received confirmation that there was a robust market for their product among a subset of consumers and that they could access consumers via direct sales.

SunBox, described in the short case at the end of this chapter, used the approach more intuitively. When they learned that their initial product was unaffordable to many of their target customers, they adapted by creating a system that enabled a solar power system (and its cost) to be shared by neighbors.

Both ventures started with limited resources and learned the importance of small tests and pivots. As a result, the founders were able to successfully adapt their models, launch, and grow. Both have also continued to apply these principles as they have expanded.

Avoiding Cognitive Bias

When using a lean approach, it is essential to maintain an objective perspective. Teams that are highly committed to the success of an idea may be susceptible to bias and incorrectly interpret information in their rush to move forward. As Reis, Eisenmann, and Dillard warn us in their "Lean Startup" article, the human brain is subject to multiple biases that impair our ability to make impartial decisions, observing that

Table 3.1 Bias Types and Mitigation Strategies[18]

Bias Type	Mitigation Strategies	Application to Social Ventures
Optimism: the tendency to overestimate the likelihood of positive outcomes and underestimate negative outcomes	Create prioritized hypothesis and launch inexpensive tests to track performance	Social entrepreneurs are particularly susceptible to this bias because of the passion they bring to their ventures. Overcoming the optimism bias helps them prioritize their efforts
Planning fallacy: the tendency to overestimate the benefits of an action and underestimate the costs, duration, and risks	Use of objective benchmarks; be wary of using estimates and seek verification	Social entrepreneurs sometimes fail to critically interrogate the benefits of their actions because of their keen focus on the mission
Confirmation bias: looking for or interpreting information in a way that validates our beliefs	Engage skeptics; explicitly consider the risk of false positives or negatives in testing	It is difficult to be skeptical in an organization with strong shared values
Sunk cost fallacy: overlooking the fact that already-incurred expenses cannot be recovered so should be ignored in going forward decision-making	Maintain an objective view on sunk costs understanding that they are no longer relevant; become comfortable with pivoting and avoid premature scaling	It can be challenging to maintain objectivity in social ventures, particularly when philanthropic resources have been expended

"while we cannot eliminate these biases, we can mitigate their impact by understanding them and employing strategies to combat them."[19] The authors describe four bias types and ways to overcome them (Table 3.1).

DESIGN THINKING

Design thinking is a human-centered iterative process that teams use to understand users, challenge assumptions, redefine problems, and create innovative solutions. It is similar to the hypothesis-driven approaches described above in several ways but it is used for a broader set of design challenges (solutions to problems and process design, for example), is less linear, and places a higher value on empathy and customer observation. As articulated by iconic design firm IDEO, the approach prescribes five "spaces" for tackling complex problems:

- Use empathy to develop a deep understanding of the problem. This involves observing and engaging deeply with stakeholders
- Define the problem
- Ideate—generate multiple ideas (We discussed several ideation techniques in Chapter 2)
- Prototype—develop inexpensive, scaled down versions of the product or features. This is analogous to the MVP discussed above
- Test the product or idea, gain understanding, and iterate

Design thinking practitioners remind us that the five stages are not always sequential and can take place in parallel. Feedback at every stage of the process sheds new light on potential solutions.

In a 2010 article in *Stanford Social Innovation Review*, Tim Brown (IDEO CEO and President) and Jocelyn Wyatt (IDEO Social Innovation Group Leader) observed that "many social enterprises already intuitively use some aspects of design thinking but most stop short of embracing the approach as a way to move beyond today's conventional problem solving."[20] The authors encourage mission-driven organizations to overcome these barriers by embracing vibrant design thinking cultures as part of the creative process, not just as a way to validate finished ideas.

CHAPTER SUMMARY

A key challenge for social entrepreneurs is moving a concept for a social venture from the idea stage to create a fully developed business model. Luckily, there are a number of tools that can help. One is the business model canvas, which enables the entrepreneur to take an objective approach to defining key elements of the venture and helps them avoid blind spots. A second tool is of hypothesis-driven concept development, which uses small, tailored, prioritized experiments to test the validity of key assumptions. Design thinking is an alternate, human-centered approach. For new products and services, creating an MVP can help to streamline venture development.

When developing a product or service, it is critically important to take a rigorous look at market potential. Too often, social entrepreneurs make blanket assumptions about how their product or service will be embraced by the market only to discover late in the process that consumer, payers, or both have little interest. Entrepreneurs must consider whether there is a genuine need, whether the value proposition is sufficiently compelling, and whether there are insurmountable barriers to implementation. Part of this process involves validating market potential by asking hard questions about how large the market of users is, determining how the market is changing over time, and verifying who will pay for the product or service and what price they are willing to pay.

Throughout the venture development process, the key to effectively shaping social ventures is an open mind and a willingness to experiment. Waafa Arbash, founder of WorkAround Online, offers us a memorable analogy—a long road trip. You probably have a clear idea of your destination but will need to make many course corrections and take a few detours. Her advice to aspiring social entrepreneurs once they know their destination, however, is: "Just start driving."[21]

KEY TERMS

Agility: willingness to adapt an idea—sometimes significantly—when an entrepreneur learns that certain elements of the emerging concept will not work.

Business model: a design for a business venture. It describes the products and services the venture is offering, the value the product or service creates and for whom, and how the venture will operate and support itself.

Business model canvas: a single page that summarizes key elements of the business model in a standard format.

Design thinking: a nonlinear, iterative process that teams use to understand users, challenge assumptions, redefine problems, and create innovative solutions.

Makerspace: a collaborative workspace that enables people to come together and use on-site tools to create product prototypes.

Minimum viable product (MVP): a product or service that provides limited functionality but is sufficient to either prove or disprove a hypothesis.

Perish: a decision to abandon an idea.

Persevere: the decision by an entrepreneur to move forward with a venture, supported by confirming data.

Pivot: a decision to adjust elements of a business model to increase feasibility.

Processes: the ways a company uses its resources.

Profit formula: a way of looking at the revenues and costs of the venture that establishes how these components interact to create a financially viable venture.

Resources: the elements that the venture must put in place to deliver the value proposition, for example, technology, equipment, people, and products.

Tenacity: an ability to work through initial barriers, relentlessly pursuing an opportunity. It takes discipline and focus to promote an idea.

Value propositions: brief descriptions of a product or service and the value it provides. It explains why a product or service is superior to other choices.

IN-CLASS EXERCISES

Exercise 3.1: Business Model Canvas

(Estimated time: 1 hour)

Purpose

The business model canvas articulates the company's design for a business in a simplified, easy to understand way. It allows entrepreneurs to quickly look at the company while constantly being able to make adjustments as the business develops. Working through the canvas enables aspiring social entrepreneurs to understand key business model elements and the interrelationship between them and to form the foundation for additional work developing their venture.

Preparation

Provide blank copies of Figure 3.4 below, large sheets of paper, markers, and sticky notes.

Figure 3.4 Social Business Model Canvas Template

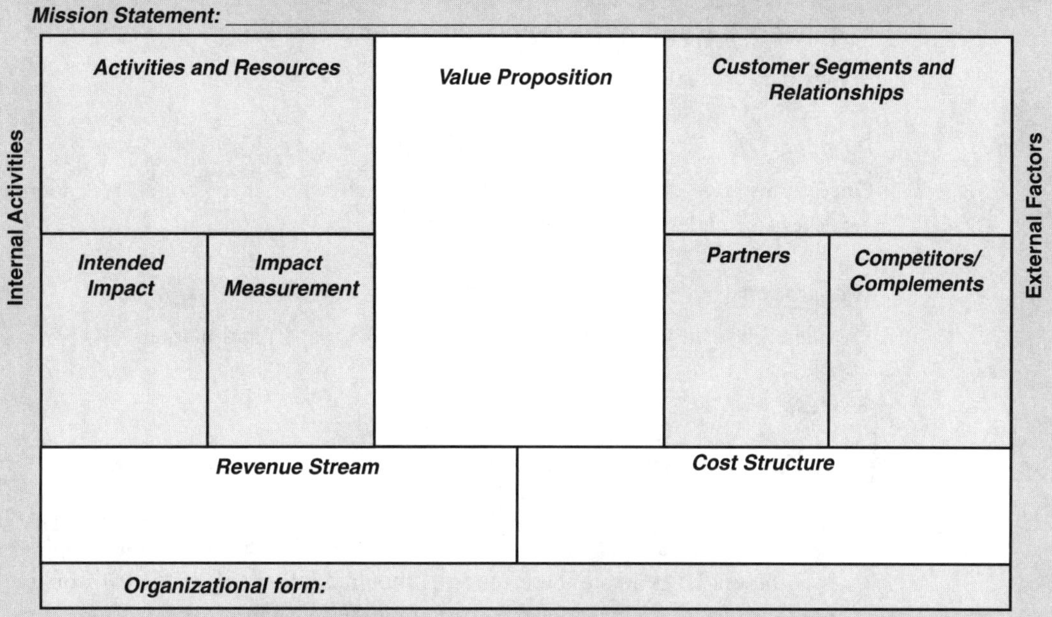

Source: Adapted from Osterwalder, A., & Yves Pigneur, Y. (2010). *Business model generation.* John Wiley & Sons.

Process

1. Break into teams of 3–5 students to complete the sections for either a social venture they are developing or a social venture they are familiar with or select a venture for all teams to use.
2. Fill in each building block of the business model canvas, starting with the mission and moving through all 9 building blocks.
3. Present the final business model canvas to the class. If the room and class size allow, a gallery walk approach, where teams display their work on large sheets of paper taped to the wall, can be especially engaging.
4. Debrief:
    a. Which building blocks were hard to complete?
    b. Which building blocks were easy to complete?
    c. In what ways did the team iterate/develop your model as it worked through the canvas?

5. Post-class: Continue to refine the business model canvas. Report back during the next class.

Exercise 3.2: Hypothesis Development and Testing

(Estimated time: 30 minutes)

Purpose

Once teams have developed their business model canvas, they can start to identify quick tests of underlying assumptions.

Preparation

Provide each team with blank copies of Figure 3.5, paper, and markers.

Process

1. Break into the same teams of 3–5 students from the previous exercise.
2. Using a social venture idea that students have been working on (or one they are familiar with or suggest an example for the entire class to use) and develop 3–4 hypotheses. To generate these, students should ask themselves: "What would I need to believe to be true for this opportunity to move forward to the next stage?"

Figure 3.5 In-Class Exercise: Testing Hypotheses Template

Questions	Hypothesis 1	Hypothesis 2	Hypothesis 3	...Others...
What would I need to believe for this idea to be viable? ⬇				
What is the easiest and least expensive way to test this? ⬇				
How will I know if my concept has succeed/failed? ⬇				
What is the priority that I should give this test? ⬇				

3. Use the Figure 3.5 template to guide the team's work.
4. Debrief: A few teams provide an overview of their results and describe:
    a. Which hypotheses did they develop?
    b. Which tests were proposed and how would they sequence them?
    c. What would the potential outcomes be and how will the team remain objective as they collect information?
    d. How would they expect to persevere, pivot, or perish based on test results?
5. Post-class: Continue to refine hypotheses and testing plan. Report back during the next class.

SHORT CASE: MAJD MASHHARAWI AT SUNBOX

Majd Mashharawi looked on as a collection of families from a local neighborhood in Gaza crowded around a laptop watching a soccer game made possible by her most recent innovation SunBox. This particular unit was the last of her company's second round of production, which sold out in just two weeks and has helped to provide power to just under 1,000 individuals in Gaza. She was proud of all she and her team had accomplished and was excited for what the future could hold for the venture in a region that desperately needs electricity.

Mashharawi was also excited about her trip the next day. She would be visiting Saudi Arabia, the Czech Republic, and Jordan to seek new markets for SunBox and engage financial partners. As she thought about her upcoming meetings she wondered—had she hit on exactly the right model for Gaza and positioned SunBox for out-of-country expansion? Had she developed a sufficiently resilient business model? And how should she go about convincing stakeholders to support her ventures?

As a youth in Palestine, Mashharawi pursued a degree in engineering and enrolled in Gaza's Islamic University. It was there that she delved into entrepreneurship with the hope of improving the lives of the residents in the region—over 100,000 of whom were left homeless by the 2014 Israel–Gaza conflict which resulted in the destruction of 17,000 homes, buildings, and roads. Mashharawi was intimately familiar with these hardships, as her family's home had been destroyed in 2008. Despite the need for new construction, accessing affordable building materials was difficult because many of the materials needed to create new buildings (like cement and gravel) were difficult to import because of security concerns. And with 2 million people living with less than 4 hours of electricity a day, reliable production was challenging. Ever the optimist, Mashharawi saw an opening and the potential to develop a new product that could improve the lives of thousands in the region and "turn the ashes of war into hope."[22]

The result was Mashharawi's first venture, GreenCake. Not deterred by what Gaza lacked, Mashharawi took stock of the resources that the region did have access to and attempted to make usable building materials out of what was readily available: paper, mud, and myriad other products over a six-month period. These tests resulted in countless prototypes which included over 150 failed tests. It was not until she noticed a pile of ash from a discarded prototype that Mashharawi thought, "Why don't we use those ashes?"[23] This led to her development of GreenCake, an ecofriendly building block with the strength of concrete constructed out of ash and rubble. Mashharawi and her partner Rawan Abdulatif decided to call the venture GreenCake because the blocks they created were dark green in color and had many air bubbles in them, reminding them of the spongy texture of cake. GreenCake quickly acquired its first major customer and by April 2019, they had built over 30 buildings, produced 50,000 blocks, and created 30 jobs. However, a major barrier prohibited GreenCake from reaching its full potential—reliable electricity.

Since 2006, Gaza had suffered from an energy crisis and most residents only had access to three to five hours of electricity a day. Mashharawi had frequently completed schoolwork by candlelight as a youth. The unreliability of electricity had caused frequent work stoppages for GreenCake. But, with the success of her first venture came international acclaim and Mashharawi was able to leave Gaza for the first time, experiencing how different life could be with reliable access to electricity. "When I was in Gaza, I used to accept it, but when I went to Japan, and I saw how many lights they have in the streets, how easy life is ... you just go to the bathroom, you have [a] hot shower, it's so easy."[24] This gave Mashharawi a new idea.

SunBox was created in 2018 to serve the Gazan market, providing "reliable, affordable and easy-to-use solar systems to families suffering from electricity shortage."[25] The company sold a solar-powered system that supplied enough electricity to support basic appliances such as lights, fans, phones, and laptop chargers, as well as a connection to the internet. The system only required three hours of sunlight to charge and did not require a technician for installation. Since the region typically experienced 320 days of sunshine a year, it was an ideal market for the launch of the product.

Experimentation was important for achieving a product–market fit. Initially, Mashharawi and her team sourced a low cost 500-watt device that had been used to bring electricity to developing countries. They quickly found that the modest amount of electricity generated—enough for a laptop and a few hours of light—was not good enough for the Gazan market, where consumers had experienced reliable electricity in the past. They quickly upgraded to an 800-watt system but found that, too, was insufficient. The team adapted by offering a more robust 1000-watt system. As they upgraded capacity, costs increased, and they knew that they also needed to address affordability. According to the World Bank, Gaza's average income had fallen from

$2,659 in 1994 to $1,826 in 2018, meaning a $350 SunBox unit would cost nearly 20% of a potential customer's yearly income. An important innovation driving early adoption was the high price of the technology (despite subsidies). In response, Mashharawi introduced the "Sharing is Caring" sales model which enabled two to three families to split the cost of a unit using a pay-as-you-go monthly model. Another innovation was modularization—a customer could purchase some SunBox components initially and then upgrade to a system with more capacity over time.

Mashharawi and her team also learned the importance of user behavior. Each backup battery in the prototype system had 800 cycles (which is the number of times the battery could be recharged). In Africa, where the system had been tested initially, this was sufficient because users typically recharged daily, giving the system a life span of approximately three years. In Gaza, customers were recharging three times daily, depleting battery life in less than a year. To respond, SunBox upgraded to 1600-cycle batteries, and advised customers to extend system life by limiting recharges. SunBox also expanded to B2B and B2G models, providing street lighting and electric power for water treatment plants and education facilities.

Despite innovations and careful sourcing, about half of the $350 cost of each SunBox unit was subsidized through a combination of crowdsourcing, international donations, and internal subsidies from SunBox's commercial products. While this kept the cost to consumers affordable, it also limited scaling potential. Despite these constraints, SunBox had installed 250 units in only two years, serving the electricity needs of 3,000 people.

Mashharawi knew that both products played a crucial role in a region where electricity is scarce and that less than 20% of the 160,000 homes destroyed in the conflict between Israel and Gaza had been rebuilt. She also knew that with a staff of nine depending on her for income, the pressure was on to make the ventures a success. As she moved to the edge of the soccer-watching crowd, she wondered: What was the best way to make the company financially sustainable? Was more innovation in order? And how should she secure the investments/working capital she needed to expand her companies' impact?

Discussion Questions

1. How did Mashharawi use experimentation to evolve her ideas?
2. SunBox is attempting to capture their next round of funding. How would you make the case for the company to potential investors?
3. What other challenges do you anticipate Mashharawi facing if she chooses to grow SunBox? Are these different or the same for GreenCake?

4. Mashharawi's innovations have come from a place of need in her community. Do you think there are limitation/issues with this approach? Are there other similar companies that have operated in this way and if so, how have they overcome existing hurdles?

NOTES

1. Edison, T. (n.d.). *Thomas A Edison Quotes*. Brainyquote. Retrieved April 11, 2021, from www.brainyquote.com/quotes/thomas_a_edison_132683.
2. Hendry, E. R. (2013, November 20). Seven epic fails brought to you by the genius mind of Thomas Edison. *Smithsonian Magazine*.
3. Brigham Young University. (2013). *First place winner owlet* [Video]. IBMC Business Model Competition.
4. Ibid.
5. Ibid.
6. Adams, S. (2017, April 26). How daily table sells healthy food to the poor at junk food prices. *Forbes Prep Talks*. Forbes Media. Retrieved from https://www.forbes.com/sites/forbestreptalks/2017/04/26/how-daily-table-sells-healthy-food-to-the-poor-at-junk-food-prices/?sh=2b4c69a21bc3.
7. Stangler, D. (2010, March 9). High-growth firms and the future of the American economy. *SSRN Electronic Journal*, 1–16.
8. CB Insights Research. (2019). *Why startups fail: Top 20 reasons*. CB Information Services.
9. Fetsch, E. (2015, March 30). *Six ways non-profit entrepreneurs are distinct from 'traditional' entrepreneurs*. Kauffman Foundation. Retrieved from https://www.kauffman.org/currents/six-ways-non-profit-entrepreneurs-are-distinct-from-traditional-entrepreneurs/.
10. Edmondson, A. C. (2011). Strategies for learning from failure. *Harvard Business Review, 89*(4).
11. BRAC Social Innovation Lab. (2019). *Failure report 2019* [Report]. Retrieved from http://innovation.brac.net/wp-content/uploads/2020/02/FAILURE-REPORT-2019.pdf.
12. Ibid.
13. Christensen, C. M., & Johnson, M. W. (2009). What are business models, and how are they built? *Harvard Business School Module Note*, 610–019.
14. Applegate, L. M., & Carlson, C. (2014, September 1). *Entrepreneurship reading: Recognizing and shaping opportunities. Core Curriculum*. Harvard Business Publishing.
15. Christensen, C. M., & Johnson, M. W. (2009). What are business models, and how are they built? *Harvard Business School Module Note*, 610–019.
16. Blank, S. (2013). Why the lean start-up changes everything. *Harvard Business Review, 91*(5).
17. Eisenmann, T., Ries, E., & Dillard, S. (2011). Hypothesis-driven entrepreneurship: The lean startup. *Harvard Business School Background Note*, 812–095 [Revised July 2013].
18. Ibid.
19. Ibid.
20. Brown, T., & Wyatt, J. (2010). Design thinking for social innovation. *Stanford Social Innovation Review*.
21. Arbash, W. (2020). *Carlson social entrepreneurship and innovation class visit*. Brandeis University, Massachusetts, USA.
22. Mashharawi, M. (2016, December 5). *Help rebuilding Gaza!* Indiegogo. Retrieved from https://www.indiegogo.com/projects/help-rebuilding-gaza#/updates/all.

23. Mashharawi, M. (2019). *How I'm making bricks out of ashes and rubble in Gaza* [Video]. TED Conferences. Retrieved from https://www.ted.com/talks/majd_mashharawi_how_i_m_making_bricks_out_of_ashes_and_rubble_in_gaza/transcript?language=en.
24. Dehghan, S. K. (2019, September 27). The Palestinian entrepreneur bringing power to Gaza. *The Guardian*. Retrieved from https://www.theguardian.com/global-development/2019/sep/27/the-palestinian-entrepreneur-bringing-power-to-gaza-majd-mashharawi.
25. SunBox Company (n.d.). [Brochure].

CHAPTER FOUR

BUILDING SOCIAL IMPACT TEAMS AND ECOSYSTEMS

Learning Objectives

- Identify the benefits that teams bring to social ventures and distinguish between human, social, and financial capital.
- Examine major challenges that founding venture teams must navigate.
- Assess ways to attract talent to entrepreneurial social ventures and identify pitfalls.
- Discuss the importance and characteristics of effective ecosystems for social ventures.

There is a popular saying that goes like this: "If you want to go fast, go alone. If you want to go far, go together."[1] While this idea rings true to entrepreneurs in general, it has particular resonance for social entrepreneurs. While individual founders can quickly make decisions and move forward, they can also be more prone to bias or narrow thinking and limited networks. During a social venture launch, these limitations can lead to constrained growth, mistakes, and possible failure.

THE BENEFITS OF FOUNDING IN TEAMS

For entrepreneurial ventures, the benefits of founding in teams are clear. Teams add a diversity of perspectives and experience as well as additional human, social, and financial capital. Most ventures are team founded. According to research by Harvard Business School Professor Noam Wasserman, 76% of private start-ups were founded by teams (in a survey of over 1,000 life sciences and tech companies in the United States and Canada), and the average size of the founding team was 2.8 founders per venture.[2] Additional studies have also confirmed the dominance of teams in new venture formation.

Teams make it possible to "go far." Consider, for example, the formation of WorkAround, a start-up discussed in a case study included at the end of this book. The team came together while participating in the Hult Challenge, a global start-up competition with an eye-popping $1 million prize that aims to solve pressing challenges related to the UN Sustainable Development Goals. The year the WorkAround team competed, the competition challenge was to create a sustainable social enterprise that would restore the rights and dignity of 10 million refugees. The team combined the deep customer knowledge of cofounder Waafa Arbush with the technical know-how of cofounder Jennie Kelly, the NGO partnership and education expertise of Shadi Sheikhsarif, and the marketing and international business understanding of Shai Dinnar. When the team discovered after their launch that they needed additional sales and marketing expertise, they developed these skills while relying on an external network of advisors to help them.

According to Wasserman, a primary reason to cofound a venture is that the founders are lacking in one of three types of capital: human, social, or financial:[3]

- *Human capital:* knowledge from formal education and skills derived from prior experience. In social ventures, this may come from a deep understanding of the customers and the context surrounding them, prior experience, or expertise in technology.
- *Social capital:* information and communication networks. In social ventures, this often comes from team member's relationships external to the team, partnerships that help them access a supportive ecosystem, or networks that enable them to attract team members, talented employees and volunteers, and key partners.
- *Financial capital:* money and other resources that can be used to establish the venture. For social ventures, this includes financial support for the early phases of a venture (often from donors) as well as earned income that helps to support the organization as it grows.

Wasserman recommends that founders carefully assess their gaps or limitations in these categories and consider filling or supplementing them when forming teams or through the addition of new team members.

For example, Sanergy's cofounders met during an orientation hiking trip they took when they were incoming graduate students at Massachusetts Institute of Technology (MIT). Bonding over their shared interests in using business as a force for social good, they took MIT's Development Ventures course together to see if they could cofound a social impact start-up.

The trio brought expertise based on their personal educational and work experiences. Ani Vallabhaneni had previously run a chain of dialysis clinics for low-income patients in the Philippines, David Auerbach had built partnerships at Endeavor and the Clinton Global Initiative, and Lindsay Stradley had expertise in sales and operations at Google and at Bridge International, a network of low-cost schools in Nairobi. Other early teammates had engineering and product design expertise. As their concept to create a new sanitation system for informal settlements in Kenya crystalized, they decided to add additional *human capital*, by expanding the team to include advisors and experts, tapping into their contacts at MIT. They increased their *social capital* by adding teammates from MIT and from the University of Nairobi, who added their unique knowledge to the venture. Together they increased their *financial capital* by winning a series of business plan contests that provided seed funds for the venture and then subsequently attracting financial resources from investors and foundations.

What about individual founders who decide to "go fast" and found alone? While they typically take more risks, they are able to avoid the complexities of group coordination and can usually launch with fewer resources. Brenna Schneider, founder of 99Degrees Custom who we introduced in Chapter 2 and discuss in a short case in Chapter 8, is one example. She decided to be a solo founder but created *social capital* by being part of the Merrimack Valley Sandbox incubator. She also was supported along the way by a very strong network of supporters and advisors and later by staff and partners. When asked why she solo founded, Schneider explained that she could not find anyone who shared her specific passion to break cycles of intergenerational poverty by creating a manufacturing business in Lawrence, Massachusetts. She also said that she did not want to share the financial sacrifices. Schneider had invested a considerable amount of her financial capital in the venture and did not take a salary for the first year of operation. She explains: "While I believed in the idea enough to do this on my own, I did not feel comfortable imposing that financial burden on a co-founder."[4]

NAVIGATING FORMATION CHALLENGES

Wasserman's "Four R's"

Noam Wasserman, in his classic book *The Founder's Dilemmas*, describes three challenges that cofounders must navigate when considering cofounding a new venture: relationships, roles, and rewards.[5] We add to this an additional category—responsibilities.

Relationships refers to whether you will you cofound with those who you have an existing relationship and how you will manage it. It is very common for social entrepreneurs who are students to cofound with classmates and for professionals to cofound with colleagues. But, as discussed later in this chapter, cofounders often find that moving beyond their initial circle gives them additional benefits. If cofounding with those you know well, particularly a friend or relative, it is important to consider whether the relationship is a benefit or a barrier, particularly when it comes to areas of disagreement. It is also worth assessing whether the relationship might suffer.

Roles refers to how decision-making powers will be allocated within the team and what functional areas each cofounder has control or authority over. While it is tempting to divide responsibilities along functional lines, in reality, most newly formed social ventures are so small that functional decision lines are fluid. Roles also refers to the decision-making model that teams will employ (for example, consensus, voting, or some other process) to manage the new venture. While the best approach will differ depending on the preferences and personalities of the team members, it is wise to consider this in advance given the potential for conflict.

Rewards in a commercial venture refers to how equity, salaries, recognition/titles, and other benefits will be allocated in for-profit ventures. But in a social venture, the upside is usually limited and in a nonprofit venture in particular, equity does not accrue to the founders or investors. Because mission is at the center of social impact ventures, meaningfully allocating awards can be more subtle and include how cofounders will be recognized, who becomes the external face of the organization, and other intangible benefits.

Responsibilities refers to the level of commitment and contribution that is expected from each founding team member. For example, the team should be clear on whether the venture is a full- or part-time commitment, and what additional contributions (of startup capital, expertise, intellectual property, contacts, and other resources) each member will be expected to make.

Heterogeneous and Homogeneous Founding Teams

An important question for founders as they seek to assemble a team is whether they aim to have a heterogeneous team (meaning diverse in character or content) or a homogeneous team (for startups, this means having common backgrounds or experience).

The benefits, particularly in the short term, of homogeneous teams include ease of formation (you likely already know your cofounders) and ease of initial communication. Shared experiences and values, as well as shared expertise, make it easier to communicate and align against a social impact venture concept. However, homogeneous teams tend to have common expertise, networks, social capital, and often patterns of thinking, which means that their new ventures may have inferior external connections or be less resilient.

Initial challenges forming heterogeneous teams include identifying team members (founders must network or find other means to create their teams), establishing trust initially, and developing ways to work together. However, cofounders' different networks, experience, and expertise can increase the odds of team success.

While social venture teams are typically created around a common vision, it may include individuals from different backgrounds that do not know each other well. For example, the WorkAround team was created during a social impact venture competition. During the initial Friday night "pitch" presentations, the team of four—which included three graduate students and one undergraduate student—rallied around Wafaa Arbash's vision to help refugees find employment through microtasks. While the students were in different academic programs, they had much in common when it came to a common commitment to social impact. But their diversity enabled them to tap into different knowledge and networks as they evolved the venture.

Similarly, the founders of Sanergy did not know each other well before they met at MIT (although two had studied as undergraduates together). However, they shared a common passion and quickly found that they had complementary skills. When they expanded the team, they were able to add knowledge and experience that increased venture feasibility. And they found that having different backgrounds, experiences, and skills enabled them to disagree constructively as they shaped the venture.

Attracting Talent to Social Ventures

As a social venture grows, the required effort can exceed the capabilities of the founding team. One of the key advantages social ventures possess is their ability to rally individuals—cofounders, team members, supporters, volunteers, partners, and others—around a mission. Unlike conventional start-ups, where the motivation for participating may be largely financial, mission-driven ventures usually rely at least in part on intrinsic motivation as they seek to expand their team.

For social venture founders looking to expand their team or recruit talent beyond their personal networks, there are several time-tested methods for finding new team members:

- *Networking:* in person and via social media (including LinkedIn) to search for particular affinities and skills
- *Partners:* funders and like-minded social venture teams can help connect founding teams
- *Board members and advisors*: often are aware of available talent and can help make introductions or recommendations
- *Hackathons*: can help founders identify talent, particularly technical talent
- *Incubators and accelerators:* natural connectors, such as coworking spaces

As social entrepreneurs attract additional talent, they should consider how and when they plan to scale, as well as the financial model they will use. Adding too much talent too quickly can easily bankrupt even the most promising venture, but having constrained human resources can inhibit growth and reduce momentum. Founding teams should be aware of several potential team attraction pitfalls:

- *Hiring employees too early:* sometimes it is better to contract or outsource work

- *Not being lean enough:* bringing too many people on board before the venture can support them
- *Being too lean:* by holding off on attracting critically needed talent and thereby constraining growth
- *Attracting the wrong people:* especially inflexible specialists, those who aren't fully on board with the mission, and those who can't accommodate the start-up culture
- *Underutilizing volunteers:* not taking full advantage of the capabilities of volunteers
- *Early title inflation:* attracting or rewarding early talent with executive titles can backfire if the organization grows and finds it harder to attract high-quality team members as it expands

Another consideration is whether newly added team members should be staff, consultants, or volunteers. All of these approaches have advantages and disadvantages. Sometimes talent can be added by partnering with external organizations or outsourcing. For example, new ventures often choose to outsource technology services, financial operations, or human resource management. Founders should make careful decisions after assessing which capabilities to develop internally (for example, to maintain control, accelerate operations, maximize learning, or reduce expenses) and which to delegate to third parties.

Ohad Elhelo, who we profile later in this chapter, has founded two high-impact ventures: a successful mission-driven venture (Our Generation Speaks [OGS]) and a venture capital-funded for-profit organization (Stuff). In both cases, he needed to recruit hard-to-find talent. He explained the difference he experienced when attracting team members:

> *The most important thing you need when growing a venture is a team you can trust. This means that they need to be highly committed to the venture and its goals. For a for-profit venture, you need to convince prospective team members that they will share in the rewards via equity, and importantly, that they are embarking on an adventure. For a social venture, the most important thing is to convince the team that the venture will happen. There is usually a lot of buzz around social impact ideas, but people will only fully commit to a startup that they think has traction. The moment a social venture has real resources behind it, and it clearly going to have an impact, attracting a team becomes easy.*
>
> (O. Elhelo, personal interview, February 13, 2020)

Similar to attracting cofounders, it usually benefits the founding team to look beyond their immediate circles to build the team. The same caveats apply—friends, family, and close associates usually share the same networks, contacts, and social capital—so moving beyond personal circles can enable founders to assemble a team with better and more diverse skill sets and increased network access.

Social venture founders should also be aware that because team members usually join because of both intrinsic motivation (belief in the mission) and extrinsic motivation (often compensation, status, and/or learning opportunities), they need to invest heavily in mission accomplishment, team culture, and team processes to keep their (often underresourced) teams performing at the highest level. While team members typically have individual contribution responsibilities, the existence of shared goals elevates commitment.

John Harthorne, the founder of MassChallenge, who we profiled in Chapter 3, has a keen sense of what it takes to hire effectively in a high-performance nonprofit. He encourages social entrepreneurs to hire very carefully, ensuring that they only have highly motivated people around them and notes that even one bad hire can be very costly, given a start-up venture's need for speed and effective teamwork. His approach during interviews is to dig deep to understand what truly motivates the candidate. He asks probing questions about their background, why they have made certain life and career choices, and even how they interact with their siblings to understand what makes them tick. And once a hiring decision is made, he seeks to motivate new hires emotionally rather than financially. For example, when encouraging high-quality candidates to join his mission-driven venture, he stressed both the organization's goals and the fact that new hires will have significant opportunities to grow and learn.

For those seeking to join a social impact venture team either as a founder or a team member, Harthorne offers the following advice: "Make sure you care deeply about the mission of the organization. Helping to get a new venture off the ground will be hard, really hard. You are likely to quit if you don't care deeply. So, it is important to be honest with yourself about your passion for the mission at the outset" (J. Harthorne, personal interview, February 18, 2020).

MANAGING SOCIAL VENTURE TEAMS

Teams typically work better than individuals when the task is complex and when it benefits from multiple points of view. In a recent book, researchers Anthony Mayo, Ranjay Gulati, and Nitin Nohria discuss how teams are defined by interdependence—how members must rely on the expertise and efforts of others to get things done. They discuss how new product development teams (which bear a strong resemblance to entrepreneurial start-up teams) prefer to include individuals with an understanding of the customer, the production process, and new technologies, enabling members to build on each other's skills.[6]

Mayo and his coauthors suggest that there is no right size for a team: the optimal size depends on how many team members are required to include the right mix of skills and perspectives. They suggest, however, that larger teams can be hobbled by communication problems and increased complexity.[7] Jeff Bezos, founder of Amazon, once famously implemented a rule that every internal team should be small enough to be fed with two large pizzas. His logic: That smaller teams work more productively and stay more on task.[8]

J. Richard Hackman, a pioneer in researching and understanding teams, identified a number of "enabling conditions" that help teams thrive. Martine Haas and Mark Mortensen elaborated on this work in their recent article, "The Secrets of Great Teamwork," by describing three of these elements in detail: a compelling direction, a strong structure, and a supportive context.[9] Let's look at each of these as they apply to social entrepreneurs (Table 4.1)

Table 4.1 Effective Teamwork for Social Ventures

Element	Description	Application to Social Ventures
Compelling direction	Challenging but achievable goals that energize and engage team members	Social entrepreneurs usually rally around a mission—seeking to solve an important problem for society—that provides this direction
Structure	The right mix and number of members, well-designed tasks and processes, and norms that create positive team dynamics	While social entrepreneurs depend on committed individuals, they must also maintain structure by assembling the right mix of expertise and capabilities and creating processes and norms that support the team
Supportive context	The "scaffolding" that enables the team to be effective: infrastructure for communication, material support for tasks, support for team development	Founders of social ventures scaffold by reinforcing the sense of purpose and by reinforcing culture and structure. Ventures often leverage external supportive ecosystems by providing space, technology, mentoring, advising, and seed funding

PROFILE: OHAD ELHELO—FROM SOLDIER TO ENTREPRENEURIAL PEACE BUILDER

Ohad Elhelo was surprised when the emails started flooding in. What had started out as a simple speech had gone viral and had received over 1 million views. He had been invited to share his perspective in front of a crowd of over 3,000 people at the Boston "Stand Up for Israel" conference. In his speech, he shared the challenges of being a soldier on the front lines of the Israel–Palestine conflict. But rather than bitterness, he talked about how terrorism and conflict were fueled by poverty and a lack of meaningful choices and encouraged the audience to support "an infrastructure of hope."

Two years earlier, as a sophomore, he had transferred to Brandeis University in Waltham, Massachusetts, to study economics. His plan at the time was to receive his MBA and secure a high-quality job after graduation. But the reception to his speech galvanized him, motivating him to pursue what he recognized as a rare opportunity to make a meaningful contribution to creating peace to the Middle East by founding Our Generation Speaks (OGS). A scant two years later in 2016, OGS launched its first cohort of Palestinians and Israelis fellows.

The design of OGS was simple. According to Elhelo: "Every year, we identify 30 of the best and brightest Israelis and Palestinians and we host them at Brandeis for the summer. They develop ideas for companies and then return home with funding and we support them as they launch the ventures" (O. Elhelo, personal interview, February 13, 2020). The OGS vision was to create a space where participants could rally around common interests and overcome conflicts, yielding both immediate benefits (in the form of new ventures that would bring services and economic growth to the region) and forming a larger grassroots movement that will catalyze change and peace.

This program design emerged after multiple iterations. A starting point was the idea of bringing participants to Boston and to accomplish this, Elhelo knew that the program would need to offer visas. The easiest way to access them was via a university partnership. At Brandeis, he also found university sponsors who shared his vision and helped to move it forward. The next step was shaping the program. The initial idea, for a multiyear degree program, was discarded when it became clear that it would not attract participants who would quickly return to the region and have an immediate impact. Eventually the design for a summer fellowship program emerged and gained broad stakeholder support.

To achieve his vision, Elhelo needed to engage an extremely complex ecosystem. By 2019 when OGS launched its third cohort, it had involved 80 volunteers (acting as coaches, mentors, and venture advisors), as well as dozens of financial supporters, important partnerships with academic partners that included host Brandeis University and the Massachusetts Institute of Technology, and an advisory board that included prominent philanthropists (with former Massachusetts Governor Deval Patrick as chair). This enabled its small staff of seven to run an intensive, well-designed program that exposed the fellows to new ideas and countless opportunities to learn from each other. Elhelo's transition from idea to reality had been made possible by his ability to attract, engage, and inspire an equally committed group of supporters.

As Elhelo reflected on his journey and the future of OGS, one thing was certain—it had not come easily. He had spent two years balancing a rigorous economics curriculum while reaching out to potential partners and polishing his strategy for engagement. Driven by an instinct that told him to leverage the relationships he made while at Brandeis into a larger network of supporters, he meticulously scheduled and prepared for meetings with potential advocates. He made sure to end each meeting outlining OGS's immediate needs, asking if this new connection knew anyone who would be interested in helping with those specific items, and finally if they would be willing to connect him with two or three people that would like to get coffee with him.

For entrepreneurs starting out, Elhelo stressed the importance of understanding and being honest about your motivations for starting a social enterprise. He explained that by interrogating your own intentions, your organization will become stronger because your honesty will shine through to those looking to understand your vision. He added, "The thing that helped me the most was to understand the concept of champions. Every business is a business of relationships, and ventures with a mission are no exception. People who contribute want to have an influence on the organization and you need to treat them very well. If you create meaningful, exceptional experiences for key supporters, they will support you and your venture and be committed to its success" (O. Elhelo, personal interview, February 13, 2020).

THE IMPORTANCE OF ECOSYSTEMS FOR SOCIAL ENTREPRENEURS

In biology, an ecosystem describes a community or group of organisms that live in and interact with each other in a specific environment. A *business* ecosystem is the network of organizations, institutional arrangements, and other elements—including suppliers, distributors, customers, competitors, government agencies, cultural context, and other elements that help to deliver a product or service through both competition and cooperation.

The business ecosystem concept was first articulated by James F. Moore in an award-winning 1993 *Harvard Business Review* article entitled "Predators and Prey: A New Ecology of Competition," in which he defined the business ecosystem as:

> An economic community supported by a foundation of interacting organizations and individuals—the organisms of the business world. The economic community produces goods and services of value to customers, who are themselves members of the ecosystem. The member organisms also include suppliers, lead producers, competitors, and other stakeholders.[10]

This article built on growing attention in the organizational literature at the time regarding systems thinking. Since then, many scholars have elaborated on this concept. The most current thinking describes business ecosystems as multi-entity, semi-permanent organizations characterized by competition, collaboration, and sometimes complementarity. They are linked by flows of data, services, and money.[11] Increasingly, business ecosystems are built around digital platforms that are not bound by traditional industry or sector constraints.

For social entrepreneurs, ecosystems can increase resilience and success. University of Tennessee Professor Philip Roundy theorizes that ecosystems can increase the chance of successfully launching and scaling by providing benefits that include assembling heterogeneous participants, diversifying investors and resource providers, creating an altruistic culture, and increasing opportunities for vicarious learning.[12]

Like traditional business ventures, social ventures operate in complex ecosystems. As we can see in Figure 4.1, the ecosystems of mission-based ventures have additional participants, and several other characteristics of social ventures make them even more complex including:

- Customers or beneficiaries are not always the party paying for a good or service. Part or all of the cost of a good or service are borne by third parties, including donors, government organizations, or other consumers.
- The community served by the mission-driven venture serves is often keenly focused on the venture's outcomes. For nonprofits organizations, where the assets of an organization are held "in trust," for the community's benefit means that that the community as a whole is an important stakeholder.
- Many social ventures rely on significant volunteer contributions.
- The competitive environment is different. While social ventures do compete—such as for funding and volunteers—there is also an expectation that they will cooperate around a larger mission. So rather than "predators and prey," as Moore characterized business ecosystems, social venture ecosystems are usually characterized by a higher degree of both cooperation and symbiosis.

This highly complex environment interlocking stakeholder groups means that social impact ventures need to navigate a considerably more complex environment than commercial ventures that need to mainly attend to the needs of investors, customers, suppliers, and employees.

Consider, for example, Victoria Hale at One World Health. Founded in San Francisco in 2000, the organization was the first nonprofit pharmaceutical company in the United States. Hale had been a senior reviewer at the US Food and Drug Administration and then a private pharmaceutical scientist. Her entrepreneurial insight was that many promising drugs were abandoned because, despite their life-saving potential in developing countries, they were not sufficiently profitable in

Figure 4.1 Ecosystem Participants

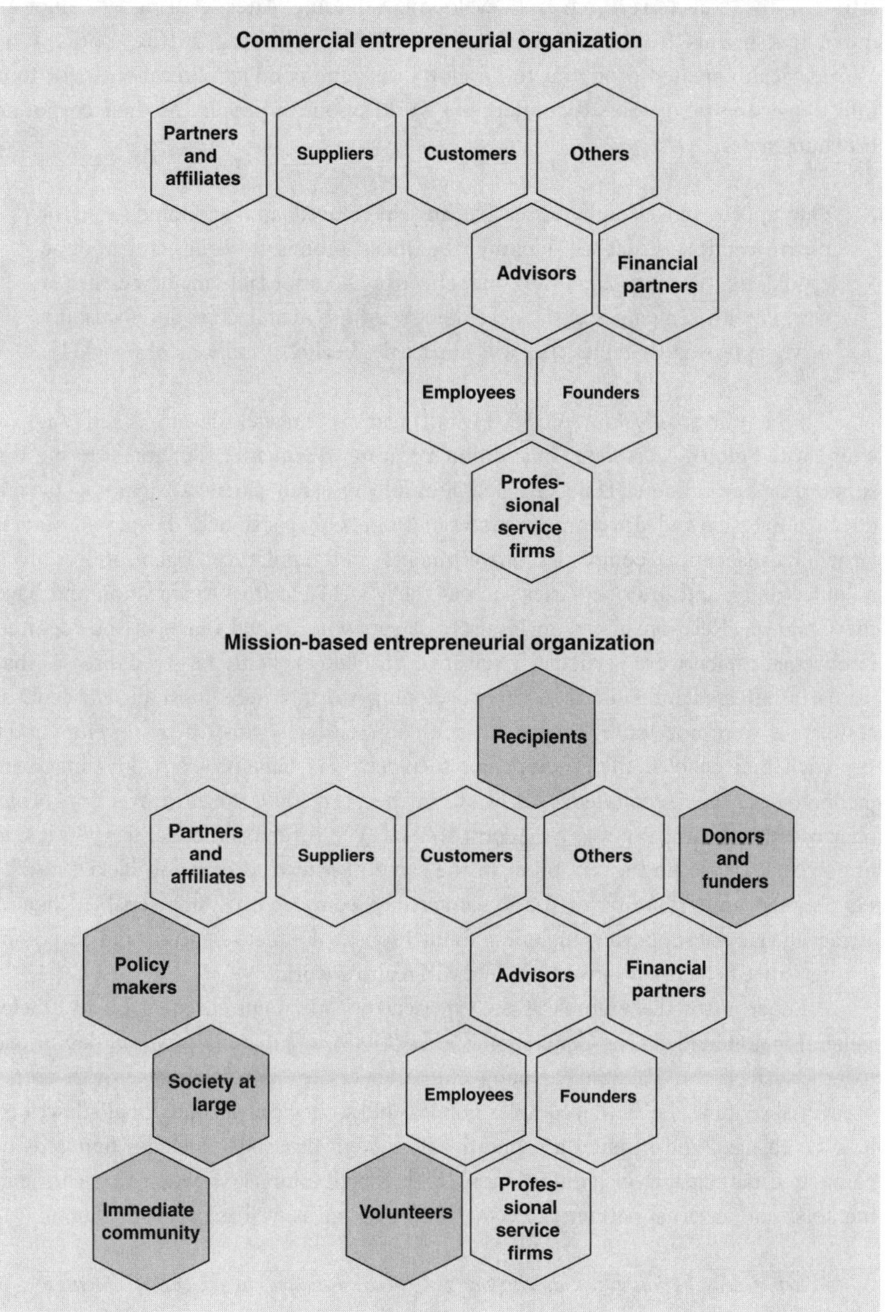

developed country markets to warrant investment.[13] Malaria alone, one of One World Health's target diseases, affected over 500 million people each year but therapies attracted low levels of research and development funding. After securing $9 million in initial investments from charitable foundations and achieving 501(c)3 status, One World Health created programs to develop drugs and conduct clinical trials for four infectious parasitic diseases that affect the world's poorest people. As their corporate brochure states:

> Our approach is simple. Assemble an experienced and dedicated team of pharmaceutical scientists, identify the most promising drug and vaccine candidates…develop them into safe, effective and affordable medicines…then partner with companies in the developing world to manufacture and distribute newly approved therapies that will impact the health of millions of people.[14]

To be effective, One World Health had to engage, develop, and align a complicated global ecosystem. In addition, creating the organization and securing the support of key funders, Hale engaged multiple research partners including over a dozen university and government research centers that spanned the globe, several large pharmaceutical companies; governments and regulatory organizations, drug manufacturers, and intermediaries such as the World Health Organization and Save the Children. Relationships with industry players who owned much of the required intellectual capital were particularly sensitive, so Hale explicitly targeted diseases that primarily affected individuals in the developing world where most pharmaceutical companies were not active. She also made cooperation a win-win by developing an approach that enabled these companies to receive tax benefits from donating their technologies. Hale recounted: "Early on, in the year 2000, the idea of a non-profit pharmaceutical company was very controversial. We ruffled some feathers. So it was important that we find a way to sit in the same nest instead of being kicked out."[15] Hale's keen understanding of the dynamics of a complex ecosystem enabled her to attract an array of supporters including foundations, volunteer scientists, and corporate partners that helped advanced One World Health's work.

Another instructive example is the experience of social entrepreneur Ohad Elhelo. When Elhelo founded Our Generation Speaks (OGS), a fellowship program that brings together Israeli and Palestinian young entrepreneurs to cocreate high-growth entrepreneurial ventures, he faced a complex political and strategic challenge. Elhelo described how he engaged and inspired a supportive ecosystem that today includes hundreds of committed participants including donors, high touch volunteers, venture coaches and mentors, staff, external partners, directors, and advisors as well as over 100 alumni:

> *When I was building initial support for OGS, I talked to dozens of potential supporters, and some patterns became clear. If you talk with ten people, three or*

four will tell you they support you, but you are not their primary interest. Another three to four will become 'committed supporters'—people who agree to help you in limited ways. One person will say 'this is a passion I can prioritize' and these individuals become your foundation builders—helping to guide the organization. And one person will say 'I've been waiting a long time for an opportunity like this to emerge and intend to fully support you.' This person will be a key funder and also deploy their entire network to help you.

(O. Elhelo, personal interview, February 14, 2020)

Other fledgling social entrepreneurs have discovered similar patterns (although the proportions may be different) and most agree that when entrepreneurs build their ecosystem, segmenting participants helps them effectively manage their contributions. Below is a typology of commitment levels. Exercise 2, at the end of this chapter, enables you to map the ecosystem for a prospective venture.

- *Rocketship partners:* These are individuals in the ecosystem that are highly committed to a social venture's mission. They donate money and time and are high-value board members. For a nonprofit, they are often the largest donors. These partners work with others in the ecosystem to increase venture feasibility and actively advocate for the venture. They also provide critical feedback to help the venture move forward.
- *Foundation builders:* These individuals become long-term advisors and often serve on the board of directors or board of advisors. They help to assemble needed resources, raise the venture's profile, and are often donors. They introduce the founding team to important resources and help refer new team members. Key partners who actively seek to further the venture's mission and who cooperate on joint initiatives are usually in this category.
- *Committed supporters:* Individuals in this category care about the venture's mission and actively seek to support it through volunteering. They help to recruit other supporters.
- *Interested bystanders:* This group is supportive of the mission but not actively engaged. They may connect the venture with resources, provide introductions, and make smaller donations. Vendors and less involved partners also fall into this category.
- *Agnostics:* This group is composed of those who have little interest in the venture and while they do not participate, they also do not actively seek to inhibit its growth.

- *Dissenters:* This final group of ecosystem participants actively seeks to prevent a social venture from starting or growing. This may be because they see the venture as a source of competition, as a disrupter in the marketplace that could potentially harm them, or because they disagree with the social venture's mission or approach. These dissenters may use multiple methods, for example, competing directly, blocking access to key resources or partnerships, or establishing regulatory barriers to inhibit a venture from moving forward.

Like Hale and Elhelo, every social entrepreneur should consider the ecosystem in which they work and determine the relationships they need to establish to function effectively. One of the most critical groups—financial supporters—is described in Chapter 6, and we discuss customers in several other chapters. Below we describe several other ecosystem players that provide important support for social entrepreneurs.

Boards of Directors and Boards of Advisors

The Board of Directors of a new social venture is critically important to its success, particularly if a social entrepreneur is inexperienced or poorly connected. The board serves a major role by signaling credibility to prospective partners, funders, and other important stakeholders. Potential funders or investors will often base their decisions to support a venture solely on who is on the board.

While it is tempting for an aspiring entrepreneur to assemble a roster of prominent individuals (in many class projects, Bill Gates and Muhammad Yunas often show up on students' aspirational board list), founders should be pragmatic about who they can attract. A small local nonprofit venture usually attracts a local board that is typically a mix of volunteers, funders, and individuals with specific expertise. If the venture grows to be regional or national (or global), the board usually adjusts to reflect this focus. If the venture is a nonprofit, major donors are often represented.

Nonprofit boards vary in size (from a handful of members to twenty or more) and members are typically not compensated. According to Guidestar (an organization that provides information on and rates nonprofits), a nonprofit board is the central decision-making body for the organization and bears ultimate responsibility and accountability for the organization's actions. The CEO of a nonprofit organization reports to the Board of Directors. Board members have three fundamental fiduciary duties:

- *Duty of care:* This means that the board member actively participates, attends board meetings, is educated on the industry, provides strategic direction, and oversees management

- *Duty of loyalty:* This requires the board member to operate in the interest of the nonprofit and not to use the position to further personal agenda.
- *Duty of obedience:* This requires the board to know the state and federal laws and regulations that apply. This includes the regulations and guidance issued by the IRS. Obedience to governing documents requires a deep understanding of the operating documents (by-laws, rules, board manuals).

For-profit boards (and those of hybrid organizations) are usually smaller and include founders, investors, and individuals with specific expertise. Social ventures' board members are typically not compensated, but some ventures do pay board members or give them a share of the company's equity. Like their nonprofit counterparts, they have fiduciary duties towards the corporation and its shareholders. Corporate offices (for example, CEO, CFO or treasurer, secretary, and president) carry out operations under the board's direction.

A Board of Advisors is a specialized board that provides advice to either a nonprofit or for-profit organization, reporting to the organization's CEO. These boards usually have responsibility for advising on a specific area. For example, when Dr. Yasmeen Abu Fraiha founded Genesis, a nonprofit organization that provides premarital genetic testing to Bedouin youth in Israel (discussed in a case at the end of this book), she assembled an advisory board that would give her credibility and also provide deep technical knowledge. The initial board included Husni Abu Samrah, Cofounder and CEO at Gravilog, which is an organization that provides medical education for the Arab world with an emphasis on pregnant women. Abu Samrah added both an entrepreneurial perspective and hands-on experience in medical education. She also engaged Professor Avishay Braverman, former President of Ben-Gurion University, who had worked with the Bedouin population for many years and understood how to engage the community and government. The list of supporters and advisors also includes key figures in the Boston ecosystem where Genesis was formed, such as Professor Kevin Tabb, President and CEO of Beth Israel Deaconess Medical Center, a prominent Boston hospital, and Mary Krauss, Interim Dean and former Provost at Brandeis University. Added to this list were other prominent individuals, fundraisers, and philanthropists.

Abu Fraiha also received support from medical partners including Professor Ohad Birk, Head of the Institute of Human Genetics in Be'er Sheva (Israel), and Dr. Naim Abu-Fraiha, Head of the Arab Medical Association in the Negev (Israel). Finally, a group of community partners pledged support including the Chief Archaeologist of Sinai and the Mayor of the Town of Hura (which was the target launch site).[16]

This web of supporters gave Genesis several advantages. First, with support from donors and partners, she was able to clearly demonstrate the venture's traction.

Second, she was confident that the medical and technical expertise of her supporters would help her hone her plans. She also knew local support would be critical to attracting participants. Finally, looking over her list of supporters, she knew not only that some would emerge as rocket ship partners and foundation builders but also that she had effectively moved several individuals from "indifferent" to "committed" simply by including them in her ecosystem.

Contracted Professionals

Newly created social ventures rely on a wide range of professionals to advise the founding team. These typically include lawyers and accountants and may also include fundraising professionals and strategy consultants as well as others. Depending on the nature of the venture, services are often provided below cost or on a pro bono basis, and contributing professionals often sit on the board of directors.

Partners

New ventures, particularly those that are resource constrained, rely heavily on an array of partners who help invent and produce the venture's goods or services.

- *Innovation partners:* those who help a social entrepreneur develop or refine their venture concept. Incubators and accelerators often provide this assistance, as do social venture business plan contests which provide feedback and sometimes launch funding.
- *Production partners:* organizations that provide goods or services to enable the social venture to deliver on its value proposition. For example, Prosperity Candle, a hybrid organization that provides employment opportunities to women in conflict regions, initially partnered with Women to Women International to identify and engage home-based entrepreneurs to produce their products.
- *Distribution partners:* those who help to deliver the social venture's goods and services to their target recipients/customers.
- *Community partners:* important connections between the venture and the community it seeks to serve, raising its profile and building trust.

The venture's ecosystem also often includes complementary organizations, which create value for the venture by increasing the value of its products. For example, organizations that provide training services enhance the value of social ventures that provide employment. Other partners may be vendors who provide goods and services to the social venture, including facilities, technology, and other services.

Universities as Incubators

It should come as no surprise to entrepreneurial students that universities often offer particularly rich and robust ecosystems. They bring together students from multiple disciplines, offer built-in mentoring, and often have expertise in technology acceleration and licensing. Effective university ecosystems act as boundary spanners, network builders, and orchestrators, developing social capital and helping ecosystem members access resources and build relationships.[17]

For example, at Brandeis University, in addition to specialized classes in social entrepreneurship, we offer training for aspiring entrepreneurs through the National Science Foundation's Innovation Corps (I-Corps™) early training program, cross-disciplinary opportunities to connect student researchers in the sciences and business programs, a maker lab, seed funding, and an array of competitions including the Heller Social Impact Challenge.

In New Zealand, the University of Auckland has taken a different approach. It was a leader in establishing the Icehouse, a coworking space that offers community building and connections for start-up and growing companies and is owned by a charitable trust. The University sponsors a center for innovation and entrepreneurship, an innovation space and maker lab and a student-led entrepreneurial development program. These initiatives together create a robust ecosystem for students interested in developing their entrepreneurial skills and making external connections.

University-led incubator programs have also been criticized as bureaucratic, prone to operating in silos, underresourced, and overly focused on academic excellence vs. student learning. Critics suggest that additional funding and a stronger focus on experiential education would help to make these ecosystems fulfill their promise.[18]

Criticisms aside, most universities do offer either formal or informal supports for students interested in founding ventures; interested students would be well advised to take advantage of the many resources available to them when they are free and readily accessible. We can see the benefits from the experience of entrepreneurs discussed in this book that include Waafa Arbash (WorkAround), Ohad Elhelo (Our Generation Speaks), Louise Langheier (Peer Health Exchange), Emiliano Iturriaga and Sebastián Muñoz (Rutopia), and Siiri Morley (Prosperity Candle). Their experience suggests that founding a venture while connected to and able to draw on the resources of a higher education ecosystem is a wonderful way to begin.

CHAPTER SUMMARY

When it comes to teams and ecosystems, aspiring social entrepreneurs have a number of advantages. First, the passion they bring to their venture and the ability to engage others committed to social impact provide a significant tailwind. But constraining factors such as the complexity of the ecosystem social entrepreneurs operate also exist.

In this chapter, we've discussed how social ventures are founded and the supportive systems that are required in order to succeed. Aspiring social entrepreneurs must make key decisions about whether to found solo or as a team and how to assemble three types of capital—human, social, and financial. They also need to determine how to structure relationships (who to found with), roles (what each member of the founding team will contribute), and rewards (who will receive recognition or financial rewards).

Every new venture exists within a context, and this chapter discusses the emergence of the ecosystem concept in business and why social ventures have complex ecosystems. A new framework for segmenting ecosystem participants according to their commitment level is introduced and key ecosystem participants including the boards of directors, board of advisors, and partners are described. And finally, the chapter touches on the benefits of supportive ecosystems at universities.

Following up on a proverb from the beginning of the chapter, social entrepreneurs who crave impact seek to "go far." Teams and ecosystems are key factors that enable them to do just that.

KEY TERMS

Agnostics: those supporters who have little interest in the venture and while they do not participate, they also do not actively seek to inhibit its growth.

Board of Advisors: a specialized board that provides advice to either a nonprofit or for-profit organization. It typically reports to the organization's CEO.

Committed supporters: individual supporters that care about the venture's mission and actively seek to support it through volunteering. They also help to recruit other supporters.

Community partners: important supporters in connecting the venture to the community they seek to serve, raising its profile and building trust.

Dissenters: these ecosystem participants actively seek to prevent a social venture from starting or growing.

Distribution partners: help to deliver the social venture's goods and services to their target recipients/customers.

Duty of care: board members actively participate, attend board meetings, are educated on the industry, provide strategic direction, and oversee management.

Duty of loyalty: requires the board member to operate in the interest of the nonprofit and not to use the position to further personal agenda.

Duty of obedience: requires the board to know the state and federal laws and regulations that apply to a venture.

Financial capital: money and other resources that can be used in the founding process of a venture.

Foundation builders: become long-term advisors and often serve on the board or help to assemble needed resources, raise the venture's profile, and are often donors.

Heterogeneous team: a team that is diverse in the character and/or content of its members.

Homogeneous team: for start-ups, this means that the cofounders have common backgrounds or experiences.

Human capital: knowledge from formal education and skills derived from prior experience(s).

Innovation partners: those partners who help a developing social entrepreneur develop or refine their venture concept.

Interested bystanders: are supportive of the venture's mission but not actively engaged. They may connect the venture with resources, provide introductions, and make smaller donations.

Production partners: organizations that provide goods or services to enable the social venture to deliver on its value proposition.

Relationships: refers to whether you will cofound with those who you have an existing relationship and how you will manage it.

Responsibilities: refers to the level of commitment and contribution that is expected from each founding team member.

Rewards: refers to how equity, salaries, recognition/titles, and other benefits will be allocated.

Rocketship partners: are individuals throughout the ecosystem that are highly committed to a social venture's mission.

Roles: refers to how decision-making powers will be allocated within the team and what functional areas each cofounder has control or authority over.

Social capital: information and communication networks.

IN-CLASS EXERCISES

Exercise 4.1: Design Your Culture

(Estimated time: 20 minutes)

Purpose

Consider a venture you would like to found or cofound, reflect on the culture you would like to create.

Preparation

Divide students into groups of 3–5, ideally based on project teams.

Process

1. Each team develops ten single word attributes that describe the kind of culture they would like to create. Examples: meritocratic, hardworking, relaxed, entrepreneurial.
2. Each team reflects on what the implications are for these choices. For example, a relaxed culture may be less driven. A driven culture may risk burnout.

Debrief

1. Each team records their culture descriptions on the board. Circle words that are common among teams.
2. Discuss the implications of the proposed cultural attributes.
3. Discuss what an organization needs to do to achieve this culture. Consider, for example, the talent acquisition process, rewards, shared decision-making, flat vs. hierarchical structure.
4. Post-class: Continue to reflect on each group's proposed culture.

Exercise 4.2: Map Your Ecosystem

(Estimated time: 30 minutes)

Purpose

Critically assess who will be in your venture's ecosystem and what role each will play.

Figure 4.2 Ecosystem Assessment	Financial supporters	External partners	Volunteers	Founders and team	Influencers (e.g., government or media)	Others
Rocket ship partners						
Foundation builders						
Committed supporters						
Interested bystanders						
Agnostics						
Dissenters						

Preparation

Divide students into groups of 3–5, ideally by project team. If teams have not yet been formed, each group should choose one prospective venture for which they will map the ecosystem. Provide blank copies of Figure 4.2 below.

Process

Take 20 minutes to map the expected ecosystem for each project.

Debrief

A few teams present their ecosystems to the class and request feedback.

SHORT CASE: CHERYL DORSEY AT ECHOING GREEN—SUPPORTING BOLD IDEAS

Cheryl Dorsey, President of Echoing Green, looked with pride at the gathering of 2020 Fellows during their first web convening. The fellows came from across the globe, working in seven different countries and territories and several cities in the United States. They had been selected from a pool of over 3,000 applicants during a 10-month vetting process. While she had great confidence in the thirteen new fellows, she also knew that they faced special challenges. They would be beginning their fellowships at a time of economic uncertainty and systems transformation due to the Covid-19 pandemic and global reckoning with structural racism. Still, she was confident that with Echoing Green's ecosystem behind them, they would be able to achieve even greater impact.

Each member of the new group of fellows was an entrepreneur with an ambitious vision for social impact. The group included Samlara Baa, Founder and CEO of for-profit Loo Works, an organization that uses plastic waste to create sanitation solutions for marginalized communities in West Africa. Xavier Henderson and Taylor Toynes had been selected as cofounders of For Oak Cliff, an organization that works to build a culture of education to increase social mobility and social capital in their home neighborhood of South Oak Cliff, located in Dallas, Texas. The class also included Charlot Magay, the Founder and CEO of Mukuru Clean Stoves. She grew up in Mukuru, a large slum in Nairobi and, after her two-year-old daughter suffered a severe burn injury caused by a traditional stove, was moved to found a venture that would provide safer cooking technologies for her community.[19]

Echoing Green's mission is "supporting bold ideas and extraordinary leaders." Its approach is to discover emerging social entrepreneurs and invest deeply in the growth of their ideas and leadership. Since its founding in 1987, Echoing Green has built a broad, dynamic ecosystem based on the insight that a group of talented and committed young people could make an enormous difference in society if they had access to funding, expert mentoring, connections, and a community of like-minded individuals. According to cofounder Dave Hodgson: "The early realization that there were so many talented young social entrepreneurs out there, and that they could be resources to one another—that was when we knew we were on to something really exciting."[20]

Echoing Green quickly established a reputation for "picking winners" among social entrepreneurs, providing early support and visibility to founders like Wendy Kopp, Founder of Teach for America, Vanessa Kirsch, Founder of Public Allies (and later, of New Profit), and Raj Panjabi, Founder of Last Mile Health. Kopp, who was selected as a fellow in 1991, described her experience: "In my first few months out of college, when it was hard to find anyone who would take my initiative seriously, Echoing Green was determined to help get Teach for America off the ground. Today, our work is helping to fuel the national movement for educational excellence and equity, and Echoing Green helped put us on this trajectory."[21] While Echoing Green initially exclusively supported nonprofit founders, in 2006, its strategy expanded to include mission-driven for-profit and hybrid organizations. According to Dorsey: "In 2006 15% of our applicants were founding for-profit ventures. Now it is about half" (C. Dorsey, personal interview, December 4, 2020).

By 2020, Echoing Green had provided more than $46 million in seed funding to emerging social entrepreneurs around the world. Seventy percent of the organizations launched by its Fellows are still in operation today, and 77% of the Fellows still work in the social sector.[22]

Dorsey became President of Echoing Green in 2001. She brought a rich background in public service and social impact, having served in two presidential administrations. Dorsey received her medical degree from Harvard Medical School, and her Master's in Public Policy from Harvard's Kennedy School. She also drew on her personal experience as a social entrepreneur. She was selected as an Echoing Green Fellow in 1992 and this experience enabled her to cofound and expand a mobile health clinic called The Family Van that still operates today bringing accessible health care to nearly 7,000 clients annually. In 2009, Dorsey was honored as one of "America's Best Leaders" by US News & World Report and the Center for Public Leadership at the Harvard Kennedy School. In 2011, she was selected by The Nonprofit Times as one of the "Power and Influence Top 50."

Echoing Green provided its fellows access to three types of capital. According to Dorsey, the individuals selected as fellows—the human capital—were outstanding. "We select best in class, ambitious social entrepreneurs. We respect them and their visions and give them the resources they need to thrive" (C. Dorsey, personal interview, December 4, 2020). In terms of social capital, Dorsey observed that Echoing Green had "created a sticky, high quality familial community where former fellows support current ones. Being associated with Echoing Green also helps early-stage entrepreneurs expand their networks. The imprimatur of being a fellow gives them extraordinary access. We are also great at building bonds among fellows" (C. Dorsey, personal interview, December 4, 2020). For financial capital, "we don't give much, but what we give—early stage, unrestricted capital—is rare and comes at a critically important time" (C. Dorsey, personal interview, December 4, 2020).

In late 2011, Dorsey began to engage the Echoing Green team in a dialogue about how to innovate to reduce racial disparities after being approached by the Open Society Foundation to participate in the Campaign for Black Male Achievement. Seeing the clear intersection between social innovation and racial equity, she saw an opportunity for Echoing Green to increase its impact. The opportunity also hit home for Dorsey because, as she described it: "First, investing to reduce disparities is consistent with my lived experience, and what I hope will be my legacy as a leader of color. Second, we had worked hard as an organization to eliminate bias and saw an opportunity to extend this work. And finally, our funders consider racial equity to be important to society, so we wanted to engage with them to develop solutions" (C. Dorsey, personal interview, December 4, 2020).

After many discussions with team members and stakeholders, Dorsey honed in on two areas where Echoing Green could make a unique contribution. The first was the lack of availability of venture funding for leaders of color, which she saw as a major impediment to scaling important social impact solutions. Along with two colleagues from nonprofit consulting firm and thought leader Bridgespan, she coauthored a report on Racial Equity in Philanthropy, and an article in *Harvard Business Review* titled, "The Problem with 'Color-Blind' Philanthropy." They observed that, while well meaning, a "color-blind" approach to grant making is ineffective. They instead advocated for funders to provide more financial support for leaders of color and to pay more attention to race-conscious solutions.[23] They observed that leaders of color face multiple barriers working with philanthropists, including inadequate networks and unconscious bias. Their second observation was that for social entrepreneurs, proximity—being personally close to the issues they hope to address—is critical for developing a deep understanding and building the trust and connections that will lead to durable solutions.

With these insights in hand, Echoing Green announced a new $50 million racial equity philanthropic fund in 2020. The fund aims to transform the field of social innovation over three years, ensuring that a heightened awareness of racial inequity would translate into sustained action and impact. As part of the initiative, Echoing Green planned to launch and scale 500 social enterprises focused on racial equity in the United States and globally, provide follow-up funding in its portfolio's most high-impact enterprises to help founders scale their solutions, provide on ramps for new leaders focused on racial equity, and increase opportunities for corporate engagement.[24]

Dorsey had also decided to limit the 2020 class of fellows to thirteen. The logic was "intentionally creating room to sharpen our work and redouble our commitment to supporting social innovators at this critical time."[25] Looking at the new class of high-potential social entrepreneurs, Dorsey was satisfied that they reflected Echoing Green's priorities in terms of high potential and proximity to the problems they planned to address. She was also confident that the availability of addition investment funds would help them scale over time. Now the hard work would begin: building a supportive community and providing the fellows with an ecosystem that would enable them to create meaningful social value.

Discussion Questions

1. Why do you think Echoing Green has been so prominent in helping social entrepreneurs launch their ventures? What have they done right?
2. Among the supports Echoing Green provides to fellows, which do you consider the most important? Is there anything missing?

3. Dorsey believes that for social entrepreneurs, proximity to the communities they plan to serve is critically important. Do you agree?
4. Echoing Green has made racial equity a central part of its work. How should the organization leverage its assets and experience to foster transformative impact to address inequities?
5. In Dorsey's shoes, what would you do to make sure the ecosystem Echoing Green provides enables incoming fellows to maximize their potential?

NOTES

1. While often cited as an African proverb, the origin of this saying is unknown.
2. Hellmann, T., & Wasserman, N. (2012). The first deal: The division of founder equity in new ventures. *Harvard Business School Working Paper, 14*(085).
3. Wasserman, N. (2013). *The founders Dilemmas: Anticipating and avoiding the pitfalls that can sink a startup*. Princeton, NJ: Princeton University Press.
4. Schneider, B. (2016). *Q&A* [Carlson social entrepreneurship class visit]. Waltham, MA: Brandeis University.
5. Wasserman, N. (2013). *The founders Dilemmas: Anticipating and avoiding the pitfalls that can sink a startup*. Princeton, NJ: Princeton University Press.
6. Gulati, R., Mayo, A. J., & Nohria, N. (2017). *Management: An integrated approach*. Boston, MA: Cengage Learning.
7. Ibid.
8. Hern, A. (2018, April 24). The two-pizza rule and the secret of Amazon's success. *The Guardian*.
9. Haas, M., & Mortensen, M. (2016). The secrets of great teamwork. *Harvard Business Review, 94*(6), 70–76.
10. Moore, J. (1993). Predators and prey: A new ecology of competition. *Harvard Business Review, 71*(3), 75–86.
11. Fuller, J., Jacobides, M. G., & Reeves, M. (2019). The myths and realities of business ecosystems. *Sloan Management Review*, Reprint 60,315.
12. Roundy, P. T. (2017). Social entrepreneurship and entrepreneurial ecosystems: Complementary or disjoint phenomena? *International Journal of Social Economics, 44*(9), 1252–1267.
13. Phills, J., & Denend, L. (2005). *Social entrepreneurs: Correcting market failures (A)*. Stanford Graduate School of Business Case No. SI72A.
14. One World Health. (n.d.). *One World health corporate brochure*. Cited in Phills, J., & Denend, L. (2005). *Social entrepreneurs: Correcting market failures (A)*. Stanford Graduate School of Business Case No. SI72A.
15. Phills, J., & Denend, L. (2005). *Social entrepreneurs: Correcting market failures (A)*. Stanford Graduate School of Business, Case No. SI72A.
16. Genesis. (2016). *Business plan booklet* [Unpublished business plan summary].
17. Roundy, P., & Fayard, D. (2018). Dynamic capabilities and entrepreneurial ecosystems: The micro-foundations of regional entrepreneurship. *Journal of Entrepreneurship, 28*(1), 94–120.

18. Thomsen, B., Muurlink, T. B., & Best, T. (2018). The political ecology of university-based social entrepreneurship ecosystems. *Journal of Enterprising Communities: People and Places in the Global Economy*, *12*(2), 199–219.
19. Echoing Green. (n.d.). *Fellows directory*. Retrieved April 11, 2021, from https://fellows.echoinggreen.org/.
20. Echoing Green. (2012). *Annual report 2012*. Retrieved from https://echoinggreen.org/wp-content/uploads/2019/08/2012-Annual-Report.pdf.
21. Ibid.
22. Echoing Green. (2020). *Announcement: Echoing green announces new racial equity philanthropic fund*. Retrieved from https://echoinggreen.org/news/echoing-green-announces-racial-equity-philanthropic-fund.
23. Dorsey, C., Bradach, J., & Kim, P. (2020, June 5). The problem with 'color blind' philanthropy. *Harvard Business Review*, Digital Article H05OJG-PDF-ENG.
24. Echoing Green. (2020). *Announcement: Echoing green announces new racial equity philanthropic fund*. Retrieved from https://echoinggreen.org/news/echoing-green-announces-racial-equity-philanthropic-fund.
25. Echoing Green. (2020, July 21). *Announcement: Innovating our fellowship*. Retrieved from https://echoinggreen.org/news/innovating-our-fellowship/.

CHAPTER FIVE

CREATING ALIGNMENT AND MEASURING IMPACT

Social entrepreneurs who want to make a difference recognize that they have a special obligation to justify their use of resources by creating innovative solutions to society's most pressing problems. This requires them to clearly articulate their mission, and how exactly their activities will help to achieve it. Taking an entrepreneurial approach—by being opportunistic, agile, and using experimentation—should not replace clear thinking about impact.

A few words of advice for social entrepreneurs as they plan their ventures and measure impact. Be pragmatic. Measure what matters. Rigorously interrogate your model and make sure that your measurement approach matches your mission and vision. Engage your stakeholders. And make sure that those responsible for execution fully understand what is being measured and the link to the venture's overall strategy.

Learning Objectives

- Explain why social entrepreneurs should evaluate outcomes and measure impact.
- Distinguish between a theory of change and a logic model as guiding tools.
- Assess different approaches for measuring social impact.
- Describe common impact measurement pitfalls.
- Contrast methods for calculating social impact.

WHY MEASURE OUTCOMES AND IMPACT?

Social entrepreneurs have a well-deserved reputation for tackling some of society's most pressing problems—from youth unemployment to refugee livelihoods to reliable energy production to disease mitigation—with creativity, innovation, and deep commitment. But, if they want to address problems in a systematic, meaningful, and scalable way, they also have a special responsibility to move from anecdote to proof. This is why it is important to develop a deep understanding of the specific reasons a given program, project, or intervention has positive consequences (and avoids negative ones.)

In the early stages of venture formation, social entrepreneurs can use impact assessment and measurement tools to decide which ventures to pursue. Scholars and practitioners have developed a set of tools (including a theory of change and logic models) and methods for measuring impact that enable entrepreneurs and their partners to compare alternatives and decide the best way to invest their time and resources.

On an ongoing basis, measurement helps entrepreneurial teams assess how well a venture is performing against its goals and uses this information to improve performance. Sound measurement improves operations, guides internal resource allocation decisions, and can increase accountability. This last point is important—the more stakeholders understand about why and how a venture works and what the costs and benefits will be, the more likely they are to support it.

Another reason to measure results is to set the stage for scaling. Growing effectively requires a clear understanding of the relationship between activity and impact and consistent measurement.

Unsurprisingly, it is much more complicated to measure impact in the social sector. While for-profit commercial enterprises can rely largely on financial measures, social ventures must consider a broader range of metrics. This is even more challenging when mission-driven organizations receive fewer, slower, and more complex market signals than their commercial counterparts. And against this backdrop, they must routinely demonstrate impact to establish and maintain relationships with stakeholders, all the while meeting expectations for a higher level of transparency.

The Planning and Learning Cycle

Figure 5.1 shows how entrepreneurial ventures plan, execute, and learn differently from their nonentrepreneurial counterparts. These organizations use a sequential approach: after they decide which idea to pursue, they develop plans, implement them, and then evaluate their efforts. This approach aligns closely with the Plan-Do-Study-Act cycle, a popular management structure for fostering continuous improvement developed by the "fathers" of the quality control movement, American physicist and statistician Walter Shewhart and business consultant and statistician W. Edwards Deming.

Entrepreneurial ventures approach this cycle differently by reducing the time for each step (thereby using fewer resources) and undertaking process steps concurrently rather than sequentially. Essentially, entrepreneurs are "building the plane while flying it" which is why the wheel on the right is smaller and the elapsed time is shorter. Entrepreneurs are constantly experimenting with new things and making adjustments, illustrated by the two small circles on the right. And by simultaneously implementing and measuring outcomes, they can improve both current operations and

Figure 5.1 Project Cycle in Traditional End Entrepreneurial Ventures

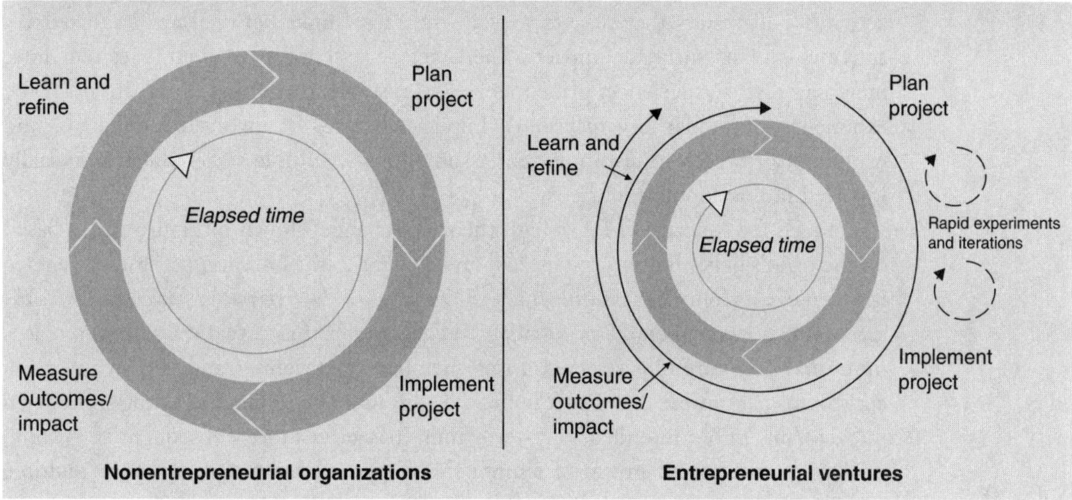

the measurement process. In addition to being faster, this approach can also increase momentum, creating a flywheel effect.[1]

USING A THEORY OF CHANGE OR LOGIC MODEL

Why Use Models and Evaluation Tools?

Using models to understand impact enables an organization to create a well-thought-through strategy that links its intended outcomes to its activities, documenting the causal links between what the organization does and what it hopes to achieve.

Theory of change models and **logic models** are terms that are often used interchangeably. While both are models used by mission-driven organizations to link their intentions to their outcomes, test their logic, and be clear about the outcomes they hope to achieve, they differ in their format and how they explain impact.

Some organizations use both, developing a high-level theory of change and then translating the ideas into a logic model format. For example, human service provider HopeWell, described in the short case at the end of this chapter, developed a high-level theory of change for communicating with stakeholders, and then translated it first into an organizational-level logic model and then into departmental-level logic models that will be used to align and guide overall operations.

Theory of Change

A theory of change is a graphical depiction of the causal relationships between activities and results that seek to explain the causal links between an organization's activities and its ultimate impact. There are several ways to identify causal links, including direct experience, prior theory and research (including observations of the experience of similar organizations), implicit theories of involved individuals, and exploratory research to test important assumptions.[2] Multiple stakeholders are usually involved in developing the theory.

Teach for America (TFA)'s high theory of change, shown in Figure 5.2, is based on the team's belief that bringing exceptional talent to the education sector will enable it to achieve its founding vision, which is: *One day, all children in this nation will have the opportunity to attain an excellent education.* TFA achieves this in two ways: first, it places motivated and carefully selected corps members in teaching and support roles in classrooms nationwide to support improved educational outcomes, creating short-term impact. But TFA's intended long-term impact is even more consequential: second, TFA aims to create a group of alumni that support educational equity in multiple sectors, creating systems level change.

What are TFA's underlying beliefs that make its theory of change work? First, it believes that through its processes it can attract highly motivated and diverse future leaders. It also believes that during their fellowships, participants will have meaningful experiences that will increase their commitment to educational equity. Finally, TFA's theory is based on its belief that alumni will translate their experience into lifelong leadership promoting educational equity. Numerous studies have demonstrated its effectiveness at achieving these outcomes. For example, a recent in-depth study demonstrated that more founders and leaders in the education sector had been

Figure 5.2 Teach for America Theory of Change

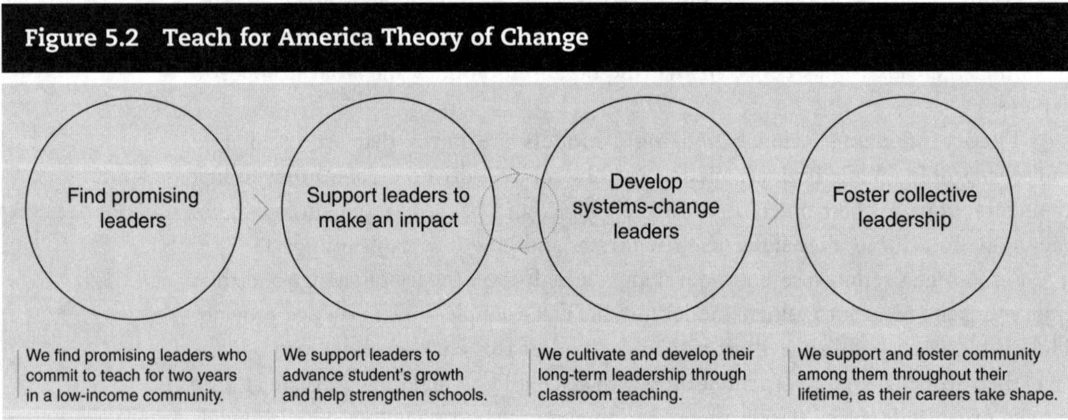

Source: Teach for America (2020). Used with permission.

participants in TFA than in any other organization or program.[3] TFA's clarity around its theory of change has also enabled its team to accurately convey the "secret sauce" that makes it effective, helping to support TFA's growth by engaging policy makers, donors, and prospective corps members.

The One Acre Fund uses a more detailed theory of change to illustrate the relationship between its efforts and its outcomes. Its earliest programs aimed to increase agricultural yields and incomes for smallholder farmers. But the leadership team learned that in order to have a comprehensive impact, they needed to consider other factors as well, including nutritional quality and sustainable farm management. The One Acre Fund's theory has enabled the organization to maximize the impact of its work, refine its programs, and design practical and effective annual measurement tools (Figure 5.3).

Figure 5.3 One Acre Fund Theory of Change

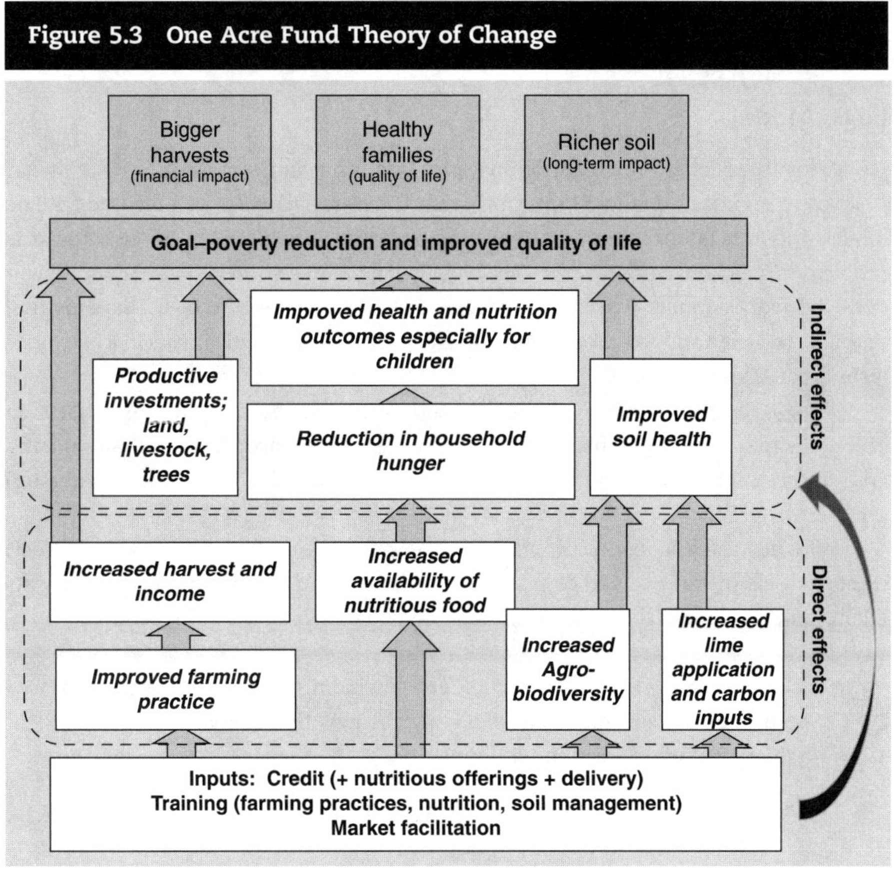

Source: One Acre Fund (2020). Used with permission.

Some financial supporters consider a venture's stage of maturity when they evaluate theories of change and expect newly created organizations to evolve over time. For example, the Edna McConnell Clark Foundations, a major funder of youth development programs, evaluates grantee's theories of change based on three developmental stages:

- *Apparent effectiveness:* In its early stages, an organization is expected to have anecdotal success stories, some preliminary data on participants, and a plausible theory of change.
- *Demonstrated effectiveness:* An organization has rigorous data comparing participants and nonparticipants and is building evaluation capacity.
- *Proven effectiveness:* An organization demonstrates impact using a well-documented theory of change and statistically significant rigorous evaluations such as randomized controlled trials.[4]

Logic Model

A logic model is an organization's plan for achieving impact. It uses a linear, descriptive approach to show how a program translates activities to outcomes. Logic models follow a tabular format, articulating an organization's assumptions about the problem it is tackling and how they see change happening, strategies (what and how it does the work), inputs (what it provides), and then linking these to the activities' outputs (what it produces), outcomes (the desired results), and impacts (what long-term broad changes result).

A logic model supports monitoring and evaluation by determining what data are collected and providing the basis for assessing progress and supporting continuous improvement. Figure 5.4 shows an example for a homeownership services program.

Whether using a theory of change, a logic model, or both, the intent is clear: create a disciplined process to help an organization understand its impact and focus its talents and resources. There are additional benefits, including the following:

- *Deeply engaging* multiple stakeholders—including the leadership team, other staff, funders, and recipients—in conversations that enable a deep understanding of mission and impact.
- *Infusing new vitality* into organizations when stakeholders' passion for the work is affirmed and renewed.

Figure 5.4 Logic Model Overview and Example: Homeownership Services

	Internal activities		External results		
	Inputs	**Activities**	**Outputs**	**Outcomes**	**Impacts**
What it is	**Resources invested in the activity**	**Implementation of the activity**	**Products of the activity**	**Direct changes that result from the activity**	**Broader or systemic change that results from the activity**
How it is measured	**Direct and human resource costs**	**Direct costs and human resource costs of delivering the activity, specific actions**	**Measurable direct results, or example, number of people reached**	**Measurable actions that demonstrate progress towards specific outcomes**	**Effects on the target or broader population**
Example: First-time homebuyer program in Cambridge, Massachusetts	*Down payment assistance fund $100,000* *Buyer training–3 full-time coaches and one external trainer. Total cost $250,000*	*First-time buyer classes including curriculum development and delivery* *Intensive 1:1 coaching program to assist buyers through process* *Down payment funds provided via banking partner*	*200 participants in training program* *100 participants in coaching program* *20 participants in down payment assistance program*	*100 first-time buyers purchase homes in year 1* *100 prospective buyers indicate readiness to buy in year 2* *75 prospective buyers improve credit score by 75 points*	*5% increase in low and moderate income ownership rate in community* *5% reduction in families leaving community due to unaffordable housing* *Higher primary school enrollment for children from low/moderate families*

- *Creating alignment* within an organization. If everyone in an organization understands the links surfaced by a logic model, implementation, commitment, and outcomes improve.
- *Enabling better external communications* by giving leaders and staff a consistent way to describe an organization's mission, strategies, and intended outcomes to those outside the organization.
- *Influencing other organizations* to improve practice.

Another important benefit of the clarity provided by these models is avoiding **mission creep**, which we describe in more detail in Chapter 7. And while focus is important, social entrepreneurs may still act opportunistically. Sometimes a unique opportunity arises to increase impact, enter a new market, or engage new stakeholders. A new revenue opportunity could increase scale, attract new talent, expand impact, or support core programs. What is important is that entrepreneurs know the difference between initiatives that support their work, grounded in their core mission and values, and those that distract from it. A clear theory of change or logic model helps venture teams decide what to do and what not to do.

IMPACT MEASUREMENT

Why Do We Measure Impact?

Social entrepreneurs have a special obligation to society to make sure that they are using resources wisely. Brian Trelstad, former Chief Investment Officer at the Acumen Fund, described social venture founder's responsibilities to funders, partners, and recipients:

- We owe it to our donors to ensure we maximize their social return;
- We owe it to ourselves to make sure we understand what is working and what isn't;
- We owe it to those we invest in to not unnecessarily burden them;
- We owe it to end users to think clearly about how we will make a difference.[5]

Different Approaches to Measurement

Randomized Controlled Trials

In 2019 economists Abhijit Banerjee, Esther Duflo, and Michael Kremer were jointly awarded the Nobel Prize in Economics for pioneering the use of randomized controlled trials to test the impact of interventions that help mitigate global poverty. Their work was described by The Royal Swedish Academy of Sciences as having "considerably improved our ability to fight global poverty. In just two decades, their new experiment-based approach has transformed development economics, which is now a flourishing field of research."[6] The three colleagues taught economics at MIT in the 1990s and Banerjee and Duflo would go on to found MIT's Abdul Latif Jameel Poverty Action Lab in 2003, with a mission of "working to reduce poverty by ensuring that policy is informed by scientific evidence."[7]

The trio were recognized for their seminal research involving randomized controlled trials, or RCT. RCT is a form of experiment where "large numbers of participants are randomized to receive either a particular intervention or a standard treatment and followed over time—to social interventions such as improving education."[8] Duflo observed that this follows the same approach as the process of testing new drugs, allowing researchers to "distinguish between drugs that work and drugs that don't work." She adds that "you can do the same randomized controlled trial for social policy."[9] Duflo and Kremer believe that what makes RCT successful is "that it involves on the ground engagement to try and engage in practical ways with problems, and it combines that with ethical rigor, and this had led to a real flourishing of the field."[10]

Their first success came in the mid-1990s when Kremer and a colleague used a RCT to highlight how mass deworming in Kenya had a positive impact on school attendance.

Intestinal worms can live in individuals' stomach and intestines and steal their nutrients. In areas where intestinal worms are prevalent, stomach pains account for a high percentage of school absences. Kremer found that mass deworming not only increased attendance by 25% in the schools that were treated, but these results also spilled over into neighboring communities where no treatment was implemented, most likely through a disruption in transmission.[11] These findings set off a tidal wave of interest in not only deworming but also in the use of RCT to improve a wide range of social programs.

Banerjee and Duflo used the same approach in India to assess the value of remedial education. While more students than ever had access to education, some still fell behind, leaving the duo to consider if improving outcomes was possible. Banerjee notes that "once you think in the scale of the Indian school system, these are massive resource implications, 600,000 schools...it's not cheap...Can it be done within the school system, with normal teachers, in the normal teaching hours?" Working with a partner NGO in the field, the team discovered that for $2.25 per child per year, average test scores could be significantly increased. Their RCT trial intervention was simple: conduct an RCT study that hired tutors who took lagging children out of the class in groups for two hours a day for remedial help. This simple solution enabled an increase of almost 10% in standardized test scores and this was just the beginning. These and similar successes have allowed the field of RTC to grow, leading Banerjee and Duflo to conduct over 70 experiments around the world.

This rigorous approach to understanding the impact of antipoverty interventions, and the use of experiments to demonstrate efficacy is consistent with the idea of hypothesis-driven entrepreneurship that we discussed in Chapter 3. There are potential drawbacks, however. One is cost: data collection for a large-scale multiyear study can be very expensive. A second is the ethical challenge of having some people benefit but not those in a control group. And finally, while randomized controlled trials are effective at assessing impact, they may not identify causality.

Practical Measurement for Complex Situations

Let's contrast the use of randomized controlled trials to the approach employed by Sanergy, the Narobi-based sanitation start-up that we discuss in a case at the end of this book.

In 2015, five years after it was founded, Sanergy regularly reported the number of toilets it had installed as well as the number of users and tons of waste removed. It also reported on jobs created. What Sanergy did not measure at the time was its impact on public health. Cofounder David Auerbach expressed his skepticism about the value of detailed measurement: "At this early stage, we've elected not to get too deep into understanding public health impact as a whole. It is too hard to measure, and even if you do, it is almost impossible to be fully attributable to us."[12] He offered an example: "Consider the way meat arrives into a slum in Nairobi. It will most likely be on the back of a motorcycle. It won't be refrigerated. So, some of the time it will make people sick. How do you separate out Sanergy's impact from improving sanitation when there are thousands of similar issues? We know that hygienic sanitation makes a difference—often a huge difference—to the health of slum residents."[13]

Strong Women Strong Girls (SWSG) also uses a practical approach to measuring impact. SWSG was founded in 2000 to create mentorship opportunities for women and girls. The nonprofit organization convenes three generations of women to create community, connections, and strength to break down barriers and imagine a broader future. Girls in grades 3–5, who are primarily from underresourced neighborhoods, attend weekly, curriculum-guided mentoring sessions with college women mentors. College mentors build relationships with professional women mentors. SWSG's multigenerational model amplifies the well-established benefits of strong mentorship for young people. The results for participating girls include increased school attendance and participation, stronger self-identity and confidence, as well as increased future orientation, including towards college and careers.

SWSG measures outputs (the number of girls and college mentors participating and the number of sites), participant demographics and outcomes (via survey data that measure participants' sense of belonging, feeling safe, and intent to help others)[14] but not long-term educational outcomes. While the SWSG team acknowledges that collecting educational metrics such as school success and civic participation would help satisfy funders and support program improvement, there are practical challenges. One is that it is difficult for external partners like SWSG to get consistent data on educational outcomes from school districts. A second is the cost: a robust longitudinal study can cost hundreds of thousands of dollars—resources the team would rather invest in current programming. According to SWSG Board Chair Kate Rogers: "We understand our impact—and we certainly know we have an impact based on what we are seeing in the field. But we are pragmatic and know that we don't have the resources to do statistically significant long term impact measurement the way we would like to if we were larger" (K. Rogers, personal interview, July 27, 2020).

Or consider the work of 99Degrees, profiled in a short case in Chapter 8. 99Degrees seeks to break cycles of multigenerational poverty by creating entry-level employment opportunities in apparel manufacturing in Lawrence Massachusetts, enabling employees to learn advanced manufacturing skills. The company employs 250 people, 98% of whom are people of color, 78% of whom are women and 97% of whom speak English as a second language. In its first five years, the company was in start-up mode with fewer than 50 employees most of whom were sewing machine operators and related production employees. During that time, founder Brenna Schneider's approach to assessing impact was "knowing it when I see it." As the leader of a small organization, she was intimately familiar with the successes and challenges faced by team members and was able to evaluate impact real time. And as a for-profit mission-driven organization without foundation or government stakeholders, she was comfortable assessing impact based on this knowledge.

However, in the 24 months ending mid-2020, 99Degrees grew rapidly, more than tripling its workforce from 70 to 250 people. This motivated Schneider to create a more systematic approach to impact evaluation while maintaining the company's entrepreneurial approach. The leadership team identified ten specific challenges faced by employees (such as access to childcare, affordable health care, and education and training) and created evaluation tools to measure progress in overcoming them, with results reported regularly to the board. To measure progress on its goal of creating a culture of advancement, the company surveys employees about their perception of whether they feel the climate supports their progression. But going further, 99Degrees set practical and specific measures, for example, aiming to promote 50 people (20% of the workforce) to positions requiring additional skills at higher pay levels in 2020. Schneider also offers an example of how promoting a culture of advancement works in practice: "Most of our employees are Spanish-speaking and many do not speak English. When a new position is available, we carefully assess whether English-language skills are actually necessary vs. nice to have. If they aren't actually needed, we remove them from the job specification. And if they are, we aim to provide language learning support to make the position accessible to current employees" (B. Schneider, personal interview, July 28, 2020).

Reflecting on her experience, Schneider offers the following advice for emerging social entrepreneurs: "When you are starting an entrepreneurial venture, it takes time to develop the systems and discipline to be able to measure impact effectively." At the same time, she encourages social entrepreneurs to be strategic about their impact and take a bold stand. "It is so easy to measure small scale and external activities (like donations to a food bank or internal statistics like demographics) and that is a good start. It is harder yet often more important to be clear about your culture and values and to express them as principles, so that your internal operations, policies, and activities have impact as well. Link your values with principles, which guide activities which leads to impact. Find simple clear measures to ensure your activities align and are delivering impact" (B. Schneider, personal interview, July 28, 2020).

Direct vs. Systems Level Impact—the Bridgespan Dilemma

Some social impact organizations make a difference by amplifying the impact of other organizations instead of directly providing services. Consider the case of Bridgespan, a leading nonprofit consulting firm. Bridgespan's mission is to "work to build a better world by strengthening the ability of mission-driven organizations and philanthropists to achieve breakthrough results in addressing society's most important challenges and opportunities."[15] Its theory of change is to improve the outcomes of organizations, leaders, systems and movements in target areas.

Bridgespan delivers on this mission by providing both consulting services and knowledge dissemination. But the partner group wondered: should they measure their impact based on how effectively they strengthened the social sector, or based on the impact of the work of its clients? According to Bridgespan partner Susan Colby, "One of the biggest debates was whether Bridgespan should hold itself accountable for specific social outcomes—like college readiness in the case of nonprofit clients working with high-school aged youth—or whether we should hold ourselves accountable for helping to develop strong nonprofits and philanthropies that work on these outcomes."[16] Ultimately, the team decided to focus on measuring two things: the success of their clients (and not their clients' clients) and how broadly they disseminate knowledge.

Measuring From Multiple Perspectives

While measuring social impact is important, it is not the only data social entrepreneurs should focus on. The financial health of their organizations is also critical. "No margin, no mission" is a truism for social ventures—if an organization's financial house is not in order, it will not be able to deliver its programs. Successful social entrepreneurs advise that "knowing your numbers" is fundamental for both sustainable current operations and growth. Other elements a social venture might measure include team support for its activities, stakeholder alignment, efficient operations, and learning. Tools might include survey-based assessments of employee engagement and stakeholder satisfaction, and metrics that track operation efficiency, reputation, or environmental impact.

A useful multiperspective approach is the Balanced Scorecard, originally developed in 1992 for private sector use by Harvard Business School Professor Robert Kaplan and consultant David Norton. Observing "what you measure is what you get,"[17] the authors suggest measuring from four perspectives—financial, internal business processes, customer, and learning and growth, each with its own set of metrics, that collectively enable a business to track progress against its strategy. Mission-driven organizations can use the balanced scorecard to track success, improve focus, and align the organization around implementation. Potential disadvantages of this tool include the cost (it takes time to customize the approach and implementation may require an external consultant) and some find the structure inflexible.

In the example shown in Figure 5.5, a balanced scorecard for the fictional first-time homebuyer program we highlighted in Figure 5.4 uses the four perspectives, each with specified goals. For example, under the customer perspective, the first goal is quality buyer training provided, and the organization could measure this by surveying customer satisfaction. In the financial perspective category, one of its goals is to maintain a cost-effective operation and it could measure this by tracking expenses as a proportion of revenues and other related financial metrics. The organization is now poised to develop a dashboard to track metrics related to each of these elements.

Figure 5.5 Example Balanced Scorecard Overview for a Nonprofit Organization

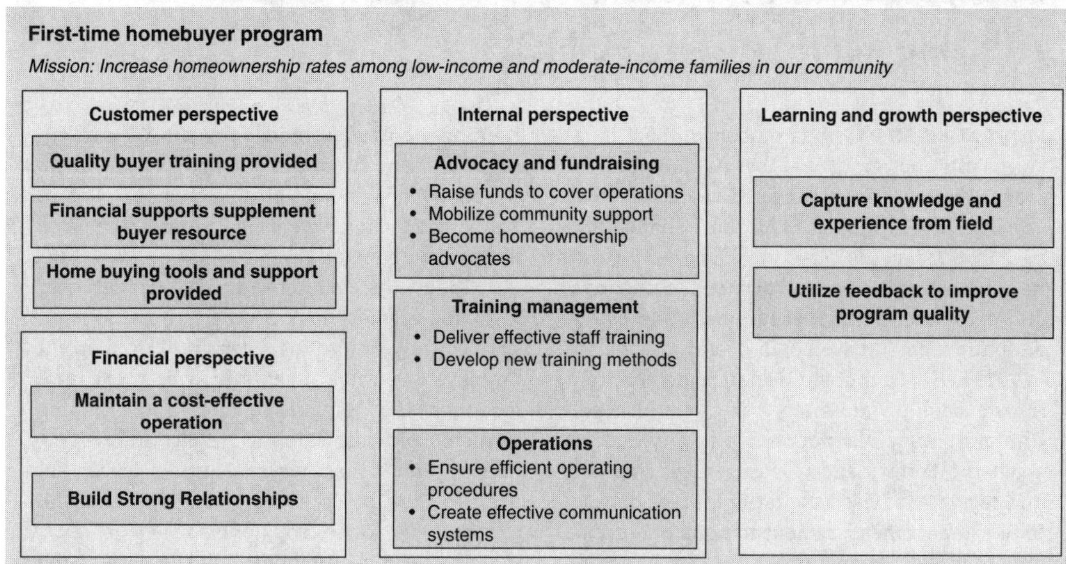

Which Measurement Approach Should Social Entrepreneurs Choose?

What separates the randomized controlled trials done by the Nobel Prize winners from the "we know it when we see it" impact measurement approach of Sanergy and 99Degrees Custom and the intentionally narrow activity and survey data collected by SWSG? Cost is a major factor. Some organizations have developed effective **proxy measures** that enable them to measure important outcomes using simple metrics. For example, to determine poverty, microlending pioneer Grameen Bank asks clients ten questions including whether they had a vegetable garden, whether their children are in school, and whether there are times of the year they go hungry to simply and effectively measure poverty.[18] Stage also matters. An early-stage start-up may not have long-term impact information in the first few years of operation simply because it takes time for outcomes to happen. How an organization is funded also matters. For example, government and philanthropic funders often require detailed impact and performance metrics.

Finally, while a focus on numbers is important, social entrepreneurs should not forget the impact of stories. Using examples of the human impact of their products or services is an important way to engage stakeholders, employees, and recipients and bring the organization's impact to life.

PROFILE: MATT FORTI—DRIVING IMPACT AT THE ONE ACRE FUND

MATT FORTI IS PASsionate about impact measurement and motivated by its potential to make mission-driven ventures more effective, scalable, and responsive. As the Philadelphia-based US Managing Director of One Acre Fund, he coordinates various global support functions, and helps oversee its measurement and evaluation function. But even before joining One Acre in 2013 he was a thought leader in the nonprofit impact field. As a Manager at the Bridgespan Group, an influential nonprofit advisory firm, he coled the Performance Measurement Practice, and regularly advised nonprofit leaders on how to use impact measurement to hone operations and improve scalability. He is also a prolific author, speaker, and blogger on these topics.

The One Acre Fund is an entrepreneurial success story. Founded in 2006, it helps Africa's hard-working smallholder farm families dramatically improve their incomes through a comprehensive agricultural bundle that includes finance, farm inputs, training, and postharvest support. One Acre Fund aspires to nothing less than eradicating chronic hunger among Africa's 50 million smallholder farm families.

Forti's relationship with the One Acre Fund goes back to its formation in 2006 by Andrew Youn, his graduate school classmate. Youn visited rural Kenya in 2005 during "hunger season," a time when staple food had run out and families were barely surviving. The idea for One Acre took seed when Youn met one farmer who was producing three times as many crops as others because she had hybrid seeds, the appropriate amount of micro-dosed fertilizer, and knew the basics of spacing seeds properly. Youn's entrepreneurial inspiration was that he could make an enormous difference simply by proving tools—initially seeds, fertilizer, and training—to rural farmers on credit. Youn asked Forti to help fundraise to support his idea. Together they launched a successful pilot in Kenya, and One Acre was incorporated as a nonprofit organization.

Today, the One Acre Fund works with over 1 million farmers in 6 countries in Africa and has gross revenue of over $120 million. It employs 6,000 field agents in over 4,500 rural locations that are responsible for enrolling farmers, providing inputs, collecting repayments, and other tasks. Farmers cover on average 75% of core program costs and the remainder is covered by donors.

Impact measurement is at the core of the One Acre Fund's work as they explain on their website: "At One Acre Fund, impact is our north star. We always seek to generate positive impact in the lives of smallholder farmers and rigorous measurement is the only way to know if we are headed in the right direction."

Forti has played a key role in evolving One Acre's data-driven innovation and impact measurement approach that is used to make sure that they are consistently delivering high-quality products and services and having a positive impact in the lives of farmers. For example, One Acre routinely conducts many physical harvest measurements per year for a group of farmers enrolled in One Acre Fund and compares it to a group of non–One Acre Fund farmers from the same villages who are subject to the same agro-ecological conditions. The innovation team also uses multiple experiments before introducing new products to the farmers they serve, ensuring, for example, that a new crop type will be successful.

The One Acre Fund initially focused on metrics related to financial impact on farmers (new farmer income generated from additional crops grown) but as they expanded, their approach became more nuanced; they now evaluate four impact areas. These are asset accumulation (their theory is that farmers are making more money through One Acre Fund and will invest it back into productive assets), hunger and nutrition (how much their work is contributing to nutritional diversity for the farmers), soil health, and climate resilience. When measuring climate resilience, the team believes farmers are most at risk from climate change, so they aim to introduce drought-tolerant seeds, offer crop insurance, and encourage crop diversification to mitigate this.

The Fund has also been studying quality of life for farmers in Rwanda and Kenya, examining health, education, nutrition, and literacy through rigorous data collection and analysis. Looking to the future, Forti plans to introduce additional "softer" metrics that measure improvements in well-being, including asking participating farmers to identify whether "I feel part of a community," "I am less stressed," and/or "I am trusted as a leader." He explains that community-level change and building local capacity make One Acre's work more durable (M. Forti, personal interview, July 24, 2020).

One Acre uses Social Return on Investment (SROI) as a primary measure. To calculate this metric, the team takes the total impact of a program in terms of new farmer income generated, and then divides it by the donor cost of operating that program. Forti believes that—despite the proliferation of measurement approaches among nonprofits—SROI is a simple, comparable tool that can help donors make sound investment decisions. They also use SROI internally (along with other measures) to help make resource allocation decisions. However, he explains that despite the benefit of simplicity, a one-size-fits-all metric like SROI has limitations; to account for differences across sites, they have modified the approach to account for stage of operations in different countries, and to consider how additional income is more impactful for those who are more impoverished.

Forti offers the following advice to aspiring social entrepreneurs: "Because measurement is about improving programs real-time, you really need to invest in building your capabilities early. If you skip this step (or delegate it) you will lose cycles of learning and improvement." He also offers a caution: "Don't get overwhelmed with the enormity of what you are trying to accomplish. Especially in the early years, get comfortable with measuring the critical few ultimate outcomes you most want to hold yourself accountable to achieving, along with all the process indicators that tell you whether you are implementing your program correctly" (M. Forti, personal interview, July 24, 2020).

IMPACT MEASUREMENT PITFALLS

Mission-driven organizations are particularly vulnerable to measurement challenges because of the complexity of their missions and frequent scarcity of resources. Three major pitfalls to avoid include measuring the wrong things, measuring without considering cost, and not using the results effectively.

Measuring the Wrong Things

In a haste for efficiency, social entrepreneurs sometimes choose simple measures or **proxy measures** to track their progress. The benefit is making it easy to collect and track data. Simplifications can save time and resources. That said, social entrepreneurs should remember that simplified measures that do not reflect mission achievement can move an organization in the wrong direction. For example, the mission of the Nature Conservancy (TNC), the world's largest private conservation group, is to preserve the diversity of plants and animals around the world by protecting habitats. Their simplification was to regularly report on just two things: bucks (the amount of charitable donations received) and acres (the number of acres it protected). These metrics showed a high level of success, and TNC consistently reported protecting millions of acres and increased revenues. But over time TNC leaders realized that using these two proxies did not align the organization to meet its core mission and in fact encouraged off-mission activities.[19] By realigning their measurement system to focus on preserving biodiversity, they were able to refocus on activities that supported TNC's core mission.

Measuring Without Regard to Cost

A second pitfall is measuring without regard to cost. Many organizations find themselves expending such a large proportion of their budget on measurement that they have insufficient resources for program delivery. As we discussed earlier, large-scale evaluation research is beneficial for high-stakes multimillion-dollar programs, but not for early-stage start-ups.

Measuring Without Analyzing or Acting

In trying to satisfy stakeholders, many social ventures find themselves measuring things that are not important, or worse, collecting so much information that data collection crowds out data analysis. Consider the quandary faced by Jenn Bender, CEO of New Sector Alliance, a nonprofit leadership development organization. In 2015, New Sector was at a pivotal point in its history having just reimagined its mission and aligned operations. Yet New Sector's small staff of ten still collected data on a granular level for its major federal funder (for example, collecting highly detailed timesheets for the fellows it placed at nonprofits), conducted over 60 surveys of fellows annually and prepared multiple, detailed reports for its board, some of which were useful and some of which were not. Bender found that streamlining the data that New Sector collected was the only way to free up staff capacity for analysis and learning.

CALCULATING SOCIAL IMPACT

Foundations, major donors, government organizations, and impact investors that fund social impact ventures use impact calculation tools to make decisions and compare alternative investments. Many investors have developed their own methodologies for deciding whether the social return of a project merits investment. Three foundational approaches are as follows:

- *Cost–benefit analysis*—is a tool used both in business and by funders to compare value across initiatives. For example, an infrastructure provider might use a cost–benefit analysis to select among alternatives for a sanitation project. The approach in its simplest form involves counting all the projected revenues and costs associated with a project and estimating when they will occur. For social impact projects, the value of social benefits is also counted. Then the net stream of costs and benefits over time is discounted back to the current period to derive the **net present value** of the investment. The theory is that if the net present value is positive, the investment is worthwhile. An alternate measure, using the same data, is **internal rate of return (IRR)**, which can be used to compare projects of different lengths. The advantage of cost–benefit analysis is that it enables investors to compare alternatives systematically.
- *SROI (Social Return on Investment)*—builds on the principles of cost–benefit analysis but goes further, explicitly valuing a wider range of social benefits, including those that accrue to unrelated parties. The formula used is the sum of expected benefits, less the investment required, divided by the investment. Variations of this approach are used by philanthropists, impact investors, nonprofits, and others to determine whether an investment will yield a positive social return. For example, REDF, a California-based job creation nonprofit created a blended SROI which has both an economic return component and a social return component. The Robin Hood Foundation, New York's largest poverty fighting organization, adapts this approach by using a benefit–cost ratio. The benefit component is an estimated total poverty mitigation benefit, including total benefits that will accrue to low-income individuals over their lifetime. The cost is the direct cost to Robin Hood. The ratio is then adjusted by a "Robin Hood Factor" which is an estimate of the portion of benefits that could reasonably be attributed to Robin Hood's role.[20]
- *Best Available Charitable Option (BACO) assessment*—The Acumen Fund, a global nonprofit impact investment fund that invests in social enterprises that serve low-income communities, uses BACO to compare potential investments. For example, if the cost of a given intervention is $10 per unit and a charitable alternative costs less, the investment will not meet their standards. Brian Trelstad, former Chief Investment Officer at Acumen explains: "The BACO methodology is important for our process in a few ways. First, it forces the team to think about who is doing the best or

prevailing work on solving the same or similar problems. Second, it forces us to think about the marginal cost decision a hypothetical donor is making… we need to think about how else the donor could have invested their money. Finally, it is a very practical tool that is easy to use."[21]

Figure 5.6 shows a highly simplified version of the three tools applied to a proposed initiative to reduce malaria by supplying treated mosquito nets in sub-Saharan Africa. The first example shows a cost–benefit analysis which lays out the cost (initial net acquisition and distribution and then replacements nets since they wear out). It then calculates a hypothetical benefit which assumes that effectiveness degrades over time (nets wear out, can be damaged, or are used less over time), and then estimates what the impact is (lives saved or medical expenses averted). Finally, the net flow of

Figure 5.6 Comparison of Three Different Approaches to Calculating Social Return

Cost-Benefit analysis	*Year 0*	*Year 1*	*Year 2*	*Year 3*	*Year 4*	*Year 5*	*Year 6*
Acquisition cost 1000 nets	($3,000)	0	0	($3,000)	0	0	0
Distribution cost 1000 nets	($1,000)	0	0	($1,000)	0	0	0
Benefit							
Sickness averted / lives saved	$0	$10,000	$5,000	$2,500	$10,000	$5,000	$2,500
Net cost and benefit	($4,000)	$10,000	$5,000	($1,500)	$10,000	$5,000	$2,500
Net present value	**$21,689**	*assumes 5% discount rate*					
Internal rate of return	**199%**						

Note: Assumes 3-year replacement cycle due to wear and tear

Social return on investment	
Total benefit	$35,000
Total cost	-$8,000
Net total benefits	$27,000
Donor dollars	$8,000
divided by net total benefits	$27,000
SROI	**3.38**

BACO (Best alternative to a charitable option)	
Loan to establish a net factory	$0.02 cost per year to protect one person
Charitable (grant) alternative	$0.84 cost per year to protect one person
BACO ratio	**42**

costs and benefits is discounted back to the current period using an assumed rate (in this example 5%).

The calculation is very sensitive to the assumptions, particularly the estimated value of a human life, as well as the cost of the nets and the choice of discount rate. This example excludes program management or administrative costs, but these might be included or excluded depending on the intent of the analyst. If these expenses were included, the calculated value would be lower.

The second example shows social return on investment for the same initiative. It compares the amount of donor dollars to an estimate of the benefit achieved. Once again, the ratio is extremely sensitive to assumptions about benefits. In this example, organizational overhead expenses are also excluded.

The third example estimates the best alternative to a charitable outcome, which compares the cost of a loan to establish a bed net factory with the estimated cost a charity would incur purchasing the nets directly as a cost per year of mosquito protection. This approach is intuitively appealing and enables easy comparisons, but does not account for several things, including failure risk or nonsponsor investment expenses.

One additional factor that many prospective investors build into their assessment is the capability of the implementing organizations. Those that invest in entrepreneurs realize that they are betting on both the "horse" (the venture) and the "jockey" (the founding team). Organizations as diverse as the Schwab Foundation for Social Entrepreneurship, Echoing Green, and New Profit all pay as much attention to who will be leading the venture as the venture's projected outcomes.

CHAPTER SUMMARY

In this chapter, we have discussed two important models—theory of change and logic model—that entrepreneurs use to clarify their intent and improve their approach. We also considered different approaches for measuring impact and consider how effective entrepreneurs balance their responsibility for evaluating efficiently *and* comprehensively. A key question for social entrepreneurs who depend on agility to launch their ventures is how they should also invest in measurement to improve operations and communicate effectively with stakeholders while continuing to use a lean approach.

There are myriad approaches to measuring and calculating impact ranging from randomized controlled trials to pragmatic measurement processes that balance the benefits and costs of data collection and analysis. Simple, clear measures based on an organization's activities can help to link values with principles. And when we seek to compare alternatives, there are numerous ways to calculating impact and each has benefits and drawbacks.

Those that lead mission-driven organizations are often reminded that "what gets measured gets better," "what gets measured gets managed," or "what gets measured gets managed." But sometimes, what gets measured is simply what gets measured. This leads to our final suggestion for social entrepreneurs: be pragmatic and make sure you measure what matters.

KEY TERMS

Internal rate of return (IRR): an organization's estimated rate of return for a project or investment over a multiyear period.

Logic models: show the links between specific inputs and outputs, outcomes, and ultimately impact. They typically use a linear format with columns for each category.

Mission creep: the gradual or incremental expansion of a project or intervention beyond its original goals.

Net present value (NPV): calculates the net value of a stream of costs and benefits over time by identifying them and discounting the stream back to the current period.

Proxy measures: substitute, indirect, or simpler indicators to track an outcome.

Randomized controlled trial (RCT): a form of experiment where large numbers of participants are randomized, receiving either a particular intervention or a standard treatment and outcomes are tracked over time and compared.

Social return on investment (SROI): builds on the principles of cost–benefit analysis but goes further, explicitly valuing a wide range of social benefits, including those that accrue to unrelated parties.

Theory of change: a one-page graphical depiction of how an organization intends to meet its mission.

IN-CLASS EXERCISE

Exercise 5.1: Create a Logic Model

(Estimated time 30 minutes)

Purpose

A logic model helps social entrepreneurs describe the link between the activities of their organization and the impact they hope to achieve. This exercise will demonstrate the importance of this process and highlight some of the challenges.

Preparation

Have blank copies of the exercise template below (Figure 5.7 Logic Model Template).

Figure 5.7 Logic Model Template

Inputs Resources invested in the activities	**Activities** Programs or activities offered	**Outputs** Products of the activity	**Outcomes** Direct changes from the activity	**Impact** Broader or systemic changes

? What would you need to believe for your projected activities to translate into expected outputs, outcomes and impact?

Process

1. In groups of 3–5 students, complete the logic model template for a proposed venture (ideally one for which the team has completed a business model canvas earlier in the course.)
2. Complete the template and iterate until the model is robust.
   Hint: While it is tempting to work left to right, teams often find that starting with desired impact in the right-hand column and working backwards enables them to be more creative.
3. Identify the underlying beliefs that drove the team's understanding of how the venture will have the intended impact. Write these down.
4. Be ready to present the analysis to the class. A gallery walk approach posting the models on large sheets of paper taped to the walls can also be used.
5. Debrief:
   a. What was difficult about preparing a logic model? What was easy?
   b. What were the underlying beliefs and what would the team do if some of them proved not to be true?
6. Post-class: Working with your team, discuss how to measure the venture's impact based on the outcome, outputs, and impacts identified in the logic model.

SHORT CASE: REINVENTION AND PLANNING FOR IMPACT AT HOPEWELL

Shaheer Mustafa and Amy Schneider and the other members of HopeWell's Executive Leadership Team shared exhausted smiles as they finished their last meeting to hone HopeWell's new theory of change and organization-level logic model. After reflecting on what they had learned at the last meeting, they turned to the challenging task at hand, which was taking one more look before presenting the documents to their board of Directors on Tuesday. Approval by HopeWell's board would be an important affirmation of their efforts to dramatically reinvent the organization and position it for the future. But, their thoughts also turned to HopeWell's 140 staff members and the individuals and families engaged in their programs. Would they be able to secure broad agreement? Would it effectively guide day-to-day actions? And how could they most effectively engage these important stakeholders around the new vision?

HopeWell Background

HopeWell was a social justice and learning organization that has grown to engage 1,000 youth and individuals annually through a variety of critical programs. In addition to foster care, HopeWell provides in-home support and stabilization services to families involved with the state Department of Children and Families (DCF), supports youth aging out of foster care by providing stable housing, education and employment support, as well as providing residential care for adults with intellectual and developmental disabilities. HopeWell's work is funded primarily via state contracts, but it also receives funding from corporate and individual donors.

HopeWell's roots go back to 1964 when founder Gerry Wright saw an urgent need for an alternative to court-involved teens being warehoused in juvenile detention centers. Determined to find a better, more humane alternative, Wright launched the state's first community-based residential program for boys. This pioneering program evolved and by the 1970s had grown significantly and become a state leader in providing intensive foster care services to children and teens with a history of serious challenges and family trauma.

In 2016, the Board hired Mustafa, an entrepreneurial new leader with an ambitious vision for what HopeWell could become. He saw an opportunity to leverage his background as a social worker, former director of a large child protection agency, and experience turning around residential programs serving youth in high-risk situations. He soon recruited Amy Schneider as Vice President of Programs, who contributed significant management and leadership experience and over a decade of experience in direct service supporting youth learning and development. Other key hires within the first year included a Vice President of Human Resources and a new Vice President of Advancement.

Shaking the Box

After six months of "careful listening" Mustafa decided to make substantial changes. With his new leadership team, he also brought a new, entrepreneurial philosophy to an organization that had experienced little change over the past decades. Believing that experimentation and iteration is the recipe for making substantial change, he immediately set out to solve a pressing problem.

Children who have been in foster care face severe challenges when they "age out" of foster care at the age of 18. Within a year of leaving, when they became ineligible for services, 40% experience homelessness. Over the course of a few months, he and the team launched a new housing-first initiative called My First Place™, in partnership with a California-based provider that had honed the model in multiple settings. The program involved renting apartments scattered throughout the community and hiring education and employment specialists to provide specific transitional services.

When My First Place was conceived, HopeWell had not secured state contracts to finance it. (Preexisting contracts were the primary way that all of HopeWell's programs were funded.) While it was clear that the new program filled a critical gap facing the youth that HopeWell supported, announcing a program without initial financial guarantees was a radical step for an organization that was accustomed to following the lead of its funders. Mustafa raised donor funds to support the program initially and once the concept was solidified, it was awarded a state contract. The visible introduction of a new program, with outside partners and a different financial model was a wake-up call for the entire organization, clearly demonstrating that innovation, person-centered programming and different financial models would be central going forward.

A New Theory of Change and Logic Model

Mustafa believed that learning and measurement would play a critical role moving forward:

> *When I started at Hopewell in September of 2016, one thing that was critically important was being able to capture the impact that we were having on the individuals that we were serving. We were certainly having impact—that was very apparent—but just knowing that in a gut sense way is insufficient and we really wanted to be able to know and capture our impact. That was the beginning of our journey.*
>
> (S. Mustafa, personal interview, July 17, 2020)

In 2018, HopeWell's leadership team conducted a series of visits to each of their eight sites to reach out to the staff. They asked questions about how to deepen their impact, what new opportunities should be considered, and what resources would be required. This was an important step for engaging the staff, hearing their ideas, and honing HopeWell's direction. A few months later, they used a similar process to develop agency values and vision and initial input for the organizational logic model.

Then, starting in 2019, partnering with Brandeis University Heller School's Center for Youth and Communities, the leadership team started work on a theory of change. This one-page document which depicted an overarching vision that started with the challenge and ended with the larger vision of what they hoped clients could achieve. An accompanying organizational-level logic model that would describe the approach in more detail and demonstrate the link between HopeWell's actions and their impact. Developing both required an intensive effort from HopeWell's leadership team, as well as extensive staff input. They had lengthy discussion about the theory's underpinnings and how exactly they would meet their mission. The team exhaustively examined and clarified each part of the model, including the meaning of terms like equity, opportunity, and innovation to bring crispness and clarity to their ideas.

Translating HopeWell's Theory of Change in to Action

Unlike a more graphic theory of change, HopeWell's draft organizational logic model followed a tabular format. It started with an articulation of collective beliefs: a set of 15 statements that included outward-facing assumptions (for example, "Having a safe place to call home is a stabilizing factor that enables individuals and families to focus on their lives, education and employment goals, build community, and establish a foundation for long-term success."), and internal assumptions (for example, "Staff who feel respected, supported, and have opportunities for leadership experiences and advancement will be valuable co-creators of HopeWell's culture of inclusion and learning and practice excellence."). Based on these beliefs, the next section was a series of organizational strategies in four categories: individuals and families, caregivers, staff, and HopeWell (organization). From these, long-term outcomes (such as safety, stability, and connection or physical and emotional health) were developed which led to "the promise" of their ultimate impact: well-being, self-actualization, and equity and opportunity. Flowing from beliefs to strategies to outcomes enabled the reader to understand the link between what HopeWell does and what it plans to achieve. The process also included developing short-term outcomes and measures.

Mustafa and Schneider believed that the best way to reinforce the staff's intense dedication will be to engage them in bringing the logic model to life. They also saw an opportunity to include representatives of individuals participating in their programs. In an unusual move, the team decided to have all parts of the organization—including internal services like finance and human resources—develop a series of more specific logic models that would cascade from the organization level logic model to provide a clear road map for each program and service. Creating these program- and department-level logic models wouldn't be easy but would ensure that the entire organization was aligned. Schneider noted:

> *Relationships at HopeWell are central. How we treat our staff and how engaged and cultivated they feel is critical. Staff need to feel our values in real-time and feel valued and appreciated in how they do their work. We need to have trust and true collaboration if we want to be the kind of learning organization we aspire to be.*
>
> (A. Schneider, personal interview, July 17, 2020)

Ultimately, the nested set of documents would provide a critical road map that they hope would enable HopeWell to achieve its vision. According to Mustafa, "this is a critical milestone for our organization and a chance to indicate our seriousness, our commitment and willingness to challenge ourselves to be better. We are here for those that we serve and do the best work that we can, and this is a way to hold ourselves accountable to that" (S. Mustafa, personal interview, July 17, 2020).

Looking to the Future

With the first part of the process behind them, Mustafa and Schneider turned their discussion to how to make sure that their investment in reimagining HopeWell would earn the support of field staff. They debated the best way to introduce the organization-level model to all staff and in particular the 70 percent of the staff that provided direct care in the field. They also wondered how quickly to move to program level–logic models. Should they give the organization-level model a chance to be socialized, or take advantage of the momentum they had created and begin the process immediately?

Finally, they considered how to measure progress towards achievement now that they had specific outcomes in place. They wanted to make sure they had objective measures of progress but were wary of imposing additional burdens on their hardworking field staff. With these questions top of mind, and realizing that their work was just beginning, they took a deep breath and took out their phones to schedule another meeting.

Discussion Questions

1. What advice would you give Mustafa and Schneider as they roll their process out organization-wide? Do you expect any resistance?
2. What do you think of their decision to create program-level logic models? How should they balance their desire for staff alignment with the additional work it will create?
3. Who else should be involved in creating the program-level models? How should this be done?
4. A well-thought-through theory of change/logic model can provide clear guidance to staff. Is there a risk that this will stifle program-level innovation? How should the leadership team guard against this?
5. Schneider and Mustafa seek to be a model for the sector to extend HopeWell's impact. What do you see as the best ways to accomplish this?

NOTES

1. Collins, J. (2001). *Good to great*. Random House Business Books. See also for a summary https://www.jimcollins.com/concepts/the-flywheel.html.
2. Coryn, C. L. S., Noakes, L. A., Westine, C. D., & Schröter D. C. (2011). A systematic review of theory-driven evaluation practice from 1990 to 2009. *American Journal of Evaluation, 32*(2), 199–226.

3. Higgins, M., Hess, R., Wiender, J., & Robison, W. (2011). Creating a corps of change agents teach for America alumni project. *Education Next*. Retrieved from https://www.educationnext.org/creating-a-corps-of-change-agents/. [Revised May 11, 2011].
4. Brest, P. (2010). The power of theories of change. *Stanford Social Innovation Review*.
5. Trelstad, B. (2008). Simple measures for social enterprise. *Innovations: Technology, Governance, Globalization*, MIT Press, *3*(3), 105–118.
6. The Nobel Prize. (2019, October 14). *Press release: The prize in economic sciences 2019*. Retrieved from https://www.nobelprize.org/prizes/economic-sciences/2019/press-release/.
7. The Abdul Latif Jameel Poverty Action Lab (J-PAL). (2020). *About us | The Abdul Latif Jameel poverty action lab*. Retrieved from www.povertyactionlab.org/about-j-pal.
8. Nature. (2019, October 14). *'Randomistas' who used controlled trials to fight poverty win economics nobel*. Retrieved from www.nature.com/articles/d41586-019-03125-y?error=cookies_not_supported&code=3b61a97d-86eb-4602-894f-715f9b9a35f8.
9. Solman, P. (2019, November 21). *How these 2 economists are using randomized trials to solve global poverty*. PBS NewsHour. Retrieved from www.pbs.org/newshour/show/how-these-2-economists-are-using-randomized-trials-to-solve-global-poverty.
10. Kremer, M. (2019, October 14). *A lot of people go into economics because they care about poverty* [Video]. YouTube. Retrieved from www.youtube.com/watch?v=Rj1clfnnbRs.
11. Miguel, E., & Kremer, M. (2004). Worms: Identifying impacts on education and health in the presence of treatment externalities. *Econometrica*, *72*(1), 159–217.
12. Carlson, C., Campbell, C. M., & Virani, P. (2016). *Sanergy: Using social entrepreneurship to solve emerging market problems*. London: SAGE Publications.
13. Ibid.
14. Strong Women, Strong Girls Boston. (2019). *Social impact report: Boston 2017 – 2018*. Retrieved from http://swsg.org/wp-content/uploads/2019/06/boston_report_web.pdf.
15. The Bridgespan Group. (2020). *About Bridgespan*. Retrieved from www.bridgespan.org/about-us/about-bridgespan.
16. Grossman, A. S., Greckol-Herlich, N., & Ross, C. (2008). *The Bridgespan group: Chapter 2*. HBS Case No. 309-020. [Revised April 2010].
17. Kaplan, R. S., & Norton, D. P. (1992). The balanced scorecard—measures that drive performance. *Harvard Business Review*, *70*(1), 71–79.
18. Kramer, M. R. (2005). *Measuring innovation: Evaluation in the field of social entrepreneurship*. Skoll Foundation.
19. Sawhill, J., & Williamson, D. (2001). Measuring what matters in nonprofits. *The McKinsey Quarterly*.
20. So, I., & Staskevicius, A. (2015). *Measuring the impact in impact investing*. Harvard Business School [Unpublished study].
21. Trelstad, B. (2008). *Simple measures for social enterprise*. Innovations: Technology, Governance, Globalization, MIT Press, *3*(3), 105–118.

CHAPTER SIX

LEGAL STRUCTURES AND FINANCIAL PLANS FOR SOCIAL VENTURES

Learning Objectives

- Appraise alternative legal structures in the United States and other countries.
- Explain the importance of cash flow as a critical resource for new ventures.
- Contrast different sources of financing for new social ventures.
- Distinguish between different financial strategies and funding models.

As they develop their ventures, social entrepreneurs face two important and interlocked decisions: how they should organize their venture and how they should finance it. These decisions, made within the context of both mission and the market in which a new venture will operate, are critically important to a venture's overall success. While it is tempting to defer these decisions, delegate them to specialists, or worse, wish them away, a disciplined approach to organizational structure, financial planning, and accountability separates entrepreneurs who poise their ventures for success from those who do not.

CHOOSING A LEGAL STRUCTURE

A Tale of Three Ventures

When Ohad Elhelo (who we profiled in Chapter 4) founded Our Generation Speaks (OGS), it was clear that he should operate OGS as a charitable organization. This decision was consistent with OGS's mission "to create an entrepreneurial generation of leaders to shape a peaceful Israeli-Palestinian future built on trust." The OGS funding model also provided guidance; OGS relies on generous contributions from committed donors. Tax deductibility of donations was important for attracting them, and being a nonprofit would increase their trust in OGS to navigate a challenging political climate with insight and integrity. Elhelo was also convinced that attracting a high-quality board was essential to

OGS's success and nonprofit formation would enable him to incorporate diverse perspectives and gain committed stakeholders.

Brenna Schneider's decision to incorporate 99Degrees as a privately held limited liability corporation (LLC) was equally thoughtful. She knew that as founder and owner she would be able to shape the company's mission to match her passion for breaking the cycle of intergenerational poverty she observed in Lawrence, Massachusetts. She wanted to attract external for-profit investors because she was confident that this would be the best way to scale the venture and its impact. An LLC structure would ensure that she did not take on personal liability. She also observed that in the conservative garment manufacturing industry, being a nonprofit would be a liability with high-volume customers and suppliers concerned about margins and reliability, and was concerned that if she organized as a nonprofit they would dismiss her operation as less businesslike and decide not to work with her.

Ted Barber, Amber Chand, and Siiri Morley chose a different path with Prosperity Candle (which is included as a mini case in this chapter). Seeking to reinforce their commitment to social mission vs. profit, but anxious to tap into a wider range of capital markets, they incorporated them as a **low profit limited liability corporation** (L3C). Later, they helped to seed a "sister" nonprofit organization called Prosperity Catalyst (of which Morley became the first executive director) when it was clear that parts of their social mission (specifically training and support for women's groups in Haiti) could be accomplished more effectively by a charitable organization.

In each of these examples, the founding social entrepreneurs made careful decisions about legal and financing structure in tandem, based on a clear assessment of the nature of their venture and their aspirations for growth and impact. It isn't easy at the early stages of a new social venture to make these decisions, particularly if the founding team is still experimenting with how to make the venture viable. That said, a clear vision for the mission and a solid understanding of the planned business model provide guidance.

Legal Forms of Organization in the United States

Mission-driven organizations face an initial choice of legal status. In the United States, the most prevalent form of nonprofit corporation is a charitable organization. But many mission-driven organizations decide instead to organize as for-profit organizations and there are many options in this category including sole proprietorships, partnerships, and corporations. In addition, several specialized and hybrid forms exist that seek to marry the benefits of nonprofit and for-profit incorporation.

Each type of organization varies in tax treatment, limitations on equity ownership, and liability. Despite these differences, entrepreneurs often don't fully understand the consequences of their selection of organization form, relying instead on simple (and sometimes shortsighted) cost comparisons when making this decision.[1]

A recent survey of over 600 US social enterprise founders and associates found that the majority (41%) of new mission-driven ventures incorporated as 501(c) (3) organizations, followed by 21% as **limited liability companies** (LLCs) and 7% as corporations. Nine percent used the hybrid B-corporation form, a further 5% were operating without incorporating or "unofficial," and 16% indicated other.[2]

Nonprofit Entities

When founders talk about forming a nonprofit, they are usually referring to creating a charitable organization under section 501(c) (3) of the tax code. Of the roughly 1.5 million nonprofit organizations in the United States, approximately two-thirds are charitable organizations. In addition to these public charitable organizations, there are approximately 30 other types of nonprofit organizations that are exempt from some federal income taxes including, for example, private foundations, chambers of commerce, fraternal organizations, and civic leagues.

501(c) (3) nonprofit organizations are tax-exempt organizations designed exclusively for the purpose of pursuing a social mission, without intending to make a profit.[3] By operating as a charitable organization, the organization agrees to benefit the public and not individual owners. A main advantage of this type of nonprofit is that it can access philanthropic funding. A disadvantage is that it cannot access traditional start-up capital investment. Nonprofits are managed by executive directors who are accountable to boards of directors that have final say on decisions. Boards are usually made up of donors, community members, and industry advisors. While charitable organizations can have earned income in addition to accepting donations, these funds must be used for charitable purposes.

For-Profit Entities

In the United States, there are 23 million sole proprietorships (most of which have fewer than four employees) and over 9 million corporations. This number includes 1.7 million traditional corporations, as well as 7.4 million partnerships and S corporations. There are only 400 worker-owned cooperatives in the United States. Each type of organization is described below.

In a *sole proprietorship* an individual entrepreneur and the business are essentially the same entity. The income earned is reported as income on the entrepreneur's tax return, meaning that the tax burden "passes through" to the owner directly. The owner also bears the liabilities of the business as an individual. While easy to form and simple to operate, the liability risks often make this a poor choice of structure.[4] When an organization begins operating without incorporating, it is by default a sole proprietorship. Examples include very early-stage ventures that have not yet formalized their structure or side businesses run by individuals.

Partnerships are business entities with two or more owners. A general partnership is treated as a sole proprietorship for tax and liability purposes. While no government filings or written agreements are needed to create a partnership, contributions to the business, the distribution of profits and losses, management responsibilities, and means of dissolution are typically laid out in a partnership agreement. Partnerships dissolve upon a material change to the partnership, including the death or withdrawal of one of the partners. All of the partners are jointly and severally liable if there is claim against the entity.[5] Entrepreneurs should be cautious that partnerships may be created regardless of any written agreement when two or more individuals act as or represent themselves as partners, and that one partner may legally bind the others if they have the apparent authority to do so. In the past, small professional services practices often operated as partnerships but most have now become LLCs to gain the benefit of limited liability.

A *limited partnership* is a partnership with general and limited partners. The general partner assumes management responsibility and unlimited liability. The limited partners are liable only for their contribution and do not engage in day-to-day decision-making. Profits and losses are distributed according to a partnership agreement and can be allocated differently from each other.[6] Unlike sole proprietorships or general partnerships, formation requires the entity to file a certificate of formation. Limited partnerships are often used for investment purposes.

A *limited liability company (LLC)* is a structure that combines the limited liability features of a corporation with the tax efficiencies and operational flexibility of a partnership. Advantages include limited personal liability, lighter registration requirements than a corporation, and fewer restrictions on profit sharing. Additionally, an LLC may be taxed as a "pass through" like a sole proprietorship and therefore avoid being taxed at both the corporate and individual level. However, a limited life (as with a partnership, when a member leaves the partnership is dissolved) and the fact that members of an LLC are considered self-employed and must make self-employment tax contributions toward Medicare and Social Security are potential disadvantages. Many professional services firms, including law and consulting firms, are organized as LLCs.

Corporations are special entities where the corporation is a separate legal entity, distinct from its owners. The corporation, not the owner, has liability. Corporations must have boards of directors, file annual reports, have articles of incorporation and comply with other regulatory and filing requirements. Traditional corporations (C Corporations) pay taxes at the corporate level and when shareholders receive distributions, they incur individual tax liability as well. Unlike partnerships, corporations are not dissolved when a partner exits due to death or retirement. The advantages of a corporation, in addition to limited liability, are the ability to raise funds by selling stock and treatment as a separate entity for tax purposes. Also, if a venture plans to exit via a sale of stock or receive venture capital, this form may be the best choice. Disadvantages include "double taxation," which refers to income taxed first at the corporate level and then at the personal level when distributed to shareholder, as well as administrative and regulatory complexity and cost.[7] Most large companies are corporations.

S Corporations have the tax status of a partnership with the liability limitation benefits of a corporation. Advantages include tax savings (only the wages of the S Corp shareholder who is an employee are subject to employment tax and the remaining income is paid to the owner as a "distribution," which is taxed at a lower rate) and an independent life. If a shareholder leaves the company, or sells their shares, the S Corporation can continue doing business.[8] There are some limitations. An S Corporation can have only one class of stock, must be owned only by US citizens, have 75 or fewer stockholders, and allocate economic benefits on a per share basis.

Specialized and Hybrid Forms of Organization

In addition to the nonprofit and for-profit forms discussed above, several specialized and hybrid forms of incorporation used by mission-driven organizations have emerged in recent years. These forms seek to combine the social accountability and tax advantages of a nonprofit organization with the flexibility and capital market advantages of a for-profit.

A *benefit corporation* is a legal form that enables a corporation to make decisions to pursue a specific social mission and broader stakeholder interests, aside from shareholder value.[9] Like a corporation, a benefit corporation has limited liability and can choose to be taxed either as a C or S corporation. This form provides an advantage for attracting investment, since it can access both traditional financial markets and impact investments. Another advantage is that this form guarantees protection of its social mission even after an initial public offering (IPO). Benefit corporations operate under traditional corporate governance requirements, although many states require that the organization appoint a "benefit director" to hold the corporation accountable to its social mission.[10]

The benefit LLC or BLLC mirrors the mandates of a benefit corporation. A BLLC must uphold a specified social mission and consider the concerns of a broader range of stakeholders including customers, suppliers, employees, and creditors. BLLCs are distinct in that the underlying form is an LLC rather than a corporation. This means that they maintain limited liability but may be taxed as a pass-through rather than face double taxation that would be triggered by corporation status.[11] As of 2020, the BLLC status was only available in five states: Delaware, Maryland, Pennsylvania, Oregon, and Utah.[12] There are important differences by state with this form.

Certified B Corps are different from benefit corporations in that a Certified B Corp is not a statutory designation but rather a certification conducted by the private nonprofit organization, B Lab. Organizations of any legal status can be certified by BLab. Certified B Corps must meet certain qualifications measured by BLab's Impact assessment test.

Recertification is required every three years. This certification is beneficial for an organization looking to hold itself accountable to a mission and seeking to communicate this mission to its customers without choosing a separate legal designation. This option is advantageous for entrepreneurs who have already started their venture in a traditional legal form. However, there are no tax benefits with this choice.

A *low profit limited liability corporation (L3C)* is a for-profit social enterprise form that incentivizes investment from the philanthropic sector. The statutory language of the L3C enables financing via program-related investments (PRIs).[13] These are tax-exempt investments from the philanthropic sector for a social purpose. It was hoped that since the creation of the L3C, the IRS would deem all investment in L3Cs to be tax exempt, thereby incentivizing investment in the entity. However, as of 2020, the IRS had not yet made this designation. As a result, the form has been less popular than expected. The L3C is available only in eight states. This form protects owners through limited liability and has pass-through tax status.

A *worker-owned cooperative corporation* is defined as a "values-driven business that puts worker and community benefit at the core of their purpose."[14] A worker cooperative may operate using a specific legal designation that is only available in 6 states, a 501(c) (12) tax designation, or an organization of any legal form that elects to adopt cooperative principles.[15] In a worker-owned cooperative, all employees have an equal share of equity in the organization and an equal vote in organizational decisions.[16] Moreover, only workers can have equity, which minimizes the impact of outside decision-makers while also limiting investments it might attract. While cooperatives may still have a hierarchical system, most work using a representative democracy approach. A worker cooperative that is "operating on a cooperative basis" benefits from pass-through tax status so dividends distributed to worker owners are only taxed once at the organizational level.[17]

Legal Forms of Organization Globally

Most developed countries have forms of incorporation that are roughly equivalent to the for-profit and nonprofit organization types in the United States with respect to liability and tax treatment. For example, Brazil, China, Germany, and Israel all have forms of sole proprietorship, limited liability companies, and corporations, although the names of different types of organizations are different in different countries. There is no reliable estimate of the global count of for-profit entities.

Some countries have similar hybrid forms to those discussed above. For example, the United Kingdom established a legal form called Community Interest Corporation in 2005, enabling organizations that operate like for-profit corporations but with legally embedded social missions. In other countries, such as New Zealand, a variety of organizations are advocating for a hybrid that fills the gap between traditional companies and public charities.

In addition, there are an estimated 10 million nonprofit organizations (also called NGOs or nongovernmental organizations) worldwide.

Which Form to Choose?

Important considerations for founders deciding what kind of entity to choose include: control (determining who has ownership interests and decision rights) and access to capital markets. Charitable organizations are owned in trust for the public good so there are no shareholders and decisions are made by a board of directors that is responsible for ensuring the organization meets its charitable purpose. These characteristics limit the ability of nonprofits to attract private capital. In short:

- The reasons to consider a nonprofit form include tax-exempt status, access to philanthropic donations, and inspiring trust.
- The reasons to consider a for-profit form of organization include control, simplicity of formation, ease of financing, the ability to build equity, and the ability to change direction more easily to respond to changes in the marketplace.

Entrepreneurs should consider in advance how they intend to organize investor and ownership rights, which approach to tax treatment of the entity is most desirable, how they would like to manage liability and the complexity and cost of different entity types. Social entrepreneurs should also consider the impact this decision will have on their ability to uphold their social mission when attracting financing. While for-profit corporations can transition from one structure to another (albeit with potentially steep administrative and legal costs), a nonprofit cannot easily transition to a for-profit (although a nonprofit can establish a wholly owned for-profit subsidiary). A for-profit can be converted under some circumstances to a nonprofit but must clearly demonstrate its charitable purpose.

FINANCING DECISIONS

Mission, capability, and focus are all critically important for a new mission-driven venture. But none of these will lead to success without positive cash flow. Whether an organization is a nonprofit, for-profit, or hybrid, it must rely on an influx of resources in order to survive. Any start-up venture should carefully plan for where its resources will come from, and what its expenses will be. Indeed, the financial model was a key element of the business model canvas that we developed in Chapter 3. A solid financial plan is even more important for mission-driven organizations for three reasons: they often find it more difficult to secure revenues and investments while staying true to their mission, financial stability is essential since they often provide important resources for vulnerable people, and they are generally held to higher standards of accountability.

A simple way to think about how start-up organizations are financed is illustrated in Figure 6.1. When a venture is first founded, it almost always incurs expenses before it experiences **positive cash flow**, which is a surplus of revenue over expenses. Initial expenses include formation expenses, office set up expenses, research and development, product development, and early marketing expenses. Up-front costs might be covered by investors, founder contributions, or grants or loans from third parties. For example, when One Acre Fund was first established, founder Andrew Youn invested $7,000 of his own money and then along with Matt Forti convinced over 100 of their classmates to donate at least $240 per year to cover initial costs. These funds, combined with business contest winnings, supported One Acre Fund's first year budget of $200,000.[18]

As a venture evolves, it attracts additional resources and continues to incur expenses, resulting in **operating cash flow**. Sources of revenue can include donations (including financial contributions by the founders and others), earned income from the sale of products or services, and donations and "investments" from related or third parties. Investments might be in the form of gifts (as is the case with investments in the GreenLight Fund, profiled in a mini-case at the end of this chapter) or investors may expect a return in the form of either repayment or equity participation if the entity is a for-profit enterprise. Ventures may also secure loans to cover expenses.

Figure 6.1 Cash Flow Curves for New Ventures

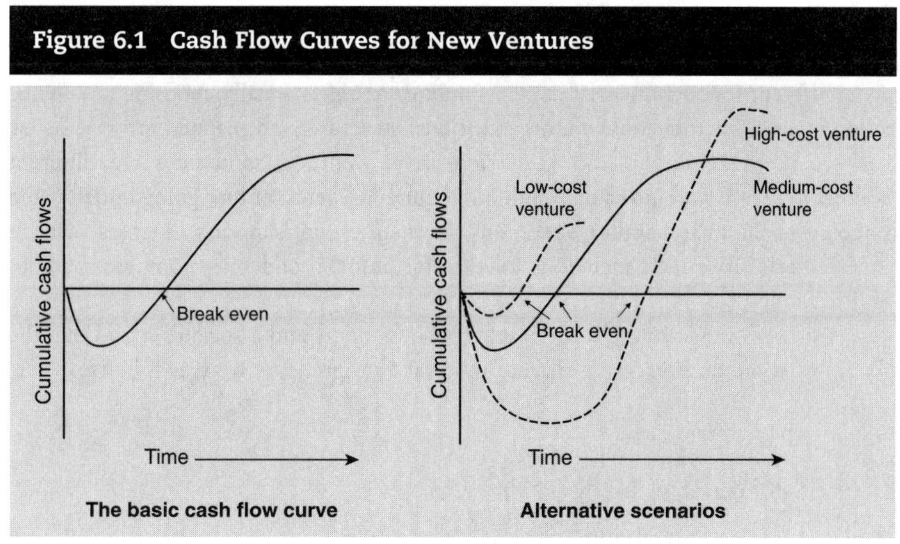

There are many possible cash flow curves, depending on the nature of the venture. One of the reasons to start lean is to make the initial dip in the curve shallower (via frugal operations) and shorten the period of negative cash flow (by using rapid experiments to speed time to market) thereby increasing the odds that the venture will be able to achieve break even before it exhausts its resources.

Every venture should anticipate its unique cash flow characteristics and try to plan its expenditures, or "cash burn," accordingly. Ventures that require few resources such as those that rely on easily developed or replicated technologies can be **bootstrapped** more easily. The line representing low- or medium-cost ventures in Figure 6.1 shows what this might look like.

In contrast, other new ventures will require substantial investments over a long period of time before generating revenues. For example, drug discovery, in which the cost of bringing a new drug to market, can take over ten years and cost billions has a long and deep deficit period. The high-cost venture example in Figure 6.1 illustrates this.

Why do these hypothetical cash flow curves flatten out over time, and in some cases move downward? Even in the best organizations, time erodes market positions. Nonprofit organizations follow this pattern as well. However, agile organizations can avoid this pitfall through continuous renewal (via new or refined products and services or geographic expansion, and possibly by seeding entirely new ventures to meet stakeholder needs.)

SOURCES OF FINANCING FOR MISSION-DRIVEN VENTURES

Funding Strategies

Different founders select different funding strategies, ideally choosing one that is a good match for their mission, organizational structure, and planned growth. As we can see in the examples above, mission-driven ventures sometimes tap different sources to secure start-up capital (funding required to get a venture going initially) and ongoing revenues to support operations. Start-up capital supports expenses that are incurred prior to launch, including, for example, initial product development, facilities and technology.

A survey of over 600 US social enterprise founders and associates found that the five most common sources of capital for social entrepreneurs were as follows:

- Grants (27%)
- Self, friends, or family (19%)
- Loans or debt (18%)

- Angel investors (11%)
- Venture capital (7%)[19]

Sources of Initial Capital and Expansion Funding

As we see in Figure 6.2, social entrepreneurs draw on multiple sources to fund their ventures. Use of *founder capital* is also called **bootstrapping**. It describes contributions from the founder or founding team before the venture achieves a positive cash flow (and in many cases, afterwards). Start-up funding from family and friends also falls into this category. In addition to cash, founders or related parties may provide goods or contribute preexisting intellectual property. For nonprofit organizations, initial founder capital usually becomes a donation to the organization. In the case of for-profits, it takes the form of founder equity or debt if the venture succeeds.

Equity investments are capital contributions made by third parties in return for a share of ownership and anticipated financial returns. Because equity investors are motivated by financial returns, this type of financing is usually available only to for-profit entities. Hybrid organizations may have trouble attracting profit-driven equity investors if the investors are concerned that the social mission of the organization may limit their upside. Exceptions are impact investors, who typically accept a lower return when investing in mission-driven organizations, and who may invest in either nonprofit or for-profit organizations.

Figure 6.2 Typical Sources of Financing for Mission-Driven Ventures

All structures	Nonprofits	For-profits	Hybrids

• Founder capital
• Earned income
  • From customers
  • Via contracts with third parties
• Crowdfunding
• Debt
• Impact investments
• Program-related investments
	• Donations / grants
	  • Foundation
	  • Corporate
	  • Individual
	• Nonequity investors
		• Equity investors
		  • Angels
		  • Venture capital
		  • Strategic investors
		  • Other investors
		• Venture debt
		• Grants
		• Hybrids
		• Investors (equity investor interest may be constrained by limited profit status)
			• Investors (equity investor interest may be constrained by limited profit status)
			• Program-related investments from foundations

Three main types of equity investors are angel investors, venture capital, and strategic investments.

- Angels: These are typically wealthy individuals or groups of individuals, often with sector expertise, who seek out and invest in early stage ventures. They help to fill the gap between founder capital and later-stage investments. Angels contributed an estimated $24 billion to 64,000 US start-ups in 2016.[20] Angel investments vary widely, from $150,000 to over $2 million.
- Venture capital and private equity (VCPE): These investors are companies that typically aggregate investors and use professional staff to identify and invest in high-potential ventures. In 2019, US venture funds raised $46 billion, funding 256 deals.[21] Venture capital is divided into five distinct stages: start-up stage, seed or early stage, growth stage, late stage, and buyouts/recapitalizations (each matches a specific phase on the cash flow curve). Because the venture investing model balances investing in risky early-stage businesses by requiring outsized returns from those that succeed, venture investors are highly skeptical of businesses that seek to balance social and financial goals. Venture capitalists typically only invest in traditional corporations.
- Strategic investments: are investments by organizations primarily for strategic rather than financial reasons. For example, investors may seek to gain future access to a new product or technology.

Impact investments are investments intended to generate positive, measurable impact along with a financial return. The estimated size of the global impact investing market was $502 billion assets under management at the end of 2018; 58% of investments were sourced from US investors.[22] Impact investors include individuals, foundations, pension funds, development finance institutions, and banks. They may do their own investing or hire asset managers to invest on their behalf. Impact investors can be divided into two groups: those that prioritize financial returns (while aspiring to have a social impact) and those that prioritize social or environmental impact while being willing to accept below market returns or take more risks.[23] Impact investors offer a variety of financing options (including equity, debt, loan guarantees, and other types) and invest in both charitable and for-profit organizations. Because those receiving impact investments need to demonstrate ability to repay investments and must have relatively sophisticated impact measurement approaches, these funds are usually available to more established organizations.

Impact investors have diverse investment targets and geographic focuses. For example, as of 2020, the world's five largest impact investors (based on assets under management) are show in Table 6.1.

Table 6.1 Examples of Large Impact Investment Funds Globally

Fund	Assets Under Management	Investment Focus
Triodos Investment Management, Netherlands	$6.5 billion	Manages over a dozen sustainable investment funds. Primary investment areas include renewable energy, sustainable food and agriculture (including organic farming), health care, and education
BlueOrchard Finance, Switzerland	$2.5 billion	Provides both debt and equity financing to businesses and institutions, emphasizing alleviating hunger and poverty, fostering entrepreneurship, establishing food production and education programs, and working on climate change issues
Community Reinvestment Fund, Minneapolis, USA	$633 million	A national (US) nonprofit certified community development financial institution providing small business loans for growth, staff expansion and energy efficiency and also funds community housing projects, health-care centers, charter schools, daycare centers, and small businesses
Vital Capital Fund, Western Europe	$350 million	Invests in developing areas, principally sub-Saharan Africa, in businesses and projects designed to enhance

(Continued)

Table 6.1 Examples of Large Impact Investment Funds Globally (Continued)		
Fund	**Assets Under Management**	**Investment Focus**
		quality of life. It invests in infrastructure, housing projects, agroindustrial projects, renewable energy, health care, and education
Reinvestment Fund, Philadelphia, USA	$126 million (outstanding debt)	A nonprofit community development financial institution, it finances housing projects, access to health care, educational programs, primarily in distressed communities in the United States

Program-related investments (PRIs) are a specialized form of impact investment made by private foundations to extend the impact of their work. A PRI can be counted (along with grants and program support costs) towards the 5% minimum annual payout required of private foundations. PRIs are made with the expectation of returns, but typically at a below market interest rate. A related investment is an MRI (or mission-related investment), which is a social impact–related investment that seeks a market rate of return. The median size of PRIs is $250,000, although the range varies widely.[24] MRI financing can take the form of debt, equity investment, or loan guarantees. The advantage for social entrepreneurs is access to capital at a lower rate. The disadvantage is that borrowers must demonstrate ability to repay the PRI or MRI, which may exclude social ventures with limited track records. In addition, foundations may prefer to fund organizations that they already have relationships with, making them less available to early-stage entrepreneurs. Foundations are the source of over 20% of impact investments.

Nonequity investors contribute to a nonprofit organization to fund start-up costs or operations. The investments can be in the form of donations or debt. For example, many churches loan out a portion of their savings at a below-market rate to provide capital to nonprofits.

Crowdfunding involves using an online platform to solicit investments from third parties, typically to provide initial capital for a venture or new product launch. Popular platforms include Kickstarter and Indiegogo, but there are many others. There are four main types of crowdfunding: donation crowdfunding (used to attract donors), reward crowdfunding (supporters receive a product sample or gift in return for their pledge), debt crowdfunding (which solicits loans), and equity crowdfunding (where a portion of company ownership is given in return for financial support). A benefit of crowdfunding is the ability to raise capital quickly and at a relatively low cost. It can also be a marketing opportunity for goods and services. The disadvantage is that not all campaigns are successful. For example, while Kickstarter has raised nearly $5 billion for successfully launched initiatives, as of 2019, only 37% of posted projects had reached their funding goals.[25]

Debt: is taken on by many ventures either in the start-up phase or to increase liquidity. Two different forms of debt are recourse debt and nonrecourse debt. Recourse debt requires the borrower to pledge personal assets to secure repayment and the lender can pursue any outstanding funds owed to pay back the loan. Nonrecourse debt limits the lender, allowing them only the ability to liquidate certain assets that have been pledged to secure the debt, usually property, but not pursue additional funds such as bank accounts if the borrower is unable to repay their debt. Venture debt is a specialized form of debt that converts to equity after a given period. It is only available to for-profit entities, typically those that are also backed by equity-based venture capital.

While debt is often part of the financial strategy for established organizations, it can be very challenging for newly created ventures without assets or experience to secure loans.

Sources of Funding for Operations

Donations or grants are a large source of funding; most nonprofits rely either partially or fully on donations. Individuals are by far the largest source of donations in the United States ($292 billion), followed by foundations ($76 billion), bequests, property conveyed by a will ($40 billion), and corporate donations ($20 billion.)[26] Although individuals comprise the largest amount of donations, the average recurring annual donation by individual donors is just $326.[27]

The benefits of using donor funds include enabling the organization to better meet its mission, and creating stakeholder relationships that support the organization's mission. For example, donors may also serve as volunteers. The challenge for new ventures is that, without an established track record, it can be difficult to get the attention and support of donors. Securing commitments from both large and small individual donors can be costly, so new charitable organizations should carefully assess their likely appeal to donors and the related cost and benefit of raising donor funds.

While for-profit organizations can seek donations, they are typically unsuccessful. These donations are not tax deductible and donors are usually skeptical about donating to for-profit entities. For-profits must also take care to not run afoul of state laws against soliciting donations without registering with the state attorney general, and must at a minimum make it clear that the entity is not a nonprofit.

Earned income is revenue received in exchange for a product or service. According to *The NonProfit Times*, nearly half of all nonprofit revenues come from fee-for-service (although the figure is skewed by large nonprofits like hospitals).[28] Earned income might cover all of the costs of producing and delivering a product (as is the case for Prosperity Candle), or a portion of the cost (for example, Healthworks Community Fitness). It is useful to think about earned income as falling on a spectrum, from covering the full cost of operations to covering none and relying on full philanthropic support.[29] Earned income can come from customers who purchase a venture's products or services, customers who purchase products, or from interested third parties (for example, through government contracts).

An example of an organization that uses fees for partial operating support is One Acre Fund, which charges a cost-based fee to farmers that use its agricultural support products but covers corporate expenses through donations.

Earned income can also be used to subsidize services to a subset of consumers. An example of an organization charging a sliding scale fee is Aravind Eye Hospital in India. The hospital provides glaucoma surgery at market rates for patients who can afford to pay and at a low cost or free for those who cannot, relying on the benefits of scale and efficiency to make their financial model work. There are both advantages and disadvantages to charging recipients fees. Potential benefits include generating income, model testing, encouraging the efficient use of a scare resource, increasing commitment, signaling quality, or screening out those who get less value.[30] However, with some social programs (for example, women's shelters, refugee services, or environmental initiatives), it may not be ethical or feasible to charge recipients.

Government grants and fee-for-services contracts are a common source of earned income for mission driven organizations. According to the Nonprofit Times, in the United States, 32% of nonprofit revenues comes from government sources, over twice the amount that comes from donors.[31] Human services organizations providing housing and social services often operate using government contracts. Benefits include stability during the contract period and the availability of significant funding from a single source. Drawbacks include often onerous operating and reporting requirements.

Social impact bonds are an innovative financing mechanism for financing social outcomes. The first social impact bond was launched by Social Finance UK in 2010 in the United Kingdom, and there are have now been over 160 impact bonds issued in 28 countries.[32] The bonds are securities in which a government agency contracts through an intermediary to pay for defined social outcomes and passes on part of the savings to investors that have provided up-front capital. If the objectives are not achieved, the investors do not see a return and lose their principal. Social impact bonds have been used to finance services that range from preventing juvenile recidivism to reduce chronic asthma in low-income children in Fresno, California. A prominent issuer of social impact bonds is Social Finance US; cofounder Tracy Palandjian is profiled in this chapter.

PROFILE: TRACY PALANDJIAN AT SOCIAL FINANCE

In 2011, Tracy Palandjian cofounded Social Finance US, acting on her belief that successful nonprofits can scale more effectively with access to private capital, enabling them to impact more people and create societal change. She also believed that governments are more effective if they position themselves to invest more in upstream prevention than downstream triage.

Palandjian's path to social entrepreneurship started when she came to the United States from Hong Kong at age 14 as a foreign student to attend high school. She then studied economics at Harvard College, worked for the consulting firm McKinsey and Co., and earned her MBA at Harvard Business School. After a stint in asset management, she joined the global strategy consulting firm Parthenon Group, now Parthenon EY, where she founded the nonprofit practice and worked with foundations and NGOs here and abroad to accomplish their missions. While working at Parthenon, the leaders of Social Finance UK, founded in 2007, approached her to see if she would start a sister organization in the United States to export their approach to impact investing, which centered on the Social Impact Bond (SIB).

Social Finance is an intermediary that mobilizes capital to drive social progress by connecting investors with on-the-ground service delivery organizations, often nonprofits. The organization was an early leader issuing social impact bonds, an innovative funding mechanism that uses an outcomes-based financing model to deploy private capital to fund social interventions that address challenges such as opioid addiction, job training for immigrants, and prisoner recidivism. SIBs work when nonprofits, investors, and governments come together to tackle an issue. They propose an initiative and jointly decide how they will define and quantify success. Investors put forward money to scale up a promising nonprofit initiative, and if specified metrics are achieved, the government reimburses investors. Otherwise, the investors forfeit their capital.

Social Finance has also pioneered Career Impact Bonds (CIBs), where investors provide capital to expand and cover the upfront tuition for career training programs for people who face barriers to education and employment. Participants who graduate and earn salaries over a preset threshold repay the cost of their education through capped payments withdrawn as a percentage of their income over a fixed period of time.

Under Palandjian's leadership, the team at Social Finance performs intensive research and analysis to study the suitability of catalyzing financing within a given issue area and geography. Then, working closely with government and service providers, they conduct due diligence to assess interventions' and providers' strengths and weaknesses. Social Finance locates investors willing to participate, and governments or providers that are willing to use capital to achieve specific impact. This approach resonates with federal, state, and local government officials, as well as sophisticated nonprofits. Although a risky proposition, some investors have embraced the chance to practice impact investing to achieve social impact and financial returns.

By 2020, Social Finance US had catalyzed over $150M across a dozen SIBs and CIBs to address a range of social challenges in criminal justice, early childhood, education, workforce development, health, and homelessness. Sister organizations in four other countries collaborate to share best practices and build recognition for innovative financing options.

Social Finance is guided by a set of core principles: clearly defining and measuring progress toward shared goals, collaborating across the public, private, and social sectors to achieve these goals, and making funding directly dependent on outcomes achieved.

Palandjian's advice for aspiring social entrepreneurs is to get comfortable with risk. But she cautions, "Know your risk. Be clear eyed about the many kinds of risks that come with new financing approaches. It is important to understand the impact vis-à-vis the status quo – or the counterfactual - and avoid the risks of creating unintended consequences for vulnerable people" (T. Palandjian, personal interview, June 27, 2020). She also points out that not every entrepreneurial idea needs to be unique. "Often, as with Social Finance, the way to launch most effectively was to build on the work of others." Finally, she counsels aspiring social entrepreneurs to be authentic: "You can be most effective when you truly believe in your mission, own your results, and trust your instincts" (T. Palandjian, personal interview, June 27, 2020).

DIFFERENT VENTURES, DIFFERENT STRATEGIES

Matching Mission and Financing Strategy

The following examples demonstrate the breadth of strategies used by mission-driven organizations.

Each of these organizations developed a business model and organizational structure that was consistent with their mission and in line with their financing strategy.

Youth Villages

Initial funding: Earned income from government contracts.

Expansion funds: Philanthropy.

Funding for operations: Earned income from government contracts.

When Youth Villages was founded in Tennessee in 1986 by Patrick Lawler, the organization's mission was clear: to provide services that would help vulnerable children and young adults succeed. Since it took over an existing program, there were minimal up-front investments required. From a small residential program for troubled youth, it has become an organization that helps 30,000 children and their families each year. The right funding model was also clear—Youth Villages funds operations through government contracts, supplemented by donor funds. Lawler's decision to incorporate as a charitable organization was also clear, reflecting their mission and the need to build trust with state governments in potential expansion locations. A clear business model and vision has helped Youth Villages expand operations to 13 states.

Genesis

Initial investment: Our Generation Speaks incubator program.

Funding for operations: Donor contributions.

Aspires to be government-supported.

Genesis (profiled in a case at the end of this book) chose a different approach. Founder Dr. Yasmeen Abu Fraiha did not want to charge her target customers for the genetic tests that would help them raise healthy children by avoiding hereditary genetic diseases. She knew that the opportunity was compelling to donors, but her long-term plan was to secure funding from the Israeli health system, which would save millions in expenses if her solution was effective. Her lean approach was to pilot a program initially using donated funds to form strong partnerships, and gain government support after proof of concept.

GreenLight Fund

Initial investments: Founder and donor contributions.

Funding for operations: Ongoing donor contributions, government funding (social impact fund grants)

The GreenLight Fund (profiled in a minicase in Chapter 7) used a different model. The cofounders believed that rather than reinvent the wheel when addressing local needs of low-income children, youth and families, it would be more efficient, impactful, and less risky to replicate nonprofit organizations that had already demonstrated impact and results in other communities. It was clear from the outset that they incorporate as a nonprofit organization and raise donations from high-net-worth individuals. This approach made the most of the passion and connections of the founders.

Healthworks Community Fitness

Initial investment: Corporate parent as a nonequity investor.

Funding for operations: Earned income and donations.

Healthworks Community Fitness is a 501(c) (3) nonprofit organization that aims to provide high-quality fitness opportunities and health education to women and children in Boston neighborhoods in order to prevent and treat chronic diseases, improve health and fitness, and promote well-being and empowerment. This nonprofit gym depends on donations to cover less than half of annual expenses and the balance is covered by membership fees that are charged on a sliding scale (from $10 to $30 per month), depending on member income.

Sanergy

Initial investment: Bootstrapping and business plan contest winnings.

Funding for operations: Earned income.

Sanergy, a start-up founded in 2010 by students at MIT and the University of Nairobi (and profiled in a case at the end of this book), created a network of low-cost sanitation centers in slums and distributes them through franchising to local entrepreneurs. Sanergy collects the waste produced, and processes it into by-products, such as organic fertilizer, energy, and animal feed. The founders funded their start-up in part using prize money gained from winning multiple business plan contests, incorporated as a for-profit organization, believing that this would enable them to scale more effectively. (Sanergy also has a sister nonprofit that enables them to accept donations towards their social mission.)

Funding Models for Nonprofit Organizations

In their excellent article in "Ten Nonprofit Funding Models," the authors lay out ten distinct funding models for nonprofit organizations that match fundraising models with organization mission (Table 6.2):[33]

Table 6.2 Typical Nonprofit Funding Models

Category	Strategy	Examples
Many individual donors	*Heartfelt connectors* utilize the organization's mission that resonates with a large number of donors *Beneficiary builders* rely on donation from those who have benefited in the past. *Member motivators* rely on member affiliation with an issue they care deeply about	Habitat for Humanity and other faith-based organizations with a broad funding base Hospitals that have created a strong connection with donors Many environmental and cultural membership organizations
A small number of large donors	*Big bettors* rely on major grants from individuals or foundations.	Wealthy individual supporters of venture philanthropy organizations. The GreenLight fund is a good example.
Government funding	*Public providers* provide essential social services. *Policy innovators* establish new ways to create value using government funds.	Contracts for human services such as youth training Youth Village's public policy advocacy work

Table 6.2 Typical Nonprofit Funding Models (*Continued*)

Category	Strategy	Examples
	Beneficiary brokers provide government funded services to beneficiaries	Employment services, community health providers
Corporate funding	*Resource recyclers* distribute in-kind donations to recipients	Food bank donations from grocery retailers.
Mixed funding	*Market makers* mediate demand between altruistic donors and recipients *Local nationalizers* that raise funds via national affiliates	Organ donation nonprofits National organizations with local chapters such as the Girl Scouts of America

Source: Foster, W., Kim, P., & Christiansen, B. (2009). Ten nonprofit funding models. *Stanford Social Innovation Review*.

CHAPTER SUMMARY

Entrepreneurs must make important decisions about how they should organize their ventures and how to finance it. Making good decisions about legal and financial structure that fit an organization's mission can make the difference between success and failure.

These decisions are crucial to the structure and survival of an organization. Over the course of the chapter, we reviewed the paths of a number of organizations including OGS (charitable organization), 99DegreesCustom (for-profit LLC), and Prosperity Candle (L3C), as well as others. In each of these examples, the organization made thoughtful decisions about the legal and financial structure that fit their mission best.

There are various forms of legal organization in the United States starting with nonprofit entities, moving on to for-profit entities and briefly discussing specialized and hybrid entities such as benefit corporations and L3Cs and most other countries have largely parallel structures. Often times, the most important considerations for founders when deciding on whether to be a nonprofit or a for-profit organization include control and access to capital markets.

When a venture is founded, it nearly always incurs expenses before it generates revenue. For mission-driven organizations, it can be more difficult to secure investments and operating funds while staying true to their mission. To the extent that social ventures provide important resources for vulnerable people, financial stability is essential. There are multiple financing models pursued by social ventures. For initial capital, many use grants, founder capital, nonequity investments and equity investments, among other sources. Ongoing operations can be funded by earned income, donations, grants, or a combination of sources; there are multiple models for this depending on the nature of the venture.

A few words of closing advice for aspiring social entrepreneurs who are considering the best way to organize and finance their ventures: choose wisely, get good advice, avoid diluting your mission by chasing funding that is a poor match for your vision and make sure that you have considered both the short- and long-term consequences of your structural and funding decisions.

KEY TERMS

501(c) (3) Nonprofit organizations: tax exempt organizations designed exclusively for the purpose of pursuing a social mission, without regard for profit. By operating as a charitable organization, the organization agrees to benefit the public and not individual owners.

Angel investors: typically wealthy individuals or groups of individuals who seek out and invest in early-stage ventures.

Benefit corporation: a legal form that enables corporations to make decisions that protect a specific social mission and broader stakeholder interests, aside from shareholder value.

Benefit LLC or BLLC: mirrors the mandates of a Benefit Corporation but must uphold a specified social mission and consider the concerns of a broader range of stakeholders including customers, suppliers, employees, and creditors.

Bootstrapping or use of founder capital: involves using funds that the founder or founding team, or related parties such as friends and family contribute before the venture achieves positive cash flow.

Break-even: the point at which a venture's initial startup costs and operating deficits are recovered.

Cash flow positive: when resources exceed expenses.

Certified B co*rps*: not a statutory designation, but rather a certification conducted by the private nonprofit organization, B Lab.

Corporations: special entities where the corporation is a separate legal entity, distinct from its owners. The corporation, not the owner, has liability. Corporations must have boards of directors, file annual reports, have articles of incorporation and comply with other regulatory and filing requirements.

Crowdfunding: involves using an online platform to solicit investments from third parties, typically to provide initial capital for a venture or new product launch.

Earned income: the funds required to support ongoing operations and is money received from recipients, customers, or third parties as an exchange for a product or services.

Equity investments: capital contributions made by third parties in return for a share of ownership and anticipated financial returns.

Impact investments: investments that are intended to generate positive measurable social impact along with a financial return.

Lean startup concept: the idea that initial lower levels of investment that preserve cash flow will help new ventures achieve break even.

Limited liability company (LLC): a corporate structure that combines the limited liability features of a corporation with the tax efficiencies and operational flexibility of a partnership.

Limited partnership: a partnership with general and limited partners. The general partner (which can be corporations or individuals) assumes management responsibility and unlimited liability.

Low-profit limited liability corporation (L3C): a for-profit social enterprise form that incentivizes investment from the philanthropic sector.

Nonequity investors: investors that choose to contribute to an enterprise or organization to fund start-up costs or operations. The investments can be in the form of donations or debt, but do not convey ownership rights.

Operating cash flow: cash generated by an enterprise's normal business operations.

Partnerships: business entities with two or more owners. A general partnership is treated as a sole proprietorship for tax and liability purposes.

Program-related investments (PRIs): a specialized form of impact investment made by private foundations to extend the impact of their work.

Recourse debt: requires the borrower to pledge personal assets to secure repayment, while nonrecourse debt relies on the assets of the venture to secure repayment.

S corporations: entities with the tax status of a partnership with the legal liability limitations of a corporation.

Social impact bonds: securities in which a government agency contracts through an intermediary to pay for defined social outcomes.

Sole proprietorship: an individual entrepreneur may select this form of organization in which the business and individual are essentially the same.

Startup capital: the funds required to get a venture going.

Strategic investments: investments by organizations primarily for strategic rather than financial reasons.

Worker-owned cooperative corporation: a values-driven business that is owned by workers.

Venture capital and private equity: capital provided to high-potential organizations by companies that typically aggregate investors and use professional staff to identify and invest in high-potential ventures.

Venture debt: a specialized form of debt that converts to equity after a given period.

IN-CLASS EXERCISES

Exercise 6.1: Legal Structure

(Estimated time 30 minutes)

Purpose

The choice of legal structure is an essential one for a new mission-driven organization. This exercise will highlight the pros and cons of different structures.

Preparation

Have blank copies of the template below.

Process

1. Break into groups of 3–5 ideally teams that have been working together on a venture.
2. Identify alternative legal structures based on the structures described in this chapter. Answer the questions in Figure 6.3 and debate the pros and cons of each option (Figures 6.4 and 6.5).
3. Present your analysis to the class
4. Debrief:
   a. Which structures did you consider?
   b. What were the high-level pros and cons of each?
   c. What else would you need to know to make a decision?
5. Post-class: Continue to refine your ideas. Report back during the next class.

Exercise 6.2: Financial Model

(Estimated time 1 hour)

Purpose

Develop a financial model for a proposed venture (or estimate the financial model for one of the organizations profiled in this book).

Preparation

Each team should have a laptop and blank copies of the template below.

Figure 6.3 Legal Structure Alternatives

Questions	Alternative 1	Alternative 2	Alternative 3	Others...
How does the structure impact my ability to stay on mission?				
How does the structure impact my investment and revenue potential and costs?				
How does the structure impact my relationships with stakeholders?				
How does the structure impact my ability to scale over time?				
Conclusion				

Process

1. Break into teams of 3–5 students, ideally groups working together on a venture. Have a copy of the template ready.
2. Go to GuideStar (www.Guidestar.org—to set up a free account) and find 2–3 organizations in the same sector as the proposed venture and look at their statement of revenues and expenses (search for the organization and click "financials," examples below). Discuss what the revenue and expense components are for these comparable organizations and why. If time allows, go to the forms 990 on GuideStar to see more detailed information on each organization.
   Based on the team's assumptions about the planned venture's activities, revenues and expenses, prepare a five-year estimate of revenue and expenses following the template format.

Figure 6.4 Financial Projections Template

Your Organization: ______________________

Revenue	Year 1	Year 2	Year 3	Year 4	Year 5
Contributions, Grants, Gifts					
Program Services					
Membership Dues					
Special Events					
Other Revenue					
Total Revenue	0	0	0	0	0
Expenses					
Program Services					
Administration					
Fundraising					
Payments to Affiliates					
Other Expenses					
Total Expenses	0	0	0	0	0

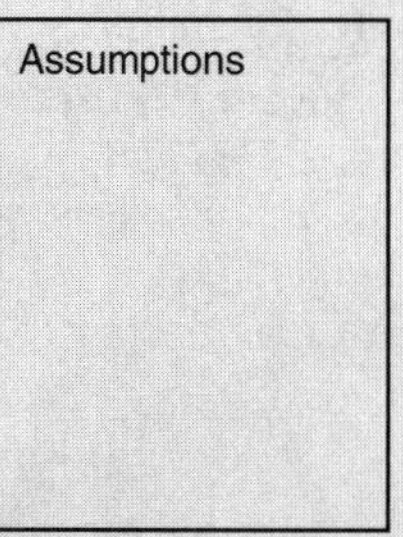

Assumptions

Hint: In making these estimates, it can be helpful to start with the unit economics—the revenue and costs associated with each unit you produce and the estimated number of units per year. To model the overhead costs, start with the number of staff you expect to have each year.

3. Iterate the model until projected revenues and expenses are balanced and the team has confidence in its projections.

Debrief

In class, a few teams should provide an overview of their proposed venture and describe:

a. The venture mission and proposed organizational form

b. What is the financial plan for the venture?

c. What was easy and what was hard about this exercise?

Post-class

If the instructor assigns it, use the template excel cash flow model to calculate cash flow for your proposed venture.

Figure 6.5 Examples From GuideStar

Revenue & expenses | Balance sheet

Youthbuild USA, Inc.
Revenue & expenses
Fiscal year: 2016
SOURCE: Self-reported by organization

Revenue	
Contributions, grants, gifts	$8,622,409
Program services	$18,052,891
Membership dues	$116,850
Special events	$0
Other revenue	$909,758
Total revenue	**$27,701,908**

Expenses	
Program services	$13,532,419
Administration	$3,913,469
Fundraising	$346,060
Payments to affiliates	$10,743,552
Other expenses	$0
Total expenses	**$28,535,550**

Revenue & expenses | Balance sheet

ONE ACRE FUND
Revenue & expenses
Fiscal year: 2017
SOURCE: Self-reported by organization

Revenue	
Contributions, grants, gifts	$55,004,094
Program services	$44,068,539
Membership dues	$0
Special events	$2,039,094
Other revenue	($891,328)
Total revenue	**$98,219,781**

Expenses	
Program services	$61,590,192
Administration	$30,456,484
Fundraising	$3,153,928
Payments to affiliates	$0
Other expenses	$0
Total expenses	**$98,006,834**

Source: GuideStar. Used with permission.

SHORT CASE: PROSPERITY CANDLE

Ted Barber and Siiri Morley sat together in Flour Bakery in the Boston Seaport district. They had just attended a day-long workshop called "Structure Lab" sponsored by the Criterion Institute, aimed at helping young organizations refine their social venture strategies.

The workshop had provided rich information about the pros and cons of organizational structure. As they took a break, they continued to debate their top-of-mind issue: how should they organize and then align the organizational structure and financial model to meet their mission of creating prosperity and reducing poverty for women in and from regions of conflict?

Company Overview

Prosperity Candle was cofounded by Ted Barber and Amber Chand. After working together for many years, they began to meet regularly to think through a new kind of business model that would help women escape poverty in shadows of war. Their goal was to find an approach that, unlike most fair trade and income-generation programs, would enable producers to move beyond a subsistence wage and truly thrive.

The team was well poised to launch the venture. Ted Barber, the CEO and lead investor, had managed and sold a successful import and trade consulting company that specialized in emerging markets, as well as spent a decade working on projects to alleviate poverty through small business development. Amber Chand was a highly respected businessperson who had previously established The Women's Peace Collection and launched "The 100 Women: 100 Hopes Campaign" supporting women who were struggling in Western Darfur, drawing on her passionate dedication to women's empowerment and economic security. They were joined by Siiri Morley, an MBA graduate with expertise in supporting artisanal businesses, whose experience included work at an international consulting firm that focused on poverty reduction and sustainable economic development, and over four years working in various parts of Africa supporting women's enterprise development and empowerment.

Prosperity Candle's founders created a simple yet innovative business model they called "shared prosperity." They envisioned an import, marketing, and distribution business specializing in meaningful gifts that prioritize social benefit to a group that is among the most isolated from global commerce—women entrepreneurs in places of distress—through ongoing support, sustained market access, and regular profit-sharing. They developed the model first and then considered a wide range of products to identify one that could match their criteria for a low-cost, scalable venture. Candle making offered women a highly scalable opportunity, had a huge international market, and could easily be home-based which was important in regions of conflict. As Morley stated, “It wasn’t a love of candles that started it, it was a desire to help women move beyond a living wage to earn a *prosperity wage.* Candles are the vehicle for creating this type of change.”

The social enterprise evolved rapidly, based on the production of high-quality candles that were sold primarily through Prosperity Candle’s website and to corporate partners. Initial production was in Iraq, where they established a field partnership with Women for Women International, an established vocational trainer. They expanded to Haiti following the devastating earthquake in 2010 and established an operation in western Massachusetts that employed refugees resettled from conflict countries. By creating high-quality candles that appeal to consumers and including stories of the women who had produced them with every candle, they were able to create an inspiring connection between producers and candle buyers as well as meeting their goals to provide training, employment, and entrepreneurial skill-building for women.

Organizational Options

With their small management team in place, Barber took responsibility for assessing organization and financing options. The venture had been initially incubated under an existing LLC structure controlled by Barber, but the partners wanted to find the right structure to transition to their next stage and to match their financing model.

With the concerns of risk, measurable impact, and financial growth, the team had to seriously assess the implications of business incorporation. Should the venture incorporate into a traditional nonprofit model or should they venture into the for-profit models? The team had considered four different options:

Traditional Nonprofit Charitable Organization: 501(c) (3) Model

The 501(c) (3) model is the common designation for a public charity. This model was appealing to the Prosperity Candle team due to its alignment with their goals and the provision of tax-exempt status for organization, saving up to 30% in tax expenses. Public and private donations to the organization would be tax-free, and donors could write off the donated amount on their personal income taxes. 501(c) (3) status also lends an air of credibility. However, they were concerned about whether a charitable organization would remain aligned with their mission, and whether bringing in an outside Board of Directors would enable the founders to maintain their focus. Barber had observed that the shifting priorities of donors often steer nonprofits in new directions and wanted to avoid that possibility, recounting: “I had personally witnessed the devastation of a ‘recalibration’ of donor support when I was volunteering in Ghana. A major funder of an economic development nonprofit had decided to update its priorities and as a result, hundreds of families that had given up their subsistence farming for the promise of a better future were left worse off than if they had never participated."

Limited Liability or S-Corporation

Setting up an alternate corporate structure would also be a feasible option, and the founders explored the possibility of an S-Corporation or continuing as within the current LLC structure Similar to the S-Corp, this designation would allow pass-through taxation to the owners, as well as granting limited personal liability.

"Hybrid" Models: L3C & B-Corporations

Two new business structures also held promise. The first, the L3C (Low-profit, limited liability company), was the newer of the two types. Designed to be a hybrid organization between a charity and a for profit business, only a handful of states had the legal designation.

This combination of private investment possibilities and the traditional funding vein of grant writing could help maximize potential fundraising opportunities for Prosperity Candle.

Another option would be to become a Benefit Corporation. B-Corporations were becoming available in multiple states. B-Corporations are required to create a material positive impact on society, evaluate how decisions affect employees, community, and the environment and publicly report their social and environmental performance.

As they assessed these options, Barber and Morley debated which would position Prosperity Candle for growth and discussed whether they would allow for the flexibility needed to distribute profit-sharing as outlined in their business plan.

Fundraising

Another issue central to Prosperity Candle's plans was the fundraising model. The team had considered several options and wanted to make sure that they selected an approach that was feasible, flexible and would enable them to scale. While longer term they intended to use operating revenue to fund operations, they needed capital to build the organization. While they had largely relied on founder capital to start operations, they knew that would not be a sustainable approach long term. As a result, they were in the midst of assessing several sources, or a combination of them:

Foundations: An avenue for many nonprofits, foundations provide grant monies for various uses ranging from unrestricted use, to very specific programmatic or operating functions. Morley had already begun researching different grants and one in particular—the Secretary's Innovation Award for the Empowerment of

Women & Girls (through Secretary Clinton and funded by the Rockefeller Foundation)

Crowd-sourced funds: Kickstarter and Indiegogo might be an option for securing seed capital through customer preorders and customer investment. While the team had serious concerns about the viability and feasibility of instituting this as their primary fundraising avenue, but for purposes of sales and networking, Morley thought this option could open doors that were previously unopened.

Investors/special events: Prosperity Candle had also started to experiment with hosting events and gatherings that help spread the word of Prosperity Candle, where the invited individuals could be potential investors or buyers. The typical model would be a presentation at a restaurant or sponsor's home where potential funders would be invited to learn about Prosperity Candle and make an investment. Initially, the team targeted investments of $10,000 or more, structured as low interest nonrecourse debt. The team also approached prospective lenders individually, usually through personal connections.

Institutional lenders: Among social ventures, there are a number of investment organizations that are willing to provide capital for investment and capacity building, especially when there is an opportunity to create sustainable economic opportunities to those in most need. Companies include RSF Social Finance, Grassroots Business Fund, and similar organizations.

Institutional lenders could also include the US Government. Government-chartered CDFIs (Community Development Financial Institutions) could allocate low interest loans and generous tax credits. Morley knew that Prosperity Candle would be working with refugees in the United States (Springfield, MA), so this avenue would be a viable option, except for the surprising fact that "low interest loans" were starting at a very high rate.

Decision Time

As Barber and Morley discussed the challenge of helping to build a full organization from the ground up, they reflected on all of the situations that had brought them to this point. What type of organization should we incorporate as? The choice of organizational structure would guide the funding model, but with so many choices, what avenue should the venture choose? What funding model would enable Prosperity Candle to pursue its mission and deliver sustainable impact while maintaining flexibility? They were concerned that, as an organization that intended to help people escape poverty, they could do more harm than good if their operating model was not financially durable. They also wondered: How fast could and should the organization grow? How much capital would really be required? Confident in their team, partners, and mission, but unsure of the future, the duo each ordered another cup of coffee and continued their debate.

Discussion Questions

1. What recommendations do you have on organizational structure? What do you see as the pros and cons?
2. What recommendations do you have on financial structure? What do you see as the benefits and risks?
3. How do you think Prosperity Candle's choices will affect their mission?
4. How do you think their choices will affect their scalability?

NOTES

1. USAGov. (2020). *Starting a nonprofit*. Retrieved from https://www.usa.gov/start-nonprofit.
2. Halcyon. (2020). *A step forward: Social enterprise ecosystems in the U.S.* [Brochure]. Retrieved from https://socentcity.org/sites/default/files/seer_2019_brochure_web.pdf.
3. Ibid.
4. Marcum, T. M, & Blair, E. S. (2010). *Entrepreneurial decisions and legal issues in early venture stages: Advice that shouldn't be ignored*. Illinois, IL: Kelley School of Business.
5. Roberts, M. J. (2004). *The legal forms of organization*. Boston: Harvard Business School Case No. 9-898-245.
6. Ibid.
7. U.S. Small Business Administration. (n.d.). *Choose a business structure*. Retrieved November 3, 2020 from www.sba.gov/business-guide/launch-your-business/choose-business-structure.
8. Ibid.
9. Mystica, M. A. (2014). Benefit corporations—the latest development in the evolution of social enterprise: Are they worthy of a taxpayer subsidy? *Seton Hall Legislative Journal, 38*(2).
10. Benefitcorp.net. (n.d.). *What is a benefit corporation?* Retrieved April 11, 2021, from https://benefitcorp.net/.
11. Brown, D., Downing, H., Haghighi, A., & Henriquez-Schmitz, C. (2019). *Mapping the state of social enterprise and the law, 2018–2019 report*. The Grunin Center for Law and Social Entrepreneurship at NYU Law. Retrieved from https://socentlawtracker.org/wp-content/uploads/2019/05/Grunin-Tepper-Report_5_30_B.pdf.
12. Grunin Center for Law and Social Entrepreneurship. (2020). *Social enterprise law tracker*. Retrieved from https://socentlawtracker.org/#/bllcs.
13. Thai, A., Suh, M., Jones, R., & Coleman, F. (2018). *Mapping the state of social enterprise and the law, 2017–2018 report*. The Grunin Center for Law and Social Entrepreneurship at NYU Law. Retrieved from https://www.law.nyu.edu/sites/default/files/upload_documents/Tepper%20Report%20-%20State%20of%20Social%20Enterprise%20and%20the%20Law%20-%202017-2018.pdf.
14. U.S. Federation of Worker Cooperatives. (2015). *Worker cooperative definition*. Retrieved from https://www.usworker.coop/what-is-a-worker-cooperative/.

15. Co-oplaw.org. (n.d.). *What are cooperatives?* Retrieved January 11, 2021 from https://www.co-oplaw.org/co-op-basics/what-are-cooperatives/.
16. *Puget Sound Plywood, Inc. v. Comm'r of Internal Revenue*, 44 T.C. 305 (U.S.T.C. 1965).
17. Ibid.
18. Jones, J., & Augustine, G. (2014). *Innovation at one acre fund: Seeing the forest for the trees*. Northwestern University Kellogg School of Management.
19. Halcyon. (2020). *A step forward: Social enterprise ecosystems in the U.S.* [Brochure]. Retrieved from https://socentcity.org/sites/default/files/seer_2019_brochure_web.pdf.
20. Huang, L., Wu, A., Ju Lee, M., Bao, J., Hudson, M., & Bolle, E. (2017). Wharton entrepreneurship and Angel capital association, *The American Angel*, 1–23. Retrieved from https://www.angelcapitalassociation.org/data/Documents/TAAReport11-30-17.pdf?rev=DB68.
21. National Venture Capital Association. (2020). *US venture capital investment surpasses $130 billion in 2019 for second consecutive year*. Blog - Latest News. Retrieved from https://nvca.org/pressreleases/us-venture-capital-investment-surpasses-130-billion-in-2019-for-second-consecutive-year/.
22. Global Impact Investing Network. (2019). *Sizing the impact investing market*. Retrieved from https://thegiin.org/research/publication/impinv-market-size.
23. The Bridgespan Group. (n.d.). *What is impact investing and why should or shouldn't philanthropists consider it?* Retrieved January 11, 2021 from https://www.bridgespan.org/bridgespan/Images/articles/what-is-impact-investing-and-why-should-or-shouldn/GiveSmart-Impact-Investing-What-Is-It-and-Should-You-Consider-It.pdf.
24. Henriques, R., Nath, A., Cote-Ackah, C., & Rosqueta, K. (2014). *Program-related investments*. The Center for High Impact Philanthropy. Retrieved from https://www.impact.upenn.edu/wp-content/uploads/2016/04/160415PRIFINALAH-print.pdf.
25. Szmigiera, M. (2019, December 3). *Kickstarter: Project funding success rate 2019*. Statista. Retrieved from www.statista.com/statistics/235405/kickstarter-project-funding-success-rate.
26. Giving USA. (2019, June 18). *Giving USA 2019: Americans gave $427.71 billion to charity in 2018 amid complex year for charitable giving: Giving USA*. Giving USA.
27. Nonprofits Source. (2018). *The ultimate list of charitable giving statistics for 2018*. Retrieved from https://nonprofitssource.com/online-giving-statistics/.
28. Hrywna, M. (2019, September 19). 80% of nonprofits' revenue is from government, fee for service. *Nonprofit Times*.
29. Dees, J. G. (1998). Enterprising nonprofits. *Harvard Business Review, 76*(1).
30. Dees, J. G., Emerson, J., & Economy, P. (2002). *Strategic tools for social entrepreneurs*. New York, NY: John Wiley and Sons.
31. Hrywna, M. (2019, September 19). 80% of nonprofits' revenue is from government, fee for service. *Nonprofit Times*.
32. Social Finance. (n.d.). *Social impact bonds*. Retrieved February 2, 2021 from https://socialfinance.org/social-impact-bonds/.
33. Foster, W., Kim, P., & Christiansen, B. (2009). Ten nonprofit funding models. *Stanford Social Innovation Review*.

CHAPTER SEVEN

SCALING AND EXPANSION

If they have a good solution to a pressing social problem, most social entrepreneurs are ambitious for growth. One of the elements that distinguishes social ventures is the nearly unlimited appetite for innovative, workable solutions to a social problem, assuming they can be scaled and funded. As we discussed in Chapter 1, effective social impact entrepreneurs are typically ambitious on two dimensions: they seek to expand social impact while at the same time increasing innovation; scale plays a role in both. In this chapter, we demystify the concept of scale, examine alternative approaches to scaling, and discuss the pros and cons.

Although leaders of mission-driven organizations usually wait until they have demonstrated success to increase scale, forward-thinking social entrepreneurs often consider scaling while developing their initial plans and link this to other inception-related organizational decisions such as the choice of organizational structure, financial structure, and team selection.

Learning Objectives

- Define scale in relation to mission-driven organizations.
- Appraise the advantages and disadvantages of scaling for social ventures.
- Distinguish between different scaling models.
- Explain important issues social venture teams should address when scaling including readiness, fidelity, financing model, and long-term vision.

WHAT DO WE MEAN BY SCALE?

In conventional businesses, securing **economies of scale** means something simple: achieving an economic benefit by being large, thereby spreading shared costs over a larger number of units. Sources of scale-related advantages include the following:

- *Specialized resources and equipment.* Larger enterprises can afford to invest in specialized resources and spread the cost over multiple units.

- *Workforce and management specialization.* It can increase productivity.
- *Marketing and brand recognition.* Higher levels of market power and presence lead to a lower marginal cost for customer acquisition.
- *Financing economies of scale.* Larger organizations can have access to lower-cost financing.

Figure 7.1 illustrates the concept of economy of scale, showing how average cost per unit declines as the quantity produced increases. The figure also shows that after production reaches an efficient level, the average cost can increase. This effect is called a **diseconomy of scale** and occurs if an organization's production becomes so large that the complexity increases average unit costs, or if increased production bids up the price of scarce resources.

A related concept is **economy of scope**, which describes savings gained by producing two or more goods or services, when the cost of doing so is less than producing each separately. This would be the case for a company that launches a distinctly new product while leveraging its managerial capacity, sales, and distribution network or customer relationships related to an existing product, thereby achieving lower overall costs.

Figure 7.1 Economic Benefits of Scaling

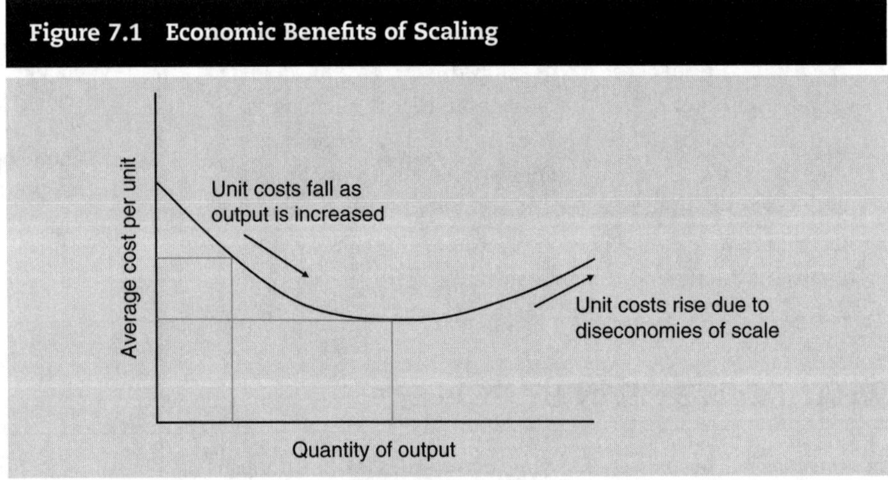

Scaling for Mission-Driven Organizations

Social ventures can benefit from the same **cost efficiencies** and scope advantages as conventional business ventures but, unsurprisingly, their options become complicated as they seek to balance social goal achievement with financial sustainability.

To illustrate these complexities, let's consider the scaling experience of some innovative mission-driven organizations.

Youth Villages is a leading provider of youth services. Its pioneering philosophy, that sustainable long-term success for troubled children and youth is most consistently achieved by working with their families to keep them in their homes and communities, has helped to redefine the child welfare landscape in the United States.[1] After demonstrating initial success, the leadership team's logic for scaling was threefold. First, they believed that Youth Villages' lower-cost, higher-impact model would enable them to meet their mission of helping children and families live successfully. Between 1986 and 2019, Youth Villages expanded from a single site to multiple sites in 13 states (and delivered through partnerships in an additional eight states), employing 3,000 staff and addressing the needs of over 30,000 children and young adults and their families via multiple programs.[2] Second, a larger footprint enabled Youth Villages to have the financial and organizational capability to better serve children and youth by offering a broader range of programs tailored to their needs. And finally, having a larger scale enabled Youth Villages to be better positioned to influence national and state policies.

The Bridgespan Group is a global nonprofit organization that launched in 1999 with a mission to strengthen the nonprofit sector to help achieve breakthrough results addressing society's most important challenges. Bridgespan collaborates with nonprofit leaders, philanthropists, and investors to develop strategies that help nonprofit organizations to improve the quality of life of those in need. To meet its goal of having a transformative impact in the nonprofit sector, Bridgespan first expanded geographically, from a single office in Boston to New York and San Francisco, and more recently established offices in India and South Africa. Yet Bridgespan chose to be intentionally narrow in one important way: by concentrating its efforts on four high-impact areas: education, children, public health, and global development. Bridgespan also works to achieve impact beyond its core consulting services by expanding its reach by developing and sharing knowledge, insights, and thought leadership.

Sanergy, featured in a case at the end of this book, is a for-profit organization based in Nairobi, Kenya, where it has created a franchised network of pay toilets in informal settlements using the collected waste to produce fertilizer, energy, and animal food. The founding team at Sanergy aimed to achieve the economic benefits of scale (reducing per unit costs) and the mission benefits (serving more customers and the community as a whole via improved sanitation) through expansion. Increasing scale has been a key focus because having more toilets enables Sanergy to secure more raw materials at a lower cost and spreads the cost of administration and fertilizer production over more units. These scale benefits have positioned Sanergy to achieve financial sustainability and supported rapid expansion.

Scaling and Organizational Evolution

Successful social entrepreneurs are ambitious when it comes to maximizing social impact. With a good team, a solid business model, favorable market dynamics, and a well-constructed plan, they can position themselves to move beyond operating as a small-scale start-up with limited impact to multiply the social benefits of the products and services they provide. Consider BRAC, which evolved from its inception as a small relief organization in 1972 to today operating in 11 countries and employing over 125,000 people and building on its experience of having reached more than 100 million people around the world. BRAC seeks to deliver on its mission, to "empower people and communities in situations of poverty, illiteracy, disease, and social injustice"[3] by scaling existing, tested innovations that help to lift millions of people out of poverty. Or consider Habitat for Humanity, which was founded in 1976 on a community farm in southern Georgia and by 2016 had become the largest private homebuilder in the United States, all while focusing on helping families build a better future by securing decent, affordable housing.[4]

What enables mission-driven organizations to scale in a way that allows them to achieve this kind of impact? It helps to break down successful growth into stages (Figure 7.2).

Figure 7.2 Stages of Growth for High-Impact Social Ventures

	Phase 1 – Inception	Phase 2 – Prepare for growth	Phase 3 – Growth	Phase 4 – Expand impact
Activities				- Document results - Disseminate information - Extend learning networks
			- Expand operations - Extend network - Measure impact	
		- Document model - Extend funding relationships - Plan for growth		
	- Attract team - Secure financing - Refine model			

Inception: In the early stages of venture formation, social entrepreneurs are keenly focused on getting the model right, assembling supporters, and commencing operations. Indeed, many social ventures never move past this point and operate small-scale programs with limited impact. Those that are unable to financially break even and pivot to growth nearly always fail, often due to poor product–market fit or an unworkable financial model.

Preparing for growth: Ventures that effectively navigate early pitfalls have earned the next step, which is to prepare for growth. This stage involves creating a platform for growth by refining their business model, documenting the operating model, and securing financial resources. For social entrepreneurs, it also requires demonstrating impact.

Growth: In this phase, ventures increase their impact through expansion. As discussed later in this chapter, there are many ways to expand, including increasing their presence in existing markets, increasing scope, expanding geographically, or a combination of these approaches. Organizations may initially select an expansion strategy that gives them a high level of control (for example, by expanding via wholly owned subsidiaries) but as their operations become more codified, aim to expand at lower cost through affiliations or partnerships. This is exactly what Peer Health Exchange cofounder Louise Langheier (who is profiled in this chapter) did by initially creating a network of branch offices but evolved to experiment with an affiliate strategy as a lower-cost way to extend their impact.

Expanded impact via innovation and dissemination: Mission-driven ventures that have successfully scaled may seek to increase their impact by leveraging their convening power, innovation capacity, and intellectual capital to have an even greater impact. Social entrepreneurs typically use this strategy after their organization is relatively mature and is in a position to exert a high level of influence.

DECIDING TO SCALE

Initial Questions to Ask

Social entrepreneurs, when weighing the pros and cons, should ask themselves a series of questions:

- *Why?* What exactly are we trying to achieve?
- *Do we have a scalable solution?* Do we aim to achieve more impact, lower costs, or both?
- *Are we well-prepared*? Have we proven and documented our model? Are we sure it will transition well to the new context?

- *Will key resources scale with us?*
- *Do we risk having a negative impact* on existing providers and constituents in target geographies?
- *What alternative approaches* to expansion should we consider?

Reasons to Scale

For social ventures, motivations for scaling include the following:

Reaching and serving more people. Social entrepreneurs can increase their venture's impact by reaching more people, either by more intense use of existing locations or by entering new markets. If they can deliver products or services virtually, they can also expand (often at a low cost) via online offerings. Crowdfunding platforms and telemedicine providers are good examples of this.

Expanding the organization's impact on current customers. This typically involves creating new products or services that address the needs of existing clients. For example, a microlender might offer mobile banking to better meet the needs of its borrowers. This was what BRAC did when it realized that microloans alone would not create financial independence for impoverished individuals. Recognizing that saving and participation in financial transactions was an important step in helping the unbanked move out of poverty, BRAC developed mobile financial services, and then extended its scope to products as diverse as microinsurance, agriculture loans, health insurance, and other financial services to help its customers.

Scaling can help to *create a more resilient organization.* Larger organizations can attract a broader donor and stakeholder base and higher caliber employees. The additional opportunities that come with increased scale can reduce operational risk and increase brand recognition. This benefits donors (who see more security in the value of their investments), employees (who have more stability and validation), and customers (who can rely on consistent operations).

Scaling can *accelerate innovation.* More specialized staff and deeper knowledge can help organizations innovate more quickly and effectively. Multiple sites can also foster experimentation so when good solutions are discovered, knowledge sharing can bring those practices to other sites. For example, Habitat for Humanity has consistently experimented with developing lower-cost construction techniques and has shared this knowledge with its affiliates.

Cost reduction. It can also be a benefit of scaling. Like their corporate counterparts, mission-driven organizations can benefit from scale-driven cost efficiencies. The ability to access specialized resources such as donor tracking software or employ consistent approaches to measurement can reduce costs and increase capacity. The ability to move beyond a stretched-to-capacity team to a more stable organization can improve morale and reduce costly turnover. Brand recognition can reduce marketing and partnership expenses. And finally, an increased ability to replicate solutions can drive startup costs down.

Disadvantages of Scaling

While increasing scale is a natural path for social entrepreneurs who aim to expand their organization's impact, there are also pitfalls. Astute observers have noted that "even before growth has been considered much less a strategy for growth laid out, social entrepreneurs and their organizations are often pulled into rapid growth by pressure from funders, demand for their products or services and pushed by their social missions to meet those needs."[5] Potential disadvantages of increasing scale include the following:

Mission creep: Poorly planned expansion endangers the clarity and mission focus of any social venture. Originally used in military operations, the term describes a gradual shift in objectives during the course of a military campaign, often resulting in unplanned long-term commitments. In social impact organizations, mission creep is the gradual or incremental expansion of a project or intervention beyond its original goals. It often shows up as "chasing dollars," moving off-mission to pursue commercial opportunities or funder interests. The result is that resources are spread too thinly and reputations are damaged if programs or services are not delivered or are inferior.

Loss of consistency: When an organization invests in geographic expansion, they may face new and challenging market conditions and possibly stakeholders who have a different vision. Ideally, an organization will have done the up-front work to ensure program **fidelity** (discussed in detail later in this chapter) to ensure that its mission can remain fully intact in a new location. But sometimes, blinded by the promises of potential supporters or drawn in by the promise of expansion, a management team does not take the time to fully assess the tradeoffs. Openness to opportunity and experimentation is usually a positive characteristic of the entrepreneurial mindset, but leaders must sometimes gate their enthusiasm to avoid ill-conceived expansion. Examples abound of entrepreneurial nonprofits that "chased the money" to establish new revenue-generating opportunities only to find that the distraction from mission did not justify the benefit.

Reduced focus on and responsiveness to local needs: Mission-driven organizations are often established initially to meet specific local needs. For example, Peer Health Exchange was founded in New Haven to solve the problem of cutbacks in health education in a specific school. Scaling to multiple geographies and expanding product offerings are great ways to magnify impact; if managed poorly, however, these can make organizations less responsive and alienate supporters.

Organizational distraction and stress on limited resources: Expansion can take a heavy toll on organizational resources, and good leaders manage this by making sure that the team is well-aligned around a shared vision and that key success factors are in place.

Establishing far-flung locations can be particularly costly. For example, in 2015, MassChallenge, a leading accelerator for entrepreneurs that we profiled in Chapter 3, was invited to set up shop in the United Kingdom. While they had enthusiastic promises of support, much of the financial support they were expecting failed to materialize, in part because their early success in Massachusetts did not translate well in a different country and culture. They were also surprised by the higher-than-expected cost of operating in London. After two years of operation, they shut down their UK operation. The MassChallenge team learned from this experience however, and has since successfully expanded to Israel, Mexico, Switzerland, and other locations.

MassChallenge's CEO, John Harthorne's advice about entering new markets via geographic expansion is to "set hard timelines and milestones for securing funding, leadership, and other resources, and roll out your commitments commensurate to achieving those milestones. Try to secure a proven leader in situ as early as possible and make sure it is someone you can trust to execute and to share progress assessments honestly. Assume you need 30–50% more resources than you initially calculate as necessary. Launching internationally brings a lot of unexpected challenges since laws and cultures are often surprisingly different, so you may need to adjust your initial strategy multiple times before you succeed. Each pivot will introduce unanticipated delays and costs" (J. Harthorne, email correspondence, July 15, 2020).

Turnover: In nonprofit organizations, the board is responsible for setting direction. If a founder and board are misaligned on their organization's scaling strategy, the result can be unproductive conflict. In some cases, the founder leaves, taking knowledge, connections, and resources with them.

Competition in crowded markets for scarce resources: In the mission-driven world, nonprofit organizations "compete" with other organizations for scarce resources at the same time that they cooperate to create social impact. In addition to serving the same clients, they often approach the same funders or government agencies for financial support. Before aggressively expanding to a new location, the team should thoughtfully consider whether they are introducing new solutions or simply competing with existing organizations. If there are already high-quality providers in place, the organization might consider expanding via partnerships or sharing intellectual capital instead of creating inefficiencies by chasing the same resources as their peers.

Linda Rottenberg learned this lesson when Endeavor, the nonprofit organization she had cofounded, expanded to India in 2007. She had decided to target India in response to pressure from her board of directors to establish a subsidiary to continue their trajectory of successful expansion beyond the near dozen countries they had already entered. As Rottenberg described their experience in a 2011 *Harvard Business Review* article, the logic was compelling: India was one of the world's fastest growing economies, it had an enormous number of newly established ventures, and mentoring young business leaders was central to Endeavor's mission. Endeavor quickly secured half the capital that was needed to launch local operations but after a short time found that multiple competing organizations, both global and home grown, had already entered the market in a way that made it difficult for Endeavor to add unique value. As Rottenberg recounts, "As the leader of a fast-growing organization I know the importance of setting an ambitious course of action and stubbornly following it. But the law of India, to me, is: You can't always will an outcome." She adds: "Sometimes knowing when to shut down a failed initiative is as vital as knowing when to start one. Sometimes embracing failure is as important as toasting success" (J. Harthorne, email correspondence, July 15, 2020).

Reputational risk of poorly executed expansion: Every time an organization expands, it takes on a new set of risks. These might involve the level of local support it can secure, how well calibrated its products or services are to a new market, the level of competition, the regulatory context, how well it can attract a qualified team, and how effectively a subsidiary can be managed at a distance. If something goes wrong, it can damage the reputation of the parent organization.

SCALING MODELS

Social entrepreneurs have multiple options for scaling, each with an array of advantages and disadvantages:

Meeting Untapped Demand by Expanding Locally

One alternative a growing organization should consider is "growing in" by expanding to meet untapped potential in its current market. Two alternative approaches are as follows:

- Identifying additional customers to serve in the current market and
- Expanding products or services to meet the needs of current customers.

When Michael Danziger, the social entrepreneur who founded the Steppingstone Foundation, decided to scale the organization, he found untapped potential in its home market of Boston. Since 1990, Steppingstone had worked with local fourth and fifth graders, enrolling them in an intense 12-month program that would then place them in top independent and exam schools and support the students through high school graduation.[6] By 2002, they had served over 600 youth and achieved remarkable results—93% of their scholars had been admitted to four-year colleges, compared to the nonparticipating students group where fewer than half graduated from high school and went on to a four-year college.[7] Danziger and his team, assisted by a consulting team from Bridgespan, wanted to expand their impact, and considered whether to expand to nearby cities that had similar low academic achievement rates. But they also wondered whether there was still room to grow in the Boston market. After conducting an analysis that used enrollment data and a series of proxies for untapped demand and assessing the supply of available placements at high-performing high schools, the team concluded that they could expand their mission effectively within their existing service area. When they decided to increase the number of Boston-based scholars, they then developed a strategy for expanding internal capacity by securing additional facilities, information technology, and management capacity.[8]

When Sanergy considered expanding its innovative sanitation solution, the team identified over 1,100 emerging market cities with characteristics that would make them good expansion targets. But before taking on the risk and expense of geographic expansion, they considered the option of expanding in the communities they were currently serving. In addition to selling toilets to local franchisees, Sanergy's management team saw an opportunity to go deeper into their existing market by partnering with proprietors and government agencies. They saw this as a cost-efficient solution to Nairobi's sanitation crisis because they could serve residents at a fraction of what the government would spend on sewers.[9] They also looked for new ways to expand impact by increasing Sanergy's scope and innovated by developing additional products. For example, they created a new technology to safely empty pit latrines owned by others and developed a way to using human waste from their toilet network to breed black soldier flies to use as high-protein animal feed.

Expanding via Owned Branches or Subsidiaries

Many mission-driven organizations have elected to expand via wholly owned branches or subsidiaries. The benefit is maintaining a high level of **operating control**, ensuring close integration among units, and maintaining a uniform culture. To successfully expand to new locations, organizations must do two things well: carefully select locations where they can be successful while understanding and integrating effectively with the existing ecosystem (including partners, funders, clients, and governments) in the new location.

For example, Teach for America (TFA) was founded by Wendy Kopp in 1990 based on ideas from her 1989 undergraduate thesis. Today, TFA operates in 52 communities across six regions. 6,000 young people participate in TFA each year, assigned as teachers at sites across the United States. The organization operates as a single nonprofit. Similarly, City Year was founded in 1988 as a national service program with a goal of uniting young adults from diverse backgrounds in a year-long full-time community service program. City Year operates in 29 US cities as well as South Africa and the United Kingdom. Its strong culture includes its visible red jackets, exercise routines, and cheers. It, too, operates as a single entity.

Why would TFA and City Year each choose to expand under a single corporate structure? A combination of factors made this a natural choice. Both organizations have a centralized funding model, relying primarily on government support, national foundations, and large corporate donors. Both also elected to have a tightly controlled operating model to maintain consistency, which was an essential element given the large number of young participants broadly distributed across TFA sites.

Expansion via Franchising or Affiliate Structures

In the private sector, companies often use franchising to expand rapidly, improve brand recognition, and avoid capital costs. Restaurants, hotels, and many types of service businesses including tax preparation and senior care use franchising as a growth strategy. When franchising, a corporation (the franchisor) sells the right to operate one or more branded units, typically in a specific geographic territory. For example, in the United States, over 40% of all Starbucks units are franchises. In a typical franchise, the franchisor provides expertise, systems, and an established brand. In return, the franchisee (franchise operator) pays an initial fee, provides startup capital, agrees to abide by contractual requirements, and pays ongoing fees for franchise participation. Franchises vary widely in terms of upfront cost and fees, as well as how tight or loose the franchise restrictions are. The benefit of participating as a commercial franchisee is reducing risk by having an established brand and operating procedures. Downsides include the cost and the lack of operational flexibility.

Similarly, nonprofits seeking to increase their impact can expand via affiliates, where "parent" organizations give or sell the right to offer a particular social program and provide related infrastructure. Affiliates operate under their own corporate structures. Like franchise agreements in the private sector, affiliation agreements define responsibilities that include how the brand can be used. Expanding using affiliates has the benefit of reducing the financial burden on the parent organizations (affiliates are usually largely responsible for local fundraising and often pay a fee) while expanding reach. Compared to creating new branches, using an affiliate approach can make it possible for an organization to scale more quickly. However, a tradeoff is the loss of control that comes from having related but independent organizations deliver services, hire their own staff, and create their own stakeholder relationships.

The I Have a Dream Foundation (IHADF) was established in New York in 1981 when Founder Eugene Lang returned to the elementary school he had attended in East Harlem 50 years earlier. Addressing a class of graduating sixth graders, he promised college tuition to every sixth grader who stayed in high school and graduated. Today, IHADF operates with 14 affiliates in nine states (each affiliate is incorporated as a separate nonprofit) and one in New Zealand. While the initial program design was a wealthy donor "adopting" a class and promising to cover college tuition, affiliates now rely on multiple funding sources and a range of program designs to meet IHADF's mission. There are common foundations that create "fidelity" to a central vision. IHADF programming focuses on four outcome pillars: academic achievement, socioemotional skills, financial literacy, and a robust community of support. But affiliates vary in the specific programs they provide and the extent to which they leverage partners rather than providing services directly. All of the affiliates consider tuition assistance to be central to the model (but use different approaches), all recognize the importance of social/emotional support for students, and all see a strong partnership with schools as central to their success. The national office's roles include providing a central brand, fostering innovation, and sharing of best practices, providing centralized services, acting as a national convener, and helping maintain an affiliate network. Eugena Oh, IHADF's President and CEO, sees this as a way to maintain local support and foster innovation while maintaining a cohesive network, observing "the strength of our program lies absolutely in the talented, passionate, and diverse people we are able to attract to our mission from around the country and world. We believe in a model of 'leading from the center' which allows all stakeholders to develop true ownership over the success of our programs and to invest whatever they can in our dreamers" (E. Ohelo, email correspondence, July 11, 2020).

Habitat for Humanity, one of the largest and most recognized nonprofits globally, has over 1,100 affiliates in all 50 US states and the District of Columbia, and in 70 nations around the world.[10] Habitat for Humanity affiliates are independent local nonprofit organizations that act in furtherance of the Habitat vision, which is to create a world where everyone has a decent place to live. All of the housing construction undertaken by Habitat takes place at the affiliate level. Affiliates agree to support the network as a whole, comply with minimum operational standards, conduct operations within a defined service area, and financially contribute to Habitat for Humanity's housing work outside the United States. A detailed policy handbook lays out policies affiliates must agree to, including standards for governance, financial management, homeowner selection, safety, and use of the brand.[11]

Sanergy has an intriguing composite structure. Most of the pay toilets in its network are owned by individual franchisees who operate their own small businesses. This creates community connection and entrepreneurial opportunities. But Sanergy centralizes waste collection and fertilizer production, thereby generating economies of scale.

There are predictable tensions in an affiliate structure. Affiliates may want to use different approaches and chafe under restrictions created by the national office. They may dislike being required to contribute financially to cover central services. Coordination issues may arise between local and central fundraising. But in practice, organizations usually find an approach that works, with some maintaining a high level of centralized control, and others being comfortable with local adaptation.

Finally, like their nonprofit counterparts, for-profit mission-driven organizations may also use an affiliate approach to expand via separate entities. However, for-profit affiliates don't have the built-in control that comes with having a nonprofit board that is legally required to protect the mission.

Licensing

Licensing is conveying the right to use a brand, know-how, or other intellectual property to another party, typically for either a flat licensing fee or a percentage of sales. Organizations may enter into agreements with manufacturers or organizations whose products are consistent with the social venture's brand image. When nonprofits enter into these agreements, their intent is usually to generate fees and possibly awareness rather than use the affiliation to increase social impact. For example, a private company might license the ability to use the Save the Children logo on apparel, or a well-known environmental nonprofit might license its name or logo to a credit card company that will use it to expand its market. Licensing is also an approach used by nonprofits like universities to charge royalties or fees for the use of intellectual property.

An example of licensing in the nonprofit sector is Mental Health First Aid (MHFA). The Australia-based nonprofit that developed the original model licenses it to affiliates and charges a fee. Twenty-six affiliates in 24 countries are licensees. For example, MHFA USA has used the licensed content to provide skills-based training on addressing mental health and substance abuse issues to 2.5 million people, demonstrating the potential of using licensed content for rapid scaling.

The advantage of licensing is that it generates income for the licensor and can enable the wide distribution of a proven model. The disadvantage is a possible loss of control over an organization's brand. For example, the American Medical Association famously licensed the use of its logo to the Sunbeam Corporation, which then used it on a variety of products for which there was no proven medical benefit. When AMA sought to terminate the deal, they were sued successfully by Sunbeam for breach of contract.

Scaling via Mergers or Acquisitions

Another way for mission-driven organizations to increase scale is through mergers or acquisitions. A merger takes place when two separate entities combine to create a new joint organization, while an acquisition refers to one organization being acquired by another. In the private sector, organizations merge or acquire to gain access to new markets, gain new customers, increase market power, or secure assets, expertise, or intellectual property. However, according to a recent article in *Harvard Business Review*, 70–90% of corporate mergers and acquisitions fail.[12]

Common motivations for nonprofit mergers are improving services, increasing their influence or market power or cost reduction. For example, hospitals often merge to improve their market positions with insurers or reduce costs by moving to common systems. When smaller mission-driven organizations merge, the rationale is usually service expansion. For example, when Boston's Pine Street Inn, a well-regarded shelter for individuals experiencing homelessness, merged with affordable housing provider hopeFound, the intent was to leverage their complementary strengths. Pine Street Inn specialized in job training but not job placement, while hopeFound had job placement services but no training. The combined entities were able to provide a better continuum of services for their homeless constituencies.

Scaling Impact via Knowledge Dissemination and Network Creation

Some entrepreneurial social ventures extend their impact by enabling other mission-driven organizations to succeed. For example, Bridgespan extends the value of its consulting work by providing a vast array of intellectual capital for free online, drawing on its experience and expertise. New Profit, a nonprofit organization founded to make venture investments in promising nonprofit organizations, hosts an annual "Gathering of Leaders" bringing together over 400 executive leaders from across the social impact sector for dynamic, in-depth dialogue and collaboration. As a platform for community building, idea generation, and agenda setting among social entrepreneurs, philanthropists, and other leaders, this gathering has become a critical driver of impact.[13] New Profit also reports that this gathering has sparked or significantly accelerated a number of breakthroughs for participants in their extended community. Initiatives like these can also drive policy change, assembling a critical mass of partners to advocate for change at the state or federal level.

Scaling via Intrapreneurship

Some established organizations scale via **intrapreneurship**, which describes a situation where employees act like entrepreneurs within established organizations. For example, Tanya Accone (whose experience we discuss in a short case at the end of Chapter 10) operated as both a strategist and entrepreneur at UNICEF, one of the world's largest charitable organizations. She established multiple innovative new ventures while working with the support of UNICEF, leveraging UNICEF's scale, reputation, and partnerships to increase the impact of their ventures. Whether intrapreneurship takes place at private companies, government organizations, or nonprofits, there are several benefits including fostering a culture of innovation and driving growth. In addition, intrapreneurship can help organizations attract and retain talented employees who are motivated by the opportunity to create new ventures within established organizations.

PROFILE: LOUISE LANGHEIER: DRIVING IMPACT THROUGH SCALE AT PEER HEALTH EXCHANGE

Louise Langheier is the CEO and Co-Founder of Peer Health Exchange (PHE), a national nonprofit organization that has a mission of empowering young people with the knowledge, skills, and resources they need to make healthy decisions. While studying for her BA in History at Yale University, she cofounded Community Health Educators, the student volunteer program out of which PHE grew.

The program's initial inspiration came directly from an expression of need. When a fellow student Sabrina Baronberg was volunteering in New Haven's Wilber High School, one of the lowest-income schools in the city, she asked veteran teacher Tom Sugrue what was most needed at his school. He responded that they had lost funding for their health program, and their biggest gap was providing basic health education to their students. Sugrue felt that college students would be uniquely positioned to fill this gap since they could relate to young people better than adults, particularly on topics such as sexual health and mental health. Baronberg, Langheier, and four other students gathered in 1999 to form Community Health Educators, a volunteer program that trained college students teach health workshops in high schools like Wilbur Cross. After the early success of the volunteer program, Langheier and another founder, Katy Dion, established PHE in 2003 to replicate and develop the model in other communities.

PHE volunteers teach a 14-workshop curriculum in which students develop skills in decision-making, communication, advocacy, and accessing resources. Today, PHE is a $10 million (revenues) organization with 60 staff and 1,500 volunteers that educate 20,000 ninth graders each year. In 2016, PHE was awarded the Society of Public Health Education Program Excellence Award, an honor given to one organization each year to recognize high quality in health education programming.

Their results have had demonstrated impact. PHE students were more likely to visit a health center, know how to access contraceptives and have greater intention to use them in the future, accurately define what constitutes consent in a sexual situation, and identify the warning signs of poor mental health. 97% of high school principals who participated in the program said they would recommend the program to other schools, and 93% of PHE volunteers said they would recommend PHE to other college students.

Because PHE deploys college student volunteers, the $450 per-student cost of program delivery is very low relative to other health education programs. To finance the model, the team at PHE relies primarily on donations, but also charges a fee to high schools. Their expansion to ten communities across the United States has been via owned sites under a single 501(c) (3) organization. In most cities, programs are supported by a local board and PHE also has a national board that provides high-level guidance.

According to Langheier, PHE's expansion has relied on a mix of strategic intent and opportunism. "We looked for communities with high rates of health challenges, unaddressed mental health issues and a lack of comprehensive health education, where we can also recruit college students that share the backgrounds of the teens and can speak to their experience." At the same time, she notes, "We also sometimes had colleges and health systems reaching out to us to try to address problems they see in their communities, and if we thought we could be effective, we worked with them to establish programs."

Despite PHE's rapid growth and documented impact, Langheier and her team are dissatisfied with the status quo. Well aware of the needs of young people and eager to show up for more young people, she has been working with her team to move to even lower-cost models that will still deliver high-quality results. One approach that PHE is experimenting with is a college affiliate model, partnering with colleges to provide the curriculum that will then implement their curriculum. This cuts the cost per student in half. Another even lower-cost approach involves leveraging technology. Their latest experiment has been for peer instructors to create short, engaging video clips, which they distribute on TikTok. So far, they have had over 100,000 views, but see the biggest opportunity as light-touch follow-up engagement for teens on specific topics.

Langheier offers the following advice to aspiring social entrepreneurs: "I find it helpful to start thinking of the next stage of expansion before we finish the one we are in." She adds: "Try to build in pilots and evaluation early and often—try things before they are perfect so you can really learn what young people want. This can help you be nimbler and more versatile to predict and adapt to new challenges." Her other advice is to "invest deeply in equity work from the start. Especially as a founder that identifies as white, I made the mistake of waiting to truly invest in a diversity, equity, and inclusion strategy until PHE had grown quite a bit. Once we did make the investment, we unleashed a whole new level of diversity and talent on our mission—from the college student young people we train to the staff we hire and the boards who guide us."

ISSUES TO NAVIGATE

Assessing Readiness

Mission-driven organizations that aspire to scale need to ask themselves whether their organization is scale-ready, determining whether they have adequately demonstrated the concept and thoroughly understand what makes it work.

In an influential article on scaling in the *Stanford Social Innovation Review*, coauthors Gregory Dees, Beth Battle Anderson, and Jane Wei-Skillern propose a five-element approach to assessing a scaling strategy:[14]

- *Readiness:* whether a social innovation is ready to expand. This process requires assessing whether the approach is effective and, if the plan is to expand via replication, is not reliant on unique circumstances.
- *Receptivity:* whether a social innovation will be well received in the target community. Many scaling attempts have failed because of unexpected barriers in a new location. An example, discussed earlier in this chapter, was Endeavor's expansion to India.
- *Resources:* whether all of the resource requirements can be met.

- *Assessing risks:* whether the innovation will be able to achieve its intended impact and assessing the negative consequences if it fails.
- *Evaluating returns:* requires an objective assessment of the approach to scaling that will provide high-quality services and maximize impact.[15]

The Importance of Fidelity

Good organizations seeking to replicate must pay close attention to the fidelity of their model prior to scaling. Fidelity describes the extent to which a program adheres to the model of the original program. This means that key program elements retain the same overall approach and quality level and are provided to a similar group of clients.

In his article "Going to Scale," Bridgespan Cofounder Jeffrey Bradach reminds readers that "the objective is to reproduce a successful program's *results*, not every one of its features."[16] This means that the organization must distinguish between the elements that must be intact for an organization to successfully replicate and those that are less important. Bradach provides a list of three elements that an organization must be able to demonstrate: that its theory of change is strong, that its outcomes are promising, and that it has systems in place to track key performance data going forward.[17]

For some organizations, the central competencies involve procedures. These should be tested and well documented and not reliant on local conditions or individual "know-how." Returning to the example of a commercial franchise organization, the franchisees are able to replicate the consumer experience (thereby maintaining brand integrity and reducing risk) by having well-defined approaches to every element of the customer experience. For example, Starbucks has strict standards for its franchisees about everything from the look and feel of its stores to coffee temperature. For mission-driven organizations seeking to expand using a similarly tight operating model, extensive documentation is essential.

Social entrepreneurs should consider: What makes their approach distinctive? What internal or external factors play critical support roles? And what could possibly be changed without jeopardizing impact?"[18] Considering the transferability to different contexts can help social entrepreneurs make key scaling decisions. Maintaining fidelity doesn't mean social entrepreneurs can't adjust a program to match local conditions, but the delivery should remain true to the original mission and critical value-creation elements should remain intact.

How a Social Venture's Financing Model Affects Growth

In their influential 2007 article in the *Stanford Social Innovation Review*, "How Nonprofits Get Really Big," authors William Foster and Gail Fine analyzed 144 nonprofits in the United States that had reached $50 million or more in revenues. The results were surprising: most of the breakout organizations they studied had succeeded by securing funding from just one type of funder. By identifying a recurring, stable funding source that was a natural match for their mission, they were able to scale more successfully than their peers. This research suggests that social entrepreneurs who want to scale should reconsider the conventional wisdom that supports building a balanced funding stream and instead build a focused and disciplined business model that is well aligned with a particular funding model.[19]

Among the high growth nonprofits studied, the largest percentage were funded by governments (40%), followed by service fees (33%), corporate financial and in-kind donations (19%), and individuals (6%). Foundations were the primary funding source for only 2%. The authors also observed that dominant funding patterns existed depending on sector. Governments were likely to be the largest funders of medical research and human services organizations as well as nonprofits meeting the needs of low-income households. Service fees, which often come from governments in the form of contracts, were the primary sources of funding for human services and health delivery nonprofits. Corporate sponsors were significant supporters of food banks and international development nonprofits, often with donations of food and medical suppliers. And individual donations were most likely to dominate for organizations that address issues that touch many people such as environmental or health-related causes.[20]

As we discussed in Chapter 6, social entrepreneurs who seek rapid growth should carefully assess their funding plans, the related choice of organizational structure, and their growth strategy to ensure that their decisions will support rapid expansion. At a minimum, they should understand the financial structure of peer organizations to identify successful growth patterns.

Thinking Long Term

In their influential 2015 article "What's Your End Game," authors Alice Gugelev and Andrew Stern ask nonprofit leaders to consider an important question: what role should your organization play in the overall solution to the social problem it addresses?[21] They discuss the importance of a theory of change and statement of intended impact and observe that this has made the nonprofit sector more focused and effective. But they caution that even the best measurement approaches can fail to specify how an organization will contribute to solving the broad social problem they have set out to address. They ask social impact leaders to specify their end game—what they hope to achieve and how they will contribute—and articulate six specific "end games' for social ventures to consider:

- *Mission achievement:* sector players are able to solve a specific problem, for example, eliminating a disease.
- *Replication:* a social venture invents a powerful intervention and then replicates it by having other organizations adopt it.

- *Commercial adoption:* a product or service with profit potential is adopted by private sector players; microfinance is a good example.
- *Open source:* a social venture invests in research and development that empowers other to implement a solution.
- *Sustained service:* an organization meets an enduring market need efficiently.
- *Government adoption:* a social venture proves its value and is adopted by a government organization to deliver at scale.[22]

For social entrepreneurs, this kind of big picture thinking can help identify opportunities to scale their programs and become more systematic about achieving outcomes. It can also drive beneficial collaborations.

CHAPTER SUMMARY

With a good team, a solid business model, favorable market dynamics, a well-constructed plan, and demonstrated impact, mission-driven organizations can position themselves to grow and multiply the social benefits of the products and services they provide. However, social ventures need to have good reasons for scaling. For some, this will be the desire to serve more people or expand the organization's impact on its current customers. For others, scaling can create a more resilient organization, help to cut costs, and even accelerate innovation. And others may seek to increase their scale to increase their ability to share information or influence policy. Founders need to consider whether scaling is right for their organization, as it is not without risks. Mission creep, loss of organizational fidelity, and reduced responsiveness to local needs are potential pitfalls.

Once a solid foundation is set, venture teams still need to consider the model they will use to scale. Perhaps scaling in their current market is the best option, as the Steppingstone Foundation or Sanergy found. Alternatively, social entrepreneurs may decide to pursue geographic expansion via owned branches or subsidiaries like TFA and City Year or expand via affiliates like the IHADF. Mergers, acquisitions, and licensing are additional options for ventures looking to scale.

Social entrepreneurs should keep in mind that scaling is not for the faint of heart. Those that want to have a meaningful impact naturally seek to push the boundaries of their organization. Social entrepreneurs should select the approach, or sequence of approaches, that are the best match with their venture and has the potential to create the greatest impact.

KEY TERMS

Acquisition: one organization being taken over by another to gain access to new markets, gain new customers, increase market power, or secure assets, expertise, or intellectual property.

Cost efficiencies: the way that a venture is able to reduce expenses by improving the ways they offer or manufacture a service or product—sometimes through economies of scale.

Diseconomies of scale: when the average cost per unit is expected to decline as the quantity produced increase. This can happen if an organization's production becomes so large that the complexity increases average unit costs, or if increased production bids up the price of scarce resources.

Economies of scale: achieving an economic benefit by spreading shared costs over a larger number of units.

Economy of scope: savings gained by producing two or more goods or services, when the cost of doing so is less than producing each separately.

Fidelity: an overarching faithfulness to the central mission of the venture and should be ingrained in all aspects of the organization regardless of location, service, date, or provider.

Growing in: expanding to meet untapped potential in a venture's current market.

Intrapreneurship: when employees act like entrepreneurs within established organizations.

Mergers: takes place when two separate entities combine to create a new joint organization.

Mission creep: the potential that expansion will endanger the clarity and focus on mission.

Operating control: ensures the close integration among units and helps maintain a uniform culture for an organization.

IN-CLASS EXERCISES

Exercise 7.1: Scaling Plan

(Estimated time 30 minutes)

Purpose

Forward-thinking social entrepreneurs should consider how they might scale long term and about the interrelated decisions around financial and organizational structure. This exercise will enable teams to consider how to scale a proposed venture and weigh the pros and cons of different approaches. It builds on the team's business model canvas from Chapter 3 and work done by teams on choosing a structure and creating a financial plan in Chapter 6.

Preparation

Have blank copies of the template below.

Process

1. In groups of 3–5, complete the templates in Figures 7.3 and 7.4 for a proposed venture (ideally a venture that the team has been developing).

Figure 7.3 Scaling Plan

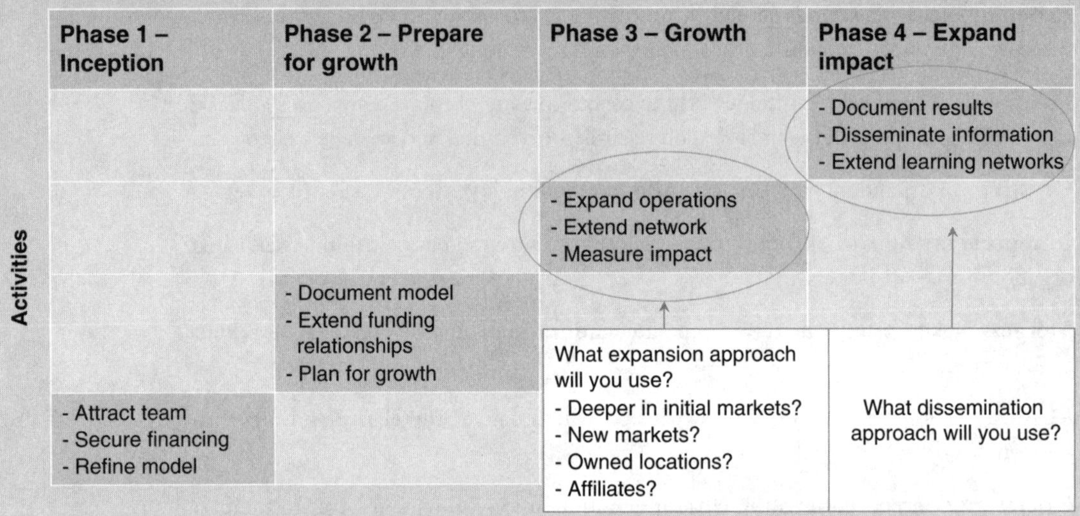

Activities	Phase 1 – Inception	Phase 2 – Prepare for growth	Phase 3 – Growth	Phase 4 – Expand impact
				- Document results - Disseminate information - Extend learning networks
			- Expand operations - Extend network - Measure impact	
		- Document model - Extend funding relationships - Plan for growth	What expansion approach will you use? - Deeper in initial markets? - New markets? - Owned locations? - Affiliates?	What dissemination approach will you use?
	- Attract team - Secure financing - Refine model			

Figure 7.4 Scaling Plan Template

For each phase please estimate:

	Phase 1 – Inception	Phase 2 – Prepare for growth	Phase 3 – Growth	Phase 4 – Expand impact
How big will the team be?				
Projected annual revenues?				
Dominant funding models?				
Planned locations?				
How many customers?				
How many products?				

2. Identify scaling alternatives. Be sure to debate the pros and cons of each. What are the implications for the organizational structure and financial plan?
3. Present the analysis to the class.
4. Debrief:
    a. What scaling alternatives did each team consider?
    b. What were the high-level pros and cons of the scaling approach?
    c. What steps would be needed to establish model fidelity to support expansion?
5. Post-class: Continue to refine ideas. Report back during the next class.

Exercise 7.2: What's Your End Game?

(Estimated time 20–30 minutes, depending on class size)

Purpose

Ideally, social entrepreneurs have a long-term vision for the end purpose of their activities. This exercise will demonstrate the importance of this process—and highlight some of the challenges.

Preparation

Be ready to consider which of the six "end games" listed below:

- *Mission achievement:* sector players are able to solve a specific problem, for example, eliminating a disease.
- *Replication:* a social venture invents a powerful intervention and then replicates it by having other organizations adopt it.
- *Commercial adoption:* a product or service with profit potential is adopted by private sector players.
- *Open source:* a social venture invests in research and development that empowers others to implement a solution.
- *Sustained service:* an organization meets an enduring market need efficiently.
- *Government adoption:* a social venture proves its value and is adopted by a government organization to deliver at scale.[23]

Process

1. In groups of 3–5 students, take 10 minutes to discuss which end game resonates the most for a proposed venture (ideally one for which the team has been working throughout the course).

2. Identify the underlying beliefs that drove the team's understanding of how the venture will achieve its end game. Write these down.
3. Debrief:
   a. Identify the end goal each team decided to pursue. Tally these and identify how many teams selected each option.
   b. Each team reports—what was difficult about identifying an end goal? What was easy?
   c. Each team reports—what are the team's underlying beliefs about how the proposed venture will grow and achieve impact?

SHORT CASE: GREENLIGHT FUND—SCALING FOR SOCIAL IMPACT

Margaret Hall was deep in thought. As she reflected on the sixteen years since she cofounded GreenLight with venture capitalist and entrepreneur John Simon, she had a great sense of pride in all that they and the team had achieved. Still, she worried about expansion. With two new cities moving toward launch and one under early consideration, she felt enormous pressure to make sure that as the GreenLight Fund continued to expand, existing sites continued to thrive and grow and sustain their impact.

GreenLight Overview

Margaret Hall and John Simon founded the GreenLight Fund in 2004 with a simple but powerful idea: how could GreenLight help communities attract the high-impact, proven social innovations they needed when they needed them? They had seen through their own experiences supporting scaling nonprofits the lack of information available to help match scale-worthy and scale-ready organizations to the cities that needed them most. At the same time, communities had no way to find out what was really working to lower barriers to and increase economic mobility for residents experiencing poverty. They believed that by creating a way to match community needs with the most promising social innovations, GreenLight could increase impact in communities and lead to greater efficiency and less risk to replicating nonprofit organizations that had already demonstrated results elsewhere. GreenLight would provide the chosen organizations with the resources and local connections needed to enable them to replicate an innovative program, achieve impact goals, and become sustainable in a new community. Hall recalled:

> *The big idea that John and I brought forward was to help cities address pressing needs of low-wealth residents by giving communities a way to identify the highest priority gaps in services and then find and import the best possible proven approach to*

meeting them. We believed that we could have a powerful impact in cities if we created an ongoing process to find and adapt proven models from other places. The second idea was equally important: if we could build cities' capacity to bring in solutions they needed when they needed them, we could enable enormous efficiencies in the nonprofit sector, and dramatically speed the scaling of good ideas and proven models.

M. Hall personal interview, July 22, 2020

Together, Simon and Hall conceived of the GreenLight Fund as a community-driven "importer" of social innovation. What this meant in practice is that GreenLight was designed as a "method" that communities would use to identify the most pressing systemic barriers to economic mobility affecting children, youth, and families experiencing poverty. This method would then take the community through a process to search the country for high-impact, evidence-based organizations that were addressing those barriers elsewhere in the US and showing results. GreenLight then conducts a rigorous diligence process to select one organization that showed the greatest potential for significant impact in the community and support its entry and early years. In its first eight years of operations, GreenLight imported six organizations that were achieving demonstrable impact on issues ranging from family economic sustainability to youth aging out of the foster care system.

Success and Expansion

GreenLight's success drew national attention and, starting in 2012, GreenLight expanded to eight other cities, averaging one new site per year, in locations that included Detroit, Cincinnati, Philadelphia, and the San Francisco Bay Area. The network operated under a single 501(c) (3).

In each new city it considered for entry, GreenLight pursued a well-defined process. First, they conducted a needs screen, collecting poverty-related statistics such as the density of poverty, the extent of income inequality, the unemployment rate, and school performance metrics. Next, they did an ecosystem screen, which involved identifying and evaluating the philanthropic, nonprofit, civic, and business communities, and their potential as collaborators and partners in the GreenLight model. Simon, Hall and the GreenLight team would have conversations with over 100 local leaders to glean local interest and buy-in before committing to opening a new GreenLight site. A key indicator of interest for GreenLight was when one stakeholder referred them to another, and the momentum continued to build. They also used the process to identify potential new hires since they knew that a local team with roots in the city was essential to their success.

The team, led by Simon, at GreenLight then conducted a funding screen to determine if they could successfully raise the $3.5 to $5 million necessary to expand. This, they knew, would provide the financial stability they would need to operate for the first four years and enable them to select three to four new portfolio investments. Only once the GreenLight team identified that there were pressing needs on the ground, a healthy institutional ecosystem, and secured local funding would they commit to an expansion.

A critical success factor is attracting a Selection Advisory Committee, which is a diverse group of local leaders (business, philanthropic, nonprofit, grassroots, public sector, people with lived experience) that advises the local GreenLight team throughout the selection process. The committee meets three to four times per year to help advise GreenLight on unmet needs in the community and provide connections to additional community resources and expertise. The GreenLight team sources and performs due diligence on potential portfolio organizations. The Selection Advisory Committee then advises on narrowing down the potential organizations based on local fit and ultimately providing input on the final decision. This approach ensures that the new office develops a deep understanding of local needs, and it created a supportive network for a newly seeded nonprofit. GreenLight also recruits an Executive Director with local roots who was deeply committed to the community. That person, along with an associate, drives the work locally and recruits the Selection Advisory Committee.

By mid-2019, after only 16 years in operation, the GreenLight Fund had invested nearly $20 million to support 29 replications of highly effective nonprofit organizations. Collectively these organizations had leveraged GreenLight's initial investment to generate nearly $108 million in additional revenue to fund their program models, reaching over 110,000 program participants each year.

Portfolio Investments

Each local office selected one new portfolio program to support each year. When an organization was selected to join GreenLight, they received a multiyear funding commitment of $600K–800K to import the organization's program model to the new location. GreenLight's local team provided significant support in addition to their philanthropic investment, including placing a GreenLight expert on the organization's local board of advisors, assisting the portfolio organization in hiring the local leader, helping to recruit the local board, facilitating community outreach to key local stakeholders, and providing early-stage operational and management support. The expansion organization benefited from increased scale, a low-risk opportunity to extend their mission and an opportunity to learn through implementation in a new market, and the benefit of being recruited into a new community.

GreenLight's national portfolio of organizations met a variety of community needs, with a focus on the well-being of children, youth, and families, but each selection was highly tailored to critical, urgent needs identified at selection time in the target community. Some portfolio organizations helped children develop early literacy skills, worked with youth transitioning from foster care to independent living, provided employment services to formerly incarcerated men and women, or helped young people to access benefits that would enable them to stay in school and complete their education.

Role of Head Office

The head office's role was to provide a strong and consistent support base that involved providing a playbook and coaching to guide implementation of and fidelity to the Method, managing a learning and support network to help sites run the process and steward local donors, and centralizing data collection and evaluation. They also provided back-office functions for all sites including financial management, human resources, and common platforms such as donor management, communications, and performance data collection.

Hall observed that there is an ongoing conversation and balance to strike around the role of the national office vs. local sites and local site autonomy vs. centralized decision-making that often gets tested: "We hire entrepreneurial Executive Directors who lead their sites through a very community-driven process. Naturally there are areas they want and need to experiment and adapt. There are other areas that require adherence to network-wide policy and decision-making for fiduciary and fidelity reasons. Once you grow past being a small organization where everyone is at the table, you naturally have to deal with decision rights (M. Hall personal interview, July 22, 2020)."

Reflecting on her decision to use a centralized model for GreenLight, Hall explained: "We wanted offices that were highly responsive to local needs, and lean. We did not want to replicate systems and operations that are more efficient to centralize (M. Hall personal interview, July 22, 2020)."

Future Scaling

Hall reflected on the GreenLight Fund and its trajectory:

> *We just opened in our ninth city and are definitely seeing a network effect and pattern recognition site-to-site that is making our work in cities better and more impactful… we haven't avoided all growing pains, but we've learned a lot about*

what works. And she added I'm encouraged that we are benefiting from that knowledge in our current sites and that it helps us open in new cities faster and better.

M. Hall personal interview, July 22, 2020

Despite the encouraging results, she was worried about the pace of growth: "We are facing the challenge that any fast-growing organization faces. We need to make sure that our growth does not outstrip our organizational capacity (M. Hall personal interview, July 22, 2020)." She recognized that building organizational capacity was essential and had already put a management team in place to support such growth. GreenLight had also invested in technology and measurement tools and developed new processes to onboard new cities. Still, she wondered what additional investments would be required to support their continued growth.

Next Steps

After spending so much time deep in thought, Hall met with her team to brainstorm how to best support the two cities they planned to enter in the next 24 months. Excited by the opportunity while aware of the challenge, she stepped up to the whiteboard and started to list their next steps.

Discussion Questions

1. How fast should GreenLight grow moving forward? Preliminary options are: pause after onboarding the next three cities, continue the pace of one new site per year, or accelerate their expansion pace.
2. Was growing through owned branches the right choice for GreenLight? What other models should they consider?
3. What are your thoughts on how Hall has balanced model fidelity with local customization?
4. If you were in Hall's shoes, what would keep you up at night?

NOTES

1. The Bridgespan Group. (n.d.). *Youth villages: Radically transforming the child welfare landscape*. Retrieved July 23, 2020 from www.bridgespan.org/stories-of-impact/youth-villages.
2. Youth Villages. (2020). *2019 annual report*. Retrieved from www.youthvillages.org/about-us/annual-report/.
3. BRAC. (n.d.). *Our vision our mission our values*. Retrieved November 25, 2020, from http://www.brac.net/vision-mission-values.
4. Croce, B. (2016, May 3). Builder 100: The top 25 private companies. *Builderonline.com*. www.builderonline.com/builder-100/builder-100-the-top-25-private-companies.

5. Austin, J. E., Stevenson, H., & Wei-Skillern, J. (2006). Social and commercial entrepreneurship: same, different or both? *Entrepreneurship Theory and Practice, 30*(1), 1–22.
6. In Boston, exam schools are high quality public schools with an exam-based admission.
7. Louh, R., & Campbell, K. (2004, April 6). *The steppingstone foundation: A case study in growing to full potential.* Bridgespan. Retrieved from www.bridgespan.org/insights/library/strategy-development/the-steppingstone-foundation-a-case-study-in-g.
8. Ibid.
9. Sanergy. (n.d.). *Impact*. Retrieved November 2, 2020 from www.sanergy.com/impact/.
10. Habitat for Humanity. (n.d). *Where we build*. Retrieved November 2, 2020 from www.habitat.org/where-we-build.
11. Habitat for Humanity International. (2013). *U.S. affiliated organization policy handbook*. Retrieved from www.hfhwhatcom.org/wp-content/uploads/2013/05/USPolicyHandbook-Non-Proselytizing.pdf.
12. Martin, R. L. (2016). M&A: The one thing you need to get right. *Harvard Business Review*, 42–48.
13. New Profit. (n.d.). *Gathering of leaders*. Retrieved May 7 2020 from www.newprofit.org/gathering-of-leaders/.
14. Dees, J. G., Anderson, B. B., & Wei-Skillern, J. (2004). Scaling social impact. *Standford Social Innovation Review, 1*, 24–32.
15. Ibid.
16. Bradach, J. L. (2003). Going to scale. *Stanford Social Innovation Review, 1*(1), 19–25.
17. Ibid.
18. Dees, J. G., Anderson, B. B., & Wei-Skillern, J. (2004). Scaling social impact. *Standford Social Innovation Review, 1*, 24–32.
19. Foster, W., & Fine, G. (2007). How nonprofits get really big. *Stanford Social Innovation Review*, 46–55.
20. Ibid.
21. Gugelev, A., & Stern, A. (2015). What's your endgame? *Stanford Social Innovation Review*.
22. Ibid.
23. Ibid.

CHAPTER EIGHT

ENTREPRENEURIAL OPERATIONS AND MARKETING

Learning Objectives

- Describe the link between strategic thinking and entrepreneurial thinking for social ventures.
- Apply key concepts in operations management to execution in mission-driven organizations.
- Explain principles of entrepreneurial marketing.
- Assess opportunities to use digital and social media to support social ventures.

In this chapter, we address how social ventures actually work as well as how they connect with their stakeholders and customers. Aspiring social entrepreneurs and their supporters usually get excited about formation issues, but those who are successful know that execution is equally critical. We like to say that the key question in strategy is "are you doing the right things?" while the question in operations and marketing is "are you doing things right?"

While the early stages of social ventures, including creating the business model and securing support, create the foundation for a successful venture, social (and economic) value is created during implementation. This means that founders must pay disciplined attention to operations and marketing, while keeping a close eye on long-term strategic decisions. Doing this is essential for translating great ideas into sustained social impact.

CONNECTING STRATEGIC THINKING AND ENTREPRENEURIAL EXECUTION

The conventional wisdom is that strategic and entrepreneurial skills are different from each other and are usually in conflict. But an examination of high-performance social ventures tells another story: great leaders combine strategic thinking with entrepreneurial execution to create agile, forward-looking ventures. An apt metaphor is that great social entrepreneurs wear bifocals. They are able to see the long view of where things are going, including evolving customer needs and broad shifts that affect the venture such as changes in technology, demographics, and the competitive environment. They pay attention to both emerging issues and "weak signals" that indicate the need to innovate and evolve. At the same time, they carefully manage the here and now with agile and effective marketing and operations. They also manage operations and marketing in a dynamic way via continuous improvement achieved through experimentation, iterative learning, and adjustment.

Figure 8.1 illustrates the interplay between strategy, operations, and marketing. These elements, along with financial management, enable entrepreneurial mission-driven ventures to move from concept to efficient operations, and then for those that are successful, to scale to increase their impact. In effect, the organization's mission is the "why," strategy is the "what," operations are the "how," and marketing is the "who."

Forward-looking entrepreneurs rethink the assumed trade-off between strategic thinking and entrepreneurial execution. By using both simultaneously, founders can position their organizations for long-term success while taking advantage of lean execution opportunities. This is especially relevant for social entrepreneurs, who must often upend traditional approaches to develop new solutions to create social change.

As illustrated in Figure 8.2, we call organizations that rely exclusively on high levels of entrepreneurial execution (but low levels of strategic thinking) *opportunists*. The pitfall is that while they may be able to create and exploit temporary advantages, unless they have a strategy, they will rarely create long-term value. We call organizations that emphasize long-range planning and operational stability *traditionalists*.

Figure 8.1 Strategy, Operations, and Marketing

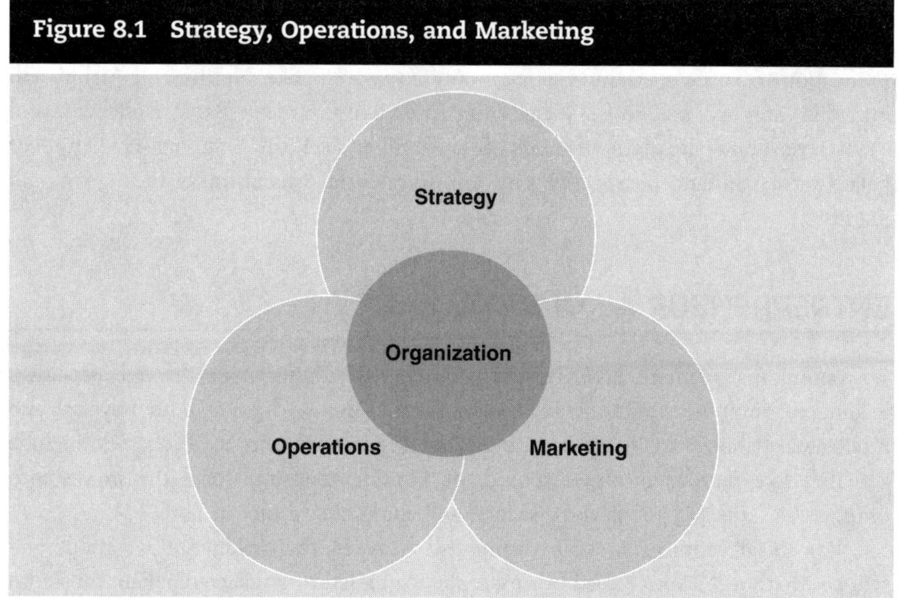

Figure 8.2 Strategic Thinking and Entrepreneurial Execution—Two Models

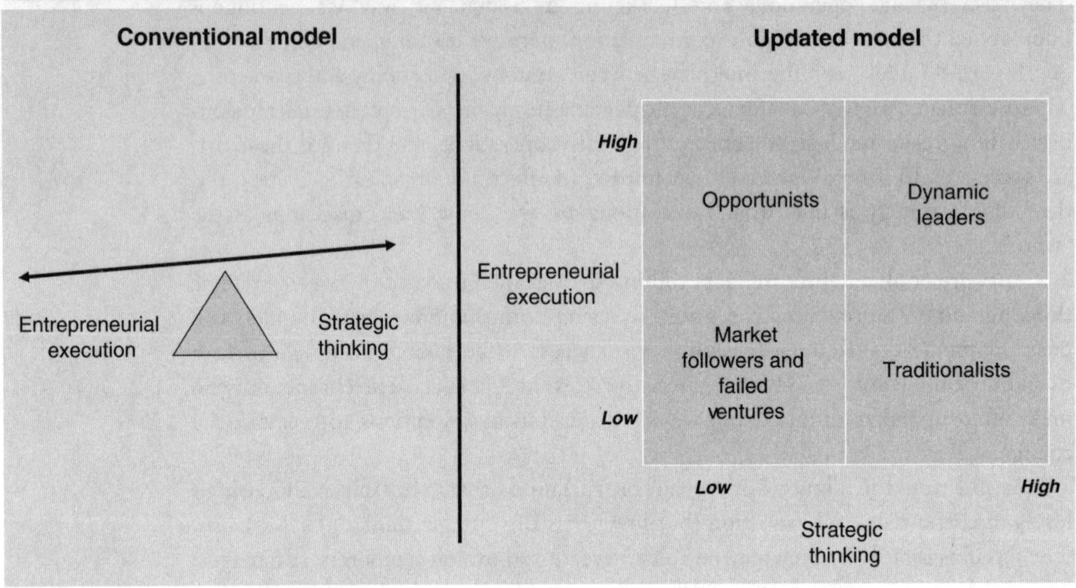

These organizations can be successful but are vulnerable to agile or disruptive competitors. In contrast, organizations that combine entrepreneurial execution with strategic thinking—characterized here as *dynamic leaders*—are able to ride a wave of innovation to success. Many new economy companies like Netflix and Airbnb fall into this category, and so do social enterprises like Grameen Bank, Endeavor, and One Acre Fund. Leaders of these organizations face the ongoing challenge of balancing a strategic perspective and entrepreneurial execution as they grow and mature.

ENTREPRENEURIAL OPERATIONS

Operations management involves taking inputs and adding value through processes leading to outputs. Inputs include raw materials, human inputs (both physical and intellectual labor), facilities, equipment, and other resources. Processes include activities like manufacturing, teaching, or farming that transform the inputs into outputs. Outputs are goods and services, and sometimes a mix of both.

For social ventures, we can distinguish between the production of goods and services that meet a social need (for example, manufacturing insect-repellant mosquito nets) and the production of goods where the social good is a byproduct of the process (for example, the job and wealth creation activities of fair-trade organizations that help artisans get paid more for what they produce).

Operations management is the process of designing, tracking, and continuously improving the processes that transform inputs to outputs. The traditional focus is on increasing predictability and lowering costs. So, what about the intersection of operations management and entrepreneurship? To understand this, we can consider two key concepts: lean manufacturing and agile operations.

A Short History of Operations Management

Operations management today can trace its roots back to the scientific management movement in the United States in the early 1910s and 1920s, that was spurred by Frederick Taylor's influential book *The Principles of Scientific Management.* Taylor was an engineer and manufacturing manager (and later a management consultant) who argued that the goal of management should be to secure maximum prosperity for both the company and each employee, resulting in maximum productivity.[1] After 1918, the Taylorist concepts of labor efficiency underpinned Fordism, named after Henry Ford and referring to his mass manufacturing system for automobiles. The principles behind Fordism included product standardization, assembly lines that allowed unskilled workers to predictably contribute to the final project, and paying a "living" wage to workers (thereby enabling them to purchase the product they produced).

In the United States, World War II spurred a massive retooling of factories from production of consumer products to the production of military products. As an illustration of the magnitude of the transition, in 1941, there were 3 million cars manufactured in the United States, but during World War II, only 139 cars rolled off US assembly lines and instead over 300,000 aircraft were produced.[2] The emphasis, guided by federally sponsored War Production Boards, was on the efficient use of scarce commodities like steel and rubber. These War Production Boards depended on workplace committees that made suggestions for efficiency improvements—presaging a key operations principle, which is to drive continuous improvement based on the knowledge of the people doing the work.

During the postwar economic boom, US factories reverted to mass production of consumer goods, churning out automobiles, appliances, and other consumer goods and even applying mass production techniques to home construction. The Taylorist and Fordism approaches of valuing front-line workforce knowledge were set aside, and the focus shifted to top-down control in most workplaces. Mass production was fueled by high-volume, vertically integrated production techniques and resulting economies of scale as they targeted growing demand from an enormous consumer market.

But in Japan, with a smaller market, scarcer natural resources, and a limited workforce, automobile manufacturer Toyota created a radically different approach that decades later would be called **lean production**. This approach was informed by the work of US expert Dr. Edwards Deming, who had the radical idea that front-line workers could examine samples of their work and be responsible for their own quality, making continuous improvement suggestions through quality circles. While this form of empowerment was rejected by US managers in the postwar years, it was embraced in Japan.

Because land was scarce, Japanese auto manufacturers could not replicate the vast scale of Ford's River Rouge complex, which company leaders had visited on a benchmarking trip. Instead of large quantities of in-process inventory, Toyota began with what we now call a "pull" from the customer and built to order. This required just-in-time delivery at each stage of the production process and an appreciation of the interplay of workers and machines. Two central themes were eliminating waste (including overproduction, excess inventories, excess time, and extra steps) and creating value by identifying improvements that add value for workers or customers.[3] These "lean production" concepts gained a global following.[4]

New Approaches: Lean and Agile

In their influential book *Lean Thinking*, James Womack and Daniel Jones described five key steps that are required to achieve lean operations:

- *Value:* Identify and create products or services that add value for a customer. Create a team to stay with each product through the entire cycle.
- *Value Stream:* Identify what creates value for each product and eliminate the wasted steps necessary to provide it.
- *Flow:* Make the product flow through the remaining steps. Eliminate steps that cause backflow, delay, or disruption.
- *Pull:* Create continuous flow between steps. Supply the work in progress to the next step only upon demand.
- *Perfection:* Continuously improve so that the process becomes even more streamlined and efficient.[5]

Today, these ideas have been extended to health care and many other sectors, with the ideas evolving and adapting in each case.[6] In health care, the optimization challenge is complicated by the multiple independent, but interdependent, parts of a health-care system. For example, different parts of a hospital could all be working with separate operational objectives and pursuing independent improvement efforts, while at the same time interacting with and depending on shared services such as the lab or radiology department in different ways. Similarly, when lean principles are applied to social impact operations, there is rarely just one customer or just one value proposition. Instead, there are many stakeholders, each with their own goals, needs, and expectations. As a result, the delivery of value in the form of social impact involves a constant process of alignment across stakeholders.[7]

Closely related to lean is the concept of **agility**, defined as "a network of teams within a people-centered culture that operates in rapid learning and fast decision cycles which are enabled by technology and a common purpose that co-creates value for all stakeholders."[8] Agile organizations are characterized by quick evolution, the constant introduction of disruptive technology, accelerating digitization and democratization of information, and competition for talent.[9] The term agility has its roots in software development where "agile" software development is used instead of traditional "waterfall" development. The waterfall approach is a linear development cycle, gradually picking up intensity until the launch of new software. In contrast, the agile approach involves constantly integrating user feedback and other considerations, with small and large pivots throughout the development process. Entrepreneurial organizations, with their typically flat hierarchies and collaborative cultures, are well suited to use both lean thinking and agility. As we saw in Chapter 3, lean or hypothesis-driven entrepreneurship is inherently agile.

Key elements of agile organizations include:

- A *common purpose*, co-creating value with and for all stakeholders.
- A *different approach to teamwork*, including cross-functional and self-managing teams and "flow-to-work" pools.
- *Rapid decision and learning cycles.*
- *Empowered employees*, acting as a cohesive community with a common culture.
- *Next generation enabling technology.*[10]

99Degrees, discussed in a short case at the end of this chapter, provides a good example of how both the lean and agile approaches have been used effectively in a mission-driven manufacturing setting. To enable rapid processing of customer orders, 99Degrees uses lean approaches that include flow, pull, and just-in-time fulfillment in its manufacturing processes. But it was the organization's agility, supported by its strong culture and the focus on cross-functional learning championed by founder Brenna Schneider, that enabled it to pivot from sportswear manufacturing to medical gown production in a few short weeks.

A series of techniques based on the ideas of lean and agile have enjoyed popularity at various times over the past few decades. These have included *total quality management* (a customer-focused approach to continuous improvement that extended the quality circle idea and became widely used in the 1980s); *Six Sigma* (an approach to standardizing process quality and eliminating defects that emerged from Motorola in the 1990s); and *supply chain management/supply chain* resilience (applying lean and agile principles to the extended enterprise). These and other approaches help organizations improve processes by aligning operations with strategy, increasing quality, increasing efficiency, reducing costs, and delivering value to stakeholders.

While the lean and agile concepts are complementary, they can be in tension as well. Lean principles depend on the standardization of steps in a process, which is necessary for continuous improvement. It is hard to improve a highly variable system since any improvement suggestion will not have predictable effects. An agile approach is disruptive to standardization so think of lean as what you do in-between agile pivots, with recalibration needed after each agile pivot.

Why are these ideas important? Lean thinking aims to reduce costs and increase value. Agility is used to increase speed, flexibility, and responsiveness. While there can be strain and contradiction between the two approaches, social ventures can employ a combination of both to lower costs and increase quality, service, and flexibility.[11]

Designing for Entrepreneurial Operations

A common mistake that first-time social entrepreneurs make is designing their ventures by first creating an organizational chart. This rarely works out well. Starting with the organization's structure instead of the customer's needs creates inefficiency and misalignment. New ventures need to be agile and early role definition can impair this. Indeed, this is the central tenet of lean thinking, where customer needs "pull" the development and delivery of products or services.

A better approach is to start by carefully assessing what customers want and what they don't care about or can do without. Based on this understanding, the founding team can define the service delivery model and decide where to invest resources. These decisions can be subdivided into production (how the good or services are created) and fulfillment (how they are delivered) and customer interface (how the organization markets, sells and then provides follow-up services to customers). Based on realistic assessments of what is required, the team can design its operations to be tailored to customer needs while minimizing low-value activities (Figure 8.3).

Lean Design in Action: Ekal Vidyalaya

In Chapter 1, we discussed Ekal Vidyalaya, which in less than four decades scaled from a single school to operate 100,000 schools in India. To accomplish this, the founding team developed an inexpensive yet agile approach for operating its rapidly

Figure 8.3 Customer-Centered Design for Operations

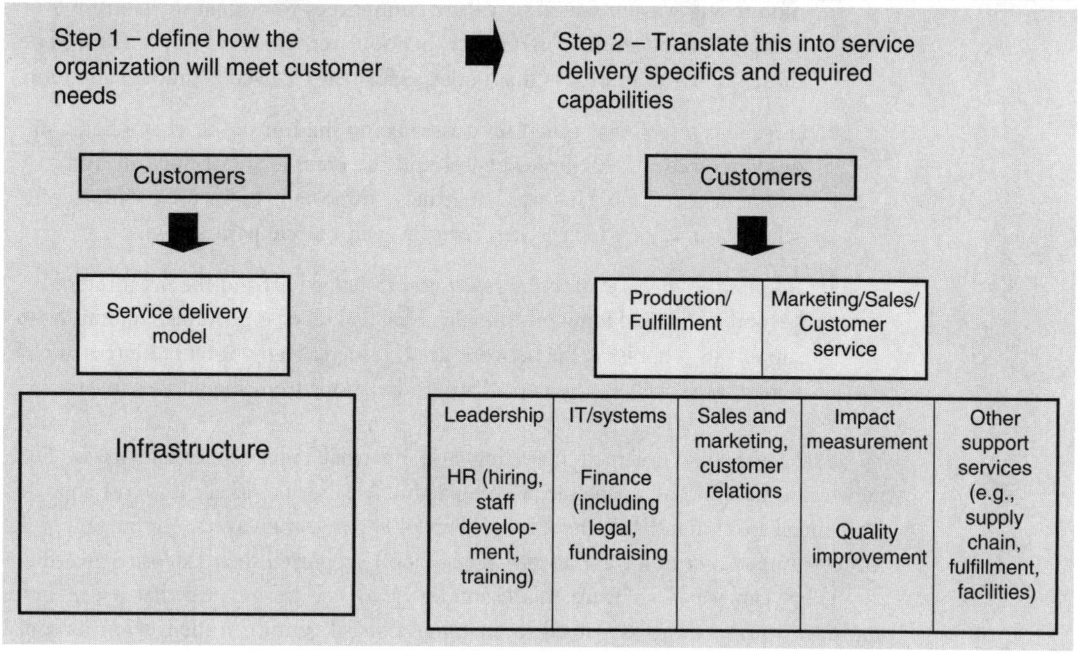

growing, far-flung network of rural schools. Early operational decisions made by the founders included:

- *The use of clusters* to balance efficient management with customization. The network was organized into groups of 30 schools within a 15-kilometer radius or less, enabling an Ekal volunteer to manage a cluster more easily while giving teachers easy access to a supportive peer group.
- *Shared resources*, including developing an expert curriculum focused on several core subjects including language, arithmetic, and health care. The curriculum was customized for local languages and traditions with individualization occurring at the state, cluster, and school levels. This created variability but was necessary to meet local needs.
- *Training to standardize program quality*, which was important to ensuring quality delivery, given the wide variety of teacher skills (many teachers had not completed high school). State-level subject matter trainers trained district-level trainers who each worked with 9–12 clusters providing hands-on support to teachers.

- *Pragmatic use of quality and performance standards and the sharing of best practices* similarly helped to keep individual programs accountable. Monthly monitoring was delegated to village committees to evaluate syllabus completion and student attendance. Schools were graded A, B, or C based on these standards and those that underperformed received additional attention.
- *A low-cost model,* that relied on classes being held in the teacher's home or outdoors, reduced facility expenses and the complexity of building and maintenance tasks. This was particularly important given the locations of schools, some of which lacked road or even bicycle path access.
- *Adapting the financial model to reflect growth* helped expand the organization beyond its original founders. Initially, Ekal had relied on national fundraising to support its schools; as the network grew, it increasingly turned to international donations as well as a greater share of donations from the villages it served.[12]

Ekal's carefully designed operating and financial approach enable its far-flung network to be efficient, adaptable, and impactful. Meanwhile, Ekal's low-cost approach (the annual cost for an Ekal school is less than $400 per year on average, a fraction of the $15,000 annual cost of a rural government school) supported their explosive growth.[13]

What can we learn from this example? Two key lessons are that a deliberate approach to operations is critical to enabling a social venture to deliver on its social mission and that a well thought through operating plan is essential for creating a platform to increase impact by increasing scale.

The Role of Experimentation

In Chapter 2, we discussed where ideas come from and in Chapter 3, we described the role of experimentation in business model development. When it comes to operations, these principles continue to apply: innovation and continuous learning are keys to improving operational efficiency and quality.

Consider TULU, a venture founded by Israeli entrepreneurs Yael Shemer and Yishai Lehavi in 2018. The concept evolved from their early idea of providing shared services, such as internet access and solar energy, to low-income multifamily housing residents in Israel. When they found that their initial plan was not financially viable, Shemer and Lehavi pivoted and created a venture called TULU that provides shared household amenities in apartment buildings, reducing the cost of living for residents and promoting responsible consumption. Initially, they collaborated with building owners to outfit TULU rooms in the basement of large apartment buildings in space-strapped New York and Tel Aviv. Residents could reserve and rent household items like vacuum cleaners, rice cookers, projectors, bikes, and electric scooters on an hourly basis instead of owning them individually.

The cofounders quickly used their experience by adapting to address initial operational challenges that included scheduling (they created a phone-based application) and security (solved via RFID tags). A significant improvement involved shifting from "hard to find" basement TULU rooms to instead using wall-mounted lockers with transparent doors. These were located in buildings' entryways or amenity floors, affording greater visibility and convenience. They also moved from a reservation-based system to an on-demand approach for most items. Subscribers could simply unlock an item using the TULU application on their phone and once the users returned the item, their account would be automatically debited. To increase efficiency by stocking fewer goods, Shemer and Levhai split the product offerings into two groups. Frequently used and highly portable items like vacuums, robotic mops, and mixers were available via the locker system (typically for $1 or $2 for a 30-minute rental), while less frequently used "host" items, like folding tables, extra chairs, and karaoke machines, could be booked for delivery from a back-office location. They also reduced operating expenses by delegating the responsibility for cleaning and basic upkeep to the host building's property maintenance teams.

TULU's cofounders made extensive use of data to adjust their model and enable continuous improvement. Using software that they called the "TULU brain," the team received real time data on the timing and frequency of use. This enabled them to understand customer needs and price sensitivity and to customize item selections at each location based on the demographics of the users. Experimentation also surfaced additional revenue opportunities, including charging fees to product suppliers for data on consumer preferences. In only two years, the use of data and experimentation (along with design thinking and creativity) enabled the founders to create a well-honed business model, setting the stage for future growth.

Leveraging External Resources

When Harvard Business School Professor Howard Stevenson defined entrepreneurship as the "pursuit of opportunities without regard to resources currently controlled,"[14] he was making an observation about how leaders of entrepreneurial organizations view boundaries differently than their more established peers. Entrepreneurial organizations are usually more adept at maintaining fluid boundaries, using outsourcing, contracts, and partners, instead of "owned" resources to help deliver their products and services. For social entrepreneurs, this often means asking volunteers, partners, and stakeholders to take responsibility for some aspects of operations (for example, customer identification, product distribution, or innovation).

By looking outside their organization's boundaries, social entrepreneurs find opportunities to reduce costs, accelerate product development, and secure access to critical resources, particularly during the early stages of their ventures. And, as we discussed in Chapter 4, a robust ecosystem exists to support them—providing mentors, assistance securing pro bono services, and access to resources like hackathons to support product development. This enables social entrepreneurs to preserve what are typically their two scarcest resources: money and time.

Management and Culture

Effective social entrepreneurs pay close attention to building lean and agile organizations. Achieving this requires effective talent management and constant attention to culture, creating open flows of information between customers and managers.

In Jeffry Timmons and Stephen Spinelli's book *New Venture Creation: Entrepreneurship for the 21st Century*, the authors distinguish between entrepreneurial organizations and traditional multilevel organizations that use a command-and-control approach from entrepreneurial organizations. They describe entrepreneurial organizations as "flat—often only one or two layers deep—adaptive and flexible; they look like interlocking circles rather than ladders; they are learning—and influence-based rather than rank—and power-based."[15]

Lean Launchpad founder Steven Blank and the author of *Why the Lean Startup Changes Everything* and *The Four Steps to the Epiphany: Successful Strategies for Products that Win* advises entrepreneurs to develop a "mission-centric culture" (in this case referring to the mission of an organization that may or may not include social impact). He observes that agile organizations operate most effectively with decentralized management and that unleashing employee initiative enables rapid and effective responses to changing conditions. He also observes that mutual trust and communication are critical to making this happen.[16]

What is the takeaway for an aspiring social entrepreneur? Coming up with a great idea and founding a potentially high-impact social venture is only a starting point. The more important test is establishing a scalable, efficient organization that with a strong supportive culture can fully deliver on its social promise.

ENTREPRENEURIAL MARKETING FOR SOCIAL VENTURES

Marketing Basics

Marketers usually follow developing a new product strategy; seeking to gain a clear understanding of market potential and constraints usually follows a specific process. The first step is to conduct a situation analysis to understand the market. A typical approach is to analyze the market using the Five C's:

- *Customer:* Assess what the customer wants or needs.
- *Company:* Determine whether your organization is well positioned to meet those needs (via, for example, product lines, or expertise).

- *Competition:* Evaluate who competes with your organization in addressing customer needs. Do they compete directly or indirectly?
- *Collaborators:* Determine outside sources that will help the company such as distributors, suppliers, or other potential partners.
- *Context:* Understand the benefits or limitations of the context affecting the organization, such as political, economic, social, or technological issues or trends.

Following analysis, marketers progress through five additional steps:

- Use data collection and other market research to fill knowledge gaps.
- Formulate a marketing strategy (using the four or five Ps, described in Figure 8.5).
- Create a detailed plan to execute the strategy.
- Implement the strategy.
- Collect continuous feedback to fine-tune approach and improve marketing implementation.

A simple but important early decision for any venture is establishing who the customer is. As shown in Table 8.1, six categories can describe the venture's high-level market strategy.

What Is Different for Entrepreneurial Organizations?

When it comes to marketing, early-stage entrepreneurial organizations are different from their more established counterparts in a few important ways. First, rather than marketing existing products and services to customers, startup entrepreneurs dedicate their early efforts to creating a business model, developing their products, and establishing initial customer relationships. This process of "building the plane while flying it" uses marketing to identify new opportunities while interacting with customers to test out the venture's assumptions. These interactions enable entrepreneurs to make important decisions about what features to offer, how to price their products, and which channels to use for distribution. As we discussed in Chapter 3, smart entrepreneurs initially focus on creating minimum viable products determining via experimentation the best way to how to maximize value for customers before locking into a single product, design, or business model.

Marketing from scratch also has its advantages. Entrepreneurs can make the first move in establishing their relationships with customers and can be deliberate about the

Table 8.1 Different Types of Ventures

Type	Definition	Example
B2B—Business to business	Provides or sells goods and services to other businesses (which often then ultimately sell them to consumers).	99Degrees (see the short case at the end of this chapter)
B2C—Business to consumer	Provides goods or services directly to consumers.	Conventional microlenders
B2G—Business to government	Government agencies contract for services that are then delivered to individual consumers	HopeWell (see Chapter 5)
B2P—Business to philanthropy	A philanthropy or donor pays some or all of the cost of providing the good or service to the ultimate customer.	Genesis (see case later in this book)
C2C—Consumer to consumer	Customers trade with each other, typically in an online environment (often facilitated by a third party).	Kiva and other crowdfunding platforms
Hybrids	Social ventures use a combination of approaches.	BAMS Fest (see the profile in this chapter) has activities that put it in four categories: B2C, B2B, B2G and B2P

impression they make. They have seen where competitors have been successful or unsuccessful and can learn from their mistakes. They also have the opportunity to establish new systems (such as fulfillment or customer service systems) using the most current technology.

What Is Different for Social Ventures?

Social ventures are unique in several ways. First, the customer relationship may be more complicated. Buyers may or may not be the ultimate recipients of the goods or services produced. As we discussed in Chapter 4, social ventures can have more complex ecosystems than mainstream ventures, often adding donors, volunteers, and recipients to the complex web of stakeholders that traditionally includes customers, suppliers, partners, investors, and employees. For social ventures that are largely funded by donations, donors may be an equal or even more important customer than the ultimate recipient of the product. These, and other important differences, are highlighted in Figure 8.4.

Refining Your Marketing Strategy

A classic tool for making marketing strategy choices is shown in Figure 8.5. It includes four critical elements: product, place (sales/distribution approach), price and promotion, and we've also added a fifth P—people—because of their contribution to brand identity, especially for social ventures.

Social entrepreneurs must be clear about what their *product* is, and whether it is the product itself that creates social benefit (this would be the case for a new vaccine, for example) or whether the process of producing the product has social value (as is the case in fair trade employment). For example, 99Degrees, discussed in this chapter, produces products such as sportswear and wearable technology as well as isolation gowns while creating employment and advancement opportunities for

Figure 8.4 Applying the Five Cs to Entrepreneurial and Social Ventures

Five C's	What's different for entrepreneurial ventures?	What's different for social ventures?
Customer	New ventures usually conduct customer discovery and product development concurrently	Customer identification can be more complex. The recipient of the social good is usually the customer, but a third party is the buyer
Company	Rather than assessing its capability, a new venture can design its capabilities around customer needs	Same as entrepreneurial ventures and can also chose a business model (for example, nonprofit, for profit or hybrid) that aligns with its mission.
Competition	Newly formed ventures can redefine their market space to make competition less relevant. Often competing against nonconsumption	Often less competition exists for social value creation due to limited or no profits, but competition can come from both for-profit and nonprofit organizations
Collaboration	Newly formed ventures have fewer pre-existing contracts so can reconfigure to leverage external resources	Typically have a larger and more complex group of stakeholders and collaborators and need to balance their interests
Context	Ability to take a fresh look and adapt for current and emerging operating context	Challenge of responding to additional contextual factors, e.g., disparities, political shifts, poverty

Figure 8.5 Marketing Strategy 4Ps + People

Product or Service	Place (sales/ distribution approach)	Price	Promotion	People
• Design • Quality • Benefits/ features • Packaging • Services • Other elements important to the venture's value proposition	• Model: B2B, B2C, B2G, C2C, other • Presence: retail, online, franchise, etc. • Sales/ distribution approach: sales force, distributor, other third parties	• Price level • Discounting • Payment terms	• Advertising • Digital marketing • Content marketing • Public relations • Sponsorship/ events • Word of mouth	• Mission congruence ("walk the talk") • Interaction quality • Consistency • Service quality

residents of Lawrence, a disadvantaged community. All three products—which must meet exacting customer specifications—are produced in service of job creation. In contrast, One Acre Fund provides services to smallholder farmers in Africa to help them increase crop yields. Its "product" is a direct service to benefit those it seeks to help.

Founders should keep in mind that even if their product offering is discounted or even offered for free, customers may usually still demand high quality products and services. Consider the case of Healthworks Community Fitness, a gym aimed at helping women in Boston's lower income neighborhoods improve their health through exercise. While the founders created a sliding fee scale based on member income (and initially provided free memberships for women on public assistance), they found through surveys that prospective members valued exactly the same things any health club consumer would: convenient hours, a range of high-quality fitness offerings, an easy to access location, cleanliness, and friendly staff. Despite having a brand-new facility, top-of-the-line fitness equipment, and a supportive community, Healthworks routinely lost clients to competitors that had longer hours, a more convenient location, or a broader range of services.

Place refers to a venture's approach to sales and distribution. For social ventures, this choice should align with its vision for social impact. For example, Mercado Global, a venture we discuss in Chapter 10, imports high-quality hand-woven handbags and accessories from Guatemala and in the process creates livelihoods for members of crafts cooperatives. The founder of Mercado, after experimenting with various forms of distribution, made an explicit decision to employ a B2B model, selling crafts to high-end retailers like Nordstrom. Her decision was a result of her past experience, which showed that this option would achieve the highest profit margin for the items and therefore enable the highest wages for Mercado's artisans.

Pricing decisions can be complicated for social ventures. First, they often have multiple funding sources including donations and earned income. If the customer is the recipient, they may not be able to afford to pay the full cost of a product. For some social ventures (for example, those that protect domestic abuse victims or promote human rights), it may be impractical or unethical to charge recipients. In other cases, recipients can afford to pay a portion or all of the cost of goods or services. This is the case at One Acre Fund, where participating farmers pay a cost-based market rate for agricultural services. (One Acre does fundraise to cover its corporate and innovation expenses.) Or consider the example of Aravind Eye Hospital, which provides high-quality cataract surgery, but on a sliding scale where high-income patients pay market rates, others pay reduced rates, and low-income patients receive services at no cost.

Promotion decisions for social ventures can be complicated because their target consumer audience is usually narrower than a commercial venture's while the stakeholder map is broader. As a result, many social ventures rely less on traditional approaches like advertising and more on targeted outreach like public relations and word of mouth. An integrated communications approach that includes social media is often the most promising marketing approach.

Another complicated question is whether to use the social mission as part of the promotion strategy. In some cases, it can help with marketing; for example, Tom's Shoes leveraged its buy-one-give-one approach to increase sales. In other cases, it can be neutral or negative.

A fifth category is *people*. This refers to those who work for or volunteer with an enterprise. The way team members, whether they are the founders, front line staff, or volunteers, interact with customers and other stakeholders is an important part of the brand. Consistency is critical, and poor alignment between mission and message can damage a brand. For example, when Tatte, a US bakery and café chain, posted messages on social media supporting the Black Lives Matter movement, it was criticized for hypocrisy, as it was accused of itself having a toxic and discriminatory company culture.[17] The CEO had to resign from her role after employees went public with their grievances.

PROFILE: CATHERINE T. MORRIS AT BAMS FEST: USING ARTS AND CULTURE TO CATALYZE SOCIAL CHANGE

Catherine T. Morris was perfectly situated to take on a major entrepreneurial challenge when she founded the Boston Art & Music Soul Fest in 2015. Morris is a Boston native who grew up around creative and entrepreneurial people. Her father was an expert commercial and residential painter, while her mother created playlists on cassette tapes and CDs. Morris is a mother, social entrepreneur, visionary, and a creative strategist who works at the intersection of arts, culture, and creative place keeping.

She gained some of the skills she would use to develop BAMS Fest when she attended Temple University's School of Sport, Tourism and Hospitality Management in Philadelphia. She had little interest in hotels but was drawn to events management. Two influential internships helped her on her path to success. The first was with the Philadelphia Mayor's Office helping to produce events for the Welcome America Festival (one of the largest outdoor free music festivals in the country) where she further developed crucial skills for operating large-scale events: sponsorship solicitation and cultivation as well as persuasive writing. At her second internship with the Philadelphia Film Society, her boss left abruptly, and it fell to her to produce 25 special events for two major film festivals. Later, after receiving a master's degree from Simmons University, and seeing an enormous gap in support for artists of color in Boston, she set out to fill the gap by creating a transformative arts and culture experiences that featured Black and Brown artists and aimed to mobilize and engage local audiences across neighborhoods.

BAMS Fest officially launched in 2015 as a volunteer-run organization and incorporated as a nonprofit in 2016. The first BAMS Festival—held at Boston's historic Franklin Park in 2018—was attended by 2,200 people and featured 21 acts. In 2019, the size of the festival almost tripled to 6,500 attendees. The festival features two separate stages: an art zone where local muralists work live; a dance zone where local choreographers teach dances from the African diaspora; a marketplace of local minority-and-women-owned businesses; and a food truck zone. For financing, the organization has relied on a mix of individual donors, city government grants, sponsorships, and foundations. Fundraising primarily supports paying artists for their time and work as well as sustaining year-around programming.

From the beginning, the largely volunteer-led team at BAMS Fest knew that they needed to market effectively to increase the festival's profile and a number of tactics were used, starting with an eye-catching logo and consistently high-quality graphical design and video. Their intention was to communicate the energy and vibrancy of the festival, using social media including a monthly email newsletter, Facebook, Twitter, Instagram, and a curated Spotify playlist. BAMS Fest also posted artist profiles and performances on YouTube. Morris also recruited MBA student interns to assist with marketing and leveraged the talents of highly skilled individuals who provided focused attention on the festival's social media presence. BAMS Fest also expanded their footprint by offering multidisciplinary programming via their Prelude Series (a traveling, thematic sequence of events meant to encourage audiences to explore different neighborhoods and even their own, all while gaining access to the arts and artists in a relevant and experimental way). This helped increase awareness and anticipation while also creating an accessible taste of things to come.

Since BAMS Fest's inception, Morris emphasized the importance of engaging the festival's audience in multiple ways. For example, food has always been a big part of their year-round programming, in part because it reinforces a sense of community and showcases its cultural diversity.

A very important underlying principle for the team has been that even though they are providing a free experience for attendees, they need to still deeply understand their customers and deliver a polished and highly engaging "product." They also found it important to consider their customers broadly, tailoring marketing not only to the audience but also to the performing artists, volunteers, and vendors.

Morris has an even bigger vision for her organization going forward: using arts and culture as an avenue for social and racial justice. She is working to create a holistic infrastructure for Black and Brown artists, including business development training and market access, in order to help increase their income and diversify their creative portfolio and impact. Her vision is that BAMS will create a "new ecosystem of arts, music, and cultural equity that is inclusive, authentic, and reflective of the people who live and work in the city" (C. Morris, personal interview, November 16, 2020).

Morris' advice for aspiring social entrepreneurs is to "follow your curiosity wherever it leads," observing: "That's where innovation happens" (C. Morris, personal interview, November 16, 2020). She urges founders to "ask a ton of questions, involve a lot of external voices, and establish a mini-brain trust to connect with external stakeholders." Finally, she recommends that nascent entrepreneurs plan carefully for how they will sell their story: "In addition to creating a powerful brand, people won't be motivated by you unless you are able to articulate why your mission is important to you" (C. Morris, personal interview, November 16, 2020).

DIGITAL AND SOCIAL MEDIA MARKETING FOR SOCIAL VENTURES

Social media is an important way for ventures to promote their goods and services. According to the Internet Advertising Board, social media advertising revenues in 2019 were nearly $125B in the United States alone, with growth of 16% over the prior year.[18] In that year, digital advertising surpassed print and TV for the first time. Additionally, by 2023, digital advertising is expected to account for over two-thirds of total media spending.[19] Globally, digital advertising spending was estimated at $325B in 2019 and projected to grow to $389B by 2021.[20] And this is just advertising spending and does not include unpaid social media promotion.

For social ventures, the good news is that it is much easier and less expensive to establish an online marketing presence today than it was in the past. Lower costs, combined with the emergence of inexpensive or free social media management tools, have leveled the playing field for establishing a social media presence. The bad news is that the marketplace is so crowded it is very difficult to differentiate a new venture (Table 8.2).

Stonehill College Professor Xin Wang, an expert on the benefits and pitfalls of using social media to promote social causes, advises social entrepreneurs to choose their platform(s) selectively. While it is tempting to try to spread messages across multiple social media platforms, this can also be time consuming (and expensive). Instead, she advises social entrepreneurs to think strategically about their brand and develop a consistent, multichannel approach based on the platforms their customers use. Tactics include both external messaging (how the organization positions itself to external stakeholders including donors and customers) and internal messaging (how the organization interacts with its internal customers like employees and volunteers), since both shape the venture's brand identity.

Most marketing professionals favor an approach called **integrated marketing communications**, using multiple strategies that reinforce each other. The idea is to convey one clear message, regardless of channel. For example, BAMS Fest invested heavily in their brand messaging up front, creating a compelling brand "personality" reinforced by high quality graphics before developing a detailed promotion plan (X. Wang, personal interview, December 14, 2020).

Digital marketing is the process of creating brand impressions and marketing products and services online. This can include a range of platforms, tools, and content delivery systems, such as: websites, blogs, email marketing, online advertising, social media, videos, and podcasts. Social media often supports a **content marketing**

Table 8.2 Free Digital Marketing Resources for Entrepreneurs

Category	Resources
Resources for nonprofits	• Google Ad Grants • Facebook Social Impact
Email marketing services	• Klaviyo
Website development	• Wix.com • WordPress
Social media keywords research	• Google Adwords
Web Analytics	• Google Analytics
Ad mockup generator	• AdParlor

strategy, which involves creating and sharing online material that does not explicitly promote a particular brand but does provide valuable and relevant content that enables stakeholder engagement and stimulates interest in an organization and its products or services.

Every organization needs a *website* where stakeholders can find it, learn more about it, and get contact information. For social ventures that sell products or services, the website is where they are introduced and where customers can access information. For organizations that sell products or solicit donations, the website can also be a key sales channel. Social ventures should ensure that their website is easy to find and navigate and also includes well-written and designed content. Many organizations use **search engine optimization (SEO)** to improve their ranking on search engines and to help customers, donors, and other stakeholders reach them more easily.

Blogging enables social ventures to increase their website's relevance (and their search results) by adding posts and articles that generate target keywords. Blogs can be part of a content marketing strategy, building relationships with stakeholders by providing them with "sticky," engaging, or useful information. Social entrepreneurs and team members can also increase their venture's profile by writing for external blogs and websites.

Social ventures may also use *email marketing* to reach customers and other stakeholders directly. Emails and newsletters can create and expand relationships, which allows for the sharing of information and encourages purchases or donations. According to Episerver's B2C Retail Benchmark report, in 2019, email had a conversion rate (outreach resulting in a sale) of 2.5% vs. 1.1% for social media. Direct referral had the highest conversion rate of 3%.[21] Email marketing can be especially effective for deepening relationships with donors and volunteers via updates and other outreach.

Some common *online advertising* types include pay-per-click ads in search engines that target terms customers may use. Additionally, some social media sites and applications will use ads on their platform aimed at reaching specific segments of their users. Yet another type of online advertising is that of the sidebar ad. These are often found on other websites and serve as a way of directing interested individuals to relevant third-party sites. Two new emerging approaches involve paid advertising on podcasts and via music streaming applications such as Spotify or Pandora. Both options provide a way of targeting individuals based on relevant interests and/or industries.

The largest players in the online ad space are Google and Facebook, with 37% and 22% of paid online advertising, respectively, in 2019. Amazon has also grown in prominence by featuring paid ads in searches for products or services and in 2019 captured nearly 9% of digital ad spending.[22] Mobile advertising has started to dominate the paid online arena as well—over half of online ads are now consumed on mobile devices and this proportion is projected to grow. In addition to paid results, search engines also generate organic (unpaid) traffic to organizations' web sites. Statistics indicate that the number 1 result in a Google search generates a click through rate of 32%, while the number 10 position generates only a 3% click through rate. If a search result is on the second page, the percentage is reduced to less than 1%.[23] While social enterprises often ignore paid advertising, for those with well-defined target markets, paid advertising via keywords can be a valuable way to attract donors or customers. Also, eligible nonprofit ventures should consider the Google Ad Grants program, which provides grants for up to $10,000 per month in free advertising.[24]

Social media is another way that social enterprises increase brand awareness, improve traffic, and generate leads. It is hard to have a high-quality presence on multiple platforms, so new ventures should consider which ones are most relevant to their target customers and stakeholders. For example, Peer Health Exchange disseminates health information to high school students, so placing short videos on TikTok was a natural way to extend its influence. BAMS Fest found that podcasts and YouTube videos were natural choices for promoting its arts and music agenda because they could convey the richness of the experience. Social media platforms can be divided into five categories:

- *Networking*—for example, Facebook, Twitter, and LinkedIn—all three of which have millions of daily users.
- *Photo Sharing*—Instagram and Pinterest fall into this category and are very effective for hosting visual content.
- *Video Sharing*—such as YouTube and Vimeo. Video content can be used very effectively to promote social causes, but production can be expensive
- *Interactive Media*—including Snapchat and TikTok. These rapid-use, mobile-only platforms include photo sharing, interactive features, and games, often appealing to younger users.
- *Blogging or Community Building*—examples include Tumblr and Reddit as well as blogs hosted on an organization's website. Blogs allow users to post about niche topics and can be particularly valuable for social ventures because they are a good way to convey impact (it is easier to engage readers around a social story than a commodity or product). They are also a good way for social ventures to connect with donors and other ecosystem participants.

Pros and cons of some of the most popular platforms are summarized in Figure 8.6.

Finally, social entrepreneurs should remember that developing and implementing detailed marketing plans is critical to successful branding and promotion.

Figure 8.6 Popular Social Media Platform Pros and Cons for Social Ventures

Platform	Facebook	Instagram	TikTok	Twitter	LinkedIn	Pinterest
Overview	Comprehensive connection, everyday use	Pictures and short video sharing	Platform for sharing user-generated short videos	Microblogging site limits post to 280 characters	Business-oriented social networking	Social site oriented towards lifestyle and style
Monthly users	2.2 billion	1 billion	850 million	326 million	260 million	250 million
Pros for social Ventures	Scale, access to older user base, large global audience	Scale, accessibility	Access younger demographic, rapid growth	Good for bite-sized content and link sharing	Global reach (70% outside US), good for professional sharing	Visual emphasis beneficial for some ventures
Cons for social Ventures	Hard to get noticed without paid ads	Content must be eye-catching to get noticed. Platform allows few links for most users	Emphasis on lip-synch and dance may not match some ventures' messaging	Must post very frequently to get attention	Professional vs. mainstream users	Visual niche, high cost of quality content production, ad-driven

CHAPTER SUMMARY

Operations and marketing can sometimes be overlooked by social entrepreneurs who are excited about forming their new ventures and plotting out strategy. However, doing so is a mistake. While a good strategy and a compelling product are starting points for getting ventures off the ground, a disciplined focus on both operations and marketing is usually the key to long-term success.

Entrepreneurial operations involve taking inputs (raw materials or human ingenuity) and adding value through processes to create outputs (final product or service). Regardless of what you make or do, ventures should always strive to improve their operations management by tracking and continuously improving these processes that transform inputs to outputs. Lean thinking can help ventures streamline operations and increase speed, flexibility and responsiveness.

This chapter also explored entrepreneurial marketing. To develop a marketing strategy, there are six steps that founders should follow well established steps to assess their markets and understand their customers. Venture teams must also decide if they are going to focus on selling directly to consumers, the government, and other businesses or function as a hybrid. A common tool for establishing marketing strategy choices is the five "P" categories (product, place, price, promotion, and people).

Once a marketing plan is formulated, a key tactic is using of social media, one of the fastest growing and most affordable ways of marketing a product or service. However, because the marketplace is so crowded, social ventures must promote a unified message with clear content and choose their platforms carefully.

KEY TERMS

Agility: the ability to operate in a way that allows a venture to rapidly learn and make fast decisions. It is often enabled by technology and a common purpose that cocreates value for all stakeholders.

Competitive advantage: established by creating organizational capabilities that support the choice of a particular competitive position in a way that is difficult for others to copy.

Content marketing: an approach that involves creating valuable and relevant content (such as how-to videos) to attract a defined audience.

Cost leadership: providing the lowest price across segments in the market. It is one of three competitive positions.

Customer interface: how the organization markets, sells to, and provides follow-up services to customers.

Differentiation: adding value across segments via higher product or service quality. It is one of three competitive positions.

Digital marketing: the process of creating brand impressions and marketing products and services online.

Dynamic leader organizations: the combination of entrepreneurial execution with strategic thinking and are able to ride a wave of innovation to success.

External messaging: how the organization positions itself to stakeholders outside of the venture, including donors and customers.

Focus: in the business sense, means making a certain part of the market your priority.

Integrated marketing communications: the process of using multiple strategies and channels in a way that aligns with and reinforces each other and the central message of venture.

Internal messaging: how the organization interacts with its internal customers like employees and volunteers.

Lean production: consists of eliminating waste (including overproduction, excess inventories, excess time, and extra steps) and creating value by identifying improvements that add value for workers or customers.

Opportunist organizations: organizations that rely exclusively on high levels of entrepreneurial execution, but low levels of strategic thinking.

Production and fulfillment: how the goods or services are created and delivered.

Search engine optimization (SEO): the process of improving a site's ranking on search engines in order to help customers, donors, and other stakeholders reach it more easily.

Traditionalist organizations: organizations that emphasize long-range planning and operational stability.

IN-CLASS EXERCISE

Exercise 8.1: Marketing and Operations Plan

(Estimated time: 30 minutes)

Purpose

Social entrepreneurs should plan how they will manage operations and market their products. The following lists enable student teams to articulate their plans for a venture they are developing.

Preparation

Have blank copies of Table 8.3.

Process

1. Break into groups of 3–5, ideally groups that have been working together to develop a venture. If not, group members should select one venture (existing or proposed) to focus on.

Table 8.3 Operating and Marketing Plans

Operating Plan	
Key Operating Questions	*Approach*
What are our main activities?	
Where will we locate initially? At scale?	
What facilities will we need?	
What will our key processes be? • What should be centralized in-house vs. outsourced?	
How will be operate our supply and fulfillment functions?	
What human resources will we need? • Initially? • At scale?	

Marketing Strategy and Tactics		
Customer Segmentation		
What Are Our Main Customer Groups?	*What Segments Exist?*	*How Will We Create Value for Each?*
Group 1 (e.g., beneficiaries)		
Group 2 (e.g., other customers)		
Group 3 (e.g., funders)		
Other groups		

Table 8.3 Operating and Marketing Plans *(Continued)*

Product		
Key Questions	*Proposed Approach*	*What Requires More Analysis?*
What are the proposed product or service offerings?		
Are they meaningfully different from the competition? How?		
What steps or timeline are proposed for launch?		
Pricing		
Key Questions	*Proposed Approach*	*What Requires More Analysis?*
What is the pricing model?		
Is a single price planned or will different buyers be charged different prices?		
Will the price be seen as fair/ethical?		
Promotion		
Key Questions	*Proposed Approach*	*What Requires More Analysis?*
What is the overall promotion strategy?		
What is the planned approach to integrated marketing communications?		
What is the planned use of social media platforms?		

(Continued)

Table 8.3 Operating and Marketing Plans (*Continued*)

Place		
Key Questions	*Proposed Approach*	*What Requires More Analysis?*
What channels are required (e.g., online, bricks, and mortar)?		
What is the distribution strategy?		
Can the approach be improved to add value?		
People		
Key Questions	*Proposed Approach*	*What Requires More Analysis?*
Who will be on the customer-facing team? How will we hire/attract them?		
How will we organize to ensure service quality and consistency?		

2. Discuss the approach for operations and marketing, guided by the questions in the template. Be sure to debate the pros and cons of your decisions. What are the implications for your organizational structure and financial plan?
3. Be ready to present your analysis to the class.
4. Debrief:
    a. What were your answers to key operating questions? Why? How does this fit with your proposed venture?
    b. What were your answers to key marketing questions? Why? How does this fit with your proposed venture?
5. Post-class: Continue to refine your ideas. Create a specific timeline for your product launch and marketing communications execution. Report back during the next class.

SHORT CASE: BRENNA SCHNEIDER AND 99DEGREES—OPERATIONS UNDER FIRE

Brenna Schneider furrowed her brow with concern as she arrived at the converted mill building that was home to 99Degrees in Lawrence, Massachusetts. It was early November 2020 and the city remained in the red zone as a COVID-19 hot spot. The cumulative number of COVID-19 cases in the city was inching towards 7,000 in a city of 81,000 people and the 7-day rolling average of cases exceeded 100 per day. To make matters worse, Lawrence is also home to virtually all of her workers. With the safety of her workers foremost on her mind, along with the larger responsibility the company had for producing customer orders, including critically needed personal protection equipment (PPE), she thought about how to keep 99Degrees' operations safe and productive in the coming weeks.

Schneider founded 99Degrees in early 2013 with a simple mission—to create a financially sustainable manufacturing company that could create quality jobs for manually skilled workers in Lawrence. The majority of these workers had a high school degree or less and spoke English as a second language. Schneider's path began in her parents' small manufacturing company in Pennsylvania. She later became a William J. Clinton Fellow for Service in India where she worked with textile artisans to reposition traditional crafts into viable market-based businesses before becoming the VP of Operations for American MOJO, a mission-driven apparel manufacturing company.

By any standard, 99Degrees had been an outstanding success since Schneider founded it with three full-time employees. After initially bootstrapping the venture and playing multiple roles (including sweeping the floor after her workers left for the day), Schneider had built 99Degrees into a stable venture that had loyal customers and a stellar record of creating employment opportunities.

She had also secured growth capital, having closed three funding rounds, one with strategic partner Reliable Source Industrial Inc., a global manufacturing leader in technical performance active wear for premium brands with over 10,000 employees worldwide. This investment and strategic partnership gave 99Degrees access to a larger network of buyers and technology and even more importantly was a partner company with compatible values. In 2015, 99Degrees was highlighted as a Game-changer by Boston *Globe Magazine* and in 2017, the company was further recognized for their ingenuity by the Massachusetts Manufacturing Caucus as part of the second Manufacturing Month Award Ceremony. By January 2020, Schneider and her team had grown the company to 150 employees producing approximately 50,000 garments per month with 10 ongoing customers.

Schneider had learned a lot along the way about agile operations. One such instance occurred when the company first pivoted from her original idea that employees would gain experience at 99Degrees and then move on to high-quality jobs in advanced manufacturing. She learned that instead, her company could become a "future factory," creating advanced manufacturing jobs with higher pay as their work evolved. Creating new production lines to produce military gear and wearable technology supported this shift.

The team at 99Degrees had also refined their understanding about how to help employees build their skills and created manufacturing lines around these insights. They found that repetition is good for training, so having some ongoing contracts with highly repetitive products enabled them to onboard new operators more quickly. Having the capacity to deliver to customers with rapid turnaround was a second capability that enabled 99Degrees to create value that justified the higher cost of US labor and created new workforce opportunities. And finally, producing wearable tech required newly skilled workers, enabling the company to pay them more and the workers to develop transferrable skills.

As Schneider evolved the business, she was prepared for many things, but COVID-19 was not one of them. In early 2020, she and the team were aware of the emerging health crisis in China and had started to see disruptions in the supply chain as things like zippers and buttons became unavailable. Soon afterwards, changes in global commerce appeared to benefit 99Degrees' rapid domestic production model. But, when it became clear that COVID-19 would become a global pandemic, and the first two cases were diagnosed in Lawrence, her sights immediately turned to the safety of 99Degrees' workforce.

In March, after extensive consultation with other business leaders, Schneider wrote an editorial in the *Boston Business Journal* asking elected leaders to shut down manufacturing to maintain safety. "I am urgently asking our elected and business leaders to shut down all non-essential businesses, mine included, under a shelter-in-place order. Pause everything for two weeks to prevent this virus from spreading. Pause everything to get enough tests in place so that we, as employers, can make informed decisions for the people who work in our companies."[25]

A shutdown of nonessential businesses followed, and Schneider started thinking about how to adapt the factory to produce certain kinds of protective products. PPE is essential for health-care workers to stay safe when treating COVID-19 patients. Types of equipment needed include masks, face shields, and isolation gowns. Starting in March, a global shortage of these essential items emerged as hospitals and other health-care providers scrambled to make sure they had sufficient supplies on hand to protect essential workers. Schneider initially considered manufacturing masks, but it quickly became clear that this would not leverage the company's strengths. However, isolation gowns provided an excellent fit with 99Degrees' cut/sew capabilities and the team quickly developed processes to safely manufacture FDA-compliant AAMI Level 1 and 2 isolation gowns.

Schneider knew the demand for PPE was high and also felt a keen responsibility to her workers, who relied on steady paychecks to support their families. Both Schneider and her workers had been deeply affected in 2018 when a natural gas explosion had forced the evacuation of 30,000 people in Lawrence. She saw that rather than leaving their homes with personal items, families were evacuating with coolers filled with the contents of their refrigerators, since they could not afford to let their food spoil. She knew that many families in Lawrence were vulnerable to economic instability and that it could compound when other household members lost their jobs. Maintaining jobs was a high priority and creating a safe workplace was vital to this.

Before making the decision to pivot, Schneider consulted with two key mentors. The first, David Parker, CEO of Entrepreneurship for All, a long-time advisor, counselled her that her first job was leading the team and that she should not even consider reopening unless she was completely confident that she could ensure her workers' safety. The second, investor Desh Deshpande, agreed about safety being essential and advised that she should be careful about which contracts to accept; she should prioritize those with the most social benefit, asking for each alternative, "Is it worth it?" (B. Schneider, personal interview, November 19, 2020).

It took three weeks in April 2020 to reconfigure the company to produce gowns. This decision immediately paid off as 99Degrees subsequently grew its workforce by 125 jobs. The company also reorganized its physical space, leasing an additional 20,000 square feet of space and renting additional storage space. Safety protocols, including mask wearing, social distancing, and cleaning and sanitizing, were developed and implemented. The team established an Infection Control Committee to integrate the most updated Centers for Disease Control and Prevention (CDC) guidelines with the team's ideas and ultimately to create evolving standard operating procedures (SOPs) to ensure a safe working environment. Seven months later, the safety protocols had worked and there had been no community spread of COVID-19 at their facilities. The company had produced over 2 million isolation gowns filling a critical safety need at health-care facilities.

Schneider had learned a lot over the nine-month period in 2020. One useful insight was that her earlier work creating a lean and agile start-up that had the capacity to iterate rapidly had paid dividends when the company had to pivot quickly. A second was that trusting her team and becoming a "master delegator" was the only way to deal with the enormous web of complex decisions they faced as they worked to create a safe workspace and formed new customer relationship. Finally, having strong values as a company and having personally earned the trust of the workforce proved critical when they needed to shift to essential manufacturing.

Once Schneider was able to catch her breath, she looked to the future. She had recently hired Mauricio Mayer as 99Degrees' new Chief Operating Officer (COO), after pursuing him for over two years. He had a sterling reputation as the manager of a large manufacturing company in Honduras that had won the Shingo Bronze Medallion (a worldwide prize for organizational excellence) and had been named second on the national list of best places to work (and 7th on the list of best places in Central America). His leadership of 99Degrees' operations would enable Schneider to rededicate her time to strategy, external relations, and sales.[26]

Schneider also had started to work with her team on an intensive strategic planning process to map out 99Degrees' post-COVID strategy. This included deciding how to leverage learnings and new relationships in the medical field, while growing their capability in a manufacturing world where their rapid production capabilities would become even more relevant. Schneider knew that as they grew, they would need to use a strategic vision to supplement the entrepreneurial agility they had relied on in the past months. Working through a process which ultimately involved representatives from every level of the company, the team defined four pillars for long-term success: speed, agility, technology, and people. They also secured broad agreement on the company's core values, which were integrity, inclusivity, innovation, quality, and investing in people. Using these frameworks to guide them, teams developed both short-term goals (including increasing speed of production and investing in the culture) and a long-term vision to create more and better jobs by diversifying 99Degrees' customer base going forward.[27] Schneider knew that in Lawrence, creating 350 new jobs would reduce the poverty rate by 1%.[28] With this as her guidepost, she surveyed the factory floor to prepare herself for another long day.

Discussion Questions

1. What about the way 99Degrees was founded prepared it for a shock like COVID-19?
2. How well has Schneider managed the operational challenges of transitioning from manufacturing garments to PPE?
3. What advice would you give Schneider's incoming COO as someone with deep manufacturing experience joining an entrepreneurial high-growth company?
4. Looking forward to a future without COVID-19, what should Schneider do to position the company for further success?

NOTES

1. Taylor, F. W. (1911). *The principles of scientific management*. Manhattan, NY: Harper & Brothers.
2. Vergun, D. (2020, March 27). *During WWII, industries transitioned from peacetime to wartime production*. U.S. Department of Defense. Retrieved from https://www.defense.gov/Explore/Features/Story/Article/2128446/during-wwii-industries-transitioned-from-peacetime-to-wartime-production/.
3. McGrath, R. G. (2013). Transient advantage. *Harvard Business Review, 91*(6), 62–70.
4. Womack, J., Jones, D., & Roos, D. (1990). *The machine that changed the World*. New York, NY: Free Press.
5. Womack, J. P., & Jones, D. T. (2003). *Lean thinking: Banish waste and create wealth in your corporation*. New York, NY: Free Press.
6. Graban, M. (2012). *Lean hospitals: Improving quality, patient safety, and employee engagement*. Boca Raton, FL: CRC Press.
7. Eric, K., Cutcher-Gershenfeld, J., & Mittleman, B. (2016). The biomarkers consortium: Dynamic tension and the art of managing collaborative complexity. *Sloan Management Review, 57*(1), 16–19.
8. Aghina, W., De Smet, A., Lackey, G., Lurie, M., & Murarka, M. (2018). *The five trademarks of agile organizations*. McKinsey & Company.
9. Ibid.
10. Ibid.
11. Narasimhan, R., Kim, S. W., & Swink, M. (2016). Disentangling leanness and agility: An empirical investigation. *Journal of Operations Management, 24*(5), 440–457.
12. Drake, D., Bhattacharya, N., Godbole, P., & Amrita Saigal, A. (2016). *Ekal Viyalaya: Education for rural India*. HBS Case No. 617021. Harvard Business School Publishing.
13. Ibid.
14. Schurenberg, E. (2012, January 9). 'What's an entrepreneur?' Here's the best answer ever. *Inc. Magazine*.
15. Timmons, J. A., & Spinelli, S. (2009). *New venture creation: Entrepreneurship for the 21st century*. New York, NY: McGraw-Hill.
16. Blank, S. (2012). *The four steps to the epiphany: Successful strategies for products that win*. Menlo Park, CA: K & S Ranch.
17. Wang, X., & Ren, Z. J. (2020). De-marketing social causes: Why companies should not promote social causes on social media. *California Management Review, 63*(3).
18. The Interactive Advertising Bureau. (2020, May 28). *FY 2019 Internet ad revenue report & coronavirus impact on ad pricing report Q1 2020*. IAB. Retrieved from https://www.iab.com/insights/internet-advertising-revenue-fy2019-q12020/.
19. eMarketer Editors. (2019, February 19). *US digital ad spending will surpass traditional in 2019*. Insider Intelligence. Retrieved from https://www.emarketer.com/content/us-digital-ad-spending-will-surpass-traditional-in-2019.
20. Guttmann, A. (2020, November 17). Digital advertising spending worldwide from 2018 to 2024. *Statista*. Retrieved from https://www.statista.com/statistics/237974/online-advertising-spending-worldwide.
21. Episerver. (2020). *B2C retail benchmark report, Q1 2020*. Episerver. Retrieved from https://www.episerver.com/globalassets/03.-global-documents/reports/b2c-retail-benchmark-report-q1-2020.pdf.

22. Insider Intelligence Inc. (2019). *Data and research on digital for business professionals*. Insider Intelligence. Retrieved from https://www.emarketer.com/.
23. Backlingo. (2019, August 27). *The #1 result in Google gets 31.7% of clicks, new study by Backlinko and ClickFlow finds*. PR Newswire. Retrieved from https://www.prnewswire.com/news-releases/the-1-result-in-google-gets-31-7-of-clicks-new-study-by-backlinko-and-clickflow-finds-300907922.html.
24. Learn more at https://www.google.com/grants/
25. Schneider, B. N. (2020, March 18). Mass. CEO op-ed: We need a shelter-in-place order. *Boston Business Journal*. Retrieved from https://www.bizjournals.com/boston/news/2020/03/18/mass-ceo-op-ed-we-need-a-shelter-in-place-order.html.
26. Schneider, B. (2020, September 8). *Carlson social entrepreneurship and innovation class visit*. Waltham, MA: Brandeis University.
27. 99Degrees. (2020). *2021 vision* [Unpublished internal planning document].
28. Schneider, B. (2020, September 8). Carlson social entrepreneurship and innovation class visit. Waltham, MA: Brandeis University.

CHAPTER NINE

BUSINESS PLANS AND PITCHES FOR SOCIAL VENTURES

An important skill for social entrepreneurs is the ability to convey their venture concepts effectively through business plans and pitches. Founders are constantly called upon to explain their ideas and why they have value; but having great ideas is not enough. Social entrepreneurs must also inspire others to support their vision, convincing stakeholder groups that include current and prospective funders, employees, board members, clients, partners, and sometimes regulators and policy makers to support their ventures. As we discussed in Chapter 4 (Building Social Impact Teams and Ecosystems), the diversity of the stakeholder group and the complexity of social ventures means that for social entrepreneurs, effective communication in the form of business plans and pitches is even more important.

Learning Objectives

- Summarize the benefits and drawbacks of creating business plans in order to understand the contents of typical sections in a social venture business plan.
- Explain how to effectively pitch a social venture concept.
- Identify how intellectual property is protected by social entrepreneurs.

CREATING BUSINESS PLANS

"I have a great idea—and I know that it will have a huge social impact. Now it is time to write a business plan." This is a common bias to action, but aspiring social entrepreneurs who move from initial concept to writing a business plan should be aware that they are skipping some important steps. Defining the business model and value proposition, researching the market and competitive landscape, and creating a well-thought-through business model canvas are critically important. All of this work will help to transform the business plan writing process from a less-than-useful exercise of committing poorly vetted assumptions to paper to the valuable process of creating a road map for their organization.

When entrepreneurial teams plan and pitch their ventures, the process ideally creates a feedback loop that enables them to refine their ideas and hone their messaging. Consider WorkAround, a for-profit venture that connects refugees with microwork assignment, profiled in a case at the end of this book. The team participated in multiple business plan contests seeking both financial support and feedback on their ideas. While it wasn't always easy to hear criticism about the venture they cared deeply about, constantly testing their plans with knowledgeable judges and advisors and using this as a springboard to discuss and refine their plans led them to make large and small pivots prior to and during launch, strengthening their venture.

There are three different types of plans (and multiple variations):

- A *short (or summary) business plan* is typically 10–15 pages and provides a summary of the plan. It is typically used to attract early supporters, as a summary to communicate the venture, or as a supplement to a pitch to attract interest from early-stage investors.
- A *traditional (or formal) business plan* can be 30–50 pages or longer and includes a detailed description of the business model, the product approach, the market and competitive positioning, planned operations, financial plan, and team board and advisor qualifications. For social ventures, a traditional plan will also provide detail on the organization's theory of change and describe how it will assess impact. The plan is used to provide detailed information to prospective external supporters, including funders, partners, and sometimes, prospective team members. A section-by-section description of this plan is included in this chapter.
- An *operational business plan* is internally focused (while summary and traditional plans are geared to external audiences). This type of plan establishes detailed financial and operational benchmarks and assumptions used to operate the venture, and identifies the resources required to launch and scale operations. It can be 40–100 pages long.

There is disagreement among experts on whether a formal business plan is necessary for all new ventures. Some believe that, unless a written plan is required by donors or investors, it has limited value. One (private sector) study conducted at Babson College examined new ventures started by alums over an 18-year period and found that there was no difference between the performance of new ventures launched with or without written plans.[1]

When considering this, it is useful to distinguish between the process of business planning (which nearly all organizations engage in, although it may be less formal and more hypothesis driven for entrepreneurial ventures) and the production of a written plan or pitch document.

In a 2008 synthesis of research on the question of whether it is better to plan in advance or learn by doing, authors Brinckmann, Grichnik, and Kapsa observed two distinct schools of approach to business formation and planning. The planning school assumes that it improves the effectiveness of entrepreneurs; the learning school advocates an adaptive and incremental approach. Based on their analysis of 46 empirical studies comprising over 11,000 organizations, they conclude that the best approach depends on the size and stage of the organization and suggest that new ventures should be prepared to do both. While observing a positive correlation between business planning and performance, they conclude that in general a "plan first, execute second" approach tends to be less successful.[2] A 2010 study by authors Burke, Fraser, and Greene based on a survey of 622 entrepreneurs in the United Kingdom demonstrated that business plan preparation promoted employment growth.[3]

What is the difference between a plan and a pitch? While both are intended to convey essential information about a venture, they are different in format, intent, and audience.

- A *business plan* is a written document that lays out the approach a new venture will take. It usually follows a prescribed format. Most business plans are used to engage investors and other stakeholders.
- A *business pitch* is an overview of the business approach delivered verbally, often accompanied by slides. Like business plans, there are multiple pitch types, ranging from situational "elevator pitches" to formal pitches delivered to prospective funders and other stakeholder groups. Unlike business plans, which are written as stand-alone documents, pitches are delivered by the venture's leadership team and give the audience an opportunity to evaluate the team as well as the venture.

Social entrepreneurs often discover that plans and pitches are even more important than for their commercial counterparts for two reasons. First, the typical funding sources for nonprofit and hybrid organizations, including foundation grants and venture philanthropy investments, often require formal plans as part of their evaluation process. Second, the more complex ecosystem that social entrepreneurs interact with makes communication and stakeholder engagement even more important.

What Are the Benefits of Creating a Business Plan?

- *Communicating with stakeholders*, as it is common to use business plans to fully explain the venture to investors, donors, and other potential partners.
- *Gaining a deeper understanding* of the venture and its market via team discussion and testing with internal and external partners.

- *Aligning the entrepreneurial team against a common vision*, which can also have the benefit of increasing team commitment.
- *Identifying potential weaknesses of the planned venture* and determining a way to fill these gaps.

What Are the Drawbacks of Creating a Plan?

- *It takes time to write the plan.* This can distract the team from other priorities. While it might be tempting to delegate plan writing to a junior team member or external resource, this reduces the plan's depth and alignment-related benefits.
- *Plans become obsolete quickly.* Once a venture is operating and adapting to market conditions, the original plan (and in particular the finance projections) may quickly become dated. It is best to treat the plan as a living document, updating it as needed.
- *Plans can encourage rigid thinking.* If following a plan is impairing the organization's ability to innovate and execute in an agile manner, it may be time to retire or rethink it.
- *Loss of control over intellectual property.* Entrepreneurs are rightfully concerned about this risk, which is discussed in more detail at the end of this chapter.

What's in a Business Plan?

Most business plans have common components and follow similar formats, but the level of detail and elements included in each section will differ from plan to plan. For example, a company entering a new consumer market will devote more space to demonstrating market potential and customer acceptance, while a company developing a health-care product will deal more explicitly with the regulatory process and related risks. Meanwhile, a venture which relies heavily on manufacturing will devote more space to the operating plan. To help ensure success, entrepreneurs should balance the ease and understandability of a common format with knowledge of their audience, and tailor the plan to make it accessible, relevant, and interesting to their targets.

Aspiring social entrepreneurs might find it helpful to think of their plan as an "argument" that demonstrates the feasibility of the venture to stakeholders. That said, the entrepreneur should not gloss over important facts, but instead provide objective and reasonable assessments of the demand for the venture, its operations, and financial feasibility. While the plan plays a role as a sales/promotional document, it should at the same time be realistic and candid about the potential for the venture, whether and how it is unique, as well as cover expected risks and market headwinds. Financial projections should be based on transparent, realistic assumptions and, where possible, supported by market research or data from early market testing. The easiest way for a venture or entrepreneur to lose credibility is with wildly optimistic, unsubstantiated financial assumptions.

There are a few important differences between conventional business plans and plans for social ventures. Social impact venture plans are upfront about their theory of change and clearly articulate how their venture will produce and measure social impact. Plans for social ventures place even more emphasis on the contributions of advisors, board members, and, in some cases, donors. Consider Genesis, the Israel-based venture described in a case at the end of this book that provides premarital genetic testing for young adults in Bedouin communities to help reduce the high prevalence of genetic disease in children. Recognizing her own limited start-up experience and that the venture's success would depend on creating a high level of trust in target communities, founder Dr. Yasmeen Abu Fraiha recruited a Board of Advisors that included experts in science and genetics as well as community leaders. Additionally, because donor-based funding was key to successful implementation, she also included prominent donors who would add credibility during fundraising.

While plans differ, there are a few time-tested guidelines on length, packaging, and writing style. In their *Harvard Business Review* article, "How to Write a Winning Business Plan," Rich and Gumpert advocate for plans of fewer than 40 pages, reasoning that adhering to a concise length will force entrepreneurs to sharpen their ideas. They also recommend the inclusion of design elements that make the plan easy to read and understand: simple sentences, use of headings and subheadings, and clear simple graphics.[4]

Social entrepreneurs should spend significant time working with mentors, partners, and colleagues as they develop their plans. They should ask for candid feedback on their assumptions, ask for help identifying weaknesses, and carefully consider the advice of outside experts. Business plan competitions are a great way for new social ventures to seek and receive feedback, and accelerators and incubators usually offer mentoring and expertise that can help to highlight and resolve gaps before the plan is shared broadly.

Section Content

Cover and Title Page: The cover should have the name of the company, contact information, and the date. Many plans also include a copy number for tracking. The title page should also include all of this information. Both should indicate that the information in the plan is confidential.

Table of Contents: This allows the reader to easily navigate the plan, so it should be formatted for clarity and include page number references. If the plan is electronic, authors may want to provide hyperlinks to each section.

Executive Summary: This is the most-read section of the plan. It is typically no more than two to three pages in length and includes a concise overview of the opportunity and a summary of each section in the plan. This section should succinctly summarize the plan. Using subheadings will make it easier to navigate. To start, the entrepreneur can describe the opportunity and why it is compelling, followed by key points from major sections. An overview of the mission and intended impact is essential and a high-level financial plan should also be included. Most entrepreneurs find it is easiest to write the summary at the end.

Venture Overview: This section can take different forms, but the intent is to clearly convey the problem that the venture is trying to solve with particular emphasis on the "pain points" that indicate a compelling need. This section could start with a story about the problem the venture addresses and why it exists, while providing context and statistics. This section could also include a mission statement and explain how the venture will be organized (nonprofit, for-profit or hybrid) and its geographic focus. The current status of the company including employees, financial status, products, and operations should also be summarized here.

Product or Service Offering: In this section, the plan should describe the products or services the company will offer. A good starting point is the current stage of development for the products or services. The plan should describe what has been accomplished to date, and what steps must be taken before the product or service can be sold. Organizations producing a physical product might include graphics or photographs to describe the product. A service company should describe in detail the service(s) that will be provided. Founders often overlook basic information that should be provided in this section, including who the buyers are, what the product does, the benefits provided, and who uses it.

Competitive Environment: If not addressed elsewhere (for example, in the Market Assessment or Venture Overview sections), the company's competitive environment should be described in detail. All ventures have competitors, whether direct or indirect. Direct competitors' size, growth, strategies, pricing, and market share should be summarized. Indirect competitors (for example, those selling substitute products) should also be addressed, as should important complementary products. If the venture is truly novel, it is competing against "nonconsumption" and the plan should describe why its target consumers will choose to purchase or use something they have not previously needed.

Market Assessment: Stakeholders will want to know that the entrepreneurs clearly understand the market they plan to enter or expand in and that they are realistic about the associated challenges and costs. The plan should provide an overview of market dynamics, including size and growth, and describe important customer segments. The compelling case for customers or recipients to buy or use the proposed product must be clearly articulated and, where possible, this information should be supported by market tests, pilots, or customer research. Social venture founders who rely on stories when promoting their ventures should also remember the importance of numbers including basic market data when making their case.

Theory of Change and Social Impact Plan: In this section, the authors should describe their theory of change (if not covered in the venture overview) and the level of impact they intend to achieve. This section should also discuss how impact will be measured.

Sales and Marketing Plan: This section should provide a clear picture of how the company will reach the client or customer and why the customer will be compelled to purchase or use the product. Building on data and analysis in the market assessment section, it should describe how customers will be reached, the cost of doing this, and what sales and marketing strategies will be used. The plan should mention if the venture has already secured initial customers. This section can also address pricing (including price comparisons with competitors) and channel strategies. While pricing is often adjusted later, data that support the proposed price range are important for demonstrating feasibility.

Operating Plan: This section provides an overview of how the company will organize itself to produce goods and services. Depending on the nature of the offering, the section might describe how the product will be produced, critical suppliers or facilities, manufacturing approach, and other important elements.

Financial Plan: This section should start with an overview of the financial plan of the company. It will always include the following financial statements:

- A *balance sheet* that shows the financial health of the company at a point in time, describing what a company owns and how those assets have been financed. In the plan, annual balance sheets can be projected, typically 5 years out from the current year.
- An *income statement* shows the venture's revenue and expense projections for both the current year and projected for 5 years, usually on an annual or quarterly basis.
- A *cash flow statement* that projects the sources and uses of cash for the same period.

Projected financial statements should include well-documented assumptions. While the financial plan is likely to change during the launch period, well-supported estimates are important for establishing credibility.

There are many templates available for financial statements, but a good (and free) set is available from SCORE at https://www.score.org/resource/financial-projections-template.

Management Team and Board of Directors/Advisors: The management team section of a business plan is the second most-read portion, after the executive summary. Readers want to know who is behind the venture and what their relevant experience is, because this is a key predictor of whether the venture will succeed. The founding team's relevant experience should be described, and the authors can increase credibility by demonstrating commitment from experts and key stakeholders. Investors are keenly interested in how the Board of Directors will help fund and guide the company, so experienced and credible directors and advisors can add depth, particularly if the entrepreneurs themselves do not have significant industry experience.

Risks: The plan should describe key market, competitive, financial, and operating risks, either in a separate section, in the financial plan section, or throughout the document, depending on the nature of the risks. For example, if most of the risks relate to operations or the performance of a major supplier, they might be discussed in the operating plan section. If the major risk is achieving market traction, risks should be highlighted in the sales and marketing section.

Appendices: Various appendices may be included to provide additional detail while keeping the main body of the plan concise. Typical appendices include summaries of market research, customer interview summaries, product mockups, and/or screen shots of an early web site. If appendices are very long, they may be included in a supplementary document.

SOCIAL VENTURE PITCHES

The Value of Effective Pitches

Social entrepreneurs are constantly called upon to explain their ideas and describe how their proposed venture will work and what difference it will make. Whether in a chance encounter in an elevator, responding to questions during a panel, meeting one-on-one with a prospective donor or advisor, or formally pitching in front of a foundation or investor, social entrepreneurs and entrepreneurial teams must always be ready to articulate what their ideas are and why they are worthy of support and attention.

In this chapter, we will focus on two common pitch types:

- *Elevator pitches* are short pitches, ranging from less than a minute in length to 3 minutes, designed to get a prospective supporter's attention and create an opportunity for further discussion
- *Formal pitches* are 6–15-minute presentations, usually using slides, delivered in a formal setting (be it a boardroom or a stage). The presentation is typically followed by a Q&A session.

In addition, there are multiple variations including short pitches, self-pitches (which involve the entrepreneur talking about their qualifications), extended pitches, and those focused on specific elements of the venture.

The Science of First Impressions

Those who meet you or your team members for the first time make rapid judgments about your capabilities; these are based not only on what is said (or delivered in a pitch) but also on how it is delivered and sometimes on unconscious biases as well. A foundational study by UCLA psychologist Albert Mehrabian suggested that only 7% of what we communicate is contained in the content of the message, while vocal tone and quality accounted for 38% and body language and facial expression for 55%.[5] More recent research by Harvard Business School professors Amy Cuddy and Anna Beninger and their colleague Peter Glick showed that the people we meet make rapid judgments based on two dimensions: perceived warmth (can I trust this person?) and competence (will they perform as I expect?).[6] Conveying a warm and competent personality makes it much more likely that a venture will receive stakeholder support.

Sometimes judgments are made even more quickly. Recent research suggests that people make immediate inferences based on the facial appearance of others—sometimes in as little as one-tenth of a second. From a half second to a second after seeing someone, those judgments, including attractiveness, likeability, trustworthiness, competence, and aggressiveness, are confirmed.[7]

What does this mean for social entrepreneurs and teams pitching their ideas? Most importantly, the pitch is not only about the idea or the material presented. Prospective funders and other stakeholders will make judgments about an entrepreneur, whether in an elevator, during a meet-and-greet event, or during a formal pitch, based on how they present themselves.

Entrepreneurs can take many steps to manage these early impressions. Warmth is conveyed by body language and facial expression. Leaning in, smiling, using natural gestures, and making eye contact (in most cultures) demonstrate that you are likable and trustworthy.

We project warmth and competence when we tell a story that we believe in. Taking the time to speak clearly and enthusiastically engenders confidence, as does the use of compelling themes, stories, and vivid language. Consider the benefits of a pitch that starts with "I grew up on a family farm and observed firsthand that..." rather than a pitch that starts with "Our product provides an agricultural solution that...." When conveying excitement and building interest, speakers should avoid monotones and use pitch and modulation to make their voice interesting.

To convey competence, speakers should provide concise, focused, and credible messages. Presenters should replace "ums" and other fillers with confident pauses. Optimal speaking pace is 150 words per minute and there are multiple online tools that measure speech speeds. Pitchers should consider physical presence as well. Additionally, good posture and appropriate dress confirm credibility.

Practice makes perfect, so social venture teams should invest time in perfecting their pitches for multiple situations and lengths. It is valuable to record sample pitches, observe what works and what does not, and get feedback from others. Finally, entrepreneurs and teams should consider the importance of authenticity. There are many ways to present your ideas; those that reflect who you are and what your core values are will most likely leave a lasting impact.

Tell a Great Story

Whether using a formal pitch or an elevator pitch, telling a great story makes your pitch memorable and impactful. There are a few important ways to make sure that your story resonates.

The first is to *know your audience, message, and intent*. Pitchers can hone their messaging by carefully considering the audience. What do they already know? What do they care about? Speakers should be clear on their key message and their overall intent. For example, some pitches seek to inspire, others to educate, and still others to challenge.

A second key to a great story is *leveraging your experience*. Pitchers can draw on their own experience to make the story relevant, describing what they have observed, what they have learned, and how they have seen problems solved by the type of product or service they will offer.

Good stories include tension. Pitchers can talk about the challenge they are trying to overcome, whether it is disease-carrying mosquitoes or intergenerational poverty. Identifying the "enemy" of social good motivates potential stakeholders to overcome it.

It is also important to *keep it simple*. Listeners will get lost if there is too much detail or too many subthemes.

Finally, all pitches should *end with a call to action or a key learning*. A call to action could be a request for funding, or could also be a request for feedback or connections.

Elevator Pitch Basics

The phrase "elevator pitch" comes, unsurprisingly, from the prospect of a chance encounter in an elevator where an entrepreneur has a short period (say, between the first and tenth floor) to convince a potential investor or partner to take an interest in their venture.

There are two common types of elevator pitches:

- The *venture pitch* describes key elements of a venture in order to secure an opportunity for a longer discussion.

- The *personal pitch* involves an individual pitching their basic qualifications (often to a potential employer).

There are many points of view about how long an elevator pitch should be, with guidance ranging from 30 seconds (appropriate for a personal pitch) to 2–3 minutes. Another common myth is that pitches are entirely one-way—an entrepreneur encounters a prospect and starts to rapidly pitch. Rather, pitches should be conversational. The person pitching should make an effort to engage the prospect in a two-way dialogue, often by asking questions (Table 9.1).

Table 9.1 Step-by-Step of Elevator Pitches

Step	Example
Step 1: Engage the Listener	Leverage a common network: *I think we both know [common connection]. She has been encouraging me to reach out to you to talk about something we've been working on together.* Make a connection: *It is great to meet you. It looks like we are both working on a solution to...* Use an intriguing hook: *We've developed a new technology that can save thousands of lives but cannot pay for itself. Can I tell you more?*
Step 2: Describe the Compelling Problem	*Subsistence farmers in Malawi could triple their incomes if they had access to a few basic tools to improve agricultural production.* *Millions of refugees are educated and have access to technology but can't find jobs.*
Step 3: Describe your Solution	*I've been working with a team on a technology that can save 100,000 lives by...* *We've developed and tested proprietary tools that increase water safety by...*
Step 4: Describe your Team	*Our team includes...*

(Continued)

Table 9.1 Step-by-Step of Elevator Pitches (*Continued*)

Step	Example
Step 5: Mention Traction you have Achieved	*So far, we have received a start-up grant from the Gates Foundation and just won $100K in a business plan contest. Our planned next steps are to…*
Step 6: **Always** end with a request	*Would it be possible for me to get in touch with you to get your feedback on our venture?* *Given your background, I would really appreciate your ideas. What do you think of our business model?* *I know you have a lot of contacts in the clean energy industry. Who would you recommend we approach to be on our board?*

Social entrepreneurs should have a variety of elevator-style pitches prepared, ranging from a single sentence to a detailed 2–3-minute overview of their venture and should be ready to deliver these pitches in both formal and informal settings. Entrepreneurs should practice until they are able to deliver multiple, compelling pitches that are engaging, clear, and captivating (and yet do not sound rehearsed).

Pitching With Slides

While pitch slide decks do not follow a conventional format, there are elements that should be included in every presentation. Pitches for social ventures aim to secure support by clearly conveying the story behind the venture while also providing the information a potential investor or partner needs to make a decision.

Most pitches are delivered using a combination of verbal and visual information. This convention has its roots in **Cognitive Load Theory**, which is based on the observation that individuals have a limited amount of working memory, and the mind processes auditory and visual information separately. This means that presenters (and educators) can make their work more memorable by using both at the same time.[8] This is why at venture showcases, entrepreneurs use pictures, demos, and models as they pitch their ventures, and why in most formal pitches, slides are used. Table 9.2 shows typical pitch deck content.

While PowerPoint slides are the most common visual supplement to a pitch, there are other presentation formats. However, given the dominance of PowerPoint, if a

Table 9.2 What's in a Pitch Deck?
Typical Pitch Deck Content
• The basic idea, often conveyed through a story about who the venture will help or how the idea was developed • An overview of why the concept is compelling. What problem does it solve? • A description of how the concept works. If the team has completed pilots or tests, these can be used to demonstrate feasibility • A compelling statement about what social impact the venture will achieve • An overview of competitors and description of how the venture is different • A discussion of the ecosystem in which the venture will operate • Scaling/growth plan • An overview of the team and why they are credible • A description of who else supports the venture including board members and advisors as well as sponsors, partners, or funders, when applicable • High-level projected financials • A slide on what you want from the pitch viewer (the "ask") • Various appendices

team elects to use an alternative, it should be a deliberate decision based on what the presenters want to convey.

Many entrepreneurs find that the best way to develop a pitch deck is to write a story. This starts with writing bullet form headlines for all of the key elements that you would like to convey. These headlines should touch on the themes above. The second step is to add essential information that supports each headline. Following that, the pitch creators can add evocative images and graphics to enhance the presentation.

Presenters should also consider whether and how to use videos, templates, and other resources. Short video clips can energize a presentation but can be distracting. Templates can be helpful for continuity but should be consistent with overall messaging and not distract from the overall flow of the presentation. Fonts and text size and color should reinforce the pitch message and, importantly, be readable by someone at the back of the room.

The Pitch Process

Preparing to Pitch

Formal pitches are high-stakes events, and social venture pitches are no exception. Experts offer the following advice to make them manageable:

Prepare From the Very Beginning. Stuart Paap from Pitch DNA is a longtime trainer and mentor for multiple accelerators, including MassChallenge. He believes that most teams wait too long to consider the important questions of what makes them special and why they believe they have an advantage. His analogy is preparing a car to be sold: he recommends that entrepreneurs avoid approaching pitches by "washing and waxing a car before the big event" and instead starting at idea conception. They should constantly debate, and pitch both within their team and externally, in effect, designing the car together. Teams should continually be probing what problem they are trying to solve, why, and for who, as this will help make the team's story well-honed and genuine on pitch day (S. Paap, personal interview, October 13, 2020).

Watch the Experts. It is easy to find video clips of social impact pitches online, either on YouTube or on sites like the Hult Challenge website. Presenters should watch how expert teams pitch and use these examples to hone their own (authentic) approaches. A key observation is that winning pitches achieve a balance of warmth, enthusiasm, and clarity.

Consider the Audience. Bozhanka Vitanova is a serial entrepreneur. She was a cofounder and CEO of TeamLift, the first HR tech company focused on improving the effectiveness of collaboration within large organizations, and was also a cofounder of Yunus and Youth, a youth-focused organization, endorsed by Nobel Peace Prize Laureate Muhammad Yunus. She estimates that she has observed, pitched, or judged over 500 pitches and has herself been judged as she pitched dozens of times. She advises teams to spend a lot of time thinking about the venture from the point of view of who will be observing the pitch. "For competitions, it is more about impact, the story and how you will grow. But for more traditional investors, the go to market strategy is critical—you need to articulate how you will reach customers" (B. Vitanova, personal interview, October 16, 2020).

Practice Q&A. One approach is to ask your team members and other mentors to pose thoughtful questions and time your response. Experts suggest that presenters aim to keep answers between 30 seconds and a minute.

Do an Authenticity Check. Interrogate your motivations. Ask why you are deeply interested in this venture. What is driving you? Grounding yourself in what is driving your passion helps you to convey it clearly.

During the Pitch

Speak Clearly and Confidently. Research by Harvard Business School Professor and Social Psychologist Amy Cuddy has shown that projecting confidence is actually one of the easiest ways to communicate effectively. In her well-received TED Talk, *Fake it till you make it*, she suggests that if a person uses assertive body language, they tend to feel more powerful, which then increases their confidence level. She concludes: "Our bodies change our minds...and our minds change our bodies...and our behavior changes our outcomes."[9] How can presenters use these insights? They can draw on reserves of confidence during practice to increase their overall confidence level. Other techniques for reducing stress include reframing (telling yourself you are not nervous, but excited, for example) and using breathing exercises to reduce anxiety.

Start Strong. Vitanova adds the following advice: "What is most important is the opening and conveying a sense of urgency about your venture. You really need to get people's attention by answering the questions why should I care? Why is this relevant? And, why is it relevant now?" (B. Vitanova, personal interview, October 16, 2020).

Balance the Content. It is easy to think of a pitch as a time slot to fill, according to Stuart Paap. Instead, he recommends that: "As a general rule of thumb, in a 15-minute segment, take a third of the time to present the idea, and the balance engaging in meaningful dialogue" (S. Paap, personal interview, October 13, 2020).

Never Read From Your Slides. Reading from slides is one of the quickest ways to alienate your audience. It also makes it difficult to make eye contact with your listeners, which is critically important to conveying your message.

If You Are Presenting as a Team, Demonstrate Team Cohesion. When teams present, the presentation is evaluated not only on what the main presenter says and does, but also on how their team reacts. Team members should aim for neutral, relaxed body language, smiling and slightly nodding, as this confirms for observers that the team agrees with the speaker. If there is more than one speaker, teams should practice coordination and handoffs and should be clear about how they will coordinate responding to questions.

End on a High Note. This enables a presenter to manage the final message and leave a lasting impression. Rather than wrapping up Q&A with "any more questions?" or thanking the panel, experts suggest that entrepreneurs prepare a final statement recapping the value of the solution and the reasons they are passionate about it.

Managing Q&A

If the presenters have practiced their Q&A responses extensively, as described above, they should feel prepared and confident. Most questioners will be genuinely interested in the idea. Sometimes questions will be off topic or aggressive, and in these cases the best strategy for presenters is to answer briefly and candidly and move on.

Most presenters find it helpful to have multiple appendix slides covering topics that are likely to be raised in the Q&A section (for example, unit economics, capital investment plans, or a detailed comparison of competitors). When a relevant question is asked, the responder can turn to the slide to explain. An important tip: rather than flipping through the slides to the relevant backup slide, access it directly (which is easy to do in most presentation formats).

Team coordination is particularly important during the Q&A. Another important tip: unless invited to by a teammate, it is best not to add to or elaborate on a team member's answer to a question. Even if these additions are helpful or clarifying, they can be perceived by viewers as "corrections" and indicate a lack of team knowledge or cohesion.

Experts recommend that teams note all of the questions that come up during their pitches (perhaps via an external note-keeper) and then use this valuable information to improve their venture concept going forward.

After the Pitch

After the pitch, there are a number of steps an entrepreneurial team can take to continue to make progress (perhaps after celebrating the milestone with the team). First, they can reflect on what went well and where opportunities exist during the pitch and treat it as a learning opportunity. It is a good time to reach out to mentors and advisors (and, if appropriate, to pitch judges) to thank them for their support. This is what Cofounders Waafa Arbash and Jennie Kelly did immediately after pitching WorkAround—a platform that connects refugees to microtasks that is profiled in a case at the end of this book—even though they had learned that they were not among the winning teams. The day following the pitch was a good time for them to take stock of the feedback they had received and use it to continue improving their business model. After failing to receive a capital commitment at MassChallenge, the WorkAround team used their learnings to go on to win several other competitions.

After the pitch entrepreneurial teams should also try to engage with important stakeholders. During the pitch, social entrepreneurs can ask select attendees: "Is it OK if I update you on [a specific topic]?" and then follow up. Asking for advice outside of the pitch format is also a great way to form relationships with important stakeholders.

Formal pitches are critically important for attracting stakeholders. Understanding your venture, your motivations, and your audience and, of course, practice, are the keys to being memorable and effective.

Tips for Presenting Virtually

Virtual presentations have special challenges; those presenting virtually should take special care to:

- Ensure adequate lighting so that facial expressions are clearly conveyed;
- Sit far enough from the camera to be able to show gestures;
- For live pitches, test connectivity in advance and "secure the perimeter" to avoid interruptions and background noise;
- If multiple team members are presenting from different locations, have each team member use a common or similar background, sit the same distance from the camera, and manage handoffs carefully.

PROFILE: RUTOPIA—CREATING THE PERFECT PITCH

On September 14, 2019, Emiliano Iturriaga, Sebastián Muñoz, Diego Espinoza, and Leslie Perez took the stage at the United Nations building in New York City to pitch their venture, Rutopia, in the final round of the Hult Prize. The stakes were high: winning the Hult Prize would give them $1 million to fund their venture and would also attract additional attention from partners, supporters, and investors. The four friends were nervous but confident as they took the stage.

Rutopia was cofounded two years earlier by Iturriaga and Muñoz after they met as students at Tec de Monterrey, Mexico. Iturriaga studied engineering and sustainable development and Munoz studied design. With these complementary interests (later augmented by Espinoza's expertise in community development and Perez' expertise in marketing) and a common passion for travel to little-known places, they were well prepared to start a venture that aimed to create more genuine experiences for people visiting Mexico.

According to Iturriaga, "I was always interested in making this kind of social difference, but when I realized that if I worked at an NGO, it would take too long to make an impact, I started to think about ideas for entrepreneurial startups" (E. Iturriaga, personal interview, October 12, 2020). After he and Muñoz completed a project as part of their final degree work on regenerative tourism, they started to explore ways to accelerate the venture.

The Hult Challenge, started in 2009, has been referred to as "the Nobel Prize for students" by Muhammad Yunus, founder of Grameen Bank. The competition aims to engage MBA and college students by challenging them to start ventures that solve a pressing social issue. Each year, a different theme is selected, with past topics including: food security, water access, energy, and education. With an attention-getting million-dollar prize, teams compete over the course of a year, initially in local and regional rounds, for an opportunity to pitch for the global prize. In 2019, the year that the Rutopia team competed, the challenge was to create a venture that would provide meaningful work for 10,000 youth within the next decade. Over 250,000 students from more than 100 countries participated. After a year-long process, six finalist teams were selected to present their pitches to high-profile judges that included former US President William J. Clinton, Founder & CEO of impact investment firm Cornerstone Capital Erika Karp, and CEO of the United Nations Global Compact, Lise King.

Rutopia is a platform that assists in the formation and operation of rural youth-run initiatives in Mexico, providing services that enable them to create and sell ecotours online. Its aim is to support jobs and local economies while providing an opportunity for tourists to authentically experience local culture. Rutopia does this by providing a platform for tour sales, tour development assistance, and marketing while at the same time broadening the market by providing tour customers with information, safety assurances, and insurance, among other services. This enables travelers from around the world to instantly book authentic and safe experiences in Mexico in just a click. Rutopía prides itself on making it as easy to book an experience in a glamping site in the middle of the forest as it is today to book a resort in Cancún. "It is all about creating an even field in the tourism industry and allow small sustainable tourism providers to thrive," according to Muñoz.

After rounding out their team to include cofounders with additional expertise, they participated in and won the campus-level Hult Prize competition, and then won a country-level competition in Monterrey, Mexico. The next stop was Hult Regionals in Madrid Spain, but they did not win. Undaunted, they participated in other accelerator programs, successfully entered Hult's "Wild Card" round, and were selected as one of 40 teams globally to participate in Hult's Global Accelerator in London, England.

"It was an intense, immersive process," Iturriaga recounted. "We pitched every Friday, in front of different groups of judges, competing against 49 other teams." The Rutopia team also practiced extensively outside of these formal rounds. "We had already worked out a lot of our business foundations and team processes, so we focused our time on refining our pitch. We would pitch every day, stopping people in the hallway and calling on multiple mentors to gain different perspectives and systematically incorporating feedback. Along the way we learned many lessons. The most important were to be flexible so not too attached to a single idea or approach, and to simplify our ideas to be able to present them clearly" (E. Iturriaga, personal interview, October 12, 2020).

The way to be successful when pitching, according to Iturriaga, is to "keep it natural and be sure that your personal passion shows through. It is also important to not to be too set on your ideas, and not to get defensive. Judges want to know that a team like ours will be adaptable and be truly open to their feedback" (E. Iturriaga, personal interview, October 12, 2020).

Muñoz advises teams to overprepare for Q&As. Once the Rutopia pitch was honed, the team worked hard to make sure they could respond to judges' questions. For example, they made a practice of using flashcards while they were socializing—questions on one side and answers on the other—to make sure that every team member was prepared to respond when needed. The team also developed cues that became second nature when they pitched. For example, when one member of the team was preparing to answer a question, they would slightly step forward, alerting the other members that they were preparing to respond.

In addition to pitch advice, Iturriaga's advice for aspiring social entrepreneurs is to "keep your focus on the problem you are trying to solve. Be passionate and persistent, while still being flexible and listening to advice. This helps you to see what you want to solve in the world and then build a business around it" (E. Iturriaga, personal interview, October 12, 2020).

PROTECTING INTELLECTUAL PROPERTY

Most entrepreneurs worry about protecting **intellectual property (IP)** when drafting and sharing their plans, and social entrepreneurs are no exception. While maintaining control of IP is valuable, entrepreneurs should keep in mind that in nearly all cases, the value of an idea itself is low and it is the execution of the idea that creates value. Sometimes their fear of a loss of control keeps entrepreneurs from sharing ideas, but if an entrepreneur wants to secure external support, they usually must share their ideas widely. It would be very unusual for a funder, whether an angel, a venture capital (VC) provider, or a foundation, to agree to confidentiality as a condition for reviewing a business concept. Indeed, most of these funders debate the value of new concepts internally and often vet them with outside parties as part of their assessment process.

Types of Intellectual Property Protection

There are four types of IP protection: patents, trademarks, copyrights, and trade secrets. Figure 9.1 shows the different types of protection available, depending on the nature of the venture. A patent applies to a specific product design; a trademark to a name, phrase, or symbol; and a copyright to a written document. In the United States, an entrepreneur must file a patent within one year of a "public disclosure" of their work (and this can include business plans, presentations, websites, emails, and other documents that they share with others).

While patents, trademarks, and copyrights can be protected by taking specific steps to secure a venture's rights, trade secrets are protected by keeping them confidential. This includes not sharing confidential information outside the organization and enforcing it by using nondisclosure agreements.

Social entrepreneurs might think that IP is unimportant because of the social mission of their venture or their intent to provide it on an open-source basis to maximize impact, but they should take the same steps to secure IP as any venture. In addition to avoiding the obvious peril of other organizations claiming rights to a venture's intellectual assets, securing IP enables a venture to maintain control of how its assets are used and ensure that its reputation isn't hijacked or damaged by a copycat organization.

Aspiring entrepreneurs should also pay attention to who owns IP that they might use in their own venture. For example, many start-ups use open-source technology, but this comes with certain requirements (often including a requirement that what is

Figure 9.1 Different Types of Intellectual Property Protection in the United States

	Product	Service	Process
Patent	✓		✓
Trademark	✓	✓	
Copyright	✓	✓	✓
Trade Secret	✓	✓	

developed using it will be open-source). Entrepreneurs should carefully assess their obligations to make sure that they are not at risk.

IP protection standards vary widely around the world, so a social entrepreneur should consider checking IP laws in all countries in which they intend to do business.

How does this influence a business plan or pitch for a new venture? At a minimum, the entrepreneur should copyright their work by adding a copyright symbol and maintaining proof of when the material was first created. If the IP involves a product design and is core to the venture, they should consider applying for a patent prior to sharing their work via a business plan, pitch, or other disclosure.

Working With University Technology Transfer Offices and Other University Resources

Nearly all universities in the United States, and many larger ones in other countries, have offices that are responsible for licensing university-owned technology. Generally, students own their inventions, unless they have created them under a university-supported grant or using university resource. Technology transfer offices will not try to exert ownership if you approach them, but they can help you figure out who owns IP that you have had a role in developing. In addition, technology transfer offices or university innovation centers can often provide support to students as they develop ventures, including advice on protecting IP, seed funding, connections to cofounders, mentors and funders, and programs that help inventors develop their ideas.

CHAPTER SUMMARY

Few things are more disappointing than seeing a great idea fail to gain traction because it is poorly conveyed. Both business plans and pitches enable aspiring social entrepreneurs to gain support for their ventures. Social entrepreneurs always have the advantage of passion for their venture and excitement about its potential. Bolstered by effective shaping and planning, as well as diligence, practice, and hard work, they are in a unique position to engage their stakeholders to turn their ideas into impactful ventures.

In this chapter, we discussed the ways in which social entrepreneurs organize and frame their business plans and pitches as well as the various forms they can take. The first steps in this process are defining the business model and value proposition, researching the market and competitive landscape, and creating a well-thought-through business model. This enables the social entrepreneur to communicate ideas to others via business plans and pitches.

There are multiple types of social venture pitches ranging from the short elevator pitch to the longer formal pitch. The entrepreneurial team should have multiple types of pitches ready for myriad scenarios and opportunities. Regardless of the situation, first impressions are key. There are many ways entrepreneurs can prepare for meetings including practicing body language and facial expressions, making sure they are speaking clearly and at an optimal pace and wearing situationally appropriate attire.

Most ventures rely to some extent on IP, and social entrepreneurs should consider how to secure it. In some instances, a patent may be sufficient, in others a trademark, copyright, or classifying certain components as trade secrets may be best. Despite the proprietary nature of an early venture, business plan or pitch, entrepreneurs should not expect funders to agree to confidentiality as a condition for reviewing a business concept. In order to secure their IP, entrepreneurs should copyright their work or apply for a patent prior to sharing their business plan, pitch, or disclosing their ideas in other ways.

KEY TERMS

Business model: the way in which a proposed venture will function and how it will deliver products or services to customers.

Business plan: written document that lays out the approach a new venture will take and often follows a prescribed format.

Business plan pitch ("pitch"): overview of the business approach delivered verbally, often accompanied by slides.

Cognitive load theory: theory based on the observation that individuals have a limited amount of working memory, but the mind processes auditory and visual information separately.

Elevator pitch: short pitch designed to get a prospective supporter's attention and create an opportunity for further discussion.

Financial projections: transparent, realistic assumptions supported by market research or product testing and usually supported by financial projections including a balance sheet, income statement, and cash flow statement.

Formal business plan: written document that provides a detailed description of the business model, the product approach, the market and competitive positioning, planned operations, financial plan, and team board and advisor qualifications. For social ventures, a formal plan will also provide detail on the organization's theory of change and describe how it will assess impact.

Formal pitches: 6–15-minute presentations, usually using slides, delivered in a formal setting (be it a boardroom or a stage). The presentation is typically followed by Q&A.

Intellectual property (IP): the creation of the entrepreneur and is often central to the business plan. It can be protected by patents, trademarks, copyrights, and labeling them trade secrets.

Investor pitch: aims to secure support by clearly conveying the story behind the venture while also providing the information a potential investor or partner needs to make a decision.

Mini business plans: 10–15 pages and provide a summary of the plan. They are used to attract early supporters, as a summary to communicate the venture, or as a supplement to a pitch to attract interest from early-stage investors.

Operational plans: detailed financial and operational benchmarks and assumptions used to operate the venture and identifies the resources required to launch and scale operations.

Personal pitches: individual pitching their basic qualifications (often to a potential employer).

Summary plans: summary of the plan and is typically used to attract early supporters, communicate the venture, or as a supplement to a pitch to attract interest from early-stage investors.

Venture pitches: key elements of a venture in order to secure an opportunity for a longer discussion.

IN-CLASS EXERCISES

Exercise 9.1: Pitch Practice

(Estimated time: 45–60 minutes)

Purpose

Being able to pitch effectively is a critical skill for social entrepreneurs. Yet, there are multiple potential pitfalls: entrepreneurs sometimes take too long to come to the point, don't effectively calibrate the pitch to the audience, or worse, "wing it" when speaking with potential stakeholders. This exercise will help social entrepreneurs hone their pitching skills so that they are ready to communicate their ideas effectively.

Preparation

Ask students in advance to be prepared to give a 3–4-minute elevator pitch on their venture or an idea they have been developing. Have copies of the instruction sheet below available to guide each group's work.

Process

1. Individually, each student should take 5 minutes to write down key message points to prepare a 3-minute elevator pitch.
2. Break students into groups of 3–5, but not into their project teams. Ask the students to assemble in a circle and assign the student to the presenter's left to be the timekeeper. The student to their right will take notes on the key points from the pitch. Each student should take 3 minutes (timed) to present to their group, followed by 5 minutes of feedback. After each student has presented and received feedback, they should repitch to their group. The total time required will be approximately 11 minutes per student.
3. In a plenary session, the instructor can ask each group what they discussed, what was challenging, and what key insights they had about how to improve their pitches.

Exercise 9.2: Advanced Pitch Challenges

(Estimated time: 30–60 minutes)

Purpose

Rather than relying on a single pitch, aspiring social entrepreneurs should have a variety of pitches available that they can deliver depending on the situation, their intent, and the prior knowledge of the audience. This series of additional challenges is intended to expand students' pitch range and depth.

Preparation

Complete In-Class Exercise 9.1—Pitch Practice before attempting Exercise 9.2.

Process

1. Break students into the same groups of 3–5 students as In-Class Exercise 9.1. Make sure that students are not in their project teams. As before, a note keeper and timer should be selected for each student.
2. Provide all groups with a challenge topic (depending on time available, choose from the challenges below). Each student in the group should present their challenge pitch (1–2 minutes depending on challenge) and then receive 2–3 minutes of feedback from their group. Total time per student should be roughly 4 minutes per challenge.
3. Announce each challenge to the students, one at a time, and in each group have each student pitch in turn while other members provide rapid feedback (2 minutes or less). If there is extra time, students can repitch. Select from the following challenges below.
4. In a plenary session, the instructor can moderate a discussion of key insights from each of the challenges and discuss how the students might incorporate lessons into a venture pitch.

Challenge 1: 2-minute pitch: Deliver your pitch in 2 minutes rather than 3, focusing on core messages (total time per student: 4 minutes).

Challenge 2: 1-minute pitch: Deliver your pitch in 1 minute, focusing only on essential elements (total time per student: 3 minutes).

Challenge 3: Passion pitch: Prepare for 1 minute; then in 1 minute or less, describe why you are passionate about the idea or mission behind your venture (total time per student: 5 minutes).

Challenge 4: Story pitch: In 3 minutes or less, tell a story about why your venture is important. This could cover how you evolved the idea or be a story about someone who will benefit. If the latter, be sure to tell the story in a way that does not marginalize the beneficiary (total time per student: 6 minutes).

Challenge 5: Personal pitch: Prepare for 1 minute and then in 1 minute or less, tell what do you want others to know about you? (Total time per student: 3 minutes).

SHORT CASE: SHRUTI SEHRA AND AMINA FAHMY AT NEW PROFIT—SELECTING HIGH-IMPACT ENTREPRENEURS

Shruti Sehra and Amina Fahmy wrapped up another call as they worked to finalize the recommendations for their 2020 selection process. They had spent the past few weeks reducing the number of potential organizations New Profit would support in this selection round from 40 to 10 finalists and would soon decide on two ventures to move into diligence.

Fahmy was a Partner at New Profit, where she helped to develop New Profit's selection strategy and oversee selection processes for incoming portfolio organizations as well as the measurement and management of the portfolio's performance. Prior to joining New Profit, Fahmy was a Research Analyst at the Brookings Institution, where she conducted research related to education and institutional reform, private sector engagement in development, and social entrepreneurship in the Middle East and North Africa.

Sehra was a Managing Partner at New Profit, where she led the education practice. Prior to that, she had led New Profit's Reimagine Learning and Early Learning Funds and its portfolio management practice. She served on the boards of CASEL, PowerMyLearning, and Zearn, and chairs the board of New Teacher Center.

Together Fahmy and Sehra were responsible for a 2020 selection round for a new set of organizations focused on advancing Wellbeing in Education. This issue area was a growing interest of New Profit's education team even before the Covid pandemic, and it took on increased urgency in the wake of the pandemic's impact on the well-being of students, teachers, and families. The process aimed to identify new nonprofit grantee partners in the education sector who provide school or instructional supports to advance the well-being of young people, educators, and families. Using an open call for letters of intent (and networking to make sure they reached a broad group of potential leaders), they received 173 proposals.

New Profit was founded in 1998 by serial social entrepreneur Vanessa Kirsch with a compelling observation: while there were many different support systems to help conventional entrepreneurs scale their ideas, the same system did not exist for mission driven organizations and nonprofits. She observed that it was difficult for nonprofits to achieve a scale that could meaningfully influence a shift in the underlying system. Her solution was to create New Profit, a venture philanthropy organization that backs breakthrough social entrepreneurs who are advancing equity and opportunity in America. Venture philanthropy is the nonprofit sector's version of VC. Instead of the VC approach of pooling funding to invest in high-potential for-profit ventures in hopes of securing outsized financial returns, venture philanthropists secure donations and pool them to make multiyear grants to help nonprofits scale rapidly and catalyze social innovation.

Since 1998, New Profit had funded 165 high-impact entrepreneurs, providing over $325 million in capital and other support. It has also sponsored multiple initiatives to help develop the nonprofit sector, including a nonpartisan policy initiative and coalition, called America Forward, which provided a platform for social entrepreneurs to advance a public policy agenda that championed innovative and effective solutions to pressing social challenges. Recognizing the complexity of important social challenges, New Profit has invested in a broad range of issue areas, but focused its efforts on supporting high-potential, primarily nonprofit ventures in the education, post-secondary, and career pathways, health, economic mobility, criminal justice, and civic engagement, with education representing the largest portion of their portfolio. Once an organization was selected, New Profit invested in the organization (with no expectation of return of funds). Its flagship Build Program provided four-year $1 million investments. For selected organizations, a member of the New Profit team would join the Board of Directors and provide ongoing strategic advising and coaching to the CEO, as well as other strategic and tactical assistance to the organization as needed. Having supported 165 organizations since the founding of New Profit, the team had a wealth of knowledge to draw upon about what would and what would not help an ambitious nonprofit grow effectively.

Since 2014, there had been a growing consensus among New Profit's board and staff that there were issues with their approach to selecting entrepreneurs and in particular that it disfavored entrepreneurs of color. New Profit also had seen from experience that "proximity is expertise" and believed that founders who are part of or close to the communities they intend to serve created more inclusive, innovative, and higher-impact ventures. This thinking informed the creation of the Inclusive Impact initiative and led New Profit to significantly increase the focus of its multiyear philanthropic investment capital and capacity building support on nonprofits led by leaders of color and leaders with proximity to the communities they served and issues they're tackling. Their aim was to build leadership in the philanthropic sector that is more representative of, and proximate to, the communities the sector serves.

Rather than reviewing business plans, as is common for other funders, New Profit's venture selection process started with a letter of intent, asking basic questions, and strategic and vision-focused questions about each organization. Paring down 173 applications to a "short list" of 37 wasn't easy. Organizations that met initial criteria were those that provided in-school or instructional support, had a full-time social entrepreneur as leader, a diversified funding stream, over $1.2M in annual revenues, and operated in two or more geographic locations. While the pool included many potentially impactful ventures, the first cut eliminated those that did not meet these binary eligibility guidelines, reducing the number to 128. These were evaluated by at least three readers, then the top third were discussed among a larger group of organization leaders, and staff members used a point-based rubric to rank those still in the pool. Four categories were assessed:

- *The entrepreneur*—including their commitment to and experience with the communities they serve, their drive and their experience making courageous, data-driven choices;

- *The impact model*—including the entrepreneurial insight, how it addresses barriers to opportunity, demonstration of promising outcomes, and commitment to evidence-based learning and continuous improvement;
- *Organizational capacity for growth*—including a track record of sound financial management and aligned leadership; and,
- *Potential for New Profit value-add*—an assessment of how effectively New Profit could support accelerated impact and the entrepreneur's receptiveness to a collaborative relationship.

After a careful review, the pool of 37 proposals was reduced to six potential organizations that received in-depth screening. Fahmy and Sehra then had 90-minute interviews with each entrepreneur. They worked with a selection committee that included a diverse group of internal staff and a parent advisory council, which is composed of six parent leaders. Again, a rubric supported their evaluation, although Sehra worried that it might be hamstringing their instincts. She added: "Based on our experience supporting dozens of portfolio organizations, we have a very good idea of which ones will be successful, but while part of this has to do with the organization, a lot depends on things that are hard to quantify on a scoring sheet" (S. Sehra, email correspondence, October 2020).

New Profit has not asked organizations to present formal pitches since 2017, replacing them with the option to submit a statement or 2-minute video as part of the application's supplementary materials. In the past, the selection team had found a formal pitch helpful for assessing the personal qualities of the entrepreneurs and make judgments about their ability to attract stakeholders and outside capital. However, Sehra and Fahmy were concerned about the burden of preparing a formal pitch and worried that it favored leaders who have come from consulting and/or finance backgrounds, potentially introducing implicit bias to the selection process. They observed that while interactions with the social entrepreneurs were key to learning about them and their leadership, they could gain this understanding outside of a pitch process.

The six finalists were all organizations led by people of color. They spanned different regions (operating in the south, midwest, east coast, and west coast), as well as different approaches (including schools, school-support programs, and parent engagement groups) and the organizations varied in age from newly minted nonprofits to 20+ year old organizations. "The challenge of moving from 37 very worthy proposals to six was really challenging" according to Fahmy, "but in the end we chose organizations that were at a stage and moment of growth which we believed we were well positioned to accelerate with both our funding and strategic support" (A. Fahmy, email correspondence, October 2020).

At the conclusion of this process, two organizations were selected for final due diligence. This process involved interviews with the senior team, board, staff, funders, and others to provide a 360-degree view of the organization. It also enabled them to articulate key questions that would cause the decision to go forward or not. According to Sehra: "This also enabled us to have conversations to build a healthy shoulder-to-shoulder relationship and build a shared perspective on how we can support the organization going forward" (S. Sehra, email correspondence, October 2020). Based on their analysis, an "investment hypothesis" memo was presented to an internal Investment Committee and the New Profit's Executive Committee of the board for final approval.

With the hard work of selection behind them, Fahmy and Sehra started to think about the future. How could they most effectively use the coming four years of partnership to enable the newly selected entrepreneurs and their teams to maximize their impact? How should they leverage their current portfolio of entrepreneurial leaders to support holistic systems change? And finally, how might they continuously innovate in their selection process to help New Profit achieve its ambitious goals going forward?

Discussion Questions

1. Do you think New Profit's efforts (and those of other venture philanthropy organizations) are effective at catalyzing change? Why or why not?
2. New Profit has chosen to focus on a small number of impact areas (and in particular education). Why do you think they made this choice vs. a more sector-agnostic approach?
3. What do you like about their selection process? Given the opportunity, how would you improve it?
4. Should they bring back in-person pitches as part of their selection process?
5. What do you see as the benefits of their work to be more inclusive? Do you have concerns?
6. If you were Fahmy or Sehra, what would keep you up at night?

NOTES

1. Bygrave, W. D., Lange, J., Mollov, A., Pearlmutter, M., & Singh, S. (2008). Pre-startup formal business plans and post-startup performance: A study of 116 new ventures. *Venture Capital Journal*, *9*(4), 1–20.
2. Brinckmann, J., Grichnik, D, & Kapsa, D. (2010). Should entrepreneurs plan or just storm the castle? A meta-analysis on contextual factors impacting the business planning–performance relationship in small firms. *Journal of Business Venturing*, *25*, 24–40.

3. Burke, A., Fraser, S., & Greene, F. (2010). The multiple effects of business planning on new venture performance. *Journal of Management Studies, 47*(3), 391–415.
4. Rich, S. R., & Gumpert, D. (2001). How to write a winning business plan. *Harvard Business Review*. HBR OnPoint Enhanced Edition.
5. Mehrabian, A., & Weiner, M. (1967). Decoding of inconsistent communications. *Journal of Personality and Social Psychology, 6*, 109–114.
6. Cuddy, A., Glick, P., & Beninger, A. (2011). The dynamics of warmth and competence judgments, and their outcomes in organizations. *Research in Organizational Behavior, 31*, 73–98.
7. Willis, J., & Todorov, A. (2006). First impressions: Making up your mind after a 100-Ms exposure to a face. *Psychological Science, 17*(7), 592–598.
8. Sweller, J. (1988). Cognitive load during problem solving: Effects on learning. *Cognitive Science, 12*, 257–285.
9. TED. (2016, July 8). *Fake it till you make it | Amy Cuddy* [Video]. YouTube. Retrieved from https://www.youtube.com/watch?v=RVmMeMcGc0Y.

CHAPTER TEN

SOCIAL ENTREPRENEURSHIP IN A GLOBAL CONTEXT

Learning Objectives

- Identify the potential economic impact of entrepreneurship.
- Assess the promise of global social entrepreneurship and its relevance for achieving social goals.
- Describe characteristics of global social entrepreneurs.
- Distinguish between different types of entrepreneurial ventures based on their scale and market focus.

It is no surprise that social entrepreneurs and the institutions that support them have focused their attention on making an impact around the world. Entrepreneurship is a powerful engine for economic growth, and social entrepreneurs are using their mission-focused skills to tackle chronic social problems ranging from addressing food insecurity in sub-Saharan Africa to expanding education access in India to addressing racial disparities in the United States. *Forbes* magazine described both the promise and complexity of this kind of problem-solving, observing that "social entrepreneurs are working in close collaboration with local communities, incubating groundbreaking (and often lifesaving) innovations; modeling synergistic partnerships with governments, companies, and traditional charities; and building business models that deploy technology and enable networking to create wins for investors and clients alike."[1]

In this chapter, we take a broad look at both entrepreneurship and social entrepreneurship around the world and examine different models that are enabling mission-driven entrepreneurs to address society's most pressing problems.

THE ECONOMIC IMPACT OF ENTREPRENEURSHIP

Global Entrepreneurial Impact

Nearly a century ago, influential Austrian economist Joseph Schumpeter theorized that entrepreneurship was a key factor in innovation and technological change. He later asserted that "the doing of new things or the doing of things that are already being done in a new way" stemmed directly from the efforts of entrepreneurs.[2] Schumpeter first coined the term "creative destruction," which describes "the essential fact" of capitalist economies which is the incessant destruction of old ways of doing business as new ones replace them.[3] His theory illustrates an essential characteristic of entrepreneurs: their willingness to question the status quo and search for more efficient paths.

Prominent American economic theorist William Baumol is credited with giving the entrepreneur a key role in mainstream economic theory. Among his many contributions (several of which build on work by Schumpeter) is his argument that institutional context influences the nature of entrepreneurship and its impact, contending that the nature and quality of institutions (for example, tax policy and protection) affects whether or not entrepreneurial activity has beneficial outcomes.[4]

Starting in the 1970s and 1980s, entrepreneurship emerged as an engine for economic growth in developed economies after a centuries-long decline. Scholars cite multiple reasons for this, including that the "growth of the service sector with its smaller scale and lower entry barriers, and increasing differentiation of consumer preferences, declining transactions costs and a trend in occupational preferences towards more autonomy and self-realization."[5] They also note that increased information and communication technologies create new business opportunities and lower costs, enabling small firms to benefit more easily from scale economies.[6]

In the United States, research using Census Bureau 2013 longitudinal data demonstrated that while start-ups account for only 3% of employment nationwide, they are responsible for almost 20% of national gross job creation. The authors observe a robust up-or-out dynamic of young firms succeeding or failing and observe that the young firms that survive grow more rapidly than their more mature counterparts.[7]

Entrepreneurship in Emerging and Developing Economies

Perhaps the most comprehensive source of information on global entrepreneurship is the Global Entrepreneurship Monitor (GEM), which has been published annually for over two decades. In their 2019/2020 global report, the authors summarize the results of over 150,000 individual interviews conducted over 50 economies. They examine factors that include attitudes towards entrepreneurship, the motivations of those starting businesses, and the level of entrepreneurial activity in each economy.

The GEM authors observe that "entrepreneurship is a uniquely powerful mechanism for economic and social development, generating incomes and jobs while enabling and enriching individuals and communities." Benefits include job and income creation, innovation, and individual autonomy, although the extent to which they are realized varies by economy.[8]

In the emerging BRIC (Brazil, Russia, India, China) economies, significant growth has been driven by entrepreneurship. Entrepreneurs' ability to access knowledge, markets, and education have all been factors enabling economic expansion.[9]

In less developed economies, necessity is often a driving force. Economists distinguish between two types of entrepreneurship: opportunity driven and necessity driven. **Opportunity entrepreneurs** are those who start a venture because they spot an opportunity in the market which they want to pursue. **Necessity entrepreneurs** are those who start a venture because they do not have another means of generating income. Opportunity-driven entrepreneurship leads to higher levels of economic growth, while necessity-driven entrepreneurship has been shown to be less promising and can even have a negative effect. Scholars have observed a downside to high levels of necessity-driven entrepreneurship. A study of 48 developing countries found a negative relationship between established business ownership rate (the percent of the population who are owner-managers of an established business) and per capita GDP and GNI, questioning whether, among other reasons, a high prevalence of necessity-driven entrepreneurship could be crowding out more productive opportunity-driven entrepreneurship and the formation of high growth ventures.[10]

The higher value of opportunity-driven entrepreneurship has also been demonstrated in multiple studies. In a 2020 analysis that followed 22 transitional and developed economies in Europe, the authors found a strong correlation between opportunity-driven entrepreneurship and economic growth.[11] An analysis of a large sample of female entrepreneurs in Mexico showed that on average, opportunity entrepreneurs had better performance and higher skills than necessity entrepreneurs and the researchers also observed that opportunity entrepreneurs achieved better venture performance and used better management practices.[12]

The Importance of Institutional and Cultural Context

For entrepreneurship to thrive, the institutional environment matters. Unsurprisingly, countries with stable governments, transparent legal systems, and strong property rights' protections are more conducive to entrepreneurship; this is also true of those with low regulatory burdens, availability of entrepreneurial education, and strong professional, commercial, and physical infrastructure. The World Bank annually ranks 170 countries on the ease of doing business. In 2020, New Zealand ranked #1, and the Democratic Republic of Sao Tome and Principe, an island country off the western equatorial coast of Central Africa, was #170. The factors the World Bank considered included start-up time and cost, ability to get credit, tax policy, and how effectively jurisdictions enforce contracts and resolve insolvency.[13]

Social norms are also important. For example, when Linda Rottenberg and Peter Kellner launched Endeavor in five countries in Latin America, they found that the countries they had entered lacked the tradition of celebrating entrepreneurs as community wealth creators that existed in many other countries and also had limited infrastructure to support entrepreneurs. "For Linda, the light bulb moment for Endeavor came in the back of a taxicab in Buenos Aires. She struck up a conversation with the driver and was shocked to learn he had a PhD in Engineering. She asked if he hadn't considered becoming an entrepreneur instead of driving a taxi. 'An empresario?' he said dismissively, using the Spanish word for a big businessperson. It suddenly occurred to her that there was no Spanish word for entrepreneur."[14] Endeavor's founders made it their mission to celebrate entrepreneurs, while building an infrastructure to support them, and today Endeavor operates in over 30 countries around the world with an impressive track record of facilitating entrepreneurial ventures and catalyzing job creation.

Across the 61 countries surveyed in 2016 by GEM, over two-thirds of the adult population believed that entrepreneurs are well regarded and enjoy high status. The most positive attitudes were reported in Africa, with 77% of respondents believing entrepreneurs are admired and 75% believing entrepreneurship is a good career choice. In contrast, a smaller proportion of adults believed entrepreneurs to be well regarded in Latin America and the Caribbean (63%) and in Europe (58%).[15]

Entrepreneurial Motivation

Motivations for entrepreneurship vary from country to country. For example, the GEM adult population survey asked entrepreneurs in 50 countries their motivations for becoming an entrepreneur. In 60% of countries, over half of the entrepreneurs surveyed somewhat or strongly agreed that "building great wealth or very high income" was their motivation. But this motivation differed country by country, with fewer than half the countries in Europe and North America reporting this dominance, while most did in the Asian and the Pacific regions as well as in nearly all of the 11 countries in the Middle East and Africa.[16]

Necessity-driven entrepreneurial formation, the drive "to earn a living because jobs are scarce," motivated more than half the adults that started new businesses in a large share (70%) of the countries GEM surveyed. There were significant regional and country-by-country differences. Half or more of the entrepreneurs somewhat or strongly agreed with the statement in every Latin American and Middle Eastern and African country surveyed, while entrepreneurs in Europe, North America, and the Asian and Pacific regions were much less likely to be motivated by earning a living. This underscores the concentration of necessity-driven entrepreneurship in less-developed nations.[17]

A third motivation, and the one most relevant to social entrepreneurs, is "to make a difference in the world." On this dimension, we counted countries where half of the entrepreneurs somewhat or strongly agreed with this statement; the percentage of countries by region was as follows:

- Latin America and the Caribbean—63%
- Middle East and Africa—45%
- Asia and the Pacific—38%
- Europe and North America—22%

The countries with the highest proportion of entrepreneurs expressing their agreement about the importance of making a difference were India, South Africa, Guatemala, and Panama (all with over 75% of entrepreneurs agreeing) closely followed by Canada, Poland, and the United States.[18]

THE PROMISE OF GLOBAL SOCIAL ENTREPRENEURSHIP

In the section above, we discussed why entrepreneurship has positive economic outcomes. Now, we'll turn our focus to social entrepreneurship as an engine for positive social change. Around the globe, examples of innovative solutions created by social entrepreneurs creating sustainable social change abound. Prominent examples include the following:

- *BRAC*, headquartered in Bangladesh, improves livelihoods by founding a series of social enterprises. Some of these enterprises, which include self-sustaining ventures in dairy production, fisheries, agriculture and seeds, silk production, and cattle insemination, among others, help give microentrepreneurs, farmers, and producers the tools, resources, and market access they need to raise their incomes. The results have been astonishing. BRAC reaches millions of the world's poorest people in Africa, India, and Asia, and its commercial ventures are largely self-supporting.
- *Aravind Eye Hospital* in Maduria, India, leveraged the profits from performing cataract surgery in a for-profit hospital to provide free services for the poorest of India's blind population. Today, the Aravind Eye Care System has treated more than 65.5 million patients and performed 7.8 million surgeries. Using a model of high volume and intense specialization, Aravind can perform cataract surgeries 98% cheaper than in the United States, with outcomes that are as good as or better than those realized in the United States and Europe.[19] Aravind is also self-supporting.
- The *One Acre Fund* was started in Kenya in 2006 by Andrew Youn with a simple observation: most families in rural Africa farm at a subsistence level, but a few low-cost improvements can dramatically increase yields. Youn was

motivated to start One Acre when he visited rural Kenya during "hunger season," a time when staple food had run out and families were barely surviving. But he also saw that some farmers achieved dramatically higher yields by using hybrid seeds, fertilizer, and crop spacing. "Smallholder farmers comprise 75% of the world' poorest citizens, including 50 million households in Africa, (most of whom) live in remote areas of the world and do not have access to basic agricultural tools and training."[20] The One Acre Fund provides a bundle of services to small groups of farmers, including seed and fertilizer access, credit, training on farming techniques, and postharvest and market support.[21] Today, One Acre works with over 1 million farmers in six countries in Africa—Kenya, Rwanda, Burundi, Tanzania, Uganda, and Malawi. One Acre also employs 6,000 field agents in over 4,500 rural locations who are responsible for enrolling farmers, providing input, and collecting payments.

- *Sanergy* was founded by a global team of young social entrepreneurs in 2010 (Sanergy's evolution is discussed in a case at the end of this book) as a hybrid for-profit and nonprofit enterprise that operates a network of franchised pay toilets in informal settlements in Nairobi, Kenya. Sanergy collects and processes the human waste that is produced to create high-quality fertilizers and animal feed byproducts. In doing so, it solves one of the most important problems in the slums by improving sanitation and reducing harmful pollution. Sanergy has "grown in" in Nairobi, increasing the number of pay toilets by expanding the use of its original franchise model as well as partnering with property owners and community institutions to make sanitation even more accessible. It currently serves nearly 140,000 urban residents daily with its network of 3,500 active toilets, removing 2,800 million metric tonnes of waste from Nairobi's slums in 2020.[22]

What can we learn from these examples? They use different approaches and operate in a range of developing nations. Some have urban operations; others operate in rural areas. Their focuses span sanitation, agriculture, and health care. But they also have common elements. Each addresses a social goal and, at the same time, creates economic opportunity for individuals and communities. Each has scaled their concept to foster significant social benefit. Each uses innovation as a foundation. This ranges from One Acre's experimentation with unique crop yield technologies to Sanergy's use of a systems approach, to bring together different elements to solve a persistent problem in a financially sustainable way, to Aravind's use of a cross-subsidized pricing model to make eye surgery affordable to very low-income individuals. And each started with the vision of a single person or small team with a commitment to make a difference in the world.

Entrepreneurship and the UN Sustainable Development Goals

The distribution of income and resources across the globe is uneven. One in ten people in developing regions lives on less than the international poverty line of US $1.90 a day. While global poverty rates have been reduced by more than half since 2000, the rate of decline has slowed. And while progress has been made in many countries within Eastern and Southeastern Asia, up to 42% of the population in sub-Saharan Africa continues to live below the poverty line. Poverty means more than just limited income—it also means lack of access to food, education, and basic services. Ten percent of the world's population is living in extreme poverty and struggling to fulfill their most basic needs. There are also gender and age dimensions to poverty, with women and children much more likely than men to live in extreme poverty.[23]

Entrepreneurship has the power to help reduce poverty by providing job opportunities and economic growth. Social entrepreneurship, in addition to creating jobs, can improve living conditions by increasing access to food, water, energy, education, and other resources.

The UN Sustainable Development Goals (also known as the SDGs or Global Goals) are 17 interlinked goals intended to be a "blueprint to achieve a better and more sustainable future for all."[24] The SDGs were established in 2015 by the United Nations General Assembly and intended to be achieved between 2020 and 2030.[25]

Figure 10.1 UN Sustainable Development Goals

Source: United Nations Sustainable Development Goals. https://www.un.org/sustainabledevelopment/. Used with permission. (The content of this publication has not been approved by the United Nations and does not reflect the views of the United Nations or its officials or Member States.)

The social ventures described above have all worked towards reaching these goals; some have addressed multiple goals. For example, Aravind Eye Hospital focuses on a single objective, Goal #3 (good health and well-being). The One Acre Fund is making progress on Goals #1 and #2 (zero poverty and no hunger). Sanergy is meaningfully addressing Goal #6 (clean water and sanitation). But along the way, it is also addressing Goal #3 (good health and well-being) and Goal #11 (sustainable cities and communities). Its impact does not stop there. By using waste products to generate its own electricity, it is contributing towards Goal #7 (affordable and clean energy) and its operations and franchise model both contribute to achieving Goals #5 and #8 (decent work and economic growth, and gender equality). Similarly, BRAC, with its multifaceted operations, helps contribute to progress on over half the goals.

Achieving the SDGs requires collaboration across sectors and social enterprises have a special role to play because they can scale rapidly and, in many cases, use financially self-sustaining models. That said, social entrepreneurship is not the only solution. Given the magnitude of the goals, social ventures are only part of an effort that requires focused and concerted efforts by individuals, companies, NGOs, governments, philanthropies, and individuals. As part of their 2020 Impact Report, the Schwab Foundation for Social Entrepreneurship (a foundation that for two decades has supported social entrepreneurs globally) surveyed 133 late-stage social entrepreneurs to, among other things, understand how their ventures addressed the SDGs. They found that 90% of the social entrepreneurs surveyed reported that their strategies are somewhat or significantly influenced by the SDGs. The focus of respondents (many of whom reported targeting multiple goals) was on the following:

- Goal 1—No poverty (51%)
- Goal 2—Good health and well-being (51%)
- Goal 4—Quality education (50%)
- Goal 5—Gender equality (50%)
- Goal 8—Decent work and economic growth (50%)
- Goal 10—Reduced inequalities (36%)[26]

The SDGs have been highly effective at catalyzing innovation and political commitment. However, progress towards the goals is not currently on track, according to the UN's September 2019 High Level Political Forum. Moreover, significant and widespread economic and social hardship caused by the worldwide COVID-19 pandemic will likely further erode progress.

Factors Supporting the Growth of Global Social Entrepreneurship

Similar to commercial entrepreneurship, there are numerous trends that have supported the growth of social entrepreneurship. A major tailwind has been technology. The availability of simple and widespread infrastructure for communicating and processing information has reduced the cost of starting ventures and the cost to reach and serve recipients and customers. Regulatory reforms that simplify trading across borders and the increased ability to enforce contracts are just a few elements that have made it easier to create new ventures.

Figure 10.2 shows how these important trends have resulted in lower business formation costs. Each year, the World Bank tracks the cost of starting new business in 190 economies. In high-income economies, the cost of starting a business (as a percentage of income per capita) declined threefold, from an average of 12% in 2004 to only 4% in 2020. The decline in low- and middle-income economies has been even more dramatic—from an average of 142% in 2004 to 25% in 2020. This means that the 2020 cost was only 17% of the cost in 2004.[27]

Constraints to Global Social Entrepreneurship

Despite this progress, social entrepreneurs continue to face impediments. One that we see in Figure 10.2 is that the cost of starting ventures remains significantly higher as a percentage of per capita income in low- and middle-income countries than in high-income countries. Another impediment is that in some countries, regulatory barriers to starting a business are persistent and, in some cases, increasing.

Figure 10.2 Cost of Starting a Business as a Percentage of Income per Capita

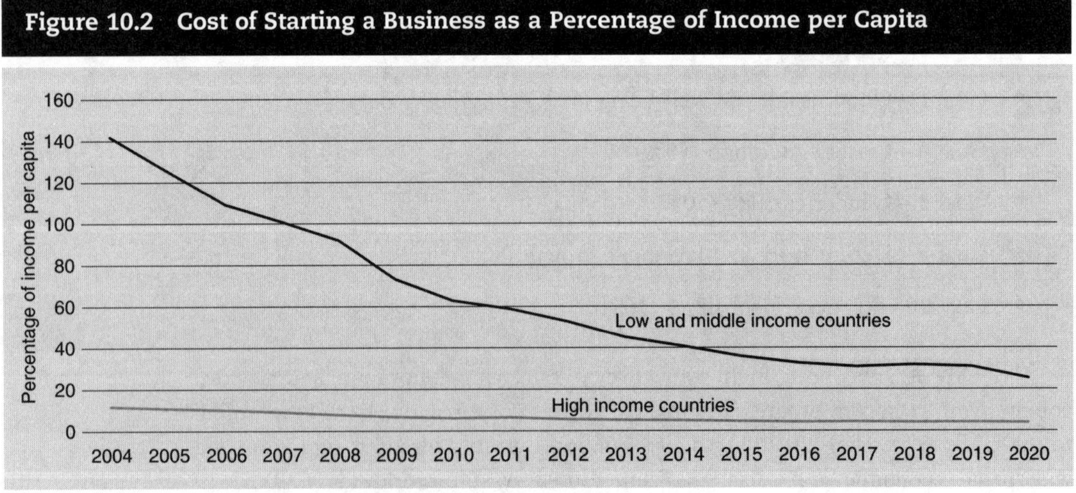

Source: World Bank. *Annual Doing Business Reports 2004–2020*. Used with permission.

In many countries, gender inequities make it harder for women to start new ventures. A lack of capital or credit can also be a significant barrier. And finally, in some countries, social norms, class structure, attitude towards risk taking, and a lack of positive role models constrain the formation of new mission-driven ventures. For example, the World Economic Forum's Global Competitiveness Index surveyed individuals in 139 countries in 2019 asking on a 1–7 scale, "In your country, to what extent do people have an appetite for entrepreneurial risk?" Results varied from lows scores of 2.40 in Mauritania and 2.77 in Haiti to high scores of 5.55 in the United States and 5.96 in Israel. Higher risk appetite had a moderately strong correlation to income per capita.[28]

Resources Supporting Mission-Driven Ventures

Mission-driven founders use a patchwork of funding sources including personal funds, friends, colleagues, and private investors (including philanthropic investors and government funds). The GEM's 2015 Report on Social Entrepreneurship found that most start-up social entrepreneurs invest personal funds, and this ranges from a high 80% of founders in Southeast Asia to a low of 64% in Western Europe. More than a third of the world's social entrepreneurial ventures rely on government funding. This source is particularly important for entrepreneurs in the United States and Australia, where, as Table 10.1 shows, 55% of entrepreneurs utilize these funds. Private investments or venture capital is used by over a quarter of entrepreneurs in the United States and Australia, Western Europe, and Sub-Saharan Africa. Founders in Southeast Asia and Sub-Saharan Africa are more likely than those in other regions to rely on family, friends, and neighbors. Relying on volunteers is another important resource, and GEM found that in all regions except for Western Europe, over half of those working for social ventures were volunteers.[29]

CHARACTERISTICS OF GLOBAL SOCIAL ENTREPRENEURS

When we consider social entrepreneurship around the world, it quickly becomes clear that there are significant differences between countries, regions, and types of economies. These differences affect who becomes a social entrepreneur, what their motivations are, and how they access the resources that they need to support their ventures.

In the 50 countries assessed by GEM and using a broad definition of social entrepreneurship (including both social and value creation goals), 3% of the adult population in these countries work in a nascent (start-up phase) social venture. The proportion varies from 0.3% in South Korea to 10.1% in Peru. The highest proportions can be found in factor-driven (developing) economies. An additional 3.7% is involved in operational (post start-up) social entrepreneurship. As a point of

Table 10.1 Sources of External Funding for Social Entrepreneurs by Region

	Southeast Asia (%)	MENA (%)	Sub-Saharan Africa (%)	Eastern Europe (%)	Western Europe (%)	Latin America/ Caribbean (%)	United States/ Australia (%)
Family	68	51	67	49	38	36	37
Friends and Neighbors	47	9	39	18	14	23	18
Employer or Work Colleagues	28	12	27	23	18	18	30
Bank/Financial Institution	37	19	42	19	25	24	27
Private Investor/Venture Capital	11	9	27	19	25	15	27
Government	25	28	38	42	43	41	55
Crowdfunding	11	11	0	14	9	7	18

Numbers add to more than 100% in each region because multiple sources of financing are used. Based on use of funding reported by social entrepreneurs (broad definition).

Source: Global Entrepreneurship Monitor. *Report on Social Entrepreneurship 2015/16*. Used with permission.

comparison, the rate of start-up for commercial entrepreneurship averages 7.6% in the world, ranging from a low of nearly 1.4% in Vietnam to a high of over 22% in Peru.[30]

If a narrower definition is used, where ventures have a market orientation and social value creation is the primary driver, the average prevalence of social entrepreneurs overall is 2.3% of adults with 1.1% in the start-up phase and 1.2% in the operating phase.[31]

Of the world's social entrepreneurs, an estimated 55% are male and 45% are female, a much smaller gap than for commercial entrepreneurship where male founders outnumber female founders by approximately 2:1.[32] Education levels differ across regions: 62% of US and Australian entrepreneurs have a post-secondary education, compared to half of those in the Middle East and North Africa, Eastern Europe, and Western Europe. In every region, social entrepreneurs are more likely to have postsecondary education than their commercial entrepreneur counterparts.[33]

Both commercial and social entrepreneurs are often young. In the Middle East, North Africa, and sub-Saharan Africa, over 50% of social entrepreneurs are in the 18–34 age range and in most other regions, over a third are in this range. The exception is the United States and Australia where 28% of start-up entrepreneurs and 18% of operating social entrepreneurs are young. In every region, the percentage of young operating phase social entrepreneurs exceeded that of commercial entrepreneurs, perhaps reflecting the idealism of young adults everywhere.[34]

In nearly all locations, both start-up and operating social entrepreneurs tend to be likely to have higher incomes than the adult population average. The exception is sub-Saharan Africa, where operating social entrepreneurs are more likely to have higher incomes than the overall population, but start-up entrepreneurs are not.[35]

The Schwab Foundation for Social Entrepreneurship's 2019/20 survey of their 133 late-stage social entrepreneurs demonstrates the diversity of issues addressed by social entrepreneurs. The top issues that they reported addressing were education (35%), economic opportunity and development (26%), entrepreneurship and enterprise development (26%), and health and health care (23%).[36] This is unsurprising based on both the high impact potential of ventures in these areas, and the existence of self-sustaining business models launched by social entrepreneurs in these spaces discussed earlier in this book (for example, India's Ekal Vidyalaya in education, Bangladesh's BRAC in economic opportunity, global player Endeavor in entrepreneurship development, and Israel-based Genesis in health care).

The same survey also identified the ten countries in which late-stage Schwab entrepreneurs are most active. The locations spanned the globe. Outside of the United States (30%), all of the ten top countries where efforts were focused were low- to middle-income economies, and the entrepreneurs were most active in India (36%), Kenya (26%), and Brazil (22%).[37]

PROFILE: MICHAEL SLY AT WILDING AND CO.—LEVERAGING A GLOBAL MARKET TO MEET LOCAL GOALS

Michael Sly credits his mother—a single parent and entrepreneur—with helping to spark his own entrepreneurial initiative. During his formative years, he watched his mother convert a small grape-growing business in Arrowtown, New Zealand, into a local wine producer, which inspired his interest in creating and growing new ventures.

Sly studied industrial design at Victoria University of Wellington and used the skills he acquired there to found several entrepreneurial ventures. First, he started a website design company called Chrometoaster. Later, inspired by his interest in textiles, he created a process to convert New Zealand flax (harakeke), a locally grown spear grass, into a new textile product. He became intrigued by this idea while he was building a client website, which focused on using new technology to extract products from plants. This led him to start working with an indigenous Maori group *(Ngai Tahu)* to help them restart the lost art of creating fragrances from native plant extracts. These diverse experiences, combined with his deep interest in environmental sustainability, created the foundation for Wilding and Co., a for-profit venture that removes invasive trees in New Zealand, and uses them to produce pine-scented essential oils. Essential oils are plant extracts obtained through distillation or pressing.

On New Zealand's South Island, the problems created by wilding pines are well documented. Over ten species of nonnative conifers were originally introduced to the area in the late 1800s to shelter homes, protect livestock, and provide timber. But the fast-growing pines proved to be prolific producers of seeds and spread rapidly, crowding out native trees and other plants, as well as the birds and insects that rely on them. The New Zealand Department of Conservation estimates that without rapid action, 20% of New Zealand will be invaded by wilding conifer forests within 20 years. Wilding conifers currently cover more than 1.8 million hectares of land and are spreading at an estimated rate of 5% a year. Approaches to reducing the spread have included the use of herbicides, removing seedlings by hand, and cutting down existing trees.

Sly's entrepreneurial inspiration was that rather than wasting the by-products of discarded pine trees, he could turn them into a commercially viable product and, as a result, accelerate their removal. Leveraging his industrial engineering background and his prior experiences, he developed a process for extracting a high-quality essential oil from cut pines.

Finding the right business model for the company was not simple. After achieving initial success selling the essential oil product on a small scale through a dedicated website, Sly discovered that the New Zealand market size was simply too small to support the levels of production that would make a meaningful environmental impact.

A chance encounter at a US perfume conference in Connecticut (USA) propelled the company forward. Sitting in a bar at the site of the convention, Sly struck up a conversation with a person who turned out to be one of the fragrance and essential oil industry's most influential advisors. When his new acquaintance showed an interest in the product, Sly followed up with samples. He recounts: "He came back and said—can you make 6 tonnes?" Through a series of operational adjustment and by engaging committed partners, Sly was able to scale up to meet this demand. Today, Wilding's Douglas Fir Oil is marketed through doTERRA, which has sold millions of units (units are equivalent to 5 ml bottles), and in the process, Wilding and Co. has removed 50,000 invasive pines a year from the Queenstown Basin. On the doTERRA website, the marketing pitch describes the fragrance and quality of the oil, as well as the social mission.

Sly recounts: "I was always interested in the connection between large scale businesses and the environment. The major reason is that it can create an engine for scale. By partnering with a multinational company and tapping into a global market, I was able to multiply our impact on a local problem. What we used to produce in a year with our locally oriented product, we now produce in a half day."

Offering advice to aspiring social entrepreneurs, Sly draws on his marketing background. "It is important to understand the power of telling a great story. Our impact on removing an invasive species makes immediate sense to consumers."

He also reflects on the challenge facing social entrepreneurs. "Starting a new social venture is a really challenging process, one that requires a lot of social and environmental fitness, as well as business acumen and an ability to work well with external partners." He adds, "Don't be afraid to think big and to partner with the commercial sector—they can help you magnify your scale."

DIFFERENT TYPES OF MISSION-DRIVEN VENTURES

There are four different types of social ventures, based on their geographic scope and the markets they serve. The most successful approach depends on the venture's mission and the nature of its products and services. The choice of venture type can also affect growth potential, although as we describe below, expanding to a new market can be an option for mission-driven ventures with proven models.

Local Ventures Serving Local Needs

The majority of entrepreneurial ventures serve a local or in-country market. There are many reasons for this including lower start-up expenses and start-up entrepreneurs' tendency to focus on solving immediate and visible problems. The majority of both commercial and social entrepreneurs serve customers primarily within their borders.[38]

Social ventures are no exception. Consider the case of OliLand, which was founded in 2018 by Amjad Dwikat with a simple observation: every year, more than 60,000 metric tonnes of waste are produced in Israel and Palestine as a byproduct of pressing olive oil. The waste can be converted into a valuable biofuel product; unfortunately, because this requires specialized equipment, the waste is usually discarded and ends up filling landfill sites and creating pollution. OliLand dries and processes the waste into briquettes that it sells to local bakeries because the high temperature and consistent size is ideal for fueling ovens. The venture is self-supporting and diverts approximately 500 metric tonnes of waste a year. OliLand operates on a small scale with a limited market, collecting waste from olive oil producers operating in a small geography, the north part of Palestine's West Bank. The briquettes that are produced are heavy and difficult to transport, so virtually all of the products are sold to users within a 60-kilometer radius of the production facility. While there may be ways to scale the concept (for example, expanding to other markets), the reliance on local inputs and a local market makes it most efficient to operate as a niche, local social enterprise.

A different example is STREETS International, located in Hoi An, Vietnam. STREETS provides culinary and hospitality training for disadvantaged youth in Vietnam, providing high-quality career paths in the hospitality industry. STREETS also runs a café and a learn-to-cook program aimed at tourists to help its students gain English language skills. While the venture provides services locally (and covers most of its expenses through earned income), it also receives charitable funding from US donors. Its 18-month training program follows a curriculum developed in conjunction with the Institute of Culinary Education in New York. By ultimately serving a tourist market via hotel employment for its graduates, as well as its café and cooking school, STREETS leverages out-of-country resources to fund a local need. Catering to the lucrative tourism hospitality market enables higher wages for trainees after graduation, and the café and cooking school create both training and language learning opportunities in addition to generating operating funds.

What can aspiring social entrepreneurs learn from these ventures? First, that meeting social needs usually requires a local focus, at least initially. Second, founders should be realistic about limitations. For example, in OliLand's case, a niche market (bakeries) and limited portability (heavy, hard-to-transport briquettes) naturally limited growth.

That said, some ventures that initially have a local focus evolve to serve larger markets both by diversifying their products and services and expanding geographically. For example, SunBox, profiled in a short case in Chapter 3, initially provided solar electricity to residences in Palestine. But over time, entrepreneur Majd Mashharawi evolved the venture, providing electrical services for hospitals and other commercial ventures. Serving a broader range of customers expanded SunBox's capabilities and this growth enabled Mashharawi to plan the creation of a for-profit solar company in Saudi Arabia.

Local Ventures With a Global Market

Many international ventures seek to create local wealth by tapping into a global marketplace. Most fair-trade organizations fall into this category. For example,

Prosperity Candle (profiled in a short case in Chapter 6) was established to enable women in conflict regions to earn a "prosperity wage" by producing high quality candles primarily for export. The founders of Prosperity Candle also established a candle factory in Western Massachusetts where they employ refugees.

Equal Exchange is one of the pioneers of fair trade that uses this model. The venture was founded as a worker-owned cooperative in 1986 by Rink Dickinson, Jonathan Rosenthal, and Michael Rozyne. Their insight (which has been widely adopted) was that small scale coffee farmers in Latin America live in unstable economic situations while their products passed through multiple intermediaries to then be sold at a premium in developed countries. They went on to develop what became the largest and oldest fair trade coffee company in the United States by establishing long-term contracts for farmers and offering higher-than-market prices. Today, Equal Exchange distributes organic gourmet coffee, tea, sugar, bananas, avocados, cocoa, and chocolate bars produced by farmer cooperatives in Latin America, Africa, and Asia. Fair trade as an approach to expanding markets and increasing incomes has grown significantly. Today, the World Fair Trade Organization has 3,000 members, who are improving the livelihoods of nearly 1 million people worldwide.[39]

A more recent example is Mercado Global, founded in 2004 by Ruth Alvarez-Degolia and CoFounder Benita Singh. Alvarez-Degolia conceived of the idea for the organization during college when she completed two summer internships in Guatemala's Highlands and saw first-hand the extreme poverty and lack of opportunity that existed after the country's crushing civil war. While still in college, she tested the market by bringing handcrafts back to campus and found that she was able to sell $5,000 worth of crafts in a single weekend, enough to send 26 local children to school for a year. Based on her experience, she wrote a business plan and won the Yale School of Management business plan contest in the nonprofit category. After graduating, she became an Echoing Green Fellow and started Mercado Global in earnest (R. Alvarez-Degolia, personal interview, October 20, 2020).

Today, Mercado Global is a nonprofit organization that works with women's cooperatives in Guatemala to create high-quality handmade products, which they sell through retail channels. All sales provide fair wages for the artisans and invest in their children's education. To support the women, they provide education on how to develop their businesses, support with asset development (for example, help purchasing sewing machines or looms), and market access.

One important lesson Alvarez-Degolia learned while expanding Mercado Global was that to work at a meaningful scale, she needed to tap into existing distribution networks, so she partnered with multiple retailers including Levi's, Free People, Stitch Fix, Target, and Nordstrom. She also learned that mission alone would not sell the product, observing: "While the story is the icing on the cake, the cake needs to be a really great product" (R. Alvarez-Degolia, personal interview, October 20, 2020). Mercado Global uses a "virtual factory" model where a network of artisan cooperatives produces products that meet the volume and quality requirements of its retail partners. An in-house design team ensures that the products are on-trend and will maximize income for artisans. And with a strong retail network firmly in place, she aims to expand Mercado Global's model to different product categories and regions.

Regional Ventures

Regional social ventures are those that serve multiple countries within a geographic area. Leveraging access across immediate borders, common time zones, and serving what are often similar economies and cultures, regional ventures are able to meet the similar social needs for a greater number of people than local or national ventures. However, because there are nearly always differences in local conditions, regional ventures must balance scope- and scale-related efficiencies with adapting to local needs.

The One Acre Fund is a social venture that has expanded regionally based on common needs. The social enterprise was founded in 2006 by MBA student Andrew Youn. After initially launching with 40 farmers in Kenya and recognizing that their solution would have regional appeal, One Acre expanded to Rwanda in Year 2. By the end of its second year in operations, the venture was serving roughly 600 farmers. Then things started to move even more quickly. Today, One Acre works with over 1 million farmers in six countries in Africa and has gross revenue of over $120 million.

Or consider the case of *BRAC* (founded as the Bangladesh Rural Advancement Committee), founded in Bangladesh in 1972. Today, BRAC is the world's largest nonprofit organization, helping an estimated 126 million people in 11 countries in Asia and Africa via health care, education, enterprise development, microfinance, and other programs. BRAC's expansion has been driven by many factors, but one of the most important has been that its demonstrated impact enabled it to attract partners (such as the Mastercard Foundation) that provided support for rapid scaling into additional countries. BRAC's efforts are concentrated in countries in Asia and Africa where its leaders believe it is best poised to alleviate poverty.

In some cases, social ventures define themselves by ethnic or cultural borders instead of national borders. For example, Genesis, an Israel-based venture that seeks to reduce the prevalence of genetic disease in Bedouin communities through premarital genetic testing (see the case at the end of this book), has started operations in Israel, where nationalized health care is expected to provide funding to support initial scaling. But the founder, Dr. Yasmeen Abu Fraiha, is well aware that there are 21 million Bedouins in the Middle East and North Africa that would benefit from Genesis' solution once the venture has proven itself and expansion funding can be secured.

Ambitious social entrepreneurs targeting international markets should also note that in all three of these examples, the venture's founders first entered one market, and then after they had proven their concept, expanded to others to gain regional scale.

Global Ventures

A handful of social ventures have established themselves as global players. The common thread among these ventures is the ability to translate a core concept or approach into a series of mutually supporting activities that meet human needs across many regions.

Endeavor is an example of this kind of geographic boundary spanner. It was founded in 1997 by Linda Rottenberg and Peter Kellner. Endeavor provides "mentor capitalist" services for high-potential entrepreneurial companies in emerging markets. It gives selected founders and teams with education, access to capital, and networks to increase the success rate of their businesses, thereby fostering economic growth, while at the same time working to promote entrepreneurship more broadly. After initially launching in five Latin American countries and refining its model, Endeavor now operates in 30 countries worldwide including countries in Asia, Africa, and the Middle East. It has helped over 2,000 entrepreneurs scale their ventures, creating 4.1 million jobs and earning $24 billion in revenues annually.[40]

One World Health, another venture with a global focus, was founded by pharmaceutical scientist Victoria Hale in San Francisco in 2000 when she saw an opportunity to develop effective, safe, and affordable treatments for neglected infectious diseases. Her insight was that many promising drugs were abandoned because they weren't lucrative for Western pharmaceutical companies, despite their lifesaving potential in lower-income countries. With funding from charitable foundations (including the Gates Foundation), One World Heath convinced for-profit pharmaceutical companies to donate abandoned intellectual property. It then created programs to develop cures for four deadly infectious parasitic diseases that affected millions of people worldwide. By conducting clinical trials and contracting with manufacturers in low-cost locations, they hoped to prove the efficacy of and then widely distribute life-saving drugs for free or at a low cost in South Asia, Africa, and South America.[41] In 2011, One World Health became a drug development affiliate of PATH, an international nonprofit global health organization based in Seattle.

Since then, other new ventures have built on Hale's insights about the unequal global availability of lifesaving treatments. For example, in 2006, Priti Krishtel, a 15-year veteran of the global access to medicines movement, and Tahir Amin, an attorney with more than 25 years of experience in intellectual property law, cofounded I-MAK, an organization that uses patent challenges and other approaches to reduce the cost of drugs in middle- and low-income countries. I-MAK has worked in 49 countries, expanding access to 33 therapies for 16 diseases and saved health systems more than $2 billion.[42]

What do all these global ventures have in common? They have a business model that leverages organization-wide intellectual capital and resources to solve an important global problem. They also have ambitious social entrepreneurs or teams at the helm who have a global vision for impact.

CHAPTER SUMMARY

In a world where millions of people live in poverty and many others lack access to essential goods and services, social entrepreneurs have the agility and motivation to fill many gaps. Entrepreneurship is an engine for economic growth and job creation around the world. Conditions have never been better: changes in technology and other factors have created enormous opportunities for social entrepreneurs to increase their impact globally. With a keen focus on solving persistent social problems and by levering entrepreneurial methods, tremendous opportunity exists for social entrepreneurs to change the world through local regional or global initiatives.

Entrepreneurship has long been a source of jobs, income creation, innovation, and individual autonomy across the globe. Starting in the 1970s and 1980s, entrepreneurship reemerged as an engine for economic growth in developed economies after a centuries-long decline. This was in large part due to lower barriers to entry, the growth of the service sector, and the prevalence of new technologies. While beneficial to many, the cost of starting ventures as a percentage of income remains significantly higher in low- and middle-income economies than in high-income economies. Countries with stable governments, transparent legal systems, and strong property rights protections are more open to entrepreneurship, as are those with low regulatory burdens, availability of entrepreneurial education, and strong professional, commercial, and physical infrastructure. Social and cultural norms are also important.

Another relevant factor is entrepreneurial motivation. Economists believe there are two main types: opportunity-driven entrepreneurship and necessity-driven entrepreneurship. Necessity-driven entrepreneurship develops where there are few other means to generate income. Opportunity-driven entrepreneurship develops in situations where a market is perceived to exist. Regardless of the location and type, the reasons that individuals become entrepreneurs are often fairly uniform. Most want to build wealth or simply earn a living; others strive to make a difference in the world. In some cases, like those of the One Acre Fund and BRAC, ventures can combine multiple goals successfully. In addition to creating jobs, these and other ventures improve living conditions by increasing access to food, water, energy, education, and other resources as well as help to achieve the UN SDGs.

There are four different types of social ventures based on geographic scope and market served: local ventures serving local needs, local ventures with a global market, regional ventures, and global ventures. The most successful approach depends on the venture's mission and the nature of its products and services. Because social enterprises can scale rapidly and provide financially self-sustaining models, they will continue to change the world, through local, regional, or global initiatives, and will likely help us achieve some of the UN's Global Goals.

KEY TERMS

Global ventures: translate a core concept or approach into a series of mutually supporting activities that meet human needs across many regions.

Local ventures serving local needs: serve a local or in-country market to help minimize start-up expenses and are often created because of an entrepreneur's focus on solving immediate and visible problems.

Local ventures with global markets: seek to create local wealth by tapping into a global marketplace with their products or services.

Necessity entrepreneurs: those who start a venture because they do not have another means of generating income.

Opportunity entrepreneurs: those who start a venture because they spot an opportunity in the market which they want to pursue.

Regional ventures: leverage access across immediate borders and common time zones to serve the similar needs of a greater number of people than those of local or national ventures—often due to the similarity in economies and cultures.

Schumpeter's theory of creative destruction: describes "the essential fact" of capitalist economies, which is described as the incessant destruction of the old ways of doing business as new ones replace them.

The United Nations Sustainable Development Goals: 17 interlinked goals intended to be a blueprint to achieve a better and more sustainable future for all.

IN-CLASS EXERCISE

Exercise 10.1: Entrepreneurship and the Sustainable Development Goals

(Estimated time: 30 minutes)

Purpose

Relate entrepreneurial opportunities to pressing global social issues, through the lens of the UN SDGs.

Preparation

Have a copy of the template below and the SDGs graphic from earlier in this chapter (Figure 10.1; Table 10.2).

Table 10.2 New Venture Ideas to Address the Sustainable Development Goals (SDGs)

	Option 1	Option 2	Option 3	Option 4
Which SDG would you like to address with a new venture?				
Why?				
Why kind of venture would support this: • Local venture/local needs • Local ventures/global market • Regional venture • Global venture				
Where would you locate initially?				
Nonprofit or for-profit structure?				
What impact do you expect to achieve?				

Process

1. Break into groups of 3–5 students.
2. Each group should select 3–4 SDGs that they would most like to have an impact on. In their group, the students should share which goals resonate and why.
3. Using the student-generated list of SDGs, the group should use the template to brainstorm entrepreneurial opportunities that would meaningfully advance the goals they have selected.
4. Debrief:
    a. Which SDGs did you select?
    b. What entrepreneurial opportunities did you consider?
    c. What was the geographic focus and scope of these opportunities?
    d. What do you see as the pros and cons of your venture ideas?
5. Post-class: Continue to refine your ideas. Report back during the next class.

SHORT CASE: TANYA ACCONE AT UNICEF—PROMOTING INTRAPRENEURSHIP AND GLOBAL INNOVATION AT SCALE

Tanya Accone looked out the window of her temporary home office near Cape Town, South Africa. It was midmorning, so she was able to reach most of her colleagues in Africa, Europe, the Middle East, and Asia during working hours, the benefit of a favorable time zone. Back at her offices in Bangkok and New York, she had found herself working very early or very late to manage time differences at UNICEF's 190+ country offices. As she sipped her coffee and worked her way through dozens of emails and text messages, one from a colleague on the UPSHIFT youth initiative required an immediate response. As she pressed "send," another email caught her eye with the subject line: "$2.6M is great, but what's next?"

UNICEF, also known as the United Nations Children's Fund, was created by the UN General Assembly in 1946 to provide emergency food and health care to mothers and children in countries that had been devastated by Word War II. Over nearly seventy-five years of operations, its mission and mandate had expanded; by 2020, it operated in over 190 countries and territories with a singular focus on improving the lives of children around the world. UNICEF's activities include providing immunization and disease prevention, enhancing childhood and maternal nutrition and health care, improving sanitation, promoting education, and providing emergency disaster relief. For revenues, UNICEF relies entirely on voluntary government contributions and donations from private individuals and companies. It had nearly 20,000 employees in 2020; total 2019 income was over $6.9 billion.[43]

UNICEF had been a major contributor towards progress in and measurement of the UN Sustainable Development goals. Attached to the goals are 169 concrete targets measured by 232 indicators, 35 of which are directly related to children. As the global leader of data for children, UNICEF is the custodian or co-custodian for 17 of the indicators.

Accone and her colleague Dr. Sharad Sapra had established an Innovation Unit within UNICEF's Communications Office in 2007 with the seed of an idea. They saw the explosion of mobile phones in developing nations and thought that this emerging technology might be used to improve health access for children. According to Accone: "We saw an opportunity to engage the organization around how mobile phones, which were then a rapidly emerging technology in developing countries, might be used to improve insights in the field." The concept quickly took hold and evolved into a program, launched in Malawi in 2008, that enabled health workers to use a SMS-based system to track health records.

Five years later, the system, now named RapidPro, was being used to track health supplies in Malawi and Uganda, and a year later was expanded to Liberia, Serra Leone, and Guinea as a core part of UNICEF's Ebola response. RapidPro collected data via short message service (SMS) and other communication channels (for example, voice, social media and other platforms like WhatsApp) to enable real-time data collection and mass communication with beneficiaries and frontline workers. The system allowed partners to gather accurate real-time information on vital areas such as health, nutrition, education, water and sanitation, and child protection—even in remote and hard-to-reach places—and use that data to reach those most in need. After demonstrating success in multiple countries, the venture was "mainstreamed" into UNICEF's health program in 2018 and manages around half-a-billion real-time data exchanges every year.

In 2015, the Innovation Unit became the Global Innovation Center (GIC) and established operations in a repurposed warehouse on Mbuya Hill in Kampala, Uganda. In her new position as Senior Advisor for Innovation, assisted by a staff of nine, Accone's focus was multifaceted. She was responsible for positioning GIC as a change maker within UNICEF, helping a large and traditional organization build innovation into its day-to-day operations while strengthening its ongoing capacity to adopt and adapt technology-based innovations. She also was committed to capturing the many innovations that were created in the field, providing support where needed to scale them across the organization. Finally, she was charged with helping transitioning innovations out of GIC to become core functions across UNICEF.

Part of UNICEF's strategic plan for 2018–2021 involved deepening their partnerships in the private sector—leveraging their core business and innovation to better serve the needs of hard-to-reach children. They also aimed to enhance the use of new technologies to strengthen systems, improve service delivery, and engage communities, citizens, and civil society organizations in public decision-making. Another priority is identifying the most promising program innovations and working with partners to adopt, adapt, and scale up the most successful approaches. Accone observed: "For UNICEF, innovation is not just a nice concept. It is really taken to heart as we see in the strategic plan, and there is a consensus that it is an important lever to both evolve our organization and expand impact. To do this we need to build the skills to help our colleagues understand how to develop and validate problems and solutions. We also need to overcome skepticism among those who are used to doing things in a more traditional way."

In her 2018 TEDx talk, Accone explained her philosophy for seeding and scaling innovations effectively. She described the importance of cocreating them by tapping into the knowledge of the communities that will be served, observing that this is the difference between creating successful innovations and failures. According to Accone, "For innovation to work, it must work in context. And when it does it can achieve tremendous impact."[44]

While her strategies had been applied successfully across a range of solutions in 90 countries, she was especially proud of her team's work on UPSHIFT, which is a program that provides 15- to 24-year-old, out-of-school young adults with informal education and training in social entrepreneurship. It started as a pilot in Kosovo, where the country team recognized the negative social impact of marginalized and disengaged youth. Over the next 18 months, the idea spread organically to neighboring Montenegro, and then to Jordan, Lebanon, and Vietnam. Having accompanied UPSHIFT, the GIC team recognized that there would be differences among countries, and therefore global value to modularize the program so that it could be adapted to meet local needs and be delivered in settings ranging from youth innovation labs to schools and nonformal education centers. Today, UPSHIFT is a core UNICEF program, operating in 35 countries and reached 1.35 million young people in 2020, and is constantly pivoting to adapt to the needs of new locations.

Accone turned back to the message from her colleague that posed the $2.6 million question. It referred to a funding commitment GIC had just received from UNICEF to seed additional innovation across the organization. While the amount seemed small within the context of the scope of UNICEF's organization and the pressing needs it faced worldwide, Accone knew from experience that if the new initiative was successful, it could easily attract multiples of that amount in matching funds from governments keen to scale high-impact ideas. She also knew that funds would go much further in developing economies.

With this in mind, she wondered about the best way to use these new resources. Should she seed a large number of new initiatives to see which ones might have merit? Another idea was to bet on a small number of winning ideas that she knew would attract support both within UNICEF and with external stakeholders. She also knew that to scale innovations successfully, they would need to ultimately have a path to being mainstreamed into UNICEF's ongoing programs and wondered whether and how to prioritize initiatives that had this potential, and especially to invest in evidence of early impact. She also wondered whether spinning off ventures to create entities independent of UNICEF might be a new way to scale. GIC had experienced recent success with this in B.O.T. (Bridge, Outsource, Transform), an initiative that had spun out of UPSHIFT as a stand-alone self-funded social enterprise that provided digital outsources services by employing marginalized youth. Finally, as always, her guiding principle was achieving maximum benefit for children around the world, and she considered how to ensure that this overarching goal would be paramount.

With these challenges top of mind, and mindful of limited resources, she took another sip of coffee and started to map out the alternatives.

Discussion Questions

1. How hard do you think it is to innovate at established organizations like UNICEF? What factors might support or constrain innovation?
2. Would you recommend that Accone use newly allocated funds to seed small initiatives or bet on winners? Why?
3. UNICEF wants to mainstream successful innovations to ensure that they scale. What do you like about this approach and what concerns might you have?
4. What is your perspective on the tension between standardizing innovations to improve efficiency and scaling them to meet local needs, particularly in a multicountry context?
5. If you were Accone, what would keep you up at night?

NOTES

1. Murphy, R. M., & Sachs, D. (2013, May 2). The rise of social entrepreneurship suggests a possible future for global capitalism. *Forbes*. Retrieved from https://www.forbes.com/sites/skollworldforum/2013/05/02/the-rise-of-social-entrepreneurship-suggests-a-possible-future-for-global-capitalism/?sh=6563ca1f348c.
2. Schumpeter, J. A. (1947). The creative response in economic history. *Journal of Economic History*, 7(2), 149–159.
3. Schumpeter, J. A. (1962) *Capitalism, socialism, and democracy*. New York, NY: Harper & Row.
4. Aeeni, Z., Motavaseli, M., Sakhdaria, K., & Idehkordia, A. M. (2019). Baumol's theory of entrepreneurial allocation: A systematic review and research agenda. *European Research on Management and Business Economics, 25*(1), 30–37.
5. Wennekers, S., van Stel, A., Carree, M. A., & Thurik, R. (2010). The relationship between entrepreneurship and economic development: Is it U-shaped? *Foundations and Trends in Entrepreneurship*, *6*(3), 167–237.
6. Ibid.
7. Haltiwanger, J., Jarmin, R. S., & Miranda, J. (May 2013). Who creates jobs? Small versus large versus young. *The Review of Economics and Statistics, 95*(2), 347–361.
8. Bosma, N., Hill, S., Ionescu-Somers, A., Kelley, D., Levie, J., & Tarnawa, A. (2020). *GEM 2019/2020 global report*. Global Entrepreneurship Monitor. Retrieved from https://www.gemconsortium.org/report/gem-2019-2020-global-report.
9. Naudé, W. (2011, March 23). *Entrepreneurs and economic development*. United Nations University. Retrieved from https://unu.edu/publications/articles/are-entrepreneurial-societies-also-happier.html.
10. The United Nations. (n.d.). *Ending poverty*. Retrieved November 13, 2020 from https://www.un.org/en/sections/issues-depth/poverty/.
11. Stoica, O., Roman, A., & Rusu, V. D. (2020). The nexus between entrepreneurship and economic growth: A comparative analysis on groups of countries. *Sustainability, 12*(3), 1186.
12. Calderon, G., Iacovone, L., & Juarez, L. (2016, April 1). Opportunity versus necessity: Understanding the heterogeneity of female micro-entrepreneurs. *World Bank Economic*

Review, 30, S86–S96. Retrieved from https://openknowledge.worldbank.org/bitstream/handle/10986/32234/Opportunity-versus-Necessity-Understanding-the-Heterogeneity-of-Female-Micro-Entrepreneurs.pdf?sequence=1&isAllowed=y.
13. The World Bank Group. (n.d.). *Ease of doing business rankings*. Retrieved November 13, 2020 from https://www.doingbusiness.org/en/rankings.
14. Endeavor Global, Inc. (n.d.). *Our story*. Retrieved November 13 from https://endeavor.org/story/.
15. Herrington, M., & Kew, P. (2017, February 4). *GEM global report 2016/17*. Global Entrepreneurship Monitor. Retrieved from https://www.gemconsortium.org/report/gem-2016-2017-global-report.
16. Bosma, N., Hill, S., Ionescu-Somers, A., Kelley, D., Levie, J., & Tarnawa, A. (2020, February 25). *GEM 2019/2020 global report*. Global Entrepreneurship Monitor. Retrieved from https://www.gemconsortium.org/report/gem-2019-2020-global-report.
17. Ibid.
18. Ibid.
19. Srinivasan, A., Staehr, H., & Meinhardt, R. (2020, November 5). *Sight to the world: How Aravind improves access to care for millions*. Retrieved from https://cdn0.scrvt.com/39b415fb07de4d9656c7b516d8e2d907/1800000007508241/4276be3ef191/Issue13_SHS_Insights_Series_Sight_to_the_world_1800000007508241.pdf.
20. Jones, J., & Augustine, G. (2014, February 17). Innovation at One Acre Fund: Seeing the forest for the trees. Chicago, IL: Kellogg School of Management.
21. Ibid.
22. Sanergy. (n.d.). *Each for equal*. Retrieved November 13, 2020 from https://mailchi.mp/saner/building-a-gender-balanced-world-one-toilet-at-a-time-eachforequal?e=bcbebc1465.
23. The United Nations. (n.d.). *Ending poverty*. Retrieved October 21, 2020 from https://www.un.org/en/global-issues/ending-poverty.
24. United Nations. (n.d.). *Take action for the Sustainable Development Goals – United Nations Sustainable Development*. Retrieved October 21, 2020 from https://www.un.org/sustainabledevelopment/sustainable-development-goals/.
25. United Nations. (n.d.). *The 17 goals*. Retrieved October 21, 2020 from https://sdgs.un.org/goals.
26. The Schwab Foundation. (n.d.). *2020 Impact report*. World Economic Forum. Retrieved October 21, 2020 from http://www3.weforum.org/docs/WEF_Schwab_Foundation_2020_Impact_Report.pdf.
27. World Bank Group. (2020). *Doing business 2020*. Washington, DC: World Bank.
28. World Bank Group. (n.d.). *TC data 360*. Retrieved October 21, 2020 from https://tcdata360.worldbank.org.
29. Ibid.
30. Bosma, N., Schøtt, T., Terjesen, S. A., & Kew, P. (2016, June 2). *Global Entrepreneurship Monitor 2015 to 2016: Special Topic Report on Social Entrepreneurship*. Retrieved from https://papers.ssrn.com/sol3/papers.cfm?abstract_id=2786949.
31. Ibid.
32. Ibid.
33. Ibid.
34. Ibid.
35. Ibid.

36. The Schwab Foundation. (n.d.). *2020 Impact report*. World Economic Forum. Retrieved October 21, 2020 from http://www3.weforum.org/docs/WEF_Schwab_Foundation_2020_Impact_Report.pdf.
37. Ibid.
38. Bosma, N., Hill, S., Ionescu-Somers, A., Kelley, D., Levie, J., & Tarnawa, A. (2020, February 25). *GEM 2019/2020 global report*. Global Entrepreneurship Monitor. Retrieved from https://www.gemconsortium.org/report/gem-2019-2020-global-report.
39. World Fair Trade Organization. (2015). *History of fair trade*. Retrieved from https://wfto.com/about-us/history-wfto/history-fair-trade.
40. Endeavor Global, Inc. (n.d.). *Impact*. Retrieved October 21, 2020 from https://endeavor.org/impact/.
41. Phills, J., & Denend, L. (2005). *Social Entrepreneurs Correcting Market Failures (A)*. Stanford Graduate School of Business Case No. SI72A.
42. I-MAK. (n.d.). Retrieved October 21, 2020 from https://www.i-mak.org/impact/.
43. UNICEF. (2020). *Funding compendium*. Retrieved from https://www.unicef.org/reports/funding-compendium-2019.
44. Accone, T. (2018) *Content is king when you're innovating to save lives* [Video]. TED Conferences. Retrieved from https://www.ted.com/talks/tanya_accone_context_is_king_when_you_re_innovating_to_save_lives.

CASE ONE

GENESIS: SEEDING A SOCIAL ENTERPRISE

Dr. Yasmeen Abu Fraiha left the conference excited; her start-up idea was coming together. She had just finished a meeting with a prominent individual in the genetic testing field, and she hoped she could convince him to become the Genesis Chairman of the Board.

Despite the traction she had achieved in this meeting and others, she was concerned. Was she pursuing the right plan? How effectively was she conveying the opportunity to potential stakeholders? And, was she using her time well—stretched as she was between meetings, fundraising, and refining the operating plan?

On the bus ride back, she reflected on her start-up and how she had come this far.

PERSONAL BACKGROUND

Ever since Abu Fraiha was a teenager, she wanted to be a doctor. When she was in high school, her mother was diagnosed with breast cancer. Throughout her teen years, she accompanied her mother to the hospital and witnessed the difference that doctors could make in the lives of their patients and in their communities. This solidified her dream to pursue a career in medicine.

But achieving this as a Bedouin teenager was not simple. Abu Fraiha knew that she would be challenged by having limited access to high-quality education opportunities in her Bedouin community and by having few professional female role models or mentors. The odds were against her in a community where it was rare for girls to receive a good education. Instead, the expectation for most families was that girls should not be educated, and instead prepare for a role raising children and taking care of the house. While some of these dynamics were changing to open more opportunities for young women, much of the community was still very traditional.

Luckily, Abu Fraiha had the strong support of her parents who believed that education was the most important gift that they could give their children. Her mother was a teacher and understood the importance of securing excellent education opportunities. Abu Fraiha's parents, despite challenges, moved to a Jewish town to enable their children to attend high-quality schools.

After completing high school, Abu Fraiha had her first taste of social entrepreneurship as Founder and Manager of a learning center in Omer, Israel, operated under the umbrella of the Hebrew Scouts Movement. The organization served children from low-income backgrounds by matching them with older volunteers to help them with their education. She was gratified to see the program have an impact and ultimately be adopted for implementation in other cities.

After two years with Hebrew Scouts, she was accepted to the Hebrew University of Jerusalem, and over the next seven years completed her medical training. In addition to the rigors of medical school, she was an active volunteer interpreter and trainer for Physicians for Human Rights, providing medical and humanitarian aid. She also founded an empowerment center for young Bedouin girls, tutored children, and led a group of young adults to help them gain leadership skills for Rotary International. Each of these experiences left an impression on her: she saw that she could create positive change for those she touched. But the experiences also made her ambitious to enact change on a larger scale.

According to Abu Fraiha, "My journey has been very challenging, but it has had its purpose. Now I can speak both cultures. I can work as a bridge and learn from one society and adapt it to my own, using my roots, history, and family as credible figures in what I'm doing" (Y. Abu Fraiha, personal interview, December 16, 2016).

GENETICS AND CLOSED COMMUNITIES

While studying medicine in Jerusalem, Abu Fraiha saw the ultra-Orthodox Jewish community and witnessed how they dealt with potential intramarriage, a problem very common in the Bedouin community as well. She observed how an organization called Dor Yeshorim, founded in 1993, was able to significantly reduce the incidence of Tay–Sachs disease (a fatal genetic disorder that occurs when two parents are carriers in 25% of births). Dor Yeshorim carried out an anonymous screening program so that couples with Tay–Sachs or another genetic disorder could avoid marrying someone who was also a carrier. Based on early success, Dor Yeshorim had expanded its testing panel to include additional genetic recessive disorders such as cystic fibrosis, familial dysautonomia, and Canavan disease, and expanded to operate in eleven countries including the United States, Canada, Europe, and Israel.

While she was intrigued by the model, Abu Fraiha also knew that it would be extremely challenging to get the Bedouin community to adopt this solution. "In the orthodox Jewish community, Rabbis are the leaders; everyone listens to them. Dor Yeshorim gained the trust and support of the Rabbis, and because of this trust, the community began to accept genetic testing" (Y. Abu Fraiha, personal interview, December 16, 2016). While she saw clear parallels to Bedouin communities, she knew that adoption might be even more complex because leadership is dispersed among families, village leaders, and Sheikhs (Bedouin traditional leaders). Different tribes are influenced by different figures and the hierarchy is not as clear as in the ultra-Orthodox Jewish community.

In Bedouin communities, it is common for marriages to be arranged by family patriarchs, and in some small communities, such as the Negev Bedouins in South Israel, 80% of young adults marry within their respective tribes, and 60% of marriages take place between first and second cousins. The result is a very high rate of birth defects because the chance that both parents carry a given disease is increased. The statistics are shocking: the number of children with genetic issues is 15% in Bedouin communities, more than ten times higher than the overall rate of genetic diseases in the Jewish community in Israel, which is slightly less than 1%.[1] In addition to the enormous personal cost for affected families, the financial cost is high: millions of dollars are spent each year on health care and disability stipends related to potentially avoidable genetic diseases. Abu Fraiha recognized that an approach like Dor Yeshorim's to test youth before marriages are arranged could be an excellent way to protect these communities. She recognized that because most of the marriages were arranged, the individuals had little to no emotional connection with their partners prior to marriage. She reasoned that prospective brides and grooms would likely be willing to accept other partners if the result was the prospect of a healthier family. But she needed to determine a way to do this that would not stigmatize those who tested positive for genetic issues.

Abu Fraiha knew that in the past Bedouin community leaders had been strongly opposed to the idea of genetic testing stemming from a lack of acceptance of technology. However, with the prevalence of smartphones and Internet access within the communities, she believed that more families have become willing to accept technology-based help to solve one of their difficult problems. Former initiatives that had tried to address the issue of genetics-related birth defects failed because the community was not receptive. Abu Fraiha knew the intricacies and complex relationships she would have to maneuver to make the community embrace genetic testing, a competitive advantage of Genesis. With her unique experience coming from a Bedouin community, her expertise as a doctor, and the opening minds of Bedouins, there was an opportunity for Genesis to succeed.

ACCELERATING THE IDEA

> *The whole atmosphere of working with other entrepreneurs and mentors and faculty members [at Our Generation Speaks] gave us so much strength, knowledge, and experience that I would not have without the incubator forum.*
>
> (Y. Abu Fraiha, personal interview, January 12, 2017)

While Abu Fraiha was convinced that the Genesis concept had potential, she was also keenly aware of the enormous divide between idea and implementation. Then, after a night shift at the hospital, she returned home to an email from a friend who worked at the Prime Minister's office. The email was about Our Generation Speaks (OGS), with her friend's addition: "This is perfect for you, you have to look into it." Too excited to sleep, she made herself coffee and started reading about the program. She applied, and after a rigorous process was selected as a member of the inaugural 2016 class. She was nervous and excited, hopeful that ultimately Genesis would be one of the projects that would be selected during the OGS residency.

Our Generation Speaks (OGS) was founded in 2014 by Ohad Elhelo as a fellowship program and incubator where Palestinian and Israeli emerging leaders came together to create high-impact new business ventures. The goal was to support the creation of innovative enterprises that generate significant social and economic value, while creating a cohort of young Israeli and Palestinian community leaders who cooperate across ethnic and political lines to build shared prosperity within the region.

Born in Ashdod, Israel, Elhelo arrived in the United States in 2013 as a Slifka Scholar to attend Brandeis University, where he received his Bachelor's in Economics and completed his Master's in Economics. He founded Our Generation Speaks to empower young Israeli and Palestinian change agents to build shared prosperity and an infrastructure of hope through entrepreneurship.

According to Elhelo:

> *My goal was to bring young high potential leaders together to form impact businesses. I decided on this approach because it is a terrific platform for building trust. A byproduct is that we are building teams that will build ventures which will create jobs, while giving young leaders credentials that will accelerate their impact. Also, there are 12.5 million people in the Region. It isn't possible to create this kind of experience to that many people, but by supporting our young leaders we expect a magnifying effect.*
>
> (O. Elhelo, personal interview, January 11, 2017)

Fellows received a fully funded three-month residency at Brandeis University's Heller School for Social Policy and Management, which included tailor-made coursework focused on entrepreneurship, communications, financial management, negotiation, and more, delivered by faculty of Brandeis University. OGS also worked in partnership with MassChallenge, the world's largest start-up accelerator, which provided mentorship, support, and exposure for fellows at the end of the academic program.

Twenty-two people came to OGS in 2016, each with their own idea. There was no guarantee that the concept that would become Genesis would be selected, but ultimately, after two intermediate selection rounds, it moved forward. Among the seven team members at OGS who prepared the initial business plan, Naomi Abraham and Maria Dyshel continued to work with Abu Fraiha to create the organizational structure and launch plan for Genesis. They each found their niche within the organization, complementing each other's strengths.

During the program, each team was challenged to develop successively more rigorous business proposals while learning about marketing, entrepreneurship, finance, and other topics. Each week the proposal was refined as the other fellows, program faculty, and mentors critiqued it, first at Brandeis and then at MassChallenge, questioning assumptions and brainstorming improvements. The Genesis team was called upon to hone the presentation of the concept in multiple pitches. Abu Fraiha was constantly pressed by her program mentors to think about how she might expand her network and gain support from other stakeholders.

> *I still say I had the best mentors in the program. I feel so lucky. First of all, I feel lucky because I got two mentors instead of one. They are a couple, but they are very different from one another. Ron, a businessman, is very supportive and he has entrepreneurial advice. Janet is a doctor and thinks about the tiniest details. Every time I sent them something to look into, she sent me two pages of detailed notes, and he just said you'll be fine you have bigger challenges. Together, she is very thorough, and he thinks about the big picture. It was the perfect combination for me. The relationship was very warm, and added to our work together. I felt very open and connected to them. I felt I could ask anything, and I still feel that way; we are still in touch.*
>
> (Y. Abu Fraiha, personal interview, January 12, 2017)

As part of the program, each fellow was assigned a US-based mentor (Abu Fraiha had two), and these relationships were intended to supplement the academic and business-building parts of the program by giving each fellow feedback and an additional, external sounding board. According to Elhelo:

> *Yasmeen has great charisma, but what is more important is that she is tenacious. And a game changer early for OGS as we developed the program was learning that we needed to identify a few champions. Yasmeen has done this as well—she has been very effective at finding and engaging a few influential people who really believe in her and the concept and can help them move forward quickly.*
>
> (O. Elhelo, personal interview, January 11, 2017)

THE BUSINESS PLAN AND THE RETURN TO ISRAEL AND PALESTINE

Writing the business plan made Abu Fraiha think of both the major and minor challenges the emerging organization would face. The business plan was necessary to mitigate financial risk, as well as address the economic, cultural, and ethical consequences of Genesis. The process of writing the pitch deck and business plan taught the team many lessons and helped them to prepare by knowing the answer to every question about the organization. Intense discussions about marketing strategy gave them a better understanding of how the team could approach key stakeholders in the community to communicate about the sensitive issue of intramarriage.

With a business plan and pitch deck in hand, the next task was even more daunting: returning home and convincing others that this idea was necessary and fundable. With the realization that this organization needed to be a nonprofit to keep the trust of the Bedouin community, they needed to find external funding for Genesis.

The day before she left Boston to return home, the team learned that they had received seed funding from the OGS program to help start the venture. Abu Fraiha would continue to work on the organization, and her teammates opted to work on Genesis in their spare time. Abraham, as an accountant and lawyer, helped with branding, legal, and financial work, while Dyshel oversaw the technology needed for Genesis to succeed. Others are helping with partnerships and fundraising efforts. The funding was not enough for Abu Fraiha or anyone to work on Genesis full-time, but it would be enough to get Genesis off the ground.

She returned home and was pitching nearly daily to various stakeholders. She viewed the pitch deck as one of the most important documents they had:

> *Dealing with partners, donors, and investors is like dating. The pitch deck is what I show on a first date, and we decide if we want to continue dating. Then the business plan, and it gets more serious. It shows people we have thought of everything.*
>
> (Y. Abu Fraiha, personal interview, January 12, 2017)

As Abu Fraiha continued to woo potential donors, the team was still fine-tuning the business plan. To them, it was a living document, and not necessarily always on paper. Each discussion with stakeholders helped identify ways to make the operations plan more efficient, or how to improve their financial plan. She recognized that external funding would be critical to both short- or long-term success and wanted to make sure that the latest version would help them achieve their goals.

MOVING FORWARD—AND A NEW CHALLENGE

> *What advice would I offer other social entrepreneurs? Two tips: First, everything is solvable. I really think that problems that seem like they can never be solved can be. We need to be optimistic. If people don't let you in through the door, you can always get in through the window. Creativity is the key to finding a solution to any problem. Never give up, and listen to people. By listening to people we found a solution to genetic testing without hurting the community.*
>
> (Y. Abu Fraiha, personal interview, January 12, 2017)

At the MassChallenge offices in Jerusalem, Abu Fraiha reviewed the most recent version of the business plan. She just finished talking about strategy with two OGS peers with whom she shares the office and who were also launching OGS-supported ventures.

She reflected on an emerging issue that had started to consume much of her time. When she and the team had originally conceived of Genesis, she had planned to partner with a prominent hospital that would provide the tests and maintain the database. But in recent meetings with community leaders, she had heard that there was a complicated history with the hospital resulting in a lack of trust. She was considering raising additional funds to establish an independent laboratory for Genesis but knew that this would involve significant up-front costs as well as ongoing expenses to staff the lab. There might also be additional benefits in the form of higher rates of adoption but it was hard to quantify those. There was also the possibility that setting up a new lab would enable them to use cheek swab vs. blood drawing for the tests. She wondered what the right decision would be and how to gather and analyze the data she would need to choose the right approach.

While extremely proud of all that she and the team had accomplished, there were also many, many questions that she hoped to address in the next iteration of the business plan. She had several pressing questions to attend to. Should she start small with a pilot or seek to start big? What would that mean for relationships with external funders and whether to expand the team? And finally, had she identified the right stakeholders, and how she should continue to engage them?

Abu Fraiha was grateful for the support that she had received, and in particular for the team she had worked with to reach this point. Now her challenge was to justify the confidence others had shown in her by pushing the venture forward and making it successful.

Discussion Questions

1. What advice would you offer Abu Fraiha to help her ensure Genesis meets its promise?
2. What do you see as the strengths of Abu Fraiha's process so far? Where are the opportunities for improvement?
3. Should she start small or large?
4. Should she establish Genesis as a nonprofit or a for-profit organization?
5. What should she do about the lab?

Acknowledgement

This case was prepared with the assistance of Teaching Assistant Seven Siegel, Brandeis University, Heller School for Social Policy and Management, MBA/MPP '16.

Note

1. Abu Fraiha, Y. (2016, August 30). *Genesis* [Unpublished business plan].

CASE TWO

SANERGY: USING SOCIAL ENTREPRENEURSHIP TO SOLVE EMERGING MARKET PROBLEMS

NEW YEAR, NEW CHALLENGES

January 1, 2015 had just passed, marking the New Year, as David Auerbach looked up from his desk to see his team still hard at work. Sanergy's office—an open, converted warehouse space in Nairobi's Mukuru slum area—buzzed with activity as the Sanergy sales team worked on their various tasks with a drive and efficiency that continued to impress him. He reflected on all that Sanergy, the start-up he cofounded in 2010, had achieved in such a short period of time. The past six months had been a whirlwind, with Sanergy opening a new fertilizer plant and expanding to the neighboring slum of Mathare, all while Auerbach was dividing his time between day-to-day operations and travelling the globe developing potential partners and raising funds.

Auerbach considered Sanergy's progress as he mentally geared up for their next operating year. Since launching its first Fresh Life Toilet in late 2011, the company had installed 600 Fresh Life Toilets in Nairobi's slums (the amount had doubled during 2014), which allowed it to remove 6 tons of waste from 26,000 daily users. Sanergy employed 200 people, over half of them residents of the communities where it operated. And it had enabled 275 entrepreneurs to start their own ventures as Sanergy franchisees.

Sanergy was founded in Cambridge, Massachusetts, in 2010 by Auerbach, Ani Vallabhaneni, and Lindsay Stradley who were then business students at MIT's Sloan School of Management, and several classmates including Nathan Cooke (industrial design) and Joel Veenstra (civil engineering). Their venture evolved quickly. In 2010, they won a variety of seed grants from many corners of MIT. Sanergy used these grants to conduct a feasibility study and survey target customers in its first pilot site of Lunga Lunga. In 2011, Sanergy raised upwards of $300,000 by winning the prestigious MIT $100K Entrepreneurship Competition, the MassChallenge, Echoing Green Fellowship, UC Berkeley's Global Social Venture Competition, and the University of Washington's Global Social Entrepreneurship Competition, among others. It also received a grant for $100,000 from USAID's Development Innovation Ventures program to implement its intervention in Nairobi's Mukuru slum. With sufficient seed funding the management team was able to relocate to Nairobi in June 2011—one week after graduating.

Sanergy's mission is to build healthy, prosperous communities by making hygienic sanitation accessible and affordable for everyone, forever. Its theory of change involves creating a comprehensive sanitation system consisting of three T's: toilets, transportation, and treatment of waste. The model involves four parts: building a network of low-cost sanitation centers in slums; distributing them through franchising to local entrepreneurs; collecting the waste produced; and processing it into by-products, such as organic fertilizer, which is sold to regional farmers. Sanergy first builds urine diverting dry toilets (UDDTs) out of locally available materials. The UDDTs collect urine and feces in two separate containers, which—along with the addition of drying material, in this case, sawdust—controls odors and maintains hygiene.

Sanergy franchises its UDDTs, known as Fresh Life Toilets, to Kenyan micro-entrepreneurs called Fresh Life Operators (FLOs). These entrepreneurs run the toilets as small businesses, or, in advanced pilots, as a value-added service for tenants or in community institutions, such as schools, which have underserved populations. Commercial Fresh Life Toilets are pay-per-use, meaning that the FLOs are responsible for charging individual users every time they use the toilets. Once a day, full-time waste collectors remove the waste from each toilet and transport it to Sanergy's central processing facility, where it is processed into fertilizer, biogas, and other by-products. Sanergy currently sells the fertilizer to commercial farmers, who have seen their crop yields increase 30–100% and have restored soil health in their fields. By building comprehensive waste management systems, creating local jobs, and generating a profit, Sanergy aspires to create socially, environmentally, and financially sustainable sanitation systems.

A SANITATION CRISIS IN THE DEVELOPING WORLD

United Nations Millennium Development Goal 7 Target C declared the world's commitment to halve, by 2015, the proportion of people without sustainable access to safe drinking water and basic sanitation. The world has met the drinking water target but is off track to meet the sanitation target. While progress has been made (between 1990 and 2015, the proportion of the global population using an improved sanitation facility increased from 54% to 68%) in 2015, 2.4 billion people were still using unimproved sanitation facilities, including 946 million people who still practiced open defecation.[1]

This is a result not only of income and geographical disparities but also from the relatively low priority given to sanitation as compared to other development problems. Drinking water, not sanitation, has dominated policy debates and commanded the attention, technical expertise, and investment of governments, the international community, social scientists, development practitioners, public health professionals, urban planners, and engineers. In fact, it is estimated that the world would have to invest another $10 billion in sanitation to reach MDG Target 7C.[2]

SANERGY'S FIRST LOCATION IN NAIROBI, KENYA

Kenya is located in East Africa and borders Tanzania, Uganda, South Sudan, Ethiopia, and Somalia. After decades of British colonial rule, it gained its independence in 1963. Kenya's population is approximately 46 million and its two largest cities, Nairobi and Mombasa, have populations of 3.8 million and 1 million, respectively.

Kenya depends on the production and export of low-priced primary goods, including tea, horticultural products, coffee, petroleum products, fish, and cement. Even though agriculture contributes less than 25% to GDP, 75% of working Kenyans are farmers.[3] Kenya has faced political and economic problems. Rampant corruption threatens to undermine its political system. Declining worldwide prices of primary goods, 40% unemployment rate, low infrastructure investment, budget deficits, inflationary pressures, and sharp currency depreciation threaten its position as the largest East African economy. With a 2015 GDP per capita of US$1,337[4] and over a third of Kenya's population living below the poverty line,[5] the country also faced serious public health problems. Several water-related diseases, including diarrhea and hepatitis A, are caused by a lack of adequate sanitation.

Kenya's capital city, Nairobi, is the center of the country's political, social, cultural, and economic life. Because of rural–urban migration, almost half of Kenya's population lives in urban centers, including Nairobi. Rapid urbanization in Kenya has led to the emergence of informal settlements, and these slums have transitory populations, high rents, and overcrowding.

SANITATION IN THE NAIROBI SLUMS

Lack of access to sanitation is an acute problem in sub-Saharan Africa and the informal settlements in Nairobi, Kenya. Sanitation coverage is less than 50% in sub-Saharan Africa and is only 32% in Kenya. Ten million people live in Kenyan slums, eight million of whom lack access to adequate sanitation. The situation is particularly acute in Nairobi where 75% of the city's population, over 2.5 million people, live in informal settlements and 70% use unhygienic and unsafe sanitation facilities.[6] As the global population of slum residents swells to 2 billion over the next 30 years[7] and Nairobi's slum population continues to grow rapidly, its sanitation problems will only escalate.

There are a number of challenges to providing sanitation services to informal settlements. Most slum residents are low-income, marginalized, uneducated, have limited assets, and work in the informal economy. In 2006, these households earned on average US $588 per year.[8] Most slum residents own few assets and lack access to credit through conventional banks.

Informal settlements in Nairobi are created in two ways. Following the rise of industry, residents needed to live closer to work and set up informal settlements on unclaimed land. Landlords have also subdivided government and private land into plots and housing units. As a result, they are ignored by Kenya's sanitation policy and the Nairobi City Council. Compounding their uncertain land tenure, most slum dwellers are tenants and migrants living in temporary residences. Only 30 of more than 200 Kenyan slums have sewage systems and less than 30% of Nairobi slum residents utilize these systems through household or shared connections.[9]

There are legal and physical challenges to providing informal settlements with sanitation. Because of illegal land tenure and unregistered plots of land, ownership of buildings and land is unclear. Settlements are characterized by haphazard physical development, including structures that violate building regulations and narrow, unpaved roads. Perilous land and infrastructure in slums pose engineering challenges to developing appropriate sanitation infrastructure. This makes it expensive to provide water and sanitation services to individual households. These challenges, combined with slum dwellers' limited ability to pay for services, result in a large gap between the costs of traditional sanitation systems and potential cost recovery.

Since few slums have access to formal sewage systems, the following sanitation practices are commonplace in Nairobi slums: open defecation, flying toilets, household pit latrines, and community pay-per-use toilets. Only 6% of slum dwellers practice open defecation, excreting within or on the border of a slum, or in drainage ditches.[10] However, these 6% endanger the health and environment of all slum residents by exposing residents to hazardous pathogens in untreated excreta. Another common sanitation practice is flying toilets, in which people relieve themselves into plastic bags and then toss the bags out their house windows.

Less than 1% of slum residents use household pour-flush toilets with septic tanks as they are very expensive. The majority of dwellers, 64%, use pit latrines.[11] Many dig their own pit latrines, which are often small holes in the ground covered with corrugated tin or wooden planks with a squat hole. As the pits are shallow and often unlined, they create environmental problems when human waste from the pits leaches into the surrounding soil and groundwater or when latrine owners empty the contents of the pits into nearby rivers, streams, and ditches, contaminating surface water.

SANERGY OPERATIONS

In 2015, Sanergy's 600 toilets provided safe sanitation over 33,000 times per day in eight slum sites throughout Nairobi (Sanergy, Management interviews, 2015). Unlike its shared sanitation competitors, Sanergy is able to provide clean, hygienic, affordable, accessible, and secure toilets. Sanergy takes a number of steps to ensure that its Fresh Life Toilet brand is associated with cleanliness. First of all, it makes FLOs responsible for maintaining the cleanliness of the toilets they operate. Sanergy representatives visit toilets once a week to monitor cleanliness and provide business support. In the rare occasion that an FLO fails to maintain a toilet's cleanliness, Sanergy will shut down the toilet—at first temporarily, and then permanently.

Sanergy promotes good hygiene practices by requiring FLOs to provide toilet paper as well as soap and water for the handwashing basin attached to each toilet. Selling sanitary products to FLOs allows Sanergy to certify that they are encouraging good hygiene, as Sanergy checks in with them on a weekly basis and verifies their soap needs. Another aspect of maintaining toilet hygiene is waste removal. The waste collection teams visit the toilets regularly to remove waste from the toilets. Sanergy provides the waste collectors with uniforms of rubber gloves, coveralls, boots, respirators, and glasses to protect them from contact with the waste. In addition, the plastic containers into which people excrete and urinate are double-sealed to prevent human exposure to harmful pathogens. This represents a significant improvement over the typical conditions faced by "frogmen," who manually empty pits with buckets.

Fresh Life Toilets are also affordable and accessible. While the FLOs have the flexibility to set their own prices, most charge the standard Nairobi slum rate of KSH 5 ($0.05USD) per use. Sanergy explains to the FLOs how changes to their revenue structure may persuade or dissuade different numbers of users from using the toilets. Accessibility is one of the major differences between Sanergy and other shared sanitation options in Nairobi settlements. Most slum dwellers, women in particular, are unwilling to walk more than 100 meters from their homes to use the bathroom. That is why Sanergy aims to establish a dense network of small-scale sanitation networks located in every block of Nairobi slums. Unlike large toilet blocks, Sanergy's individual toilets fit in the cramped spaces of the slums.

Sanergy markets sanitation through its sales team. The sales team is comprised both of people from the communities where Sanergy works and people with prior sales experience. Their understanding of the local context and access to local networks enables them to effectively market sanitation to potential users. For example, Sanergy uses a strategy called "edutainment" to reach a wide swath of community members. A Fresh Life jingle plays frequently on local radio stations, telling people about the benefits of using FLTs as part of a healthy and happy lifestyle. Another large part of Sanergy's marketing strategy has been creating an aspirational brand to meet consumer preferences.

Surveys of potential users demonstrated consumer desire for clean toilets and willingness to pay higher prices for tidy, odor-free toilets. The organization chose the name Fresh Life and the accompanying logo because users associated both the name and the logo with cleanliness. The toilets themselves are painted in bright blue, making them aesthetically pleasing and eye-catching. In addition to marketing Fresh Life through edutainment and salespeople, Sanergy works with FLOs to help them market their individual toilets to their neighbors. In particular, it supports the role of female entrepreneurs, as it believes that women are powerful advocates for community health. To this end, almost half of the FLOs are women.

Franchising toilets to FLOs is a cost-effective, time-saving, and labor-saving way of extending sanitation coverage in informal settlements. Sanergy constructs and installs the toilets, selling them at cost to FLOs: $600 for one toilet and $1,100 for two. Those prices include the cost of providing FLOs with a waste collection service for a year and providing FLOs with product branding, community-wide marketing, training, and business support. As the toilets are prefabricated, they can be assembled and functional within one day as compared to ablution blocks which take several weeks to assemble and bio-centers which take several months. Sanergy has partnered with the international microfinance organization Kiva to assist FLOs in purchasing the toilets. These organizations have been extremely successful in expanding slum residents' access to credit. In fact, the microfinance loans of the 73 FLOs that applied for credit via Kiva were all filled within an hour of appearing on Kiva's web portal. At the average rate of 50 users per day, FLOs owning two toilets—which the majority of them do—can earn $2,000 annually, a generous living in a slum where the average resident earns far less.

MEASURING IMPACT

Sanergy regularly reports number of toilets, number of users, and tons of waste removed. It also reports on jobs created. What Sanergy had not measured is the commercial toilet's impact on public health. Auerbach was skeptical about the value of detailed measurement: "At this early stage, we've elected not to get too deep into understanding public health impact as a whole. It is too hard to measure, and even if you do it is almost impossible to be fully attributable to us" (Sanergy, management interviews, 2015). He offered an example:

> *Consider the way meat arrives into a slum in Nairobi. It will most likely be on the back of a motorcycle. It won't be refrigerated. So, some of the time it will make people sick. How do you separate out Sanergy's impact from improving sanitation when there are thousands of similar issues? We know that hygienic sanitation makes a difference—often a huge difference—to the health of slum residents.*
>
> (Sanergy, management interviews, 2015)

But, skeptical as he was about measurement, Auerbach wondered about whether additional investments in measuring outcomes were needed. As Sanergy increasingly partners with NGOs and foundations, they are pressed to provide more data on outcomes. Auerbach wondered what approaches to measuring impact would meet these needs while focusing on data that would be inexpensive to collect and provide realistic information.

COMPETITION

Sanergy's comprehensive solution means that, rather than competing in a single market, it actually competes in multiple areas: as a toilet provider, a waste remover, and a seller of by-products such as fertilizer and energy.

The most straightforward competitive market is Sanergy's consumer-facing toilet market. In this arena, it competes with other solutions that slum dwellers use to meet their toilet needs. These include household latrines and other providers, in addition to nonuse (open defecation and flying toilets). Competitors in the pay-per-use space are public pit latrines constructed and operated by small service providers, including community-based organizations, nongovernmental organizations (NGOs), and other private entities. An example is private company Ecotact, which has partnered with the Nairobi City Council to provide ablution blocks, large installations with several pour-flush toilets connected to septic tanks. Umande Trust has built bio-centers, which, similar to the ablution blocks, feature a number of pour-flush toilets. These toilets flush to an onsite biogas digester which converts them into methane for cooking. While these facilities also charge KSH 3-5, they are not well utilized by slum dwellers as they are located in schools and the commercial areas of slums. The majority of other small service providers, mostly landlords and youth groups, do a poor job of constructing and maintaining toilets and properly removing and disposing of waste. They charge users KSH 3-5 for shoddy versions of pit latrines, small holes that flow directly into unlined pits or waterways. Most shared pit latrines are overcrowded, unhygienic, and do not offer people dignity or protection.

Sanergy also faces competition in waste transport and removal services. Current waste removal and transport practices of pit latrines are costly, infrequent, unhealthy, and dangerous for workers. Infrequency of disposal causes the sewage to leach into the water table and attracts disease-spreading flies and mosquitos. During rainy season pits flood bringing sewage into the streets. The most common type of waste removal is drainage directly into waterways. Independent providers also offer manual waste removal services that consist of removing waste bucket by bucket without safety gear, which exposes workers to disease vectors. This can cost anywhere from KSH 1,000 to 5,000 per exhaustion.[12] Private companies, NGOs, and the government also offer mechanical removal and transport, but transportation is challenging and infrequent, and costs are even higher. Sanergy's contained waste collection infrastructure is low-cost, frequent, and healthy. Sanergy toilets are designed with a UDDT where urine and feces are automatically captured into 30-liter barrels. Barrels have a capacity of 100 visits, and a team of local waste collectors removes the barrels on a regular basis. Compared with manual and mechanized removal and transport, Sanergy's removal cost is only KSH 9,000 (about $USD 90) per year, for regular removal services (Sanergy, management interviews, 2015).

Sanergy also faces competition as it seeks to process waste for fertilizer. Sanergy's treatment and reuse system to produce fertilizer is technologically efficient, has a high productive capacity, and a high market value with guaranteed pricing. Through anaerobic digestion, waste was converted into organic fertilizer and sold to commercial and smallholder farms around Nairobi for $500 a ton. The waste collected from two Fresh Life Toilets in one year produced around one ton of fertilizer.

SCALING SANERGY

If there was one thing Auerbach had learned in five years working in Kenya, it was that the reality of running a business often diverges from the rosy picture painted by the business plan. This was especially true when starting and scaling an innovative for-profit enterprise in a complex, ever-changing environment. Nevertheless, based on the founding team's clear vision for impact and the experiences of the past year, Auerbach and his cofounders were confident that they could continue to scale rapidly. Their plan was to expand its network size to 1,000 toilets in Nairobi by the end of 2015 and serve over 46,000 people daily.

The first option for scaling was "growing in." With this option, Sanergy would focus on reaching 100% coverage in communities where it already operates by developing additional distribution models to reach more people in a concentrated area. This approach made both economic and social sense, as it capitalized on the existing investments the Sanergy team had already made in the communities in which it operates.

The second option was "growing out," that is, taking Sanergy's model to other parts of the world: India, West Africa, or other parts of East Africa. Sanergy had already identified 1,100 cities in Africa and Asia where its model would be applicable. While this would help achieve the international scale Sanergy thought would support quick expansion, it could also lead to diluting the product and services Sanergy offered. Despite the success of the current operating model, Auerbach did not want to ignore the complexity—and potential cost—of meeting the needs of a larger and more diverse set of stakeholders. "We've been lucky because Sanergy is innovative and interesting enough that we've had a chance to pick and choose our partners. But as we scale, this may become more difficult" (Sanergy, management interviews, 2015).

Auerbach was also worried about government. Government relations had taken an increasing amount of his time, particularly since Sanergy had become large and prominent enough to attract local and national government attention. Even if these governments did not participate directly, they needed to be managed carefully, since there was always the risk that they could implement or change policies so as to create barriers to Sanergy's expansion.

Finally, attracting financial partners consumed a great deal of Auerbach's attention. As a start-up social enterprise, Sanergy's early growth relied on winnings from business plan competitions, sales, and some funding from foundations. It also received funds from impact investors. As a for-profit business, Sanergy's long-term ability to receive equity funding depended on its business's profitability. Auerbach hoped that with additional proof of concept and changing practices at NGOs and foundations (which had started to recognize the potential of for-profit mission-driven ventures), Sanergy would be able to attract additional funding partners. The tantalizing prospect of becoming cash flow positive within the next year was also exciting, particularly since this would enable Sanergy to attract additional private investors and scale more quickly.

EXPANDING TO NEW MARKETS

Having proven the positive social, financial, and environmental aspects of its model, the Sanergy management team wondered whether it was the right time to expand their innovative concept to additional markets. Having observed the entry of copycat ventures in Kenya, they were concerned about losing first-mover advantage if they did not expand to other countries in the near future.

An obvious target was India, a potentially huge market for Sanergy. India had a serious urban sanitation crisis particularly in slums. Indian cities are growing and so are their slum populations. In India, there is a major gap between the growing population and the development of basic sanitation infrastructure in both rural and urban environments, but particularly in slums.

According to the Registrar General of India, 68 million people, or one in six people, live in slum communities (Sanergy, Management interviews, 2015). In many states slum populations represent a high percentage of total urban population. Only 50% of slums have any drainage system, and 75 million people (81% of the slum population in India) lack access to any kind of toilet.

Despite increased attention to the issues of urban sanitation, the national government development policies that favor large-scale real estate and commercial developments for the rising middle class do not sufficiently support affordable and efficient basic sanitation for poor urban slum dwellers. Ironically, it is these large developments that create slums in the first place since most slum dwellers are rural migrants who have come to the cities to work as day laborers for large construction projects in the informal economy.

There are significant economic costs to inadequate sanitation in India, particularly for slum dwellers. Diarrhea, intestinal worms, and acute lower respiratory infections have significant impacts on the livelihoods of poor slum dwellers. According to the Water and Sanitation Program, urban houses in the poorest quintile bear the highest per capita economic losses due to inadequate sanitation: 1,699 INR or $37.50.[13] India has the highest number of diarrhea deaths worldwide. More than 30% of all deaths of children under the age of five are diarrhea related.[14]

There are reasons to believe that Sanergy's model would be well received in India. Poor people in Indian slums are very enterprising and would benefit from Sanergy's franchise model. Other franchise and micromodels have been successful in India, such as microfinance institutions, and cooperative finance models that include women's self-help groups and producer groups. In addition, due to caste inequalities, Indian slums have their own economic hierarchies. In this context, Sanergy's waste collection system may also provide a better livelihood to lower-caste and "untouchable" individuals who are relegated to dealing with waste.

The Total Sanitation Campaign (TSC) was launched by the government of India in 1999 with the goal of achieving universal sanitation coverage by 2012. While the TSC has been met with uneven success, reports by the Government of India's Water and Sanitation Program indicated that universal sanitation would be achieved by 2018.[15] Their inability to achieve the goal by 2012 is widely considered to result from government inefficiency at both local and national levels. The TSC also focused mostly on poor rural environments, leaving room for social enterprises such as Sanergy to fill in the gaps in India's urban slums.

In 2014, the Indian government launched a second national sanitation campaign, *Swachh Bharat Abhiyan* (Clean India Mission), to clean the streets, roads, and infrastructure of the country. This campaign aimed to accomplish the vision of a "Clean India" by 2 October 2019, the 150th birthday of Mahatma Gandhi. It was expected to cost over US$9.3 billion. The objectives of the campaign included eliminating open defecation, converting sanitary toilets to pour-flush toilets, 100% collection and processing of waste, and a behavioral change in people regarding healthy sanitation practices, among others. In addition, the government has committed to facilitating private-sector participation in operation and maintenance of sanitary facilities.

Organizations with a similar mission to Sanergy's have met with some success in the Indian market. For example, the nonprofit organization Sulabh International successfully installed and continued to operate over 8,000 public toilets in India through its commercially viable business model reliant on consumer demand.[16] But unlike Sanergy, Sulabh's financial viability depended on local branches of the government paying for toilet installation and users covering maintenance costs through fees they pay every time they visit a toilet.

Sulabh's story holds some important lessons for Sanergy. It successfully provided work to lower caste and untouchable individuals, engaged community members, and coordinated between local governments and organizations. Sulabh was able to influence government and get funding and recognition for their pay-per-use toilets. However, it also made mistakes. Just like the TSC, Sulabh built toilets without properly gauging demand in certain areas. It introduced the toilets in markets where they were not sure if people would pay to use them or not. Sulabh also faced the issue of improper knowledge about maintaining the toilets.

In India, fertilizer is highly abundant and the cost is subsidized, but it is of the highly chemical variety which has long-term negative effects on the environment and on productive crop yields over time. Sanergy's organic fertilizer could provide a good sustainable alternative to chemical fertilizers used by both commercial and small-scale farmers. But Auerbach was not sure whether demand for higher quality organic fertilizer would enable Sanergy to make an adequate return.

An alternative was to expand to other countries in East Africa. Uganda, Tanzania, and Rwanda all looked promising. They had similar cultural dynamics to Kenya, so it appeared that Sanergy could apply its operating model easily. But Auerbach considered that entering a potentially enormous market like India would verify the broad applicability of their model and also enable the company to achieve an impact on a much larger scale.

AUERBACH'S RESOLUTIONS

With 2015 only a few days old, it seemed like a good time for Auerbach to make the decisions that would guide Sanergy in the coming year. He knew that significant growth would be part of the equation. While the short-term operational imperatives were clear, the best way to prepare for long-term growth was still an open question. As he watched his marketing team at work, he pulled out a sheet of paper, wrote a series of resolutions at the top, and started to fill in the page.

Discussion Questions

1. Do you agree with the overall model of for-profit companies providing services traditionally delivered by governments or nonprofits? What are the trade-offs?
2. What elements enabled the creation of this entrepreneurial venture?
3. How effectively, in your opinion, has Sanergy assessed the market for its services?
4. Is Auerbach's pragmatic approach to measurement appropriate? How does its organization as a for-profit influence this?
5. In Auerbach's shoes, how would you prioritize your time? Where would you focus?
6. Should Sanergy expand? If so, where and when?

Acknowledgments

An earlier version of this case was published by Sage Publications. Used with permission. An earlier version of this case was prepared with the assistance of Brandeis University, Heller School for Social Policy and Management students Pooja Virani and Cameron M. Campbell.

Notes

1. United Nations. (2015). *The United Nations Millenium goals progress report 2015*. Retrieved from https://www.un.org/millenniumgoals/2015_MDG_Report/pdf/MDG%202015%20rev%20(July%201).pdf.
2. Cross, P., & Morel, A. (2005). Pro-poor strategies for urban water supply and sanitation services delivery in Africa. *Water Science and Technology*, *51*(8), 51–57.
3. Nations Encylopedia. (n.d.). *Kenya – agriculture*. Retrieved June 1, 2021 from https://www.nationsencyclopedia.com/economies/Africa/Kenya-AGRICULTURE.html.
4. World Bank Group. (n.d.). *GDP per capita (current US$) – Kenya*. Retrieved June 2, 2021 from https://data.worldbank.org/indicator/NY.GDP.PCAP.CD?locations=KE.
5. World Bank Group. (2018, April 11). *Poverty incidence in Kenya declined significantly but unlikely to be eradicated by 2030*. Retrieved June 3, 2021 from https://www.worldbank.org/en/country/kenya/publication/kenya-economic-update-poverty-incidence-in-kenya-declined-significantly-but-unlikely-to-be-eradicated-by-2030.
6. Vallabhaneni, A., Auerbach, D., & Zira, J. (n.d.). Turning waste into profits: A potential model for creating a sustainable sanitation cycle in urban slums [Unpublished white paper]. Cambridge, MA: Massachusetts Institute of Technology.
7. Nderitu, T. (2010, December 27). *Kenya sanitation: 'Flying Toilets' insulate women from rape*. Women News Network. Retrieved from http://womennewsnetwork.net/2010/12/27/kenya-flying-toilets-women/.
8. World Bank Group. (2006). *Kenya inside informality: Poverty, jobs, housing and services in Nairobi slums*. Retrieved June 1, 2021 from https://documents.worldbank.org/en/publica

tion/documents-reports/documentdetail/450081468047364801/kenya-inside-informality-poverty-jobs-housing-and-services-in-nairobis-slums.

9. Kirimi, M. (2007). *Proceedings from 18th regional water and sanitation seminar: Water and sanitation in urban Africa: Emerging approaches for reaching the un-served poor*. Mombasa: ATPS Communications Dept.
10. Szánto, G. L., Letema, S. C., Tukahirwa, J. T., Mgana, S., Oosterveer, P. J. M., & van Buuren, J. C. L. (2012). Analyzing sanitation characteristics in the slums of East Africa. *Water Policy*, *14*(4), 613–624.
11. Ibid.
12. Sanergy. (2011). *Sanergy business plan* [Unpublished manuscript].
13. World Bank. (2010). *A decade of the total sanitation campaign: Rapid assessment of processes and outcomes, volume 1. Main report*. Water and sanitation program. Retrieved from https://openknowledge.worldbank.org/handle/10986/17289.
14. Prasad, U., & Basu, S. (2013, March 29). A new approach to India's water sanitation crises. *Stanford Social Innovation Review*. Retrieved from https://ssir.org/articles/entry/a_new_approach_to_indias_water_sanitation_crisis_part_1.
15. World Bank. (2010). *A decade of the total sanitation campaign: Rapid assessment of processes and outcomes, volume 1. Main report*. Water and sanitation program. Retrieved from https://openknowledge.worldbank.org/handle/10986/17289.
16. Sulabh International. (2012). Retrieved December 1, 2016 from www.sulabhinternational.org.

CASE THREE

WORKAROUND: STARTING A NEW GLOBAL VENTURE

Wafaa Arbash and Jennie Kelly tried to keep their expressions neutral, but the truth was that they were both very disappointed. They had just learned that WorkAround—the nascent venture that together they had spent months honing—had not been selected as one of the top 16 teams to split the US $1.5M nonequity prize money from MassChallenge as they had hoped. They had been optimistic about their prospects as they went into the competition, and the feedback. While the feedback from several of the judges was supportive, other judges either did not share their vision for how to create social change or saw the technical complexity of their venture as a liability. What, they wondered, should they do next?

THE GENESIS OF WORKAROUND

WorkAround is an online platform that connects small but growing companies with a pool of skilled workers to handle a variety of business needs that can be done more quickly and with higher quality and at lower cost through microwork. WorkAround built on the example of businesses like Uber, Airbnb, and countless other gig economy startups, which connect providers of services (in this case refugees) with customers for their services (in this case businesses), and were responsible for contracting with the clients, processing payments for the workers and ensuring quality control. WorkAround's approach is to contract with companies for a large number of tasks and then break them down into microtasks to make them available to several refugee workers.

Arbash conceived of the original vision for WorkAround as she studied the refugee crisis afflicting her home country of Syria and realized that there was a significant population of talented, educated, and motivated workers who lacked access to employment opportunities.

Arbash was a Coexistence-Sustainable International Development dual MA student at the Heller School for Social Policy at Brandeis University. She had been working part-time during her academic program for an organization located in the same building as the Cambridge Innovation Center (CIC), a co-working space for entrepreneurs and start-up enterprises. She started attending Venture Café sessions at CIC where she met entrepreneurs and learned about the unfilled needs of their businesses. She started to see the potential of microtask completion to both assist growing businesses and help people who needed jobs, namely, refugees living abroad. According to Arbash:

> *I came from an economically unstable household in Syria and recognized the impact of not having predictable resources. But in my experience, I found the solutions provided by NGOs in places like Syria to be episodic and ineffective. I was working on my graduate thesis on an education-related topic, but as I started to think about the needs both of refugees and of businesses, I changed my focus to the global refugee crisis.*
>
> (W. Arbash, personal Interview, December 12, 2017)

THE GLOBAL REFUGEE CRISIS

The Hult Prize is an initiative that generates start-up ideas from students and other young adults to sustainably solve the world's most critical social challenges. According to the UN Agency for Refugees, as of 2019 there were nearly 80 million people worldwide (40% of were children) that have been forcibly displaced from their homes.[1] People are displaced for reasons that include conflict situations, environmental conditions, and a lack of economic opportunity. Circumstances can be as varied as the civil war in Syria, religious persecution of the Rohingya in Myanmar, droughts in southern India, and natural disasters in many parts of the world. In addition, hundreds of millions more survive daily chaos and crisis and have left their homes to live in refugee camps, informal settlements, or in perpetual transit. In the broadest definition, refugees can be either internally displaced within their home country or have migrated beyond their national borders to reside in other countries.

Governments and nongovernmental organizations have responded to the swelling refugee population worldwide with foreign aid and social services. According to the OECD, development aid spent on hosting refugees in donor countries increased 27.5% from 2015 to 2016 to reach $15.4 billion.[2]

In their materials for the 2017 Hult Prize competition on the global refugee crisis, Hult identified five distinct losses that refugees experience along the path of displacement that generally are not addressed by the traditional foreign aid system: place, community, ownership, learning, and work. Statistics show that as many as two-thirds of refugees worldwide have been displaced for more than five years, and over 85% are living in the developing world. The presence of large numbers of refugees can add to already tenuous social, economic, and political situations in host countries and the consequent problems are further stoked by fears of the refugee as criminals or as a draw on already limited resources.[3]

Although the refugee demographic is diverse, among them are many individuals with education and skills but without access to opportunities to earn a living for their families and end their dependence on often unreliable foreign aid. A lack of access to jobs has larger repercussions for vulnerable refugees; it leaves them at risk of exploitation and trafficking or of entering conflict situations directly as combatants. Conversely, employment can restore dignity to refugees and facilitate their integration into the host society, leading to a safer and more tolerant world. Innovative and entrepreneurial solutions such as WorkAround's are being developed to provide refugees with an alternative pathway out of economic instability.

THE WORKAROUND SOLUTION

As the digital economy has evolved, working across borders has become easier, and economic opportunities that once were available only to people in fixed geographies have expanded. A classic example of this is outsourcing, where companies seek to reduce costs or improve efficiency by shifting tasks, operations, jobs, or processes to an external contracted third party for a significant period of time. Examples include software development outsourced from the United States to India, or call centers outsourced to multiple locations.

In addition, a major labor market shift towards "the gig economy" has led companies and workers to develop new ways of working together that upend traditional employer–labor relationships. As part of this trend, technology has enabled approaches to distributing and outsourcing work to employees and independent contractors that would have been unthinkable a decade ago.

An additional evolution has been the emergence of microtasks. According to Wikipedia, microtasking is the process of splitting a large job into small, repetitive tasks that can be distributed over the Internet to many people. Appropriate tasks are those that are large volume, can be broken down into independent segments, and require human judgment.[4]

Since the inception of the concept of microwork, many online services have been developed that specialize in different types of microtasking. They typically rely on a workforce composed of Internet users from around the world, and because judgment is required, the tasks cannot be fully automated. For example, workers can identify or tag objects in a photo or video, perform data deduplication or transcribe or translate audio recordings more accurately than machines.

There are several competitors in this space. For example, Mechanical Turk, an Amazon company, was an early entry; this company enables workers to choose and perform simple tasks online, reporting directly through a web-based platform to be paid.

Building upon the example of other microwork start-ups, WorkAround seeks to connect a skilled, but economically disconnected, refugee population with the opportunity to complete microtask work remotely. This enables WorkAround's target workers to both generate income and develop a work history that will facilitate their economic integration into their host country. Target workers are well positioned to perform the work: in its pitch deck (see Appendix D), WorkAround cites a UNHCR report that found that 90% of refugees in the Middle East and Northern Africa region have access to 3G Internet and 68% have smartphones. WorkAround also found from internal surveys that 90% of their workers have higher education.[5]

EARLY SUCCESSES

While Arbash had what she thought was the seed of a great idea, it was not until she signed up for the Heller Startup Challenge in November 2016 that she was able to assemble a team with the shared vision to help her move it forward. The Heller Startup Challenge is an intensive three-day workshop for social entrepreneurs intending to start mission-driven organizations, both for-profit and nonprofit. Students from across the Brandeis University community participate and can arrive on the first day with an idea or seeking to join another team. Arbash's concept quickly resonated with the other students participating in the Startup Challenge; there, she found a team that included Heller MBA-SID student Jennie Kelly ('17), Brandeis undergraduate Shai Dinnar ('20), who later left the team, and Heller Co-existence-SID student Shadi Sheikhsaraf (MA '17) to build WorkAround from an idea to a fully developed social enterprise concept.

The WorkAround team was thrilled to win first prize of $2,000 at the Heller Startup Challenge and also gained much needed feedback and coaching.

The team went on to compete in the Heller-Hult Challenge in December, which provided accelerated entry to the main Hult Challenge, an initiative of the Clinton Global Initiative, where teams compete for a $1 million prize to solve a global social problem affecting over 10,000 people. The theme of the 2017 Hult Challenge was the global refugee crisis, creating provided an opportunity to further develop the WorkAround concept. The team did not win Heller-Hult but enjoyed the competition experience and was inspired by the other presenters to put even more energy into their new venture.

INCUBATING THE VENTURE

One of the benefits of winning the Heller Startup Challenge was expedited entry into the SPARK program at Brandeis University. SPARK is designed to encourage and support entrepreneurial activity within the Brandeis community; eligible grantees include students (graduate and undergraduate), postdocs, faculty, and staff. The seed funding provided by the program is intended to help bring innovative ideas and entrepreneurial ambitions to life with the goal of transitioning those ideas into a viable start-up. In addition to funding, all SPARK teams receive support through participation in entrepreneurship curricula, professional mentoring, and pitch training.

The team took full advantage of SPARK program resources, received additional mentoring and pitch coaching, and eventually won a SPARK prize of $10,000 to invest in the WorkAround venture. According to Rebecca Menapace, Associate Provost for Innovation at Brandeis (and Director of the SPARK program),

> *WorkAround is a prime example of the importance of supporting students with innovative ideas aimed at solving pressing social needs. I am proud that Brandeis Innovation has played a role in helping launch this startup.*
>
> (R. Menapace, email correspondence, December 28, 2017)

The team was challenged by the demands of advancing their venture while balancing graduate degree completion, job searches, professional responsibilities, and other imperatives. Kelley said, "We didn't get a lot of sleep and really needed to be good at time management."

The team also entered another three-day start-up weekend in the Spring of 2017, this one sponsored by Brandeis's International Business School, and won first place. They had also been participating in MassChallenge's Bootcamp for Underserved Communities along with seven other teams. Both events won them entry into the main MassChallenge competition.

Evolving the Business Model

The WorkAround business model had evolved significantly since Arbash initially conceived the idea and partnered with her classmates at the Heller Startup Challenge. Early in the process the team had used a business model canvas to articulate their ideas and make sure that they had considered all the important elements, and they continued to refine it (see Appendix C).

According to Kelly:

> *There were a lot of things we tried initially. For example, at first our potential customers included both organizations and individuals, and we thought that universities and libraries would be big potential customers.*
>
> (J. Kelley, & W. Arbash, personal interview, January 3, 2018)

They learned through trial and error in the marketplace that their initial customer targets were wrong. "Universities were too bureaucratic" according to Kelley, "and libraries were already well served by other microwork vendors" (J. Kelley, & W. Arbash, personal Interview, January 3, 2018). Eventually they settled on start-ups, which could make decisions quickly, as their initial target market of early adopters. Kelly and Arbash learned that the best way to pitch these and other high potential customers was by going to start-up events and artificial intelligence, machine learning and big data conferences. According to Kelly:

> *We would volunteer for the conferences so we could attend for free, and because we were familiar faces as volunteers, we had an opening to discuss our value proposition with attendees. We got an average of five solid leads and one sale from each conference we attended.*
>
> (J. Kelley, & W. Arbash, personal interview, January 3, 2018)

Another element WorkAround evolved was its economic model. Initially they charged companies per task (too complicated) and planned to use first 10% and then 20% of revenues to fund operations. As client and worker needs became clearer, they moved to a model where they would charge \$10 per hour (discounted for large contracts) and would pay \$3 per hour to the workers (derived based on the minimum wage in markets where their workers lived), with the \$7 per hour difference intended to fund operations.

Arbash and Kelly also needed to consider how workers would join the system. They had advertised only once on Facebook and attracted 300 workers but wanted to hold back on further advertising until they had a steady stream of jobs to offer. Worker applicants would fill out a form with basic information, and then Kelly and Arbash would observe their initial task completion to ensure quality control.

The current model for matching workers with jobs was described by Kelly as "extremely cumbersome." It was a slow semimanual process. But because they were trying to stay lean, they did not want to invest a lot in a technology platform. "We are currently looking for a developer who can make this process easier, but we might want to find someone who will do it on a volunteer basis or for equity" (J. Kelley, & W. Arbash, personal Interview, January 3, 2018), added Kelly.

The founders elected to establish the company as a LLC (limited liability company) incorporated in Delaware and registered in MA. They selected a for-profit organizational approach to maximize their flexibility and to signal their intent to be commercial partners to potential business customers. They also did not want to need to rely on donations to sustain and grow the organization. However, they realized that choosing a for-profit model would make it impossible to qualify for most charitable grants and other funding sources that are available only to nonprofit organizations.

THE CHALLENGE AT MASSCHALLENGE

MassChallenge likes to describe itself as the most start-up-friendly accelerator on the planet. Founded in 2010 by two former Bain consultants, it now has offices in Boston, Texas, Israel, Mexico, Switzerland, and the UK MassChallenge has a zero-equity position, meaning it only provides grant funding and nonfinancial support but does not take equity in the start-up companies it incubates. The Boston accelerator program takes place from June to October and MassChallenge requires that at least one team founder consistently work out of the shared MassChallenge workspace during that period. The program culminates in a series of competitions that teams advance through to win prize money and make important connections to potential partners and investors.

"Over the past seven years, MassChallenge has graduated more than 1,200 entrepreneurs from our intensive accelerator, enabling them to create enormous impact around the world," said John Harthorne, Founder and CEO of MassChallenge. Speaking about the class of 2017, which included WorkAround, he added: "We are proud to welcome such a high-potential class of startups to MassChallenge and are excited to help them define their future and maximize their impact."[6]

According to Kelly:

The nice thing about the competitions we participated in is that each judging and mentoring panel has a different perspective on what it takes for a venture to succeed. This enabled us to carefully refine our business model, while thinking about it from different angles. The WorkAround concept is very simple on the surface, but enormously complex in implementation, so this kind of feedback was essential. And MassChallenge in particular helped us hone in on the question of whether we really had a customer.

(J. Kelley, & W. Arbash, personal interview, January 3, 2018)

Arbash added:

SPARK and MassChallenge helped us to focus our business model. As students we were pretty focused on research, and our mentors encouraged us to stop researching and start solving the practical problems of business formation.

(J. Kelley, & W. Arbash, personal interview, January 3, 2018)

MassChallenge participation started in July, 2017 and involved a four-month process of mentoring, funder introductions, and sharing ideas with other teams. At this point most of the effort came from Arbash and Kelly. Dinnar was returning to being a full-time student, and Sheikhsaraf had committed to a full-time job with UNHCR and then relocated to Iraq. Kelly reflects: "Waafa and I were fully immersed as we worked to take advantage of the resources provided by MassChallenge and actually start the business. At the same time, I was running an entrepreneurship boot camp for high school students at Brandeis and that contributed to my learning as well."

Kathleen Healy was the team's main mentor at MassChallenge and helped them to think through their customer segments and how to make their presentation as compelling as possible.

According to Arbash, honing their concept amidst the high-stakes environment of MassChallenge also tested their thinking:

> *We thought that helping refugees would be an automatic plus and that others would share our vision. But in fact, we needed to overcome biases—potential sponsors and customers were worried about the stability of our workers, and whether we could deliver secure products. So, the social story behind our venture was not an automatic win—we needed to overcome many concerns to get customer buy-in.*
>
> (J. Kelley, & W. Arbash, personal interview, January 3, 2018)

MassChallenge also helped the team to make needed connections. In fact, the first three clients for WorkAround services were other MassChallenge start-ups.

THE BIG EVENT

The selection period at Boston MassChallenge in late September 2017 was exhilarating. 128 teams were participating over three days and were huddled in final preparation to present their ventures via a 6½ minute pitch to a judge panel of five or six experts, who would share their feedback and advice as well as help decide which teams would move forward. According to Kelly:

> *There was a real buzz around MassChallenge as we worked towards selection day. You could feel the energy as teams practiced their pitches in the hallways. It was intense but still supportive. And you could see how nervous everyone was by the fact that available snacks (which typically went quickly) remained un-eaten as the day went on.*
>
> (J. Kelley, & W. Arbash, personal interview, January 3, 2018)

Arbash and Kelly were nervous yet confident in their vision as they took one last look at the slides they planned to present. But at the end of the day, when the winners were announced, WorkAround was not among them.

According to Arbash:

We were actually shocked that we did not proceed to the next round. We saw our solution as really innovative. But we did not win. The judge feedback was mixed—many of the evaluators loved our concept, but others were focused on the operational challenges of the model.

(J. Kelley, & W. Arbash, personal interview, January 3, 2018)

Judge feedback (see an anonymized version in the appendix) included many supportive comments, such as, "You are on to a great idea" and "[you have a] unique and viable business with an outstanding social impact," and provided high ratings for the problem WorkAround would solve. Judges also raised concerns about legal barriers and payment transfer constraints. Some cited the complexity of getting the business platform up and running and were disappointed not to see a prototype. Some also mentioned that it might be better to partner with an existing player, either a competitor or a refugee-serving organization.

Kelly reacted:

I was pretty surprised by some of the feedback. It made it clear that we were not communicating the concept as well as we could and had more work to do.

(J. Kelley, & W. Arbash, personal interview, January 3, 2018)

Arbash and Kelly shared disappointed glances, and then signaled to each other that they would need to meet later that evening to decide what to do next.

WHAT HAPPENED NEXT?

After their initial disappointment, Arbash and Kelly rallied. Kelly recalled:

We were disappointed for five or ten minutes. But then we decided to move forward. We were really confident in our idea, and actually stayed at the MassChallenge office until late that night defining our next steps.

(J. Kelley, & W. Arbash, personal interview, January 3, 2018)

After a few days of writing thank-you notes and updates to the many people who had supported them along the way, they started to work through the judge's feedback and consider how they might strengthen their business plan.

The next step was for Arbash to pitch WorkAround at Hubweek (Boston) during their Beantown Throwdown event where they competed against eleven other teams and won $12,000. A few days later they were surprised to hear from one of their mentors who offered them a free extra ticket to an expensive social impact conference in San Francisco. Kelly flew out to attend the conference and made even more connections. They next competed in a SheStarts Boston event and won $5,000 in legal services. They also received a number of other benefits, including mentoring, professional and potential client connections, and a year-long gym membership at a high-end fitness club for women. ("We will definitely be making full use of that!" said Kelly.)

Other wins followed—including an unsolicited offer for office space at the CIC, which had heard the "buzz" about WorkAround and wanted to offer their support.

By late 2017, WorkAround had achieved significant traction. They had registered as an LLC, signed up nearly 300 refugees from 30 countries as workers (40 were actively accepting work assignments), and attracted several high-profile clients. One such client was Zoominfo, which hired WorkAround to review news stories and tag relationships. Relationship tagging provided an excellent example of the power of microtasking. Zoominfo was able to use software to identify any time two target companies appeared together in an online posting, but the software was unable to determine the nature of their relationship, while a human microtasker could quickly do this. Another client was America's Test Kitchen, which hired WorkAround to find pirated versions of their content on the Internet, remove it and report it.

Arbash and Kelly continued to evolve the business concept (see Appendix A for the most current revenue model). "We are redesigning the web site and hope to migrate some customers to a subscription model (which will stabilize revenues)." The subscription model was particularly appealing. Arbash and Kelly believed that it would help them achieve a more predictable cash flow and workflow (which would enable them to more carefully calibrate when to add workers) and also mitigate the problem that clients might sign up for WorkAround services but then not use them. A subscription approach also would support their goal to move to higher volume clients.

The team was also concerned about financing. They had bootstrapped operations to date using cashflow and business contest earnings (and by not taking salaries). But they also wanted to invest in the platform, technology and operations, and needed additional funds to do this. They were hoping to receive funding from the Brandeis Innovation Center which was setting up a loan program for alumni business ventures, but the timing of this was uncertain. In addition, they had identified two grants that could support their expansion but did not require them to be a nonprofit; they saw these as longshot opportunities.

Many challenges remained if they were to meet their 2018 goal of attracting 1,000 workers and 100 clients. As they looked towards the new year, Arbash and Kelly started a list of questions.

DISCUSSION QUESTIONS

1. What is your assessment of WorkAround's overall approach? Do you think this model has potential to help refugees?
2. If you were part of the team, what questions would you put on their list?
3. What would you recommend for WorkAround's funding strategy? Should they continue to bootstrap or approach investors? What are the pros and cons?
4. How should they grow their customer pool and worker pool together?
5. What do you see as the biggest risks moving forward?

APPENDIX 1: WORKAROUND TEAM BIOS

Wafaa Arbash

Cofounder and CEO

Arbash is a Syrian woman who moved to the United States in 2013. Prior to WorkAround, she spent five years working on social development programs where she spearheaded several projects to empower local citizens and to increase their leadership and advocacy skills. Arbash holds a dual Master's degrees in Sustainable International Development and Conflict Resolution from the Heller School at Brandeis University and a BS in Education and Curriculum Design from Damascus University.

Jennie Kelly

Cofounder and Director of Operations and Finance

After graduating from William & Mary with a BA in Literary and Cultural Studies, Kelley spent seven years in adult education, primarily working with recent immigrants to the United States on English Language Skills, or in International settings from Albania and Liberia to Saudi Arabia, also teaching English. She also spent several years in the for-profit space in jobs ranging from construction and housing renovations to media and publications. Following these experiences in both the public and private spheres, Kelley returned to school and received a dual MBA in nonprofit management and an MA in sustainable international development, where she learned the skills and made the connections necessary to fulfill her role as Director of Operations and Finance at WorkAround.

Shadi Sheikhsaraf

Cofounder and Director of Partnerships

Sheikhsaraf has been working with the UN in various capacities since 2002, including work with both the UNHCR and UNFPA. She has been a program assistant and coordinator, as well as a monitoring and evaluation consultant. She received a BA in English Translation from Khorasgan University in Iran, and a dual MA in Sustainable International Development and Coexistence and Conflict Resolution from the Heller School of Public Policy at Brandeis University. She now uses her skills in project management and familiarity with international and academic organizations, specifically within the field of refugee and conflict situations to lead WorkAround's partnership strategy.

APPENDIX 2: WORKER DEMOGRAPHICS

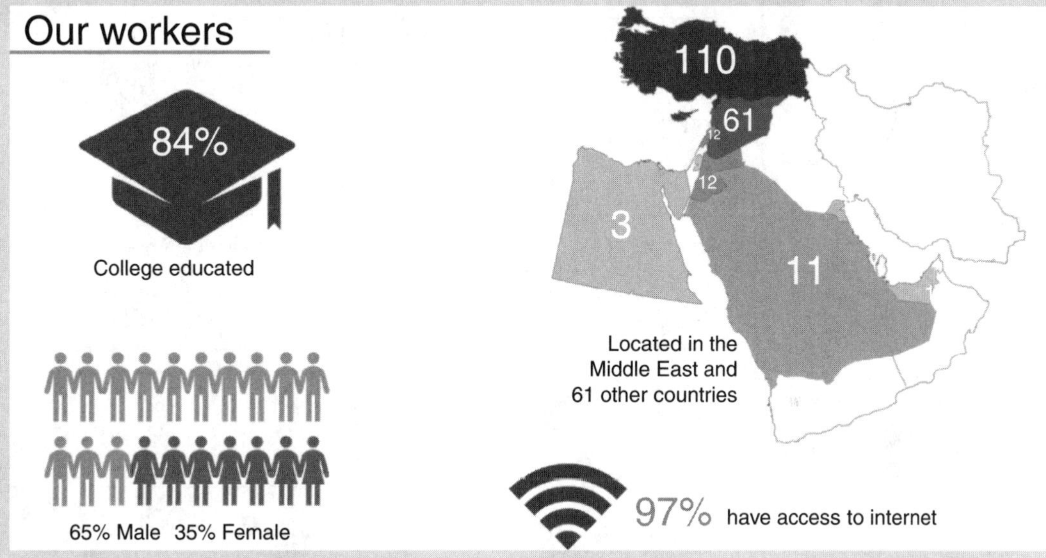

APPENDIX 3: WORKAROUND BUSINESS MODEL CANVAS

Business canvas_v2
October 4, 2017

<table>
<tr><th>Problem</th><th>Solution</th><th>Value proposition</th><th>Unfair advantage</th><th>Customer segments</th></tr>
<tr>
<td rowspan="3">1. Data input and management is time-consuming/costly
2. Accurate input is hard to ensure
3. Communicating instructions and training for outsourcing and managing the results take time and energy

Existing alternatives:
• In house
• Mturk
• Other crowdsourcing</td>
<td>Low-cost easy-to-use platform with built-in quality control and customer support.</td>
<td rowspan="3">Help companies get quality data services for less

High level concept:
Outsourcing for those who want to upsource the world's talent</td>
<td>Access to unique workers gamification of platform</td>
<td rowspan="3">1. Developers of machine learning driven products or services.
2. Managers of large data research sets or analytics services.
3. Curators of online stores or product inventories.

Early adopters:
Familiar with Mturk, connection to social mission</td>
</tr>
<tr><th>Key metrics</th><th>Channels</th></tr>
<tr>
<td>Active refugees
Retained refugees
Subscriptions
Convert from project to subscription</td>
<td>1. AI, machine learning conferences/associations
2. Blogs, media exposure, speaking engagements</td>
</tr>
</table>

Cost structure	Revenue streams
Worker payment – $3/hour Website hosting/maintenance costs – $200/year Bank and transfer fees – $5/worker People costs – $120K/year	Subscription: 1000 hours = $8,000 (1 part-time equivalent) 2000 hours = $14,000 (1 full-time equivalent) Project based: $50 + 10/hour

APPENDIX 4: WORKAROUND PITCH DECK

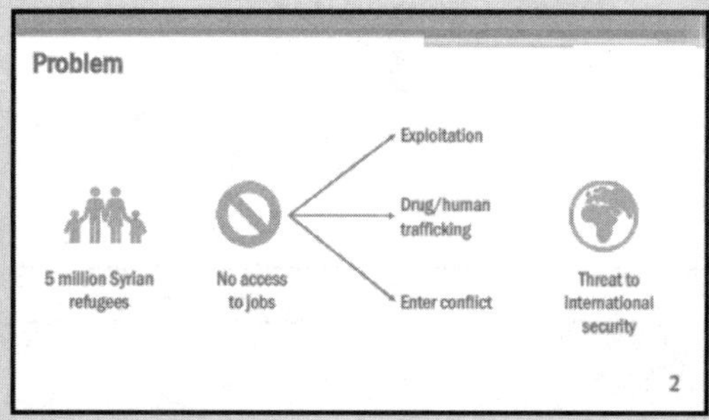

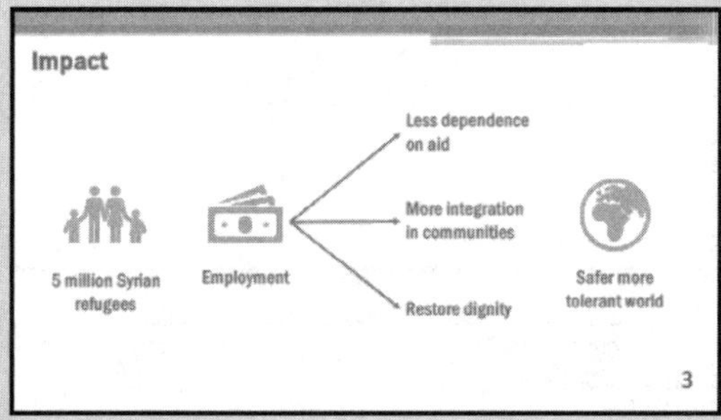

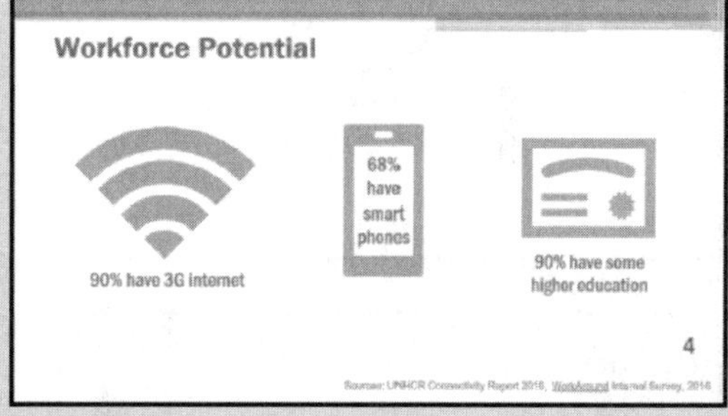

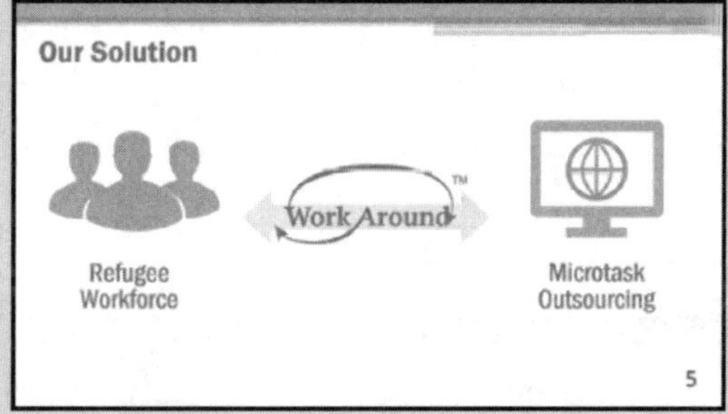

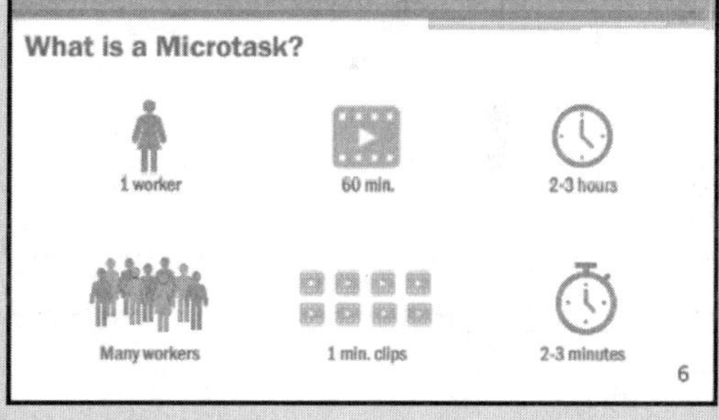

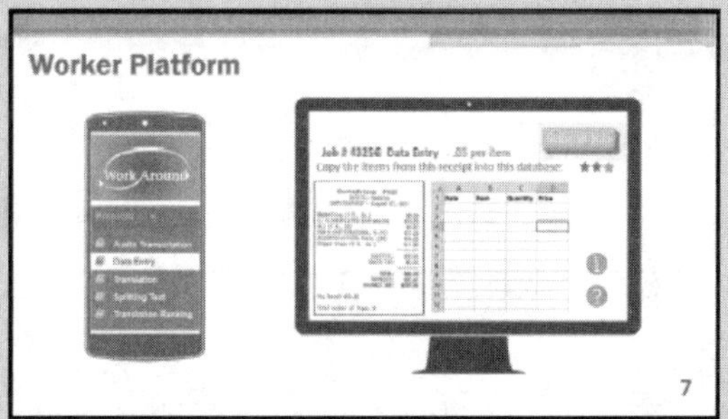

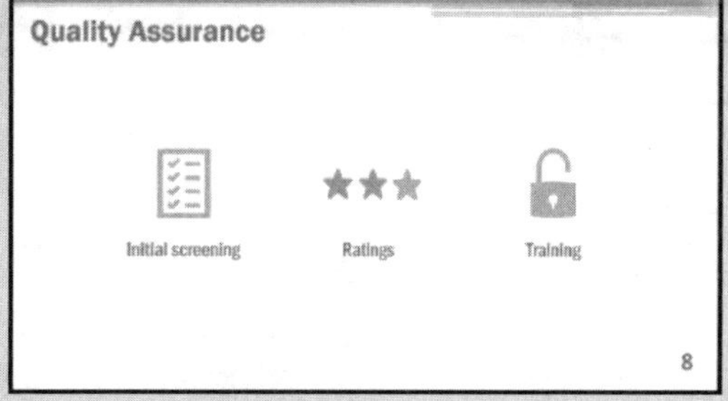

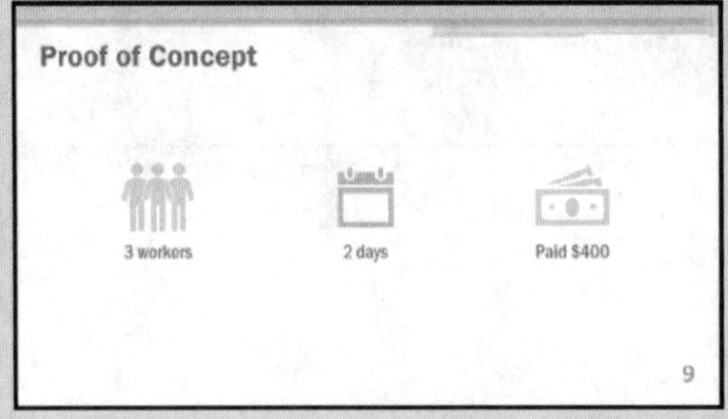
Proof of Concept
3 workers
2 days
Paid $400
9

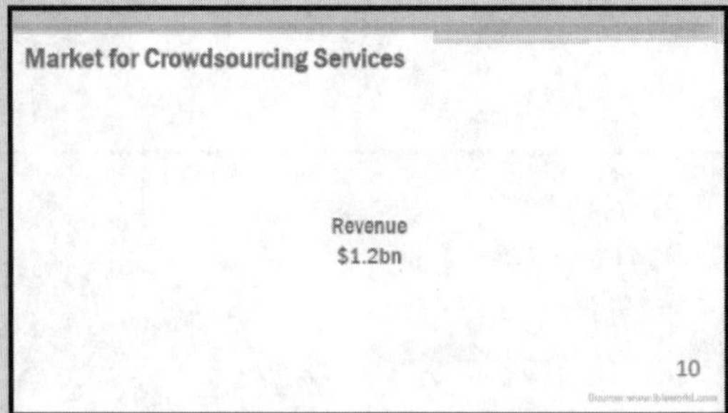
Market for Crowdsourcing Services
Revenue
$1.2bn
10

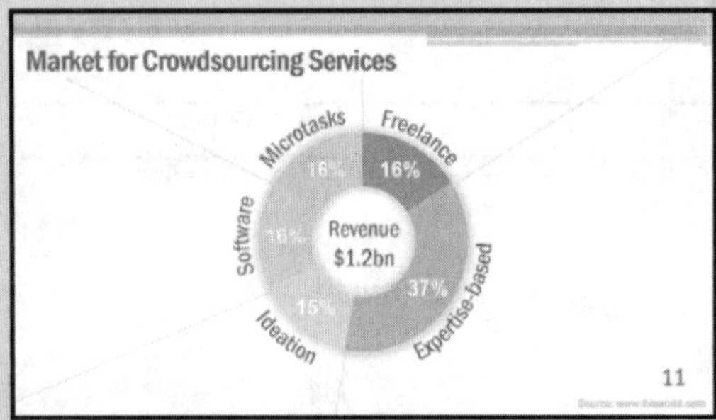
Market for Crowdsourcing Services
Microtasks
Freelance
Software
Ideation
Expertise-based
16%
16%
16%
15%
37%
Revenue
$1.2bn
11

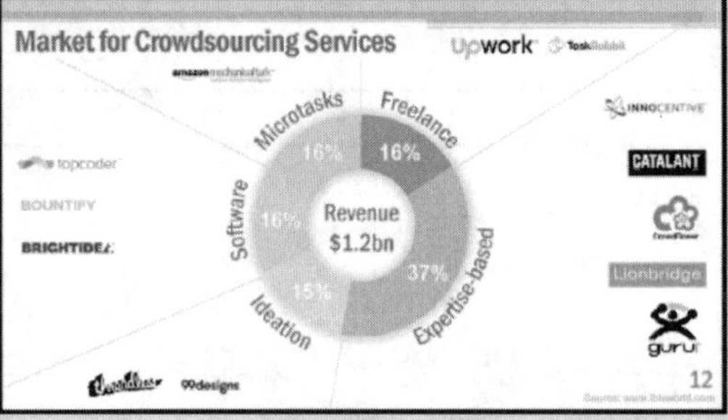
Market for Crowdsourcing Services
Upwork
topcoder
BOUNTIFY
BRIGHTIDEA
INNOCENTIVE
CATALANT
Lionbridge
guru
99designs
Microtasks
Freelance
Software
Ideation
Expertise-based
16%
16%
16%
15%
37%
Revenue
$1.2bn
12

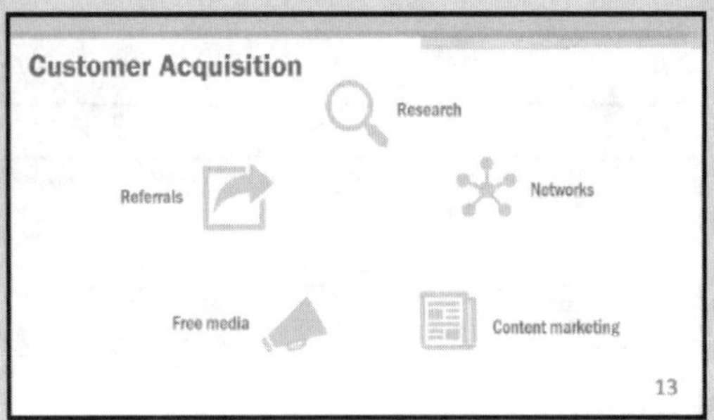
Customer Acquisition
Research
Referrals
Networks
Free media
Content marketing
13

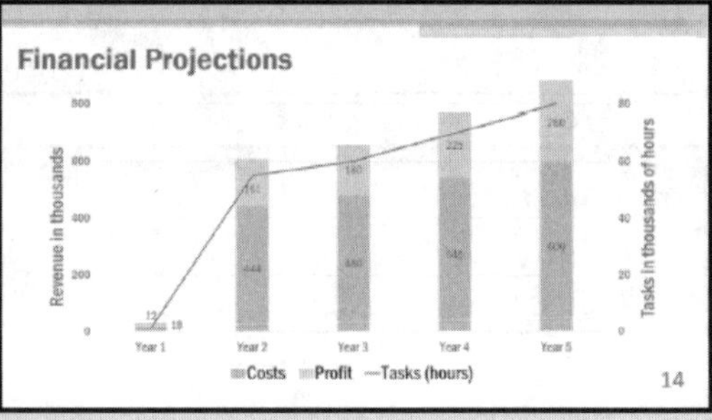
Financial Projections
Revenue in thousands
Tasks in thousands of hours
800
600
400
200
0
80
60
40
20
0
12
18
225
Year 1
Year 2
Year 3
Year 4
Year 5
Costs
Profit
Tasks (hours)
14

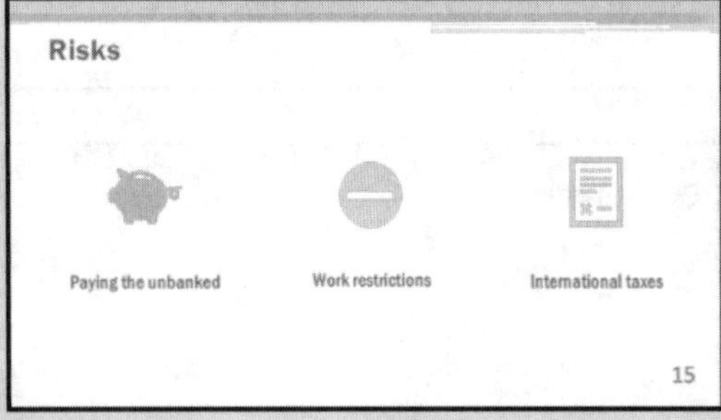
Risks
Paying the unbanked
Work restrictions
International taxes
15

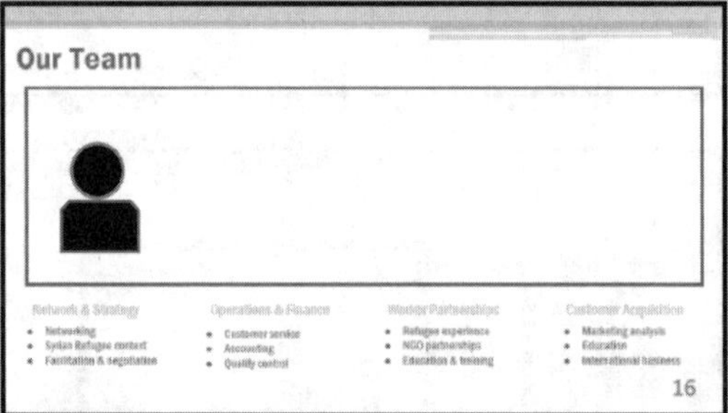
Our Team
Network & Strategy
Networking
Syrian Refugee contact
Facilitation & negotiation
Operations & Finance
Customer service
Accounting
Quality control
Worker Partnerships
Refugee experience
NGO partnerships
Education & training
Customer Acquisition
Marketing analysis
Education
International business
16

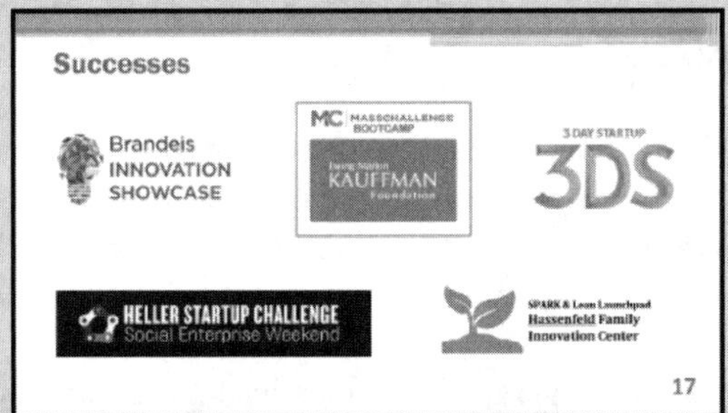

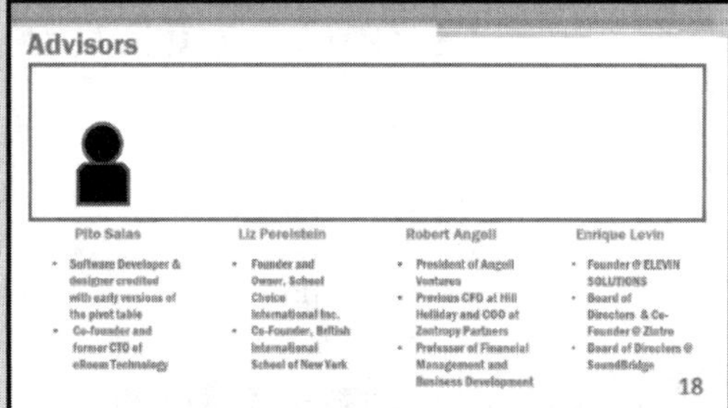

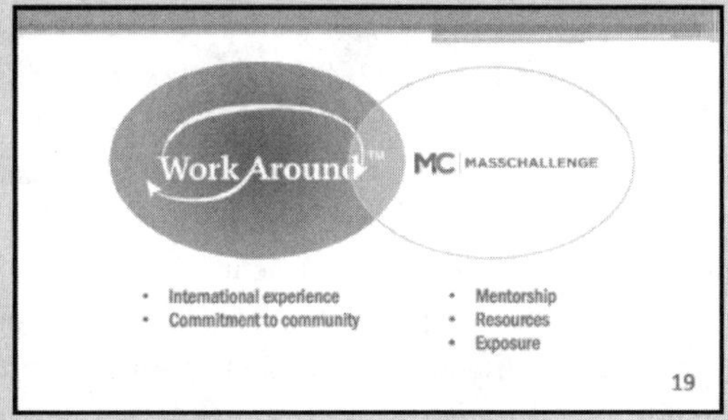

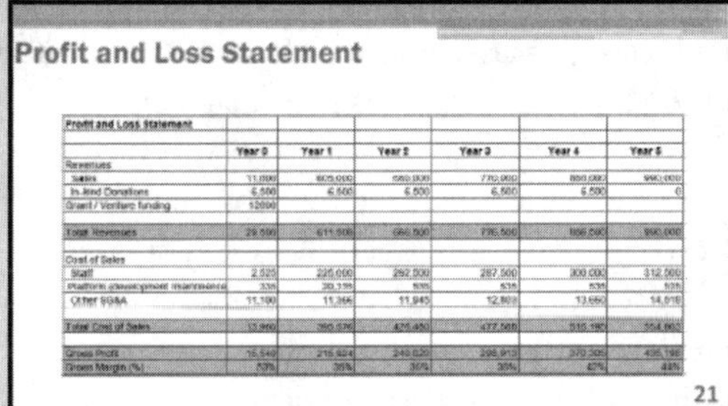

Profit and Loss Statement						
	Year 0	Year 1	Year 2	Year 3	Year 4	Year 5
Revenues						
Sales	11,000	605,000	680,000	770,000	880,000	990,000
In-kind Donations	6,500	6,500	6,500	6,500	6,500	0
Grant / Venture funding	12000					
Total Revenues	29,500	611,500	686,500	776,500	886,500	990,000
Cost of Sales						
Staff	2,525	225,000	292,500	287,500	300,000	312,500
[illegible]	335	30,135	535	535	535	535
Other SG&A	11,100	11,366	11,945	12,803	13,660	14,018
Total Cost of Sales	13,960	395,576	425,450	477,588	516,190	554,862
Gross Profit	15,540	215,924	240,020	298,913	370,306	435,198
Gross Margin (%)	53%	35%	36%	38%	42%	44%

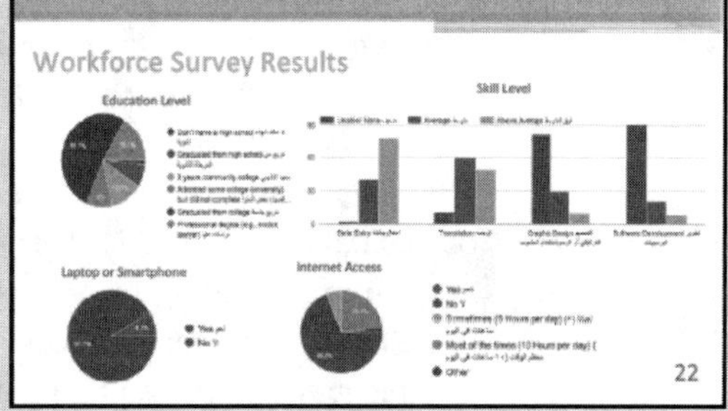

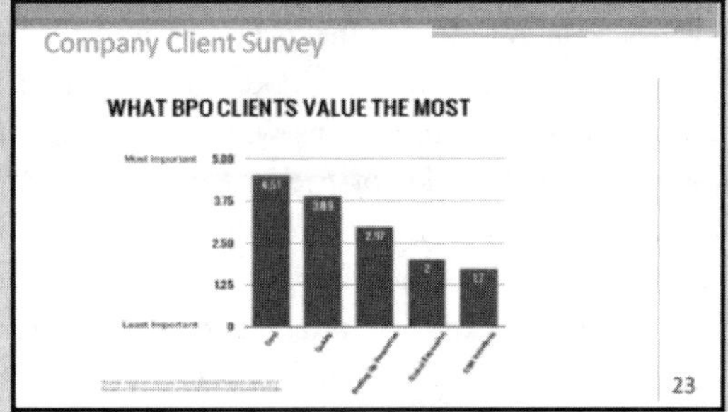

APPENDIX 5: MASSCHALLENGE SELECTED JUDGE FEEDBACK (ANONYMIZED)

Judge 1: "Great team with a great idea. I think you are on to something whether it's to benefit refugees, new immigrants or other underserved communities. I'd like to see more about the technology your platform will use but like that you don't have much competition. I think you underestimate your market potential. I am interested in seeing where this concept goes."

Judge 2: "Super important issue. I think you're still trying to find a single business model—felt a little split between economic development and helping people who have abilities but are displaced. I think it's hard to serve multiple problems like this. I would address the competition much earlier in your presentation. Given that you're paying wages above market equilibrium, I'd mention this in the competitive landscape."

Judge 3: Dear founders, your aspiration and passion is infectious and we should try this out. Suggest you focus on platform, business model, and understand KPO (knowledge process outsourcing) third tier competition in India better.

Judge 4: "I appreciate the intention for your company; however, I felt that you started your company for a specific social reason and during your pitch it got a bit lost. You indicated that while you are trying to find work for displaced refuges, anyone can use your platform. It was unclear how your business model will work and scale and why companies will utilize your 'employees' versus going to a known entity. (Also) there are several non-profits and other for-profit organizations that help to serve refuges. How do you differentiate? Have you considered partnering with them?"

Judge 5: "You outline what seems to be a unique and viable business with outstanding social impact. It is very early as you are not yet in market, and you will need to raise funding (or grants) to end your 'volunteer' status. I encourage you to forge ahead (whether in MassChallenge or not!)."

Judge 6: "Have you thought of any regulatory or legal barriers to your business? Paying non-US persons for work done outside of the US might have hidden costs that could impact the operational efficiency of your business model. While the 'pain' for the refugees is clearly palpable and it is very important to bring good work to them, I am not sure if the 'pain' for your customers (i.e., corporations who would want to outsource that work) is as high… There might be a lot of friction in reaching out to these corporations in terms of having a large marketing budget, etc. only for them to outsource a relatively small amount of work. Have you thought about partnering with people like upwork for this? More importantly though, it'd be good to see if you already have a working platform, or if you are at the idea stage. I couldn't tell from your material how far along the platform might be. You have a very strong and diverse team, but along with showing the diversity of nationalities, it'd be important to show the diversity of your expertise (such as, so and so is a computer expert, so and so is a business development expert, etc.).

Definitely a very important endeavor, and I encourage you to think about alternative ways of reaching your goals (such as partnering with other providers)."

	Judge 1	Judge 2	Judge 3	Judge 4	Judge 5	Judge 6
Customer Pain and Solution	7	10	7	4	9	6
Overall Impact	6	9	6	4	10	7
Customer Needs and Acquisition	7	8	8	4	9	7
Industry and Competitors	7	7	6	4	9	6
Financials/Business Model	7	6	4	3	7	6
Regulation and IP	6	N/A	7	3	8	7
Team and Advisors/Investors	8	7	5	4	9	7
Traction and Progress	N/A	6	N/A	4	N/A	N/A

Acknowledgment

This case was prepared with the assistance of Teaching Assistant Ariela Lovett, Brandeis University, Heller School for Social Policy and Management, MBA/MPP '18.

Notes

1. United Nations High Commission on Refugees. (2020, June 18). *Figures at a glance*. Retrieved from https://www.unhcr.org/en-us/figures-at-a-glance.html.
2. OECD. (2017, November 4). *Development aid rises again in 2016 but flows to poorest countries dip*. Retrieved from https://www.oecd.org/dac/development-aid-rises-again-in-2016-but-flows-to-poorest-countries-dip.htm.
3. Hult Prize. (2017). *2017 case challenge*. Retrieved from https://www.hultprize.org/en/compete/2017-prize/2017-case-challenge/.
4. Microtasking. (2018). In *Wikipedia*. Retrieved from https://en.wikipedia.org/wiki/Microwork.
5. WorkAround. (2017). [Unpublished pitch deck].
6. MassChallenge. (2017, May 21). *MassChallenge announces 2017 cohort*. Retrieved from https://masschallenge.org/media/masschallenge-boston-announces-2017-cohort.

INDEX

A
Abed, Fazle Hasan, 53, 54
Abu Fraiha, Yasmeen, 10, 11, 13, 39, 101, 239, 280, 291–297
Accommodating styles, 45
Accone, Tanya, 285–288
Adaptability, entrepreneurs, 6
Agbaria, Lobna, 18
Aiken, Louise, 16–17
Ākina Foundation, 16–17
Akula, Vikram, 16
Alvarez-Degolia, Ruth, 279
Amabile, Teresa, 36, 38
Anderson, Beth Battle, 188
Angel investors, 150
Anthony, Scott, 43
Aravind Eye Hospital, 268
Arbash, Wafaa, 42, 103, 312–321
Ashoka, 8–9, 15–16, 18, 25
Assimilating styles, 45
Auerbach, David, 121, 299–309
Avi, Rakib, 53–57

B
BACO assessment. *See* Best Available Charitable Option (BACO) assessment
Banerjee, Abhijit, 119–120
Bangladesh Rural Advancement Committee (BRAC), 268
  innovation, 57
  mobile money, 56–57
  origin of, 53–54
  social enterprises, sustainability, 54
  Social Innovation Lab (SIL), 53, 55–56
  social ventures, 66
Barber, Ted, 37, 141, 167–171
B-Corporations, 169
Bedouin communities, 10
Beninger, Anna, 243
Ben & Jerrys, 3
Bermas, Neal, 40–41
Best Available Charitable Option (BACO) assessment, 129–130
Bezos, Jeff, 93
Bhide, Amar, 19
Bhumi Bondhu, 66
Biodiversity, 42
Blank, Steven, 73, 212
Blogging, marketing, 221
Board of Directors, 100–102
Boards of Advisors, 101–102
Bootstrapping, 149
Boston Art & Music Soul Fest, 218–219
Braindumping creativity, 46–47
Brainstorming creativity, 46
Brainwriting/brainwalking creativity, 47
Braverman, Avishay, 101
Bridgespan Group, 175
Brinckmann, J., 236–237
Brown, Tim, 76
Business ecosystems
  agnostics, 99
  assessment, 106–107, 107 (figure)
  Board of Directors, 100–102
  Boards of Advisors, 101–102
  committed supporters, 99
  community partners, 102
  contracted professionals, 102
  definition, 95
  dissenters, 100
  distribution partners, 102
  foundation builders, 99
  innovation partners, 102
  interested bystanders, 99
  mission-based ventures, 96
  participants, 97 (figure)
  pharmaceutical companies, 98
  production partners, 102
  rocketship partners, 99
  systems thinking, 95
  university-led incubator programs, 103
Business formation costs, 272, 272 (figure)
Business model, 68 (figure)
  activities and environment, 70
  canvas, 68, 69, 69 (figure), 78–79, 79 (figure)
  customers, 70
  definition, 67
  financial and organizational approach, 70–71
  mission, 69–70
  processes, 68
  profit formula, 68

resources, 68
value proposition, 67, 70
Business Model Generation, 68
Business pitch, 237
cognitive load theory, 246
deck, 246–247, 247 (table)
elevator pitches, 242, 244–245, 245 (table)–246 (table)
formal pitches, 242, 244
during the pitch, 248–249
postpitch, 250
PowerPoint slides, 246–247
process, 247–248
Q&A responses, 249–250
virtual presentations, 250
Business plans
benefits, 237–238
business model and value proposition, 235
competitive environment, 240
cover and title page, 239
definition, 237, 238
disadvantages, 238
executive summary, 240
financial plan, 241
financial statements, 241–242
market assessment, 240–241
operating plan, 241
operational business plan, 236
product/service offering, 240
sales and marketing plan, 241
short (or summary) business plan, 236
table of contents, 239
theory of change and social impact plan, 241
traditional (or formal) business plan, 236
types, 236
venture overview, 240
Butler, Tim, 7

C

Career Prep program, 14
Caseres, Wences, 26
Cash burn, 148
Chand, Amber, 37, 141
Christensen, Clayton, 39, 67
Clark, Tim, 68
Climate change, 16–17, 41
Cognitive bias, 74–75, 75 (table)
Cognitive load theory, 246
Colby, Susan, 123
Collins, Jim, 19
Commitment and determination, entrepreneurs, 6
Content marketing, 220–221
Convergent thinking, 34–36, 35 (figure), 49
Converging styles, 45
Corporations, 143
Cost–benefit analysis, 129
Cost efficiencies, 174
Courage, entrepreneurs, 6
Craig, Nick, 20
Creativity
braindumping, 46–47
brainstorming, 46
brainwriting/brainwalking, 47
components, 36, 37 (figure)
dot voting, 48 (table)
enhancement, 38
experiential learning cycle, 46
learning styles, 45
mashups, 48 (table)
mindmapping, 48 (table)
mission impossible, 47 (table)
reverse/opposite thinking, 48 (table)
role plays, 48 (table)
storyboarding, 47 (table)
thinking skills, 36–37
Crowdfunding, 152–153, 170
Cuddy, Amy, 243
Cultural capital, 26
Cultural context, 266–267
Customer-centric design, 15

D

Daily Table, 12–13, 21, 63, 65
Danziger, Michael, 181
Debt, 153
Dees, Gregory, 2, 188
DeGraaf, Leonard, 60
99Degrees, 207, 229–232
Deming, Edwards, 206
Demographic shifts, 43
Design thinking, social ventures, 75–76
Dickinson, Rink, 42, 279
Digital marketing, 220–221, 221 (table)
Dillard, S., 74–75
Divergent thinking, 34–36, 35 (figure), 49
Diverging styles, 45
Donations/grants, 153
Dorsey, C., 16, 18, 21, 107–110
Dor Yeshorim, 13
Double taxation, 143–144
Drayton, Bill, 8–9, 18
Drayton, William, 21
Duflo, Esther, 119–120
Dwikat, Amjad, 277
Dyer, Jeffrey, 39

E

Earned income, 154
Echoing Green, 16, 21, 107–110
Economic changes, 43
Ecosystem builders
  Ākina Foundation, 16–17
  Ashoka, 15–16, 18
  Echoing Green, 16
  New Profit, 15
  Skoll Foundation, 15
Edison, Thomas, 60
Edmonson, Amy, 66
Edna McConnell Clark Foundations, 118
Education access, 42
Eisenmann, T., 74–75
Ekal Vidyalaya, 15
  lean design, 208–210
Elevator pitches, 242, 244–245, 245 (table)–246 (table)
Elhelo, Ohad, 18, 91, 94–95, 98, 100, 103, 140–141, 294, 295
Email marketing, 221
Endeavor Catalyst Philanthropy, 27
Endeavor Entrepreneurs, 26
Entrepreneurial insights, 33–36
Entrepreneurial leadership
  characteristics, 5–7
  motivation, 7
  self-assessment, 24–25, 24 (table)
Entrepreneurial marketing, 225–226, 226 (table)–228 (table), 228
  advantages, 213–214
  digital and social media marketing, 219–223
  place, 216–217
  pricing, 217
  promotion, 217
  situation analysis, 212–213
  social ventures types, 214–215, 214 (table)
  strategy, 215, 216 (figure)
Entrepreneurial motivation, 267–268
Entrepreneurial operations, 225–226, 226 (table)–228 (table), 228
  agility, 207–208
  culture, 212
  customer-centered design, 208, 209 (figure)
  99Degrees, 207
  execution, 203, 204 (figure)
  experimentation role, 210–211
  external resources, 211–212
  lean, 206–208
  lean design, 208–210
  management, 205–206
  skills, 202
  social ventures, 204
  strategy, 203, 203 (figure)
Entrepreneurial ventures, project cycle, 114, 115 (figure)
Entrepreneurship, definition, 2
Environmental, social, and governance (ESG), 3
Equal Exchange, 42
Equity investments, 149
Espinoza, Diego, 251–252
Evidence-based model, 43–44

F

Fahmy, Amina, 258–262
Fetsch, Emily, 65
Fidelity program, 179
Financial capital, 87, 88
Financial changes, 43
Financing, 163–165, 165 (figure)
  angel investors, 150
  cash burn, 148
  crowdfunding, 152–153
  debt, 153
  donations/grants, 153
  earned income, 154
  equity investments, 149
  founder capital, 149
  funding strategies, 148–149
  Genesis, 157
  government grants and fee-for-services contracts, 154
  GreenLight Fund, 157
  GuideStar, 166 (figure)
  Healthworks Community Fitness, 157
  impact investments, 150, 151 (table)–152 (table)
  mission-driven organizations, 146–147
  mission-driven ventures, 148–154
  nonequity investors, 152
  operating cash flow, 147, 147 (figure)
  positive cash flow, 147, 147 (figure)
  program-related investments (PRIs), 152
  Sanergy, 157–158
  social impact bonds, 154
  sources, 149, 149 (figure)
  strategic investments, 150
  venture capital and private equity (VCPE), 150
  Youth Villages, 156
Fine, Gail, 189–190
Formal pitches, 242, 244
For-profit organization, 44–45
Foster, William, 189–190
Founder capital, 149

G

Galinsky, Lara, 18
Genesis, 157
  business plan, 296
  closed communities, 292–293
  concept, 294–295

Gig economy, 42
Giridharadas, Anand, 11
Global entrepreneurial impact, 264–265
Global Entrepreneurship Monitor (GEM), 265, 273
Government-funded schools, 15
Government grants and fee-for-services contracts, 154
Grameen Bank, 4, 5, 11
GreenLight Fund, scaling, 157
  community, 196
  ecosystem, 197
  future scaling, 199–200
  head office's role, 199
  portfolio investments, 198–199
  Selection Advisory Committee, 198
  social innovation, 197
Gregersen, Hall, 39
Grichnik, D., 236–237
Gugelev, Alice, 190
GuideStar, 166 (figure)
Gulati, Ranjay, 92
Gumpert, D., 239

H

Haas, Martine, 93
Hackman, J. Richard, 93
Hale, Victoria, 96, 98, 100, 281
Hall, Margaret, 18, 196–200
Harthorne, John, 71–72, 92, 180
Harvard Business Review, 7
Health care, 42
Healthworks Community Fitness, 157
Hedgehog concept, 19
Heterogeneous and homogeneous founding teams, 89–90
HopeWell, 134–138
Human capital, 87
Human rights, 42
'Hybrid' business model, 27
Hypothesis-driven entrepreneurship, 67, 73–75, 120–121

I

Idea generation. *See also* Creativity
  associating, 39
  creative thinking skills, 36–37
  discovery skills, 39
  double diamond model, 50–52
  experimenting, 39
  expertise, 37
  motivation, 38
  networking, 39
  observing, 39
  passion, 38
  products and services, 36
  questioning, 39
Ikigai diagram, 19–20, 23, 23 (figure)
Impact Enterprise Fund, 17
Impact investments, 17, 150, 151 (table)–152 (table)
Impact measurement
  for complex situations, 121–123
  direct *vs.* systems level impact, Bridgespan dilemma, 123
  disadvantages, 127–128
  funders, partners, and recipients, 119
  homeownership services, 124, 124 (figure)
  mission-driven organizations, 124
  nonprofit organization, 124, 125 (figure)
  proxy measures, 125
  randomized controlled trial (RCT), 119–121
  social impact, 128–131, 130 (figure)
  survey-based assessments, 123
Innate personality characteristics, 6
Innovation
  divergent and convergent thinking, 34–36, 35 (figure)
  macro-level factors, 44
  micro-level factors, 44–45
  prepared mind, 33
  social impact, 41–44
  social ventures, 33–34
  solutions, 52, 53 (table)
Innovators
  characteristics, 12
  Daily Table, 12–13
  Sanergy, 13
Institutional context, 266–267
Integrated marketing communications, 220
Intellectual property (IP)
  protection types, 253–254, 253 (figure)
  university technology transfer offices, 254
  venture capital (VC), 252–253
Internal rate of return (IRR), 129
Iturriaga, Emiliano, 103, 251–252

J

Jobs, Steve, 49
Joe, Trader, 63
Johnson, Mark, 67
Jones, Daniel, 206

K

Kapsa, D., 236–237
Kaufmann Foundation, 65
Kellner, Peter, 25, 266–267
Kelly, Jennie, 87, 312–321
Kirsch, Vanessa, 16
Kolb, David, 45–46
Kopp, Wendy, 16, 18, 38, 182
Kremer, Michael, 119–120

L

Langheier, Louise, 103, 187–188
Lawler, Patrick, 43
Leadership, entrepreneurs, 6
Lean, 206–208
  design, 208–210
  production, 206
Lee, William, 6
Legal structure, 163, 164 (figure)
  benefit corporation, 144
  benefit LLC/BLLC, 144
  Certified B Corps, 144–145
  charitable organizations, 146
  99Degrees, 141
  for-profit entities, 142–144
  low profit limited liability corporation (L3C), 145
  nonprofit entities, 142
  OGS funding model, 140–141
  of organization, 145–146
  Prosperity Candle, 141
  Prosperity Catalyst, 141
  in United States, 141–142
  worker-owned cooperative corporation, 145
LEGO Group, 3
Limited liability companies (LLCs), 142, 143
Limited Liability/S-Corporation, 169
Limited partnership, 143
Logic model, 115, 118–119, 136–138
  creation, 133–134, 133 (figure)
  homeownership services, 124, 124 (figure)
Low-profit, limited liability company (L3C), 169

M

Management Leaders for Tomorrow (MLT), 14
Māori, 16–17
Martin, Roger, 1, 2
Mashharawi, Majd, 81–84
MassChallenge, 71–72, 92, 180, 297
  WorkAround, 318–319, 328–329
MATT FORTI, 126–127
Mausco, Joseph, 6
Mayo, Anthony, 92, 93
McLean, Murdith, 12
Mehrabian, Albert, 243
Microfinance, 4
Minimum viable product (MVP), 73, 74
Mission creep, 179
  logic model, 119
Mission-driven organizations, 141–142, 146–147
Mission-driven ventures, 148–154, 273
  global market, 278–279
  global ventures, 281
  local needs, 277–278
  regional ventures, 280
  types, 277
MLT. *See* Management Leaders for Tomorrow (MLT)
Mobile money, 56–57
Moore, James F., 95
Morley, Siiri, 103, 141, 167–171
Morris, Catherine T., 218–219
Mortensen, Mark, 93
Motivation, entrepreneurs, 6
Muñoz, Sebastián, 103, 251–252
Mustafa, Shaheer, 134–136

N

Nairobi, 38
Natural environment protection, 42
Necessity entrepreneurs, 266
Net present value, 129
New Profit, 15, 38, 258–262
Newton, Isaac, 21
Nohria, Nitin, 92
Nonequity investors, 152
Nonprofit organization, 44–45

O

One Acre Fund, 126–127, 268–269, 280
Online advertising, 221
Operating cash flow, 147, 147 (figure)
Opportunity entrepreneurs, 266
Opportunity-focused solutions, 42–44, 53 (table)
Opportunity obsession, entrepreneurs, 6
Osberg, Sally, 1, 2
Osterwalder, Alexander, 68

P

Palandjian, Tracy, 155–156
Partnerships, 143
Pattern recognition, 9
Peer Health Exchange (PHE), 187–188
Peredo, Ana Maria, 12
Perez, Leslie, 251–252
Piner, Yves, 68
Pitch, 257–258
Pitch deck, 246–247, 247 (table)
Plan-Do-Study-Act cycle, 114, 115 (figure)
Political and policy changes, 43
Positive cash flow, 147, 147 (figure)
Poverty, 42
Poverty Action Lab, 38
Problem-focused solutions, 41–42, 53 (table)
Problem-solving approach
  BRAC's Social Innovation Lab (SIL), 56
Program-related investments (PRIs), 152

Prosperity Candle, 279
B-Corporations, 169
decision time, 170–171
fundraising, 169–170
Limited Liability/S-Corporation, 169
Low-profit, limited liability company (L3C), 169
nonprofit charitable organization, 168–169
organizational options, 168
shared prosperity, 167

R

Randomized controlled trial (RCT), 119–121
Rauch, Dave, 63
Rausch, Doug, 10, 12, 21
Relationships, 88
Rental model, 61
Responsibilities, 89
Retail purchase model, 61
Rewards, 89
Rice, John, 14
Rich, S. R., 239
Ries, E., 74–75
Rohingya refugee crisis, 54
Roles, 88–89
Rosenthal, Jonathan, 42, 279
Rottenberg, Linda, 18, 21, 25–28, 180, 266–267, 281
"Round robin" style writing process, 47
Roundy, Philip, 96
Rozyne, Michael, 42, 279
Rutopia, 251–252

S

Sanergy, 13, 38, 121, 157–158, 175, 182, 269, 299
competition, 305–306
measuring impact, 304–305
mission, 300
in Nairobi, Kenya, 301–305
new markets, 307–309
operations, 302–304
sanitation crisis, 300–301
scaling, 306–307
urine diverting dry toilets (UDDTs), 300
Scalers
characteristics, 13
Ekal Vidyalaya, 15
Management Leaders for Tomorrow (MLT), 14
Scaling
advantages, 173–174
commercial adoption, 191
decisions, 177–179
disadvantages, 179–181
diseconomy of scale, 174
economic benefits, 174, 174 (figure)
economies of scale, 173
economy of scope, 174
fidelity, 189
franchising/affiliate structures, 183–185
government adoption, 191
intrapreneurship, 186
knowledge dissemination and network creation, 186
licensing, 185
mergers/acquisitions, 185–186
mission achievement, 190
mission-driven organizations, 174–175
open source, 191
operating control, 182–183
organizational evolution, 176–177, 176 (figure)
owned branches/subsidiaries, 182–183
plan, 193, 194 (figure), 195
readiness, 188
receptivity, 188
replication, 190
resources, 188
returns evaluation, 189
risks assessment, 189
social venture's financing model, 189–190
sustained service, 191
untapped demand, 181–182
Schneider, Amy, 134–136
Schneider, Brenna, 67
S-Corporation, 144, 169
Search engine optimization (SEO), 221
Sehra, Shruti, 258–262
Self-assessment, 19–20
Shared economic development, 16
SIL. *See* Social Innovation Lab (SIL)
Simon, John, 18, 196–200
Singh, Benita, 279
Six Sigma, 208
Skoll Foundation, 15
Sly, Michael, 276–277
Smith, Alan, 68
Snook, Scott, 20
Social activism, 3
Social capital, 26, 87, 88
Social entrepreneurs, 18, 19
Bedouin communities, 10
cause branding, 12
criticism of, 11
ecosystem builders, 15–17
ecosystems (*See* Business ecosystems)
funding sources, 274 (table)
impact assessment, 113–114 (*See also* Impact measurement)
innovation and impact, 9
innovators, 12–13

measurement tools, 113–114
opportunity-focused solutions, 42
problem-solving approach, 10
replication and dissemination, 11
scale and scope, 11
scalers, 13–15
social goals, 11–12
types, 12
Social entrepreneurship
change agents, social sector, 2
definition, 1
environmental, social, and governance (ESG), 3
low-cost health insurance program, 4
microfinance, 4
self-sufficiency, 4
social activism, 3
social pressure, 4
social service provision, 3
stakeholder capitalism, 3
themes, 2
transformational benefit, 2
triple bottom line, 3
UN Sustainable Development Goals, 5
Social finance, 155–156. *See also* Financing
Social impact bonds, 154
Social Innovation Lab (SIL), 53, 55–56
Social justice, 42
Social media, 219
platforms, 222, 223 (figure)
Social movement, 16–17
Social pressure, 4
Social Return on Investment (SROI), 129, 130 (figure), 131
Social service provision, 3
Social value, realigning systems, 13
Social ventures, 59
adaptability, 63
agility, 60, 61
attributes, 64
BRAC, 66–67
business model (*See* Business model)
business pitches (*See* Business pitches)
business plans (*See* Business plans)
CBI Insights, 65
concepts, 61 (figure)
culture design, 106
customer segmentation, 66
design thinking, 75–76
digital and social media marketing, 219–223, 223 (figure)
entrepreneurial marketing (*See* Entrepreneurial marketing)
failure, types, 66
financing decisions, 146–148
funding models, nonprofit organizations, 158, 158 (table)–159 (table)
hypothesis development and testing, 80–81, 80 (figure)
hypothesis-driven entrepreneurship, 67, 73–75
innovation, 33–34
intrinsic motivation, 92
legal structure, 140–146
makerspace, 60
market assessment, 62–64
market potential validation, 64–65
mission-driven organization, 65
mission-driven ventures, 148–154
nonprofit organizations, 64–65
rental model, 61
retail purchase model, 61
team attraction disadvantages, 90–91
teams, 92–93, 93 (table)
tenacity, 60, 62
time-tested methods, team members, 90
Sole proprietorship, 142
Southern Cone expansion strategy, 25
SPARK program, 315–316
Spinelli, Stephen, 6
Stakeholder capitalism, 3
Stern, Andrew, 190
Stevenson, Howard, 2, 7
Stradley, Lindsay, 299
Strategic investments, 150
STREETS International, 40–41
SunBox, 74, 81–84
Supply chain management, 208
Survey-based assessments, 123

T

Taylor, Frederick, 205
Teach for America (TFA), 182–183
Teamwork, 38
Technology, opportunity-focused solutions, 43
Theory of change, 136–138
apparent effectiveness, 118
demonstrated effectiveness, 118
models, 115
One Acre Fund, 117, 117 (figure)
proven effectiveness, 118
and social impact plan, 241
Teach for America (TFA), 116–117, 116 (figure)
Timmons, Jeffry, 6, 212
Todd and Tindall Foundations, 16–17
Total quality management, 207–208
Trelstad, Brian, 119
Triple bottom line, 3

U
UNICEF, 285–288
University-led incubator programs, 103
UN Sustainable Development Goals, 5, 44, 86, 270–271, 270 (figure), 283–284, 284 (figure)
US Environmental Protection Agency, 8

V
Vallabhaneni, Ani, 87, 299
Value proposition, 62–63
Venture capital and private equity (VCPE), 150

W
Wang, Xin, 220
Wasserman, Noam, 87, 88–89
Wei-Skillern, Jane, 188
Womack, James, 206
WorkAround, 320–321
  BIOS, 322–323
  business model canvas, 316–317, 324
  Coexistence-Sustainable International Development, 312–313
  global refugee crisis, 313–314
  Heller-Hult Challenge, 315
  MassChallenge, 318–319, 328–329
  pitch deck, 325–327
  solution, 314–315
  SPARK program, 315–316
  worker demographics, 323
Wyatt, Jocelyn, 76

Y
Youth Villages, 156, 175
Yunus, Muhammad, 4, 5, 11, 18, 21, 38